'A politi... world, remindi... future for London. It's also full of intriguing facts, always beautifully written and adventurously illustrated. Rowan Moore should be M...'

'Rowan Moore's *Slow Burn City:* ... an architectural study in the nob... ledgeable argumentative tour of ... any time in its history'

'Each chapter of Rowan Moore's book is a striking architectural set piece . . . Moore writes persuasively on public spaces and the increasing, troubling tendency to ... out of them . . . [he] is at his best examining why certain ... have worked, why we flock to them and find them congenial and welcoming . . . [his] portraits of individual buildings ... *Literary Supplement*

'An eloquent, sweep... *Literary Review*

'Moore can't be bettered . . . bri... *Country Life*

'Fun to read, packed with entertaining asides and ... piced with waspish invective' ... *die Review of Books*

'Moore knows London better than most. There is a great argument in this book – and an important one' *Sunday Times*

'[Deserves] to be celebrated for enriching our understanding of the city we live in . . . *Slow Burn City* by Rowan Moore looks at how our metropolis is changing, and the terrible damage being done by soulless corporate developments and volume house-builders. The book argues that London is something like an organic entity that goes through long cycles of expansion and decay. Today, after a period of untrammelled growth, Moore concludes that ambitious action is needed to ensure the city remains healthy and sustainable' *Evening Standard*

'I'd heartily recommend Rowan Moore's brilliant *Slow Burn City*'
Rohan Silva, *Guardian* Books of the Year

Slow Burn City

Rowan Moore is the architecture critic for the *Observer* and previously for the *Evening Standard*. He is also a trained architect, and was formerly the Director of the Architecture Foundation. His award-winning book *Why We Build* was published by Picador in 2012. In 2014 he was named Critic of the Year by the UK Press Awards.

Also by Rowan Moore

WHY WE BUILD

Rowan Moore

SLOW BURN CITY

LONDON IN THE TWENTY-FIRST CENTURY

PICADOR

First published 2016 by Picador

First published in paperback with a new prologue 2017 by Picador
an imprint of Pan Macmillan
20 New Wharf Road, London N1 9RR
Associated companies throughout the world
www.panmacmillan.com

ISBN 978-1-4472-7020-1

9 8 7 6 5 5 4 3 2 1

A CIP catalogue record for this book is available from the British Library.

Map artwork by ML Design
Printed and bound by CPI Group (UK) Ltd, Croydon, CR0 4YY

Visit www.picador.com to read more about all our books
and to buy them. You will also find features, author interviews and
news of any author events, and you can sign up for e-newsletters
so that you're always first to hear about our new releases.

For Ann and Richard, without whom

Contents

The Liberal City   *xi*

Maps   *2*

MADE BY TRADE

1: *City of the Present*   *9*

2: *The Disembodied Economy, Embodied*   *34*

3: *New Sybaris*   *74*

THE PUBLIC GOOD

4: *Water*   *103*

5: *Fire, Air, Nature*   *131*

6: *Darkness*   *167*

DAS ENGLISCHE HAUS

7: *Exile*   *195*

8: *At Home in London*   *223*

9: *The Values of Value*   *266*

SMART CITY, DUMB CITY

293   *Note on Planning*

297   *10: Mipimism*

330   *11: Public and Publoid*

357   *12: You've been Heatherwicked*

CITY OF TEN MILLION

401   *13: Subtle Substances*

439   *14: You Burned Your Own Town*

474   *15: Slow Burn City*

495   *List of Illustrations*

502   *Bibliography and Sources*

513   *Acknowledgements*

515   *Index*

The Liberal City

You don't realize how vital some things are until they are in danger.

With London it is easy to overlook its best values: its openness, multiplicity, generosity, freedom. It is a place where, in principle, anyone can find a niche, define themselves, make a home, a business, a life. It allows, within the limits of peaceful co-existence, religious, cultural and sexual identities that might be commonplace, conventional, esoteric or to non-adherents mystifying. This is the idea of London, present in the provision of needs – shelter, a job – and of social pleasures: cuisine, markets, music.

The city offers fulfilments of body and soul, chances of enrichment, wonderlands of unrestrained imagination. London is dazzling, sometimes beautiful, unconventional, fluid, endless, its range of moods and possibilities approaching the infinite. It fertilizes knowledge, understanding, discovery and creation, the exchange of ideas and beliefs. It is a testing ground for medicine, science and law. It is a supreme achievement of civilization.

Its qualities are built into its fabric, in its open spaces, in the places made for entertainment and enlightenment, dignified schools and gilt theatres, and in its slack places, the railway arches and industrial remnants where makers and artists can try things out. They are in the range of its housing – Georgian and Victorian terraces, the interwar semi-detached, post-war council housing, warehouse conversions, esoteric one-offs.

London is a Liberal city, which means it stands for values in peril. Multiplicity, co-existence, knowledge and freedom are the qualities that terrorists want to tear apart. Extremist politicians in the United States and Europe, obligingly rising to provocation, slash at them. The leaders of the Philippines, Turkey or Russia conduct their own assaults. The majorities who hold Liberal values, but find the territory shrinking where they are upheld, look around for places to go. Canada? Germany? London, although not a country, is one.

By now some readers will be incredulous. If you live outside London, and very possibly if you live inside, you may not recognize this description of a shining city on a hill. You might see it as greedy, harsh, unfriendly, arrogant, alien, self-absorbed, as a noisy brat that bends the economy of a country to its demands. It is the nest of those elites that have trashed the lives of many. Now that 'Liberal metropolitan elite' has become a term of insult, it is clear that London is guilty on all three counts. It is Liberal, metropolitan and houses elites.

London, like Liberalism, can be its own enemy. In recent years the city has exemplified the conflation of Liberalism with neo-liberalism and freedom with the free market. 'The market', which might describe any kind of commercial transaction, corporate or individual, abstract or concrete, productive or parasitic, meant in particular property speculation and the financial services industries of the City of London. Politicians of both right and left, betting the city's economic future on its expertise in finance and property, tried to make conditions as favourable as possible for these sectors. The consequences included the erosion of some of London's strengths, its availability and openness, in particular but not only through the cost and scarcity of homes.

So London enacts an internal conflict of modern liberal societies. Freedom becomes economic freedom, which becomes the reduction of freedom (or of opportunity, identity, happiness, security) for significant sections of the population, some of whom respond by challenging the principles of openness that underlie those societies. It requires other definitions of liberty than the purely economic to counter these tendencies.

London's flaws give ammunition to the right-wing mainstream media – the *Mail*, *Telegraph*, *Express*, *Sun* – which, conveniently overlooking the privileges of their own proprietors and journalists, assault attempts at reasoned argument as the 'whingeing, contemptuous, unpatriotic' outbursts of 'a well-heeled group of London "intellectuals" which is used to having everything its own way – and which has ignored the ordinary voter for decades'. London-based judges, honestly doing their job, are called 'enemies of the people'. London-based experts are derided.

London encapsulates the strengths of Liberalism, its vulnerabilities, contradictions and self-inflicted wounds. It also has the capacity to rise to its challenges and to reinvent what a Liberal city might be. It could show how to live together in a contemporary world fraught by urges to fragment and demonstrate how useful such things as expertise and openness can be. It could be, in the shape of a living, churning city of more than eight million people, the most powerful possible counter-argument to the lethal ideologies of the present. It can give hope.

But first it helps to understand how it got to be what it is now.

In the early twenty-first century, London became the global city above all others – not, as before, one of several. By which is meant that money and people from all over the world flowed through it, that its land and homes were tradable commodities on international markets, that it became a transit lounge and stopping-off point for the world's migrant populations, rich and poor – all to a greater extent than anywhere else. 'London is to the billionaires as the jungles of Sumatra are to the orang-utans,' boasted its former mayor. 'It is their natural habitat.'

To be global now means to be 'globalized', in the specific sense that describes the tendency of borderless financial forces to turn to their maximum advantage the resources and people of the world's localities, for example the way in which a phone is assembled out of the minerals, labour and skills of four continents. London, as the world's leading financial centre, played the major role in promoting globalization, but now this homeless phenomenon was coming home: London itself was becoming the plaything of the forces it had helped to set free. If for Londoners globalization had once been about far-away sweatshops providing cheap clothes and pangs of conscience, now it was about beautiful neighbourhoods bought by owners who barely lived in them and towers of flats sold sight unseen at marketing events in South-East Asia.

London was an originator and a recipient, the doer and the done-to. It despatched finance and consultants to reshape distant cities, who then returned to operate their techniques on the mothership. It became the best place to understand the way the world's cities are changing – Exhibit A, Patient Zero, Experimental Subject Number 1.

Its transformations were creative. London became a place of desirability, a New Sybaris where the industries of pleasure reached new levels of refinement, where there were more types of ceviche than in recorded history and where the art of mixology reached an unprecedented height. It became a place of invention and opportunity where people were desperate to live. Its centre was clean and safe. Its schools flourished. It attracted people of talent, energy and ambition. It had architects who were world-famous, and others who were good, and even some who were both good and world-famous. It was a marvel, fantastical, fascinating, beauteous. Its population rose to new levels.

They were also destructive. London became a wonderland at which too many of its citizens could only stare, as if through plate glass. The city's more attractive areas tended to become luxury products. New construction, though abundant, failed to create places whose qualities would match the old. Its grand natural assets, its river and sky, were assaulted by ill-considered towers. Its places of creation and recreation, its workplaces, studios and pubs, were squeezed by residential property development. The idea of home was corrupted, turned from a place where you might nurture your hopes and affections into a unit of speculation, or else into a meagre square-footage, determined by the intersection of the maximum affordable and the minimum tolerable.

From the 1980s on the city's growth had been based on the idea that the free market can build a city, more or less by itself. House-price inflation was treated as an economic engine and a self-evident good. A generation of politicians who had done well out of buying and selling homes – perhaps starting with a flat in Clapham, moving on to a little house in Fulham, attaining the edges of Notting Hill, buy-to-letting a second home – saw in their mounting profit evidence of their own cleverness rather than good luck, and so thought trading residential space was a model form of both business and home-making. Property development was seen as the supreme tool of shaping a city and property developers were charged with delivering social goods like affordable housing and public space. Now this idea has encountered its limits. The market, even if prodded and cajoled by government, is not proving equal to the task of building the homes and creating the neighbourhoods that the city needs.

'We've got to be quite up front,' said the British housing minister late in 2015, 'about the fact that, in London, we have got a finite space and if people want to live and work in and around London it's actually making a judgement call about what you can afford and where is right for you.' Which breezy statement effectively says that the country's capital might not be 'right for', that is affordable for, you, and that you are effectively barred from it. It echoes the comment of mayor Robin Wales, addressing homeless citizens of his own east London borough: 'If you can't afford to live in Newham you can't afford to live in Newham.'

In the summer of 2016 I found myself sitting on a panel at the conservative thinktank Policy Exchange, as we listened via Skype to Marwa al-Sabouni, a courageous Syrian architect who had written a book about her city, Homs. Her argument was that the seeds of its destruction had been sown over decades, through the politically motivated segregation of a previously integrated population, such that people of different faiths and classes who previously had daily contact with each other were now dispatched to isolated zones, which made it easier for mistrust, fear and eventually war to ferment. She said that the town-planning theories of Le Corbusier, which sought to separate the functional elements of a city, played a significant (but not the only) part. We were invited to reflect on the relevance of her insights to London.

Most of the panel, especially the fiercely anti-modernist philosopher Roger Scruton, seized on this last point. Indeed Corbusian theory should not escape its share of blame, but they found it harder to see that other forces are pushing the fragmentation of London. Among them is the Conservative government's Housing and Planning Act, which had just received Royal assent, which obliges local authorities to sell off council homes in high-value areas (that is, the central and fairly central parts of London) in order to subsidize the sale of homes at reduced prices which, after a few years, could be re-sold at the full market value. Its medium-term effect will be to increase the polarization of the city by income. One of the panel was a former policy adviser to the Prime Minister, who had played a central role in the preparation of the act, which helps to explain the desire to flog the dead horse that is the no-longer-current theory of a long-dead Swiss architect.

London may not be in imminent danger of becoming a Homs but in recent years the direction of its travel has been towards disaggregation and fracturing, to a diminution in the contact and sharing of space between its classes. This is the antithesis of the Liberal city. An eloquent diagram of this can be seen in VNEB, or Vauxhall Nine Elms Battersea, an area of intense property speculation on the south side of the Thames, around the location of the new American Embassy. Here poorly planned public spaces and a violent impact on the Thames-side skyline contrast with a highly publicized glass swimming pool, several storeys high, bridging two exclusive apartment blocks. Here the general public is invited to gawp at the privileged bodies above their heads, even as other forms of inter-action are designed out of the project.

The relationship of London to the rest of Britain can also be like that of the swimming pool to the pavement. It became, through the decades of its financial triumph, a city-state that made and followed its own rules, unmoored from the nation of which it was the capital. It was called a 'death star'. Nationalist parties fed on the resentment London generated outside its borders, even as the country as a whole fed off its revenues. The many who dislike London, among Britons who live outside it, often say that 'you can smell the money' – it seems to be a place not for them. The city became both a fantas-tical wealth machine and a flesh-eating capitalist monster.

Anger is directed at 'elites', a term used indistinguishably to describe overlapping but not identical entities. An elite might be financial, political or cultural. It might be a 'liberal metropolitan elite', which for some reason attracts more hostile attention than the no less substantial conservative elites. If there were some among the financial elites who robbed the economy and some politicians who fiddled their expenses, mistrust falls equally on all.

Everything associated with elites, sinister or blameless, including knowledge, expertise, tolerance, public spirit and indeed liberalism, comes under suspicion. And the place where these elites gather, their watering hole, is London.

In the months after the hardback edition of this book was published, two events crystallized the nature of London and its challenges. One was the choice by the city's voters of a Muslim mayor, Sadiq Khan, thereby rejecting a pernicious campaign by his opponents to link him to extremism. At a time when the successful American presidential candidate could call for a ban on Muslims entering his country and a French presidential candidate could support a ban on swimwear favoured by Muslim women, and however successful Khan turns out to be as a mayor, this was an eloquent demonstration. It showed that, calmly and reasonably, the people of a major Western city could narrow the gap between the Islamic and non-Islamic worlds, a gap which extremists are so keen to make wide, deep and absolute. Or rather, London's voters could act as if the gap was barely there at all.

The other event was the referendum in which the electorate of the United Kingdom as a whole voted to leave the European Union while London, along with other big cities, voted strongly to remain. Among the good and bad reasons for the country's choice there was a reaction against the openness of London and its welcome to foreigners. And the Brexit vote was seen, with reason, as in part a rebellion against the alien and overweening city state that many in the rest of the country believed London to be. Which to some degree was a tragic misunderstanding: some Brexit-voters might have thought that all Londoners were feeding from the same gilded trough, whereas there were plenty of people both inside and outside the city who were on the losing side of its financial power. Really, they had a common cause.

The referendum result was followed by half-serious calls for

London to declare independence from the rest of the country such that it really would become a city state, or at least to receive dispensations that would allow it to function much as before. The vote also threatened to slow the growth in prosperity and population that has been the recent history of the city. In which case the city's issues of housing and availability take on different but also demanding forms.

At its best London is a city that burns slowly – it renews through consuming itself, through changing its physical and cultural fabric, its buildings, neighbourhoods and traditions, from one thing into another, but without devastating what is already there. Its past is the raw material of its future. It tends to avoid the tabula rasa, the clean slate or scorched earth. Crucial to its slow burning is its separation of powers, the way it proceeds through the creative interplay of private trade, popular protest and public action. It is idle to decide which plays the biggest role. It is all three, together.

Consider, for example, the green spaces for which the city is famous, its parks, woods and commons. These are shared places, part of the communal life of the city, offering physical and mental release whoever you are, and whether you are alone, in a couple or in a group. On summer evenings one might fill with the smoke of disposable barbecues, bought from the Turkish supermarket at its edge. There will be kite-flying, ball-kicking, reading, snogging, drinking. Another might include a bowling green, its tournaments sponsored by funeral directors, played both by elderly white Londoners and by Asians who discovered the game late in life. In some there might be undercurrents of conflict, such as invisible territorial boundaries between local gangs, or tension between gentrifying incomers and established populations. A park can't resolve all these conflicts, but it can create a space which promotes co-existence over division.

These green spaces are taken for granted, as if it is as natural as air that they should be there, but they don't exist without intent and struggle. Some, such as Hampstead Heath, Epping Forest and many more obscure patches of grass and trees, are there because of the prolonged nineteenth-century campaigns to protect common land from development, fought by coalitions of (for example) the philosopher John Stuart Mill, the bookseller W. H. Smith and the Willingdale family of Loughton, who made their living from lopping trees.

Sometimes there was violence, as when crowds in 1866 forced down railings around Hyde Park and helped convert it from an aristocratic preserve to a popular park, or when, in 1897, thousands stormed a hill in south London and set fire to a golf course that was colonizing previously open land. There was milder civil disobedience: in 1981 campaigners tried to plant a single primrose on Primrose Hill, in contravention of official rules and regulations, to make the case for wilder forms of nature to be allowed into the city. Their struggles led to the creation of places like Camley Street Natural Park in King's Cross which, once attempts to destroy it had been fought off, became a primary attraction for the redevelopment of the area.

These struggles provoked reaction. They were bad for business, it was said, impeded growth and interfered with rights of property. But if they had failed, and if London has lost its shared wildernesses and green spaces, it would have been impoverished economically as well as spiritually. Its businesses would find it harder to attract talented employees from abroad. And green spaces are good – if this is your main concern in life – for property prices.

Alongside the achievements of impromptu gatherings of citizens are those of government, without which the city could not exist in its present form. Of these the best known and most impressive are the sewage systems and Thames embankments created under the engineer Joseph Bazalgette in the mid-nineteenth century, in order to relieve the city of appalling smells and of epidemics that killed tens of thousands. There are others: the building acts following the Great Fire that shaped the growth of the city in the following centuries, the mass building of schools following the introduction of universal education in 1870, the invention of council housing, the green belt that encircles the city, post-war new towns, the Clean Air Act of 1956 that would eventually reverse the flight of the middle classes from London, the protection of historic buildings, the construction of bridges, libraries and museums.

Again these initiatives were opposed, as too expensive and interfering and as obstructing the course of providence. They were not only ambitious and vast but also radical and imaginative – although they drew on the experience of other cities, nothing exactly like them had happened before. In the case of Bazalgette's sewerage the engineering work required the creation of a new form of London-wide administration, the Metropolitan Board of Works. Once realized these works and policies came to seem integral to the fabric of the city, which it would be inconceivable to do without. They also became models for other cities to follow around the world.

The private sector built the many square miles of terraces and squares into which Georgian and Victorian London grew and the avenues of semi-detached houses of the city's expansion between the wars. It built hotels, stores, banks and the first railways. It nourishes the endless creativity that goes into feeding, distracting and entertaining Londoners. An entrepreneurial spirit lies behind the city's art, from the efforts of street artists to the creation by Damien Hirst, with the portion of the wealth he has amassed as an artist-businessman of genius, of a fine new gallery that the public is free to enter.

London's friendliness to trade, to import, export, exploitations and opportunity, has given it a special flexibility, a looseness, a diversity of fabric, which more regulated and directed cities lack. Its districts can change in response to the demands of a time, becoming industrial, artistic, crowded, depopulated, transient, established, more or less criminal, poor or posh and more or less associated with an ethnic, social or religious group. But the private sector didn't achieve all this all by itself.

It might state the obvious to say that a city owes its existence to its citizens, governance and trade, but the modern tendency to credit business above the others requires a correction. Not that each operates in isolation. More often the city grows through hybrids and cross-overs between categories, such as the Jacobean public–private partnership that brought the fresh water of the New River into London. Much of London's housing might have been built by speculators, but was given form and order, not to mention basic levels of safety and comfort, by government regulations. The London Underground owes its modern form partly to Charles Tyson Yerkes, an aggressive, risk-taking, Trumpian tycoon from Chicago, but also to Frank Pick, chief executive officer of the London Passenger Transport Board, a fastidious and puritanical public servant.

London evolves in cycles. Typically free enterprise is given its head, allowed to do its thing, to create growth, opportunity and attraction until it generates crises – fire, cholera, bad housing, pollution, chaotic transport, civil disorder, destruction of the countryside – that it is unable to deal with alone. Then public actions, drastic and unprecedented, intervene, until the state agencies become sclerotic and themselves in need of reform.

Now it is at the turn of another cycle in which its politicians are groping after the initiatives that will address its current needs. There is widespread agreement that the problem is to do with the numbers and affordability of new homes but, still fixated on the idea that the property market will provide, they haven't yet come up with a Bazalgette-sized response to what is a Bazalgette-sized problem.

The basic question is how to accommodate a population bigger than it has ever been, and which by 2030 might be 50 per cent more than it was in the 1980s, within boundaries fixed by the existence of a green belt. There are also multiple answers – make both outer suburbs and council estates denser, use existing stock better, add additional storeys onto the large tracts of London that are two and three storeys high, make inhospitable arterial roads into boulevards, build towers, create new towns outside the city, expand carefully and cautiously into a small proportion of the precious green belt, which is more than three times the area of the city it is supposed to serve.

All are possible and none are easy, because wherever they go they will affect the people and the physical assets already there. Their effects could be either positive or negative – building outside the city's limits can create either garden cities or sprawl, a tower can be a landmark or an eyesore, and densifying a council estate might be regeneration or social cleansing. The difference is in how it is done, which means planning and design, which usually means some degree of public involvement. They also require use of public land and public investment.

Of course, the past history of state-led planning has had its share of disasters – waste, grandiosity, indifference to the fate of people affected. Invoking Bazalgette, indeed, should be done with caution, as there was a brutal aspect to his approach that is neither desirable nor possible to replicate. So intervention in London has to work with and not against its patterns. An example of how not to do it is the Thames Tideway Tunnel, the colossally expensive, crude and environmentally damaging 'supersewer' that the privatized monopoly Thames Water is building under the river. An example of how to do it might be the counter-proposals put forward by opponents of the TTT: a plan for slowing the run-off of rainwater from the streets and buildings of the entire city, with the help of planting, permeable surfaces, pools and water-butts, which would relieve pressure on the sewers without heavy engineering and make the city as a whole more pleasant.

New planning could also learn from Walter's Way and Segal Close, two small 1980s developments in the borough of Lewisham, guided by the architect Walter Segal. He devised a way in which people could build their own homes, using standard elements from builders' merchants, such that they were both beautiful and cheap and gave their residents the fulfilment of creating their own living space. An essential element of these projects was the provision of land by the local authority. Here the role of government was not to do everything itself but to help communities and individuals pursue their own destinies. It is a principle that could be applied at a much larger scale, for example by designating areas of land for new self-built neighbourhoods.

If it seems frivolous to talk of such slow-burning responses when the needs of the city are large and urgent, in reality they are more essential than ever. Ponderous, blunt, insensitive infrastructure projects have a way of grinding extremely slowly to completion due to the opposition, usually well-founded, that they provoke. Incremental transformations are more likely to win support and can offer tangible improvements sooner rather than later.

It might also be asked how large-scale public interventions can be paid for and achieved, at a time when the country has become used to the idea that its government doesn't have enough money. But spending on housing is an investment in a long-term capital asset that is more productive than the huge sums currently paid in housing benefit to private landlords. There is value that can be tapped in land already owned by public bodies. And public spending has proved possible for large rail and airport projects: it only requires a shift in attitude to see that housing is equally urgent.

There are signs that the city is indeed tapping its ingenuity and resilience. In the same Camley Street that contains a pioneering natural park, a group of businesses got together, in 2016, to present an alternative to the ubiquitous luxury housing that is the usual fate for industrial sites such as the one they occupied. This group – made up of wholesalers of fish and meat, a commercial laundry, an architectural modelmaker, a muesli factory, a plumbing supplies store, car repair workshops – showed how their site could be redeveloped to provide more workspace than it currently has, plus about a thousand 'meaningfully affordable' homes. The key to its success was to invest in community benefits the portion that a developer would take as profit. It wasn't a fantasy – institutional investors backed it and property companies vouched for its viability. The London Borough of Camden, which owned the site, would get a good deal out of it too – they only needed to be persuaded of the strengths of the proposal.

If the London 2012 Olympics proved that ambitious public works can be successfully achieved it remains to transfer that ability to projects of everyday life. The last few years have also seen a resurgence in the building of homes by local authorities such as Camden, Hackney, Enfield and Brent, to a higher quality than most of that achieved by developers. The idea that the public sector is always less competent than the private is simply false.

What has Liberalism ever done for us? Nothing, apart from peace, prosperity, justice, relief from disease, the advancement of knowledge, the reduction of disadvantage, the growth of freedom – achievements often hard won in the face of opposition from vested interests and their media allies. The transformation of Victorian London's sanitation was opposed with bogus science and specious philosophy by journalists of the time. The same thing is happening now with the useful idiots and flat-out liars of the Conservative press, who abuse their educations at ancient schools and universities to twist the facts about, for example, climate change and the European Union.

A single city cannot address alone all the turbulent forces of the world we now inhabit, but it can both lead by example and strive to achieve whatever it can with the powers it has. It can aim to live by the best of its nature and history. It can create alternatives to the dominant narratives of the time.

London is miraculous. It embodies a form of metropolitan society that cannot be taken for granted. In the past it had an ability to invent responses to the conflicts and problems it generates. Now it has to do this again. If, as its financial boosters like to call it, it is a 'world-class city', it also demands 'world-class' approaches to housing and shared space. It is time to apply to its planning and building the brilliance and invention that goes into its cocktails.

December 2016

SLOW BURN CITY

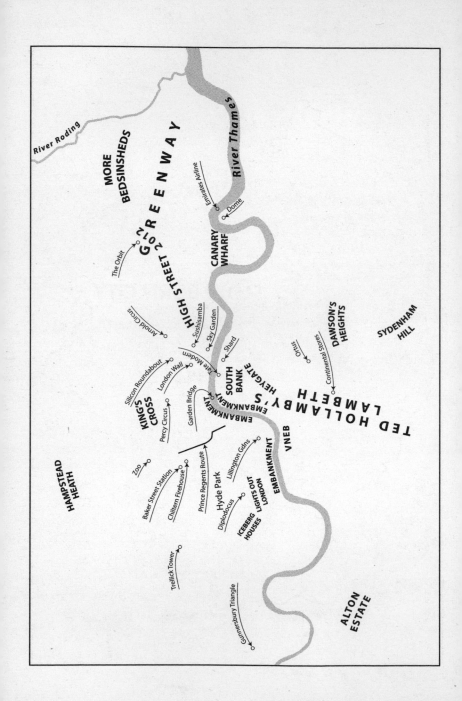

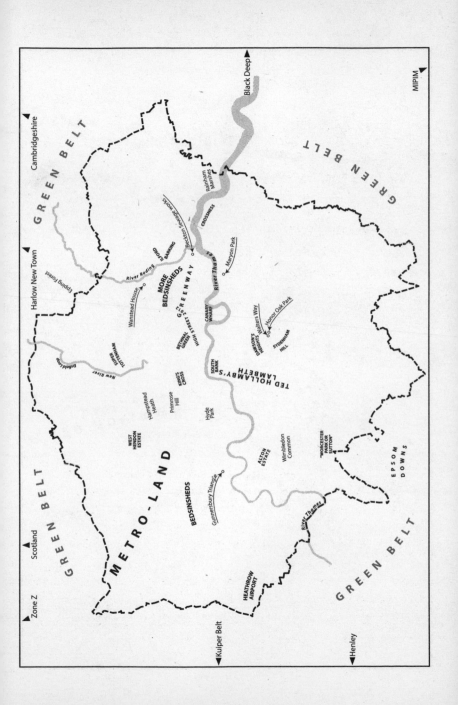

MADE BY TRADE

1: City of the Present

Inside the Snowdon Aviary at London Zoo, the building fades. There is a walkway, sloped and zig-zagging, and a slice of park landscape that tips towards the Regent's Canal beneath, dramatized with a rocky waterfall and made exotic by sacred ibis, black kite and brolga crane. The birds wouldn't stay if it wasn't for the building and the nets it hangs between its steel struts, but the enclosure recedes from the mind. It captures a zone rather than makes a room, a Middlesex-tropical fusion in which you can feel the English weather and hear buses on a nearby road while sensing the ripe guano of the foreign birds and their horse-like cries. It is a rare trick, making a building disappear when you enter.

Seen from outside, in vistas along the canal, the aviary is conspicuous, a work of tetrahedral Gothic nestling in foliage, a folly in the tradition of the English picturesque. It is a wonder of tensile engineering, in which everything seems to hang from everything else. It is a Grade II* listed structure, erected between 1962 and 1965 to the designs of the brilliant young architect Cedric Price, the young engineer Frank Newby and the Queen's brother-in-law, Lord Snowdon, in an alliance of establishment and rebels of a kind that can realize the exceptional in London.

It is an episode in the struggles inherent in the zoo's being: between reason and nature, human and animal, cruelty and care, science and entertainment. It is inscribed with attitudes of social class. It materializes with steel and feathers the zoo's relationship to

Tetrahedral Gothic

the world, the planet being a trove from which wonders can be imported and then admired by people also from anywhere. This relationship, colonial in origin, was justified in the name of enlightenment and came to be tempered by a troubled conscience about the ethics of acquiring and enclosing rare creatures, to be salved by work on conservation. In which respect – the making of a local territory open to global fluxes, to the import and export of knowledge and exploitation, its issues of havoc and control – the zoo stands for the city in which it sits.

Exotic beasts were imported to London before the zoo was invented in the early nineteenth century. They had been objects of royal fascination and prestige since the Middle Ages, with a collection kept in the Tower of London, and commodities to be exploited by travelling showmen, exhibited for a charge at fairs and eventually installed in commercial menageries inside the city's ordinary street buildings. It helped that London was a major port, with captured animals added to the cargos of ships. The practice of walking elephants through the streets (for example), from the docks to the zoo, continued into the twentieth century.

The main attraction of seeing strange animals seems to have changed little through those centuries, which is not that different from the motivation of tourists and children at the zoo now. It was to gawp. It was to satisfy the human desire to connect with another form of life, especially if strange, in order to find some comfort that the world is not atomized and disjointed. Hence the common tendency to anthropomorphize, to dress apes in clothes and give animals human names.

Nor in all this time did the treatment of the living exhibits change much. As described in Hannah Velten's *Beastly London*, it was typically atrocious, sometimes sadistic, sometimes the result of ignorance about diet or housing or of misguided scientific curiosity. An elephant was fed on a gallon of wine a day, in the belief that this would protect it from the English cold, and it died. An ostrich was fed nails to test the theory that it could digest iron, which it couldn't. An orang-utan was given beer. James I had a baiting yard built, where mastiffs and lions could maul each other. Chunee the elephant, flatulent, sexually frustrated and raging, was executed by a firing squad of keepers, soldiers and policemen, who in the course of the hour required to finish him off fired 150 bullets. There were health and safety hazards – a monkey escaping into an oyster shop, a leopard at large in Piccadilly, buffalos in Mayfair, a tiger in Limehouse, neighbours' complaints about the noise and stench of a first-floor menagerie in the Strand, a girl debrachiated by a lion, a mail coach attacked by a stray lioness.

The Zoological Society of London, founded in 1826, and the zoological gardens in Regent's Park, which it opened in 1828, set out to be different. The society would pursue 'a correct view of the Animal Kingdom at large'. It would be about serious enquiry rather than spectacle, and order would be applied not only to nature but also to social class: initially there was no public admission, 'to prevent contamination' by the 'poorer classes of society'. The Zoological Society's founders included leading scientists; they were led by Stamford Raffles, the colonial adventurer and administrator who in his forty-five-year life also founded the port of Singapore.

The zoo's high-mindedness (and snobbery) did not stay perfectly intact. The public was admitted from 1846. Animals became named celebrities – Tommy the chimp, Jumbo the elephant, Chi-Chi the giant panda – and inspired hippo waltzes and giraffe-print dresses. Chimpanzees' tea parties were first held in 1925. There was no more lion-baiting, but Victorian children could still watch live rabbits being fed to snakes. Strange science persisted, with the attempt during the First World War to train sea lions to detect submarines, and inappropriate diets. A contributory factor to the death of Guy the Gorilla in 1978 was tooth decay caused by the sweets fed to him by the public.

The zoo is both a repudiation and a continuation of the tradition of royal and commercial menageries. The Zoological Society's desires for more humane treatment and better understanding of animals were and are sincere, but it remained exploitative. It assumed a right of dominion over the creatures of the world, extracting them from their habitats and restricting their freedom. It failed to abolish the urge to gawp and now lives off it, with much of its revenue coming from admission fees. Until they were discontinued in 2015, the Society made a reported £800,000 a year from Zoo Lates, Friday-night parties where guests could 'laugh like a hyena at the improv-sets in The Comedy Den' and 'shake their tail feathers at the Silent Dance Off'. The Lates were criticized for disturbing animals' sleep; more so when a man poured beer over a tiger and another tried to swim with penguins.

The zoo's values and contradictions are embedded in its physical fabric. Over nearly two centuries it has acquired a menagerie of notable architecture in parallel to its animal collection. Many are now protected as listed buildings, possibly to the frustration of the zoo's administrators. Some were prototypes of ideas that would later be applied to the human population of the city – there is social housing in north and east London, for example, whose designs develop from buildings in the zoo. All take a position on the relationship of civilization to nature and of science to spectacle.

The zoological gardens' original layout and its earliest buildings took their cue from Regent's Park, the then-new assemblage of speculative housing and greenery created by the Prince Regent. The zoo's architect was Decimus Burton, who with John Nash had designed the park's luxury terraces and villas, and who distributed the homes of animals in a picturesque landscape of winding paths and surprising incidents somewhat as he had the homes of humans.

In the 1830s he created the Giraffe House, whose basic elements – brick arches, shallow slate roofs – are those of a simple villa, adjusted to the scale of the animals. Three arched openings of unusual height are set in an oblong building in a brownish palette similar to the giraffes' hide, whose regularity complements their graceful habit of mirroring each other's movements. Burton may not have meant it – he may only have been seeking a practical and elegant way of housing the strangely proportioned beasts – but he achieved a harmonious choreography of flesh and brick.

The Giraffe House put exotic nature in a frame. Eighty years later, in 1914, the idea behind the Mappin Terraces was to create a rocky landscape as similar as possible to the natural habitat of bears, goats and deer. Although credited to John Joass of the architects Belcher and Joass, their design owes much to the direction of the Zoological Society's secretary Peter Chalmers Mitchell, and to the 'Hagenbeck Revolution' of Carl Hagenbeck, a German businessman, animal trader and maker of zoos and circuses, who believed in breaking down barriers, removing visible caging and simulating nature. The structures are prompted by their unusual brief to be innovative in their use of reinforced concrete and revolutionary in form, man-made mountains that anticipate the fantastical crystal cathedrals and Houses for the People later conceived by Germanic expressionists such as Bruno Taut, Rudolf Steiner and Hermann Finsterlin. They precede by decades the free-form works of Frank Gehry. As it was for Burton their brilliance is partly inadvertent, a reward for the unselfconsciousness that can come when working with dumb animals.

Like the later aviary, the bright white Penguin Pool of 1934 is the offspring of outsiders and the establishment. In this case the architect was Berthold Lubetkin, born in Tbilisi, a still-socialist émigré from the Soviet Union and the boldest apostle of continental modernism in 1930s Britain, who had a partner in his practice who was the son of the politician Herbert Samuel, through whom he was introduced to the zoo's leadership, who commissioned several buildings. Also crucial to the pool's success was the engineer Ove Arup, born in Newcastle to Danish parents and educated in Denmark on an English model, who made its daring structure possible.

The pool was the Zinoviev Letter of architecture in Britain, only more successful and not fake, smuggling the dangerous foreign ideology of constructivism under the guise of creating a fun structure for lovable flightless birds. A gracious ellipse, with a central intersection of helical ramps made for the scurrying and jumping of the penguins, it was the most admired and popular modernist building in pre-war London. It is, as Lubetkin himself said of his zoo works, 'a vision of nature tamed, not with a fist but with a smile'.

It has something of the Giraffe House in that its geometries announce themselves as the work of calculating man, and something of the Mappin Terraces in that its ramps are an attempt to create the sort of landscape that its fauna would enjoy. It adds the idea of spectacle, a heightened awareness that this is a place where people entertain themselves by looking at animals. The ramps make performance art out of feeding time. Or did, until the birds were moved to the new, larger, Penguin Beach in 2011. Knowledge of habitats had moved on, and what was considered animal-friendly in the 1930s was no longer sufficient.

The Snowdon Aviary, coming from the post-war continuation of the zoo's commitment to pioneering architecture, pushes further the ideas both of a naturalistic environment and, in the exceptional engineering of its tensile structure, of the power of human reason. It develops, too, Lubetkin's interest in the experience of the spectator: having passed through an ingenious two-layer entry that stops the birds escaping, the visitor is in the same space as them, not separated by nets or bars.

To judge by the fact that it is still serving its original purpose,

This is not a Penguin Pool

the aviary was one of the more successful of the zoo's innovative buildings. (As is the Giraffe House, whereas the Mappin Terraces, which were not in practice friendly to their intended animals, have been awkwardly repurposed for smaller creatures.) But the aviary and its contemporary the Elephant House turned out to be the peaks of the zoo's architectural boldness. John Toovey's Lion House of the 1970s still has flickers of ambition: with upside-down arches, cantilevered canopies and intersections with trees and water, it gives the big cats what could be, if it were less tatty, a Blofeltian luxury villa in the Bahamas. Since the Millennium Conservation Centre of 1999 most of the zoo's architecture has been carried out by Wharmby Kozdon. They're not Lubetkin or Decimus Burton and don't pretend to be, but they seem to do what the zoo wants them to do, in terms of both animal habitat and visitor attraction.

The zoo now is a multiple hybrid. It is global and local, with the exotic and familiar turned upside-down. Beyond the black-and-flame flashes of Nile Red Bishops rises the 1850s church of St Mark's, a work of unbending Kentish Gothic of the kind Victorians scattered across the world without regard for climate or locality and which looks no more at home here than does a similar one in (for example) Grahamstown, South Africa. The visitors are mostly from outside London, whether from Lancashire or China, for whom everything is strange. 'They do have the funniest rain here, don't they,' says a North American accent to her child.

From the other side of the zoo you can see the dome and minaret of Frederick Gibberd's Regent's Park Mosque, finished in 1978, which looks no more or less foreign than the church. The eighteenth-century picturesque, of which Regent's Park is a significant descendant, liked to cushion disparate styles in lush greenery (Gothick, Hindoo, Chinese) such that they achieved equality of

meaning or insignificance; here, half-accidentally, the idea is taken to its conclusion. Everything is diverting. Nothing is more important than anything else.

The zoo is a zone of altered geography and altered nature. The Regent's Canal, a work of industrial infrastructure, becomes a forested ravine. A tunnel, which serves the practical task of taking zoo-goers under a public road, makes them into burrowing creatures; narrow bridges give them an approximation of flight. Animals are juxtaposed which would otherwise be thousands of miles apart. They are sometimes met face-to-face, but also glimpsed obliquely, like people in the rear windows of terraces, or the park lovers framed by David Hemmings's camera in *Blow-Up*.

It is compelling and unnerving. It is festive, like a funfair, a nice day out with the kids, but with anxieties that cause parents to invent needless prohibitions. Reminders of scientific dignity, like the Francophile elevation of Belcher and Joass's 1910 library, are punctured by the Carry-On ribaldry of donkey erections and poo smells. 'You just have to get used to their bottoms,' says a mother about the Sulawesi crested macaques, who through their black fur present gross globs of flesh, pressable like the controls of a games console. If there is a thrill to be had from seeing creatures that could kill you with teeth or poison, tigers and tarantulas, there is the obscure fearfulness of missing something, getting lost or not having a good time. There is unease that these animals might not be happy in their cages. The information panels pound out their amphibrachs and spondees of doom: ENDANGERED, ENDANGERED, EXTINCT.

The zoo's cool omphalos is Lubetkin's Penguin Pool, now an engine of disappointment. The sign still says PENGUIN POOL, because the raised steel sans-serif letters are integral to the design and so part of its Grade-I-listedness. They can't be removed. Historic England would never allow the zoo to prefix them with THIS IS NOT A. The proportions wouldn't be right. So crowds peer over Lubetkin's constructivist ha-ha, only to find a water feature where the birds once gambolled.

'There's nothing there, sweetheart, it's just where they used to be.'

The Elephant House, designed by Hugh Casson, is also anti-climactic. For all that the architect shaped the copper roofs such that they resembled a gathering of trunks at a watering hole, and built the walls of pachydermic concrete, there was something about the distribution of space that the large mammals didn't like. In 2001 they were sent to the Zoological Society's other zoo in Whipsnade, Bedfordshire, which left London, for the first time in centuries, elephantless.

The zoo provides explanatory labels of its architectural specimens, much as it does of its animals, but there is a resentful tone. 'The Casson is a listed building, which means we can't alter its appearance much.' Another label apologizes for the 1960s concrete, actually Piranesianally wonderful, at the north entrance to the pedestrian tunnel. The zoo's modern administration has different priorities, seen at their best in Wharmby Kozdon's new Penguin Beach, which offers gravel shoals and shallows, based on a South American beach, for wallowing and burrowing.

The modern zoo doesn't want only to make better habitats for the creatures, but also to give itself the trappings of the safari experiences and theme parks with which it competes. Having almost closed due to financial pressures in 1992, and receiving no public subsidy, it had to fight to lure visitors, charge high admission fees and then justify them with enhanced attractions. So there are bouncy castles and inflatable slides, decorated with pictures of monkeys. There are jokey signs with primary-school lettering and sweetie-coloured information panels buzzing with their high sugar content. There is a tiger gift shop selling tiger earrings tiger gold-plated pens tiger freeze-glass storm lanterns tiger eco-friendly wooden rulers. There is a condescending display about the zoo's enlisting of African villagers to help them find pygmy hippos.

There are some appearances of the Hopkins Hat, a tent-like architectural device in Teflon and steel cable that appeared in the 1980s on the Mound Stand of Lord's cricket ground, not far from the zoo. It was designed by the architect Michael Hopkins, a former partner of Norman Foster's who developed his own, highly crafted version of Foster's high-tech style. The version at Lord's, summery, festive, and at once modern and traditional, made sense, but the hat became a cliché, popping up on shopping malls and leisure attractions, a device for denoting the presence of Fun in a way that tells you that fun is what you are not going to have.

There is BUGS (Biodiversity Underpinning Global Survival). Here are true marvels, the nebulae of sea anemones and jellyfish, mantises, the radical ugliness of naked mole rats, who look like foreskins with teeth. But you have to fight to appreciate them through a storm of info-graphic gunk, a tornado in a Fisher-Price toy box, seconded by queasy combinations of carpet, wood, plastic and glass and the dumbest of all dumb uses of the Hopkins Hat. It is indoors, so its role of protecting from sun and rain is redundant. Whatever attempt there might be at reconciling the hat's parabolic curves with the oblong panels they abut, is abject.

There's a term for much of this, which is patronizing junk. Do children have to be sugared and harried into looking at animals? Does it help to watch a butterfly if you have first seen a bad cartoon of it? Does it respect nature to put it in a game-show set? This ingratiating-hectoring muzak gives no space to think or imagine, no time for quiet wonder.

It is not that habitats should remain unimproved, or that zoo animals should be condemned to live in the outdated environments of Casson, Lubetkin or Joass, just because they are listed. The Penguin Pool's greatest fans would have to admit that the birds look happier, and offer a richer range of behaviours to the spectator, in Penguin Beach. But the zoo is extraordinary and essential in its encounter of the wild and the urban, in the altered perspective it gives on civilization. It is good for a city to acknowledge the beast in its nature and the possibilities of chaos over which its superstructures of enlightenment are built. The zoo is a space of strangeness and fear, as well as beauty. From the Giraffe House to the Aviary architects took account of these phenomena in different ways. Now the instinct is to obliterate them, and fill the mysterious gaps between humanity and animals with multicoloured noise.

The zoo can be compared to other institutions, such as the British Museum, which, combining the idea of enlightenment with imperial instinct, assumed that the best way to understand the culture and nature of the world was to bring trophies of them to London, whether marbles from the Parthenon and bas-reliefs from Mesopotamia, or rare species from Asia and Africa. The zoo can also be compared with nineteenth-century housing reforms that similarly sought to tame barbarous and chaotic practices and, like the zoo, would develop their own exemplary architecture to embody their values.

The desire to improve the world was genuine, as was the belief that certain nations and classes were better qualified to do this than others. Which belief became eroded by self-doubt and external criticism. Challenge came not only from the formerly excluded, but also from pressures of the market, for which the values and knowledge of the leaders of the zoo, or of museums, or of social housing, were an obstructive freemasonry that got in the way of choice and the movement of wealth. And so regulations and privileges were dismantled and ideals discredited.

Before the zoo there was the disordered combination of royal whim and commercial barbarity with which exotic animals were treated. Then there was the earnest but paternalist zeal of the

Zoological Society, which created a radically new institution. There was revision and reform, driven by concerns about the well-being of animals and the ethics of capturing and enclosing them. Then there was crisis, followed by a demand to follow the market. Commercialism returned; if no longer barbarous, it was still corrosive.

These shifts had their architecture – first the ad-hocery and adaptation of unsuitable premises by commercial menageries, then the classicism of the early zoo, followed by attempts at naturalism, the early modern movement, further attempts at naturalism and, finally, a present which, while trying hard to achieve best practice, is Disneyfied.

This story is like that of London as a whole.

A plaque behind me commemorates the generosity of the property company British Land in sponsoring the restoration of an agreeable 1920s tea-house in a red-brick-and-white-paint style that owes something to Christopher Wren. In front, the Arctic-African mountain range of the Mappin Terraces makes a high horizon. Aeroplanes loop above towards Heathrow. Behind this horizon, between the hybrid geography of the Mappin and the internationally regulated airspace above, is the rest of London.

A teenager is leaving by the northern gate, in a white football shirt that says BEAST 30 on its back, and I follow him out. This exit leads to Primrose Hill, a place whose name could have come from a children's book – the home, indeed, of spotted dogs in *101 Dalmatians* – whose houses have children's book colours, pale blue, pink, lemon, peach, and a perfection that tells of the wealth of the owners. Some are famous, or were when the newspapers were fascinated with tales of wild parties among the actors and models whom they called 'The Primrose Hill set'. The zone called Primrose Hill Village (children's book multiplied by estate agents) offers cakes and pastries as Las Vegas offers slots. Continental pavement culture, long longed-for in London, is here. The colours are pastel on pastel, the shop signs cute lower-case: iloveyougorgeous, sweet things. Or you can leave this sugared land and climb the eponymous hill, which, like the Mappin, offers pure horizon: the ground meets the sky directly.

A round mound – with peripheral distractions edited out by trees, and despite lamp posts and asphalt paths – the hill retains a pre-urban essence that a Druid might recognize. Martians were attracted to it too, when they chose it for their last encampment in *The War of the Worlds*. Silhouettes are running up the slopes, or enjoying their couple-ness, conducting the business of being alive with added intent. At the top, turning round, there is the view, a theatre of construction. Visitors comment on the number of cranes – perhaps sixty or seventy. The blurring of distance makes them hard to count.

They see an old city. They can pick out its cathedral and parliament and discern the texture of its streets. They see many trees in the foreground and a backdrop of distant grey hills, and might infer a river in between. They can see the zoo, with the aviary at its most stately and entire. The church of St Mark reappears. But the thing that commands attention is the fabric formed in the last fifty years, with an accelerating havoc of towers.

By the standards of Asian or American cities, the height of these towers is nothing exceptional. The tallest, The Shard, slightly surpasses the Chrysler Building of 1930, which puts London eighty years off the pace in the race for height. What impresses are extent and distance. You can see structures an hour's journey away, which are still part of the same shabby-majestic artefact. The Shard seems to be in conversation, if a garbled one, with Canary Wharf, off to the left, which in turn has something in common with two remote splinters in Ilford, further left and distant, which have a relation with

Paddington Basin, nearby on the right. Hard and angular though these objects are, their composite has the quality of meteorology, a grounded cloudscape whose layers light up and fade with sunshine and shadow. Illumination makes fleeting alliances of objects miles apart. But the view is also ugly, in a way that the blessing of atmospherics can only partly mitigate.

It contains styles of architecture, theories of planning and political ideologies, each one of which might have imagined it was The Answer in its own time. In front is the trio which stakes out Tottenham Court Road – Centre Point, the BT Tower and the Euston Tower – which reflect a short-lived 1960s idea that it was good to plan tall buildings as slender objects standing alone. Canary Wharf, with its fat silver obelisk flanked by grey posts, is formed by the 1980s rediscovery of the grand axial planning of the nineteenth-century École des Beaux-Arts, with a corporate uniformity made possible by the fact that the property is in the ownership of a single company. In front of it is the City of London's response to competition from the Wharf, an upward thrusting of floor space into odd shapes, at the urging of the City's whimsical chief planner. There is the convex Gherkin, the concave Walkie-Talkie and, created by the same British Land who sponsored the zoo's tea-house, the pointy Cheesegrater.

There are try-ons, punts and gambles. Much is shaped by the huge companies that dominate the property business as South Korea's industry is by its dynastic chaebol conglomerates. There are also individual efforts. The London Eye, right of centre, was pushed into the air by the determination of husband-and-wife architects. The Shard was conceived by a formerly bust property developer who, never having proposed much more than low-rise business units in Warrington and Portsmouth, formed a series of unlikely deals to realize, on a wonky, barely there site next to a railway station, the tallest building in Europe. The red steel 367-foot sculpture called the

Orbit, leftward and more distant, is an Olympic ejaculation reportedly stimulated by a conversation between two men, Mayor Boris Johnson and the steel tycoon Lakshmi Mittal, at adjacent urinals at the World Economic Forum in Davos.

This view is multinational, the clusters of buildings echoing the polyglot spectators on the hill, and the zoo's recruitment of Macaques from Sulawesi and an architect from Georgia. The tower at Canary Wharf is by an Argentine-American architect working for developer brothers who had been born in Vienna, prospered in Tangier and prospered still further in Toronto. The Shard grew from the alliances of a London developer, a mayor from Cricklewood, an Italian architect, the Qatari sovereign wealth fund and a Hong Kong hotel chain; the Orbit from an Indian businessman, an Etonian mayor, a Mumbai-born artist, a Sri Lankan-British engineer, a Scottish architect and that Swiss toilet.

It is a truism about London, but also a truth, that it is international and multicultural. At least since the early Blair years its boosters have glibly celebrated its curries and rap, its 300-plus languages. Less flatteringly, it has been called Londonistan, an incubator of Islamist extremism. In the years around the 2008 crash, Canary Wharf was called 'Wall Street's Guantanamo', a compound where the most dangerous financial terrorists were sent and where, unlike the prisoners in the real Guantanamo, they were free – encouraged – to wreak further damage. The city contains versions of Poland, Syria, Dubai and Switzerland. Its residential property is traded on world markets like tulip bulbs or currency, with physical effects that include the ghost streets and iceberg houses of Belgravia – properties made vaster and emptier as their often absentee owners grow richer – and a flurry of towers of flats whose owners might buy without visiting the property. It is an import–export business of people, ideas, skills and goods. London consultancies and contractors help build Doha and Qatari funding helps build London.

The great Irish writer Flann O'Brien wrote of a policeman so habituated to his bicycle that man and machine exchanged molecules: parts of London are similarly part-Gulf and parts of Doha are partly Londonized.

It is another truism, not as perfectly true, that London is above all a city of trade, a great port which, even though the cargo ships now offload elsewhere, still cranes and traffics weightless bales of finance in the same spirit that it once did bananas and spice. According to this reading, London owes its physical substance to the pursuit of profit – the Georgian and Victorian terraces built by great landowners and speculative builders; the underground railways created by gambling and bankruptcy.

In 1934 the Danish architect and writer Steen Eiler Rasmussen published *London, the Unique City*, the greatest book there is on the city's built fabric. Rasmussen argues that 'the commercial city, London, became the antithesis of Paris, the city of absolutism', and 'London is the capital of all capitals which has resisted absolutism and maintained the rights of the citizens within the state'. He traces this free spirit to the Norman Conquest and King William's pragmatic decision not to fight the already-powerful city, but do a deal which would win its support in return for rights and privileges. Ever since, argues Rasmussen, the city has resisted rigid plans imposed from above, and has followed laws 'organically developed out of the life of the people'.

> Through the whole history of London we find a latent power, a desire to make the town healthy, and it has been able to act because London in contrast to other capitals was self-governing and independent of the Crown, and no standards for her development could be forced upon her.

The result, in Rasmussen's reading, is a city whose commercial nature is linked to a respect for citizens' rights, is responsive to change, trade and individuals' needs, favours private houses over apartment blocks, and whose unmanicured, quasi-natural parks invite people to pursue their sports and loves as they would wish.

London indeed has fluidity and adaptability arising from its looseness. It was without city walls for longer than most continental cities, meaning that it could spread with less meticulous management to become what Rasmussen calls a 'scattered city'. Never subjected to an overarching plan, it is rather a series of responses to the demands of particular times and places, which leave behind a variegated geology that can be inhabited and reinhabited in ways none could have predicted.

There are, for example, the stucco districts of west London, built in the mid-nineteenth century for prosperous residents which, falling victim to successive crashes, became slum tenements in multiple occupation, inadequate shelters for Irish and Caribbean immigrants, then bohemian quarters and, at last, the luxury homes they were first meant to be. Or the industrial buildings made without regard for anything but function and profit that converted well into studios for creative start-ups and designers, or flats for similar people. (Before becoming, also, luxury homes.) Or the twentieth-century council flats left to rot by neglectful authorities, apostrophized as disastrous, but then bought by their occupants and later sold to adventurous buyers unable to afford more conventional options, before becoming luxury homes. (There is a pattern here, of which more later.)

London can offer networks of lanes that retain their medieval shapes even as the plots they define are built and rebuilt into money factories of ever-greater size and technical sophistication. It has mute streets whose elevations look away, with a discreet cough, from whatever lurid lives may be going on behind them. The city has, or has had, old factories, dispersed suburbs, empty churches and cinemas, railway arches and wharves which can adapt to unforeseen fluctuations of wealth, population and work. It has districts that can light up and dim in response to the demands of a moment. A 'tech city' can form in mediocre buildings around an ugly traffic roundabout. It does so almost invisibly, with minimal outward signs of change, and it is helped precisely by the ordinariness of the built environment. The architecture's lack of preciousness lends itself to reinvention.

But, if the city is accommodating, available and open for business, it has also been made by radical actions in the name of the public good. After the city burned in 1666, building regulations were introduced to reduce the spread of fire. When law enforcement was inadequate, the first modern police force was created. When it was afflicted by cholera and appalling smells, a comprehensive network of sewers and river embankments was created. When it was decided to bring education to swathes of the population who had had none, an elegant and repeatable way of building schools was devised. In response to slums, the concept of council housing was invented. When privately run transport was chaotic and uncoordinated, London Transport was formed. In response to sprawl, a Metropolitan Green Belt was decreed. After bombing, new housing and new towns were planned. When smog was killing people and making streets opaque, laws on clean air were passed. When too much of the old fabric was being wrecked, protections of historic buildings and areas were created. Rasmussen, indeed, for all his admiration of London's trading spirit, also saw its local government and public institutions as equally important in maintaining its freedoms.

Often interventions were prompted by popular actions, such as the occupation of exclusive parks, campaigns to preserve historic buildings, and the decades-long struggle to prevent the enclosure and development of open spaces. Such interventions form the fabric and appearance of London, as much as those of the industrious and brilliant entrepreneurs, and the dreamers, makers, grabbers and chancers of the private sector. The characteristic front of a brick London house, in the placing of its windows and the details of its parapets and roofs, is governed by building acts. There are graceful inter-war underground stations, famous museums, thoughtful council housing, the granite balustrades and cast-iron lamp posts of Thames embankments and the trees on the streets. The tourists' image is formed by London Transport graphics, red buses, policemen's uniforms, the Houses of Parliament and such as remain of the red telephone boxes that made technical equipment civic.

In each case the response was creative and unprecedented: public authorities, sometimes under pressure from popular campaigns, devised new methods to address new problems. They were also huge in scale. They usually involved both the challenging and the accommodation of vested interests. They were not just functional but generated structures and spaces that help shape London's visual and social culture.

London is sometimes portrayed as an anarchic free-for-all, whose spirit and vitality would be betrayed by any kind of public action or direction. It is not. It is a competitive and creative interplay between capital, citizens and visions of the public good. From Primrose Hill you can pick out local authority housing estates and NHS hospitals among the new towers, not to mention the Palace of Westminster. The setting for the view is the verdant hill itself, preserved as public open space by an Act of Parliament.

There is also, guiding the bunching and scattering of towers, the London View Management Framework, a policy which creates zones where tall buildings can and cannot be built, in order to preserve key views of monuments. One of these views is of St Paul's from Primrose Hill, although you have to position yourself carefully to catch it. Seen from here, in fact, the policy seems Canute-like. For the message of the most recent changes to this view is that, if London is an arena of contest between public and private concentrations of

wealth and power, it is the latter that is winning. The biggest, the newest, the shiniest and most attention-grabbing structures are almost all built for profit.

London's genius is to be the City of the Present, too pragmatic to be a utopian ideal of the future, too messed-up to be a model from history, but able to give shape to whatever forces are running through the world. If, now, a central struggle of cities is that between the productive and destructive powers of borderless finance and the specificities and liberties of a place, it is vivid and complex in London – the more so as the city combines its openness to trade with an inherited fabric of buildings and politics that is intricate and resistant. As an example of the way the world goes, London has a special significance. To be optimistic, it also has in its present state – as it has in the past – the potential to generate responses to the social and economic forces that belong to the present. Such responses would be provisional, as they always have been, but they

would also have the ability to create new models for cities almost everywhere.

Scenography, however, only tells so much. To know more you must descend Primrose Hill and leave the area, its sugar houses and celebrity spottings, its vulture squawks and Dalmatian howls, to explore elsewhere.

2: The Disembodied
Economy, Embodied

During the 2014 campaign for Scottish independence, it was clear from what independence was sought. It was not from England as a whole – there was little sign that Scots minded being part of the same country as Ipswich or Middlesbrough – but from London.

Alex Salmond, then First Minister of Scotland, quoted Professor Tony Travers of the London School of Economics: 'London is the dark star of the economy, inexorably sucking in resources, people, and energy. Nobody quite knows how to control it.'

He also quoted the business secretary of the British government, Vince Cable, for whom the capital is: 'a kind of giant suction machine, draining the life out of the rest of the country'.

Gordon Wilson, Salmond's predecessor as leader of the Scottish National Party, said: 'today the grip of the London octopus is so powerful that the rest of the UK exists to serve it regardless'.

This death star, this suction machine, this octopus, this thing so frightful it mixes metaphors, had two hearts, the 'Westminster elite' and the financial centre usually described as 'The City' which, as well as the square mile of the historic City of London – the place that did an epochal deal with William the Conqueror – was now augmented by its rivalrous sibling Canary Wharf. Salmond and Wilson, like many others, identified this financial centre as the place from where bankers, traders and speculators grew rich on recklessness, leaving the rest of the world to pick up the bill, and still do.

Since 2007, Salmond continued, 'London's economy has grown approximately twice as much as the rest of the United Kingdom's. And growth is again being driven by consumption rather than investment; by a housing bubble as opposed to the real economy.'

Irvine Welsh, writer and supporter of independence, wrote: 'Scots are showing they won't go on committing their taxes or oil monies to building a London super-state on the global highway for the transnational rich, particularly when it's becoming unaffordable to their Cockney comrades, driving them out of their own city to the M25 satellites.'

To know the place they described, contemplate Canary Wharf. Its central silver obelisk is often used as an image of London's financial industry, especially its more sinister side. It appears in views reminiscent of the famous shot of St Paul's Cathedral shrouded in Blitz-smoke, only with a different message, bright and imperturbable amid a penumbra of unsettled weather and east London shabbiness. Canary Wharf also generated some of the most memorable images of the Lehman Brothers collapse, when the windows of the bank's headquarters filled with tailored *fesses*, hands fidgeting behind suit trousers or pencil skirts, as they heard their fates. The facades of such buildings are usually inscrutable – that for once one of them betrayed its inner life showed how torn was the fabric of the financial universe.

Next to the obelisk is the HSBC tower, one of the grey posts visible from Primrose Hill. Seen from closer it is a sleek tube designed by Norman Foster, the architect who in the 1980s achieved worldwide fame for designing the headquarters in Hong Kong of the Hong Kong and Shanghai Banking Corporation, as HSBC was formerly known. Where the earlier work had been elaborate and legendarily expensive, however, being in part a statement about

Hong Kong's assertion of faith in its future, the Canary Wharf version is plainer.

Greater interest lies inside. Its boardroom, to judge by images available online, is unsettling: a grey-black room and an oval table ringed with decision-makers before a wall-sized world map, the continents light against darker oceans. Have they not seen the War Room in *Dr Strangelove*? Worse, have they seen it and been inspired?

In the tower's foyer is the 'History Wall', a relatively early work by the prodigy of British design Thomas Heatherwick, a plane thirty metres by seven on which are displayed almost 4,000 images from the bank's archives. The Hong Kong and Shanghai Banking Corporation was founded in 1865 and in the course of its existence took over some older banks, so the archives go back some time. The images include fragments of documents and banknotes, all swirly copperplate and sepia tones, profiles of directors, stiff group photographs of staff in suits, forested tropical coasts bearing the first straight lines of colonial city building, cast-iron banking halls, ports of steam and sail and other props and sets for the novels of Joseph Conrad. The images are crisply printed on sharp little aluminium flags, a frozen flutter set perpendicular to a mirrored backdrop. Approached obliquely they make a vibrant fuzz; seen straight on they prettily disappear, such that you can see right through to the reflection or, through a transparent section of the wall, into the lift lobbies behind.

According to one explanation, the aims of this installation were to:

- build stature and credibility for HSBC
- demonstrate that HSBC is a global brand with a unique experience – a multi-local approach that is very different from the standardizing, homogenizing approach of other multinationals

- showcase and celebrate the diverse background of the Group – its continuous growth and development through amalgamation and acquisition since 1762.

It is considered a success. It 'perfectly illustrates the company's brand message "The World's Local Bank"' and provides 'rare and intriguing glimpses of the financial sector and gives social and cultural context to the business'. It also 'impacts the built environment by exuding character and humanity throughout the imposing head office foyer, making it a "warmer" environment for visitors and staff'.

It fits the bank's ambition, as the advertising publication *Campaign* put it, 'to appear global yet approachable,' which would also be supported by advertising that saturated the world's airports with images of tribal masks, wizened Orientals, babies, classical torsos, ballet dancers and gay men kissing. It was part of a triumph of brand-building: *Campaign* said that in five years the HSBC brand went from non-existence to an estimated value of $8.7 billion.

Which is all charming, except that the History Wall's version of history glides over many things not-nice with which the bank might have been involved in the last two centuries. It doesn't stress the fact that the Hong Kong and Shanghai Banking Corporation was founded in the immediate aftermath of the Opium Wars, in which the British used violence and destruction to force the Chinese government to accept a devastating narcotics trade. Among the upshots was the making of Shanghai into a treaty port, with special provisions for foreign trade, and of Hong Kong into a British colony. If the bank was not responsible for the wars, it benefited from the business they facilitated.

The Opium Wars are as rarely recalled in Britain as they are often remembered in China. At the time and since they have been seen as some of the darkest episodes in British imperial history. There have also been revisionist attempts to portray them as regrettable necessities for the Empire's civilizing influence on mankind. But, even if one is as generous as possible to the latter arguments, there is at the very least some moral complexity in the matter. Of which the wall gives little clue.

The wall is 'a requisite part of new employee learning' and 'employees are required as part of their performance contract to demonstrate the values and character of HSBC (illustrated by the History Wall)'. This implies that employees' career prospects can suffer if they don't absorb the incomplete truths of the aluminium flags, an almost Pyongyangian exercise in obedience and propaganda. In view of this inculcation with ethical amnesia, it is perhaps not surprising that HSBC returned to making profits from addiction. In 2012 the US Department of Justice announced in a Deferred Prosecution Agreement that it had handled billions of dollars of illicit cash, on behalf of the evil Sinaloa drugs cartel in Mexico as well as rogue states like Iran, Libya, Sudan and Burma. Its Swiss subsidiary was later found to be assisting systematic tax avoidance. It seems that the bank took too literally the idea of adapting to local customs.

The History Wall is an example of the politics of the picturesque: if you make something pretty, you might stop people noticing what lies behind it. It is also an episode in the vaster creation of Canary Wharf, which is made possible by the many dollars, whether clean or dirty, generated by HSBC and similar institutions, as well as tax breaks, government investment in infrastructure and some spectacular bankruptcy. And the first thing to say about the physical environment of Canary Wharf is that it is in many ways pleasant.

It is composed of large blocks organized formally around planted spaces, some with tended lawns and clipped and espaliered trees. One area is of North American character, with rough boulders, winding paths and conifers. The buildings often have broad arcades at their base – a simple but effective device that is surprisingly underused in London, given its patchy weather. The Wharf is inward-looking, but allows views from time to time of the water of the old docks. Smaller, more Mediterranean courts feed the larger square, where trees are now mature enough to make a canopy, and their expanding root balls pleasingly bulge the pavement. With a bit more dust, you could start a game of boules here.

It has most of the desirables of model modern urbanism: bike racks, artworks, mown grass, safety, Wi-Fi, good signage, considered street furniture, controlled smoking, mixed uses, accessibility, film screenings, an ice rink in winter, the smell of woks. It is very clean, with staff picking fallen petals from the bowls of cyclamen and polishing the steel and granite. There is a balance of transport modes – train, tube, bus, bike, foot, car. None dominates another, the well-behaved hum of the motor traffic being almost agreeable. The development follows a plan which set a strong pattern from the outset, but which also allows some degree of variation.

Its architectural styles go through stages. The earliest, designed in the 1980s by large American practices, is in Edwardian prefab, a style in which the modern technique of prefabricating chunks of building in factories was employed, while the aesthetic evoked buildings from the beginning of the twentieth century. Later, responding to criticisms that the architecture was insufficiently British and too retrograde, Norman Foster and other locals were hired to clad the blocks with sheens of metal and glass. Later again, a new kind of normal was established, with unexciting buildings in an updated version of post-war corporate modernism. At every stage, regardless of style, the finishes are considered, well made and enduring.

In the middle is the obelisk, One Canada Square, designed by César Pelli, who was born in Argentina and is based in New Haven, Connecticut. On completion in 1991 it was the tallest building in Britain. Aiming to draw attention to Canary Wharf's off-centre

location, it succeeded. It is now complemented by bon-bons of im-aginative commissioning: a bridge floating on high-tech pontoons by the visionary practice Future Systems, a deep blue reflective hat placed over an underground shopping mall by the diverting designer Ron Arad.

Canary Wharf has its oddnesses. The strong axis and heavy classicism of the first phase reminded some journalists who worked there of Ceaușescu's Bucharest, and they called it 'The Avenue of Capitalist Victory'. The geometrical shrubs look as if, like HSBC's employees, they are on performance contracts. Canary Wharf's urbanity can feel pixelated, as if rendered by the computer tech-nology available at the time of its inception, nearly thirty years ago. Those nice arcades mostly turn out not to have the shops and cafes you expect in such spaces and which are mostly located in a under-ground mall, this being standard practice in the harsh climate of Toronto, which is where Canary Wharf's development company were based. The separation of arcades and shopping creates a strange effect: there is the thing that looks like a setting for urban activity, which is the superstructure of squares and arcades, and the place where activity happens, which is the mall.

Central to Canary Wharf's commercial concept is the idea that its buildings can be calibrated to meet the desires of the office market. They can attain the right size and proportions, achieve the optimum distance from lift core to exterior wall and offer unrivalled provision of data servicing. Each floor can be the same, so that managers can relocate departments from one to another without having to think about rearranging the layout. The buildings are grey or beige, so they don't compete with the corporate colour of who-ever might move in. Canary Wharf can do this because it is built on the open space of former docks, whereas office buildings in the City have to twist and dodge to fit into medieval street patterns.

The Wharf's blocks are therefore machines, the skills of leading architects being applied mostly to superficial differences of facade and lobby. The HSBC tower (Norman Foster, modernist, red logo, 108,000 square feet of floor area, 656 feet high) is essentially identical to its companion the Citi tower (César Pelli, faintly deco, mostly white logo, 108,000 square feet of floor area, 656 feet high). Part of the role of the open spaces is to provide the difference and diversion – one might call it the humanity – that the office buildings might be felt to lack. One aspect of Canary Wharf's particular atmosphere, its android urbanity, is this coexistence of technically determined space and the wish to look like a city.

There is also security. If you drive in, you encounter a checkpoint redolent of Cold War spy movies: winding down of window, scrutiny by guard, barrier upswing. Once inside you see a private police force, who but for slight variations in the uniform look like real police. You can tease them by playing the tripod game, which is to look as if you are about to take a serious photograph. Like kittens seeing a ping-pong ball, they feel obliged to take action, except when you cross an imperceptible line, for example next to the Underground station, when you are no longer on the Canary Wharf Estate. Even though you can take almost the same photograph that you might from one metre closer, you are no longer their problem.

In some places it is taboo even to use a hand-held phone camera, as at the entrance to HSBC. Two charming bronze lions flank the revolving doors, clones of a pair installed outside HSBC's Shanghai office in 1923, and as I frame a shot a large man fills more and more of the screen.

'It's the main entrance you can't take pictures of the main entrance.'

'It's just that I like the lions.'

'The lions, that's all right. Just not the main entrance.'

So these almost-police contribute to the feeling that this is an almost-*polis*, somewhere that feels as if clever cyborgs had scanned

'It's just that I like the lions'

human cities and reconstituted their data into a three-dimensional reality. Which is then modified by the incidents added to the open spaces: the art, stalls selling 'Indian street food' or falafels; one day, an installation raising money for the homeless, the last jarringly incentivized with a goodie bag of free Godiva chocolates and the chance to win dinner for two at The Ivy. If you had any thought that the world of the Wharf was unspontaneous or uncreative or lacked conscience, these moments are designed to reassure you.

There has been criticism of Canary Wharf for establishing this privately controlled zone, albeit one not created by seizing land that was previously public. The site was part of the West India Docks, which an Act of Parliament of 1799 stipulated should be protected by a wall thirty feet high and a moat, relative to which the current development is accessible and free. It has also been criticized for its disconnection from its surroundings and the brutal contrast between its well-tended order and the still run-down neighbourhoods a short distance away – when Bloomberg News asked workers there what London borough they were in, most didn't know. To which George Jacobescu, chairman and chief executive of the Canary Wharf Group, has responded by saying that his development 'has made enormous, enormous change' to the area, but that 'it takes time, it takes a lot of effort'. It is, in Jacobescu's view, a work in progress.

The people who use the Wharf don't seem too bothered by its possible lack of authenticity. The place makes physical the modern deal which, most of the time, most people accept, at least in a prosperous city like London: your life will be made pleasant and comfortable, with the help of diversions and stimulations that are well calculated and sometimes brilliant or charming, as long as you obey certain corporate rules, surrender some trivial freedoms and forget about asking how these things come to pass. You receive donations you didn't ask for and may find annoying or intriguing –

a U2 album on iTunes, a software upgrade, an art installation – and you shrug at this little claim on your spirit and carry on.

Canary Wharf's origins can be traced to 20 March 1969, when the leftish magazine *New Society* published a special issue called 'Non-Plan: an Experiment in Freedom'. Here the same Cedric Price who had helped design London Zoo's aviary teamed up with another group of collaborators – the planner Peter Hall, the critic Reyner Banham and the magazine's editor Paul Barker – to attack the then-dominant approach of city planning directed by high government authority and their professional consultants and to ask if it would not be better to make no plan at all. Rather, they said, let people choose the kind of places where they would live.

One of the successors of 'Non-Plan' was the idea of the enterprise zone, developed by Peter Hall, whereby minimal planning would be combined with tax incentives to revive failing areas of cities. During the 1970s, meanwhile, the decline of London's docks was creating one of the largest such failing areas in the country, making it the object of projects of renewal. In a TV film, for example, made by the novelist and producer B. S. Johnson three years before his suicide in 1973, the architects Alison and Peter Smithson look into the camera with perfect glumness, as if posing for mugshots, and call for a 'leisure pleasure zone' in the old docks. The Conservative leader of the Greater London Council, Horace Cutler, wanted the Olympics to go there. J. G. Ballard set his novel *High Rise*, in which the safari-jacketed architect Anthony Royal presides over the feral self-destruction of a luxury residential development, in the old docks. Then, following Margaret Thatcher's election in 1979, she and her charismatic environment secretary Michael Heseltine saw Hall's idea as a way of solving the area's problems.

They made much of what was now called 'Docklands' into an

NEWsociety

March 1969 No 338 1s 6d weekly

Robert Holman   WRONG POVERTY PROGRAMME
John Berger   MAGRITTE RECONSIDERED
David Marquand   EDUCATION BACKLASH

Rayner Banham   NON-PLAN:
Paul Barker   AN EXPERIMENT IN FREEDOM
Peter Hall
Cedric Price

enterprise zone and put a seven-mile stretch of land, on both sides of the Thames, into the care of the unelected London Docklands Development Corporation. The concept was an intellectual alliance common in that phase of Thatcherism, of an anarchistic reaction to centralized planning by free thinkers of the 1960s and 70s, with her belief in making conditions favourable to the operations of the markets. In this philosophy there seemed little contradiction – what people wanted and what the market provided were seen as identical, their common enemy being the misguided instructions of state bureaucrats. The belief in engaging local people with shaping their future neighbourhoods, as proposed in the *New Society* article, was, however, largely absent from the concept of the Docklands Enterprise Zone.

At first the zone had the effect that was probably intended, the building of an urban scrubland of low-level industrial units and housing estates. But in 1984 Dr Michael von Clemm, who was chairman of both Credit Suisse First Boston and the Roux Brothers' restaurant business, had lunch in a Thames barge moored next to Canary Wharf, a dock facility built in 1936 to serve the fruit trade. His object was to find a site for a food-packaging factory but, reminded of an area of Boston harbour that had been converted into back-up offices, wondered why the same thing couldn't happen on the waterfront he could see from his table. His lunch companion Reg Ward, the chief executive of the London Docklands Development Corporation, liked the idea.

Von Clemm then held a meeting at which his bank's property adviser, the Kentuckian developer G. Ware Travelstead, spoke up. Travelstead had once planned a ski resort in Iran with the Shah, and during his multilawyered bankruptcy in the 1990s would become known among his creditors as Beware Travelstead. 'Visionary he certainly is,' his second wife would tell the *Baltimore Sun* by the time that he was on to his third and youngest, 'and to make visions come true, I guess a visionary has to be a little bit of a con man.' He was, at any rate, unafraid of big and unusual ideas. He had also recently been frustrated in building as he wanted in the City of London and now asked why the main office of a bank like Credit Suisse First Boston could not be located at Canary Wharf.

The plan was no less startling than a ski resort in Iran, at a time when the area looked isolated and desolate, a dark continent as far as people who might work for CSFB were concerned, populated by who knew what savages. The Isle of Dogs, where Canary Wharf is located, was especially disconnected, being mostly ringed with water and having little public transport. Its name sounds anciently sinister. But Travelstead pushed on and developed a proposal for an office development of ten million square feet with a large central tower. In 1987, when CSFB and Morgan Stanley withdrew their backing, the project was taken over by Olympia and York, the Canadian property company set up by the Reichmann brothers, Jewish refugees of Hungarian origin who had arrived in Toronto after a successful period trading currency in Tangier. Olympia and York had built the tallest building in Canada. They had created Battery Park City, a new district of Lower Manhattan erected on landfill in the Hudson River, which in turn had been formed from the excavations for the twin towers of the World Trade Center. Battery Park City is an ordered, highly managed zone and the plan was to create something similar in London's old docks. Where the New York project has many apartments, however, Canary Wharf was to be almost all offices.

Olympia and York started building. They raised the tower. They went into liquidation in 1992 with a debt of $20bn, but the Reichmanns managed to be part of the consortium, now called Canary Wharf Group, that took over in 1995. It took time for the development itself to become the bankers' haven of which Travelstead had dreamed, due partly to the fact that it wasn't connected

Aerial view of proposed Canary Wharf in the year 2025 by Carlos Diniz, 1988

to the London Underground until 1999. In its early years newspapers took much of the space, as part of their dispersal from their traditional home in Fleet Street. Journalists would wander its halls like lost souls, their natural scruffiness out of place amid the North American shine, deprived of the connection with city life that was at the heart of their work, and with little to cheer them by way of bars and restaurants.

It was only in the new millennium that the Wharf really flourished. More easily than the City of London, which was constrained by its historic fabric, it could offer the wide floorplates and large buildings of a million or so square feet that contemporary financial institutions – then becoming enormous through mergers and growth – demanded. On this flat, open territory, on a gridded plan, the developers could realize the Platonic ideal of the modern office building, much as it had once been possible, in the same location, to achieve efficient and functional banana warehouses.

Banks, lawyers and consultants moved in: Allen and Overy, ANZ, Bank of America, Barclays, Cantor Fitzgerald, Citi, Clifford Chance . . . The Wharf exceeded Travelstead's hopes by growing to fourteen million square feet, and it filled with restaurants and shops, making it a destination at weekends as well as on working days. In 2012 the *Financial Times* reported that it was overtaking the City of London as the largest employer of bankers in Europe. It grew into the water of the adjoining docks and expanded onto their further shores. Canary Wharf Group started developing a residential district nearby, Wood Wharf.

And so the speculations of some hairy 1960s thinkers combined with the arm chancing of North American developers and the relentless logistics of financial institutions to create the most significant and influential intervention in London for a generation. It was helped too by both gigantic bankruptcy and government subsidy and support, in the tax breaks and other financial incentives of the early years, and the Underground line extension and other transport investments that have helped the Wharf work. To see it as a work of pure capitalism, unaided and unrestricted by the state, is too simple.

Its effects have spread far beyond its boundaries. It has influenced, for example, the rebuilding of Beirut after the Lebanese civil wars and the growth of Chinese cities. The concept of very large private developments, under a single ownership, within whose boundaries everything from security to street food to public art to the building of skyscrapers is directed by the management, which aspires to the scale and attributes but not all the freedoms of a city, is now a principal agent of urban expansion across the world. Canary Wharf is not only a pioneer of this concept, but it is one of the most significant examples.

In London it had an immediate effect on the City, the place whose snubbing of G. Ware Travelstead had led to his vision of what the Wharf could be. Even before construction started on its upstart rival, the prospect of competition drove the City to serve the demand for abundant quantities of up-to-the-minute office space that accompanied the deregulation of the stock exchange in the 1980s. As much as possible in what is the oldest part of London, veined like ripe cheese with protected historic buildings, its outdated substance was removed and replaced.

The market wanted wide buildings, allowing expansive trading zones and generous heights between floors to give space for data cabling and other services. Buildings from the 1960s, barely twenty years old, now looked skinny and obsolete and started to disappear. London Wall, a strip of stunted autopia conceived by post-war planners for a bombed-out part of the City, where gridded glass boxes rhythmically lined a dual carriageway that was part of a larger but never implemented road scheme, was rebuilt in stages. First came Alban Gate, a pink granite jukebox perched over the road, then

London Wall, in 1962 and 2015

88 Wood Street, where the office of Richard Rogers reworked the themes of their Pompidou Centre in Paris as an elegant office building for the Japanese investment bank Daiwa – a people's palace of culture remade as corporate refinement. Further buildings ensued over the 1990s and 2000s, always adding mass and architectural elaboration, until the road became a canyon of swagger. It was now far from the vision of London Wall's 1950s planners, which had aspired to the discipline of the Bauhaus architect Ludwig Karl Hilberseimer, yet there was also a gleam of futuristic fantasy in their conception that the later buildings amplified.

In the 1980s the demand was for groundscrapers, medium-height blocks that swelled to the edge of their property line in order to create as much trading floor as possible. Towers, in what turned out to be a temporary lull, went out of fashion, with nothing that might be called a skyscraper appearing between the completion of the 600-foot NatWest Tower in 1980 and One Canada Square in 1991. The latter, however, was another goad to the City. It rediscovered its enthusiasm for height and from the later 1990s its planners started encouraging and approving towers, which were built over the next decade.

In the time of Margaret Thatcher her radical politics were combined with the trappings and look of tradition, and so it was with the City's new buildings. A similar Edwardian prefab was favoured for the groundscrapers to that used in Canary Wharf, often delivered by a handful of large American architectural practices who, knowing better than the natives how to make money factories, shouldered their way into London. Sometimes old facades, even of average quality, would be propped up while steel financial engines were inserted behind them, as happened with the offices of the Japanese holding company Nomura. Close to venerable sites like St Paul's Cathedral the preferred style would be pushed back in history, to make animatronic versions of Georgian or baroque architecture.

HSBC

Gherkin

Freewheeling capital chose over time to express itself in other ways. In the 1990s it discovered the chaste-ish modernism then practised by Norman Foster and his company. From the new millennium it embraced iconic architecture, the notion that good buildings are (a) extraordinary-looking and (b) designed by architects recognized as good, the surest imprimatur of which is the $100,000 Pritzker Prize awarded each year by the family who own the Hyatt hotel chain to an architect who, 'irrespective of nationality, race, creed, or ideology . . . has produced consistent and significant contributions to humanity and the built environment through the art of architecture'.

A key figure was Peter Wynne Rees, the chief planning officer of the City of London from 1985 to 2014. Early in his career he upheld the idea that financial revolution should take place behind traditional-looking facades, insisting for example that the American chaebol practice of SOM should clad their work in Portland stone when in sight of St Paul's, and keep their modernistic steel for the back streets. Later he urged celebrity architects to express themselves. The Square Mile is now a game reserve of nicknamed shapes – Gherkin, Cheesegrater, Walkie-Talkie – and it has the work of five winners of the Pritzker Prize within its borders and of two more nearby.

Part of Rees's motivation was to differentiate from Canary Wharf. If part of the latter's attraction was its industrial efficiency, the City could offer distinctiveness, fascination, vibrancy. Two towers, both created by Foster and Partners around the turn of the millennium, illustrate the difference. In the City the Rees-influenced Gherkin is striking, memorable, odd, 'iconic' and in terms of such criteria as its useful floor area or construction cost not completely efficient. The HSBC tower is determined by parameters of function and market, given a stylish wrap by the Foster flair. One is an artistic table lamp, the other a practical fridge-freezer.

In the competition to attract business, not only with Canary Wharf but also with foreign cities such as Frankfurt and New York, it was necessary to make the City into an attractive place for highly paid employees to spend their days. Here business interest allied with architects' rediscovery, in reaction to modernist city-planning, of 'urbanism' – of what they saw as the qualities of traditional cities. Where modernism was accused of creating sterile, functionalist environments, with different uses separated into zones, a return was now urged to the patterns of old cities, where shops and restaurants, for example, might combine with office premises and where the shaping of shared spaces such as squares and thoroughfares, where chance encounters might take place, was as important as the design of individual buildings.

This tendency went back to the hymning of humble streets in *Death and Life of American Cities* of 1961, the hugely influential book by the activist and urbanist Jane Jacobs. By the 1980s it included a revival of what is called Beaux-Arts planning, the nineteenth-century approach of structuring a city with recognizable geometric devices, such as squares, circuses, avenues and boulevards. Hence City developments like Broadgate and Paternoster Square, where geometrically defined and welcoming open spaces were populated by places to eat and drink and enriched by art and performance. In these places paving materials are high quality, the design of such features as seating, lights and bollards considered and coordinated. Professional maintenance and security teams keep them clean, in good repair and free of bad behaviour.

Canary Wharf and the City's remaking both set precedents for the rest of London. They established the idea that developers would be London's primary city-makers, companies who, lightly guided by

Paternoster Square

planning authorities, would create not only individual commercial buildings, but also the roads and open spaces between them, determining their appropriate mix of uses and managing their maintenance, cultural programmes and security. Through the mechanism known as planning gain, whereby developers pay for affordable housing and other public projects as a condition of receiving planning permission, they would dispense benefits to the hinterland of their developments. In this world property companies could become de facto municipalities.

The shaping of London by big landowners has the respectability of history. Much of the most admired parts of the city, such as the streets and squares of Bloomsbury, Fitzrovia and Belgravia, were created by the great estates, the aristocratic families who, finding themselves lucky enough to own the fields into which London expanded, wanted to maximize their value. At their grandest these speculating aristocrats were royal. Of these the most ambitious was the Prince Regent, the future George IV, who also ruled the country during his father's mental illness.

In the early nineteenth century, in addition to the park that bears his title, he and his architects created the mile-and-a-half sequence of urban spaces that leads to it, running like an uphill stream from St James's Park through streets, circuses and crescents before swelling into the 410-acre pool of leafiness that occupies the foreground of the view from Primrose Hill. Regent's Park and its long approach are the nearest London came to the large-scale set-pieces that Pope Sixtus V imposed on Rome, or that Baron Haussmann and Napoleon III would on Paris.

It was the work of a decadent prince and his corrupt architect, John Nash, but, this being in Rasmussen's terms a 'commercial' and not an 'absolutist' city, it had distinctive characteristics. It was in part a property speculation, with the aim of enhancing the value

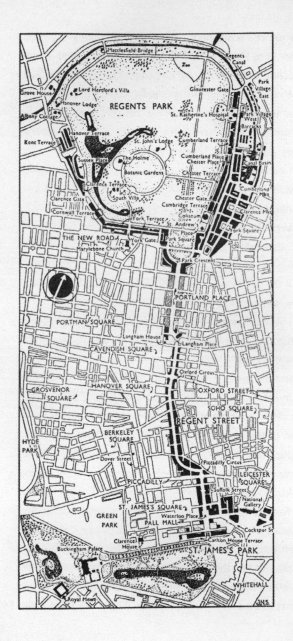

of land in the prince's possession, the site of the park having been taken from monks by Henry VIII and remaining in royal hands since. George was acting as much as a privileged private landowner as a monarch, motivated by both public and personal interests.

There was intent to achieve a public benefit, in the form of wider, better surfaced, less crowded thoroughfares and to discipline the sometimes rackety and dangerous areas through which they ran, on which basis the project was supported by an Act of Parliament. There was a desire to aggrandize the crown and the nation, with a 'National Valhalla' and a royal palace. But the prince seems also to have seen the park as a gated playground, an early Bel Air, which would also enhance the value of developments around its edge and along the approach route. The project's priorities can be inferred from the fact that the Valhalla and the palace proved optional to the pursuit of profit and were never built.

Where an absolute ruler might have thrust a single straight line from one end of the ensemble to the other, the developer-regent was obliged sometimes to weave round pre-existing buildings and ownerships, and the avenues and crescents which in other regimes could serve military displays here sustain retail and residential development. His sequence is opportunistic, commercially and architecturally. In this it was helped by the application of picturesque principles, recently developed in the design of landscape gardens for country houses, which gave value to surprises, asymmetries, chance incidents and the as-found. Nash's line starts straight and formal, up steps to the column commemorating the famously fatuous Duke of York and on to Piccadilly Circus, but then ducks left into the quadrant of Regent Street, which, curving back rightwards, restores the line's roughly northward direction. The street, ideally straight, bends slightly before proceeding past Oxford Circus and executing a deft swivel, left then right, around the conical

Park Crescent

spire of All Souls Langham Place. Next the composition enlists the pre-Nash Portland Place, broad and straight, and at its far end opens into the near-perfect semi-circle of Park Crescent (Nash again), which opens into a green square, which opens into Regent's Park.

The park is itself ordered by picturesque devices. Symmetrical villas in off-white stucco are half-hidden by artfully scattered groves. Intimate spaces alternate with open ones, straight lines with sinuous, and a boating lake of uterine form with the precise 360 degrees of road called the Inner Circle. Defining the perimeter and also appearing between trees are the terraces. These aspire to disguise the fact that they are rows of houses by taking the form of palace facades, with grand centralized compositions of pediments, corner pavilions and giant orders of Ionic and Corinthian columns.

Theatre and make-believe are part of the park's artistry of architecture and real estate. The terraces pretend to be palaces and their stucco pretends to be stone, an illusion ended when you see their blunt brick rears. If Nash was casual with details and construction – and he was – they still pretend to quality. These stage sets create an image of elegance that succeeded in making them valuable homes, which has since helped fund the remaking of Nash's original jerry-building such that they became in some sense well built. Perception has shaped reality.

Greenery is used to soften differences between architectural styles as now it does between mosque and zoo. It also achieves a social effect. The park contains or has contained the homes of such people as the United States Ambassador and Prince Jefri Bolkiah of Brunei, and the property developer Christian Candy wanted to make an entire terrace into a single home of 50,000 square feet, but at the same time it is an everyday park, used for office softball tournaments, strolling and picnics. Vegetation and picturesque planning ease the co-existence of the popular and the exclusive.

Rasmussen called it 'The People's Park'. He praises the wisdom and generosity of the decision to preserve so much green space – naively, as these were not virtues for which the prince was famous. The park was not available to the public until the reign of his successor William IV, but eventually like other parks it became an undisputed common asset, a shared territory where the city gains a sense of itself.

Regent's Park might be seen as vindication of the idea that a city built by major landowners will in the end serve the public, but only if it is acknowledged it was not at first such a place, and that it took further public actions to achieve Rasmussen's ideal. When completed it looked similar to large modern developments like Canary Wharf in the way it combined limited public intentions, the taming of unruly neighbourhoods, and property speculation based on pushing up values.

Dr Michael von Clemm did not live to see his barge-borne lunchtime lightbulb moment become its present reality: he died in 1997 of a brain tumour which his friends, including the future mobile phone magnate Richard Branson, thought could have been caused by his early adoption of mobile phones. Canary Wharf has, however, not forgotten him and he is honoured there with a tablet that bears his profile in bronze bas-relief. It lacks von Clemm's line, which perhaps should be chiselled with fine serifs, when selling his vision in 1986: 'I'd say London has lucked out.'

As sheer constructional achievement Canary Wharf is stupendous, a gigantic, thriving place made out of almost nothing in twenty-five years, professionally delivered. Strikingly, for something descended from 'Non-Plan', it benefits from a degree of planning and coordination no longer seen in state-led projects. It brings investment, creates jobs, pays taxes and makes productive what might otherwise be blighted land.

It is also the object of criticism aimed at its visible divisiveness, at the impossible-to-miss difference between its prosperous order and the degraded environments outside its boundaries. Thus Owen Hatherley, in the *Guardian*:

> Canary Wharf has been for the last twenty years the most spectacular expression of London's transformation into a city with levels of inequality that previous generations liked to think they'd fought a war to eliminate. Very, very few of the new jobs went to those who had lost their jobs when the Port of London followed the containers to Tilbury; those that did were the most menial – cleaners, baristas, prostitutes. The new housing that emerged, first as a low-rise trickle in the 80s and 90s followed by a high-rise flood in the 00s, was without exception speculatively built. Inflated prices, dictated by the means of a captive market of bankers, soon forced up rents and mortgages in the surrounding areas, a major cause of London's current acute housing crisis.

'The ludicrous nonsense of "trickle-down economics"', continues Hatherley, 'is exposed in Canary Wharf more than anywhere else in Europe.' He then describes the poor state of three architecturally notable nearby council estates. 'If anyone in any of these estates has seen anything trickle down it would be an unpleasant-smelling liquid running from a great height.'

Anna Minton, in her 2009 book *Ground Control*, talked to residents of the Isle of Dogs who felt disenfranchised and not enriched by this wealth-machine in their midst. 'It's just gone from docks and council property to conglomerates and private buyers,' said one; '. . . local people don't get a look in where jobs are concerned.' Minton concluded that 'trickle-down hasn't worked in Docklands, or in any of the other places . . . where the same model of economic

Trickle-down

growth based on increasing property values has been rolled out'. Which wouldn't have troubled the construction magnate Nigel Broackes, the first chair of the London Docklands Development Corporation, who announced that 'we are not a welfare association but a property-based organization offering good value'.

Canary Wharf Group retort that they have created thousands of jobs, of which some are held by residents of Tower Hamlets, and have contributed to affordable housing and public transport. They receive some support from Queen Mary College of the University of London, whose research into corporate philanthropy found that Canary Wharf's businesses 'are deeply engaged in the well-being of communities in east London, particularly in education, training and the mentoring of young people'. One 'school-based respondent' told them that

> I sort of chortle about the fact that we're in a wonderful triangle. We've got the Olympic Park, we've got Canary Wharf and we've got the City, and we're right in the middle! . . . This is where London is happening and we're there. You can either passively watch it or engage with it, be excited by it.

The college's research concluded that 'over time strong relationships can be built between corporations and local community organisations, reducing the friction between welfare and profit, and shaping the development of people and places'.

Their main cautions were that such philanthropy could not be guaranteed to survive financial fluctuations, that it was 'selective', that it left the role of local government uncertain and that it was particular to the situation of Canary Wharf and the East End and might not be repeatable elsewhere. This last point is striking – usually the contrast between the great wealth of the Wharf and the poverty of its surroundings is the thing that provokes disquiet, but here the suggestion is that the scale of the difference is that very thing that makes this somewhat Victorian version of philanthropy possible.

Rushanara Ali, the Labour MP for the nearby constituency of Bethnal Green and Bow, says that Canary Wharf's tenants 'could be much more ambitious about getting local graduates into jobs', but she does not condemn the development as a whole or wish it undone. When she was growing up in the area in the 1980s and early 90s, she says, 'we hated journalists coming round. Every time you picked up a paper it would be about how the area was poor and deprived, or about racism. Now it has a more positive image . . . When I was growing up it felt like a sink here, a dark place, a stuck community' and a benefit of the gentrification led by Canary Wharf is that it has 'probably led to more mixed schools and brought a wider range of activities and occupations. There is a feeling of more integration with the rest of London.'

Amazingly, given that it is the greatest urban experiment of the last thirty years, that it raises such profound economic and social issues and that it is now a prototype for development across Britain and beyond, conclusive research on the benefits and faults of Canary Wharf is sparse. Tides of money have flowed through it, a portion of which has irrigated its hinterland. It has raised property values, pushing out people who can't afford them. It has benefited from huge government subsidy, in the form of tax breaks and investment in transport. But it is impossible really to know, because the evidence is not there, what is the balance of its successes and failures. For a subject that provokes statements of certainty, both for and against, the available information is blurry.

Canary Wharf is an emblem of the well-known political dilemma of modern market economies, the dependency on financial institutions whose power exceeds that of elected governments, which contributes to the widening gap between the rich and everyone else. The Wharf's tenants illustrate the problem: they generate wealth and jobs and there is no likely economic system that can do without their services. But, as hardly needs elaborating, some also break laws and bring about financial calamities with impunity. The Wharf's buildings, shining amid gloom, look the part.

But the fact that the physical fabric looks the part does not mean that it exactly plays it. Heatherwick's History Wall, and the almost-*polis* of the development as a whole, might contribute to a removal from other realities that creates an atmosphere favourable to financial crimes, but art and architecture are hardly their primary cause. They also take place in other, different, urban environments.

The Isle of Dogs and east London were poorer and more isolated before the Wharf arrived, the dock jobs having by then disappeared, and it is not obvious how the area would be better off had it not been built. Its construction on underused quays displaced little by way of homes, employment or public assets. The arguments against it are therefore partly ones of degree: it might do more to benefit surrounding communities and to soften the contrasts between its buildings and its neighbours. Sometimes it seems that Canary Wharf's greatest affront to the liberal conscience is its visibility. If these same businesses were housed in posher places a few miles west, or in Midtown Manhattan or in Frankfurt or in Nihonbashi, Tokyo, they would be no less rapacious and disparities of wealth no less great. But they would not lend themselves to those heart-tugging Dives-et-Lazarus shots of glass and grot.

There is the unease inspired by its immaculate open spaces, the highly surveyed La-La Land of driving corporate ambition, by this stage set for *The Apprentice* and target of accusations of 'sterility'. I find these qualities weird too – but as one of many different kinds of territory all over London, one with which many of its users are content and as a small proportion of the total land area, it is not too menacing.

The most shocking things about Canary Wharf extend beyond

its boundaries and are matters for more than just its management. One is the collapse of almost anything resembling urban planning as soon as you step outside its boundaries, the unconsidered spaces in which non-Wharfites are expected to spend their days. These, perhaps, contribute as much to feelings of resentment as does the dazzle of the corporate zones. Another is the London-wide problem that regeneration equates to rising property prices equates to gentrification equates to exclusion of people on low or middle incomes. The will has so far been lacking to find serious answers to this question.

These two issues arise not only because business is powerful but also because government is weak, to which the standard political response has been to give more and more power and responsibility to property companies to shape the physical and social fabric of the city, on the grounds that only they have the competence and resources to do so. In this context Canary Wharf is now a model to be followed almost everywhere, at which point its other effects become menacing after all. What might be reasonable for a specialized enclave in a particular place is less so when rolled out across London. The controlling, excluding, exploitative spirit of the high-walled dock compounds, translated into a zone of money factories, is no way to make a city.

Canary Wharf, like the Prince Regent's developments and like the old docks, is an example of the power of landowners in London and the ways in which the city is made by trade. The Wharf and its surroundings also show the limitations of developers' logic. They show the need for creative interventions on behalf of the public, of a kind for which London has had a genius.

There will be more on these. But first, let's eat.

3: New Sybaris

If as cliché has it skyscrapers are penile then where am I now, in the express elevator of the Heron Tower, on the way to its rooftop bar? Shooting past the corpus cavernosum, surging towards the urethral opening? And what am I, hurtling upwards, with others? It doesn't bear thinking about.

At pavement level one passes the glass wall of a high reception area, with escalators and a truck-sized fish tank, before reaching a velvet rope and name-checks. Next a lobby as tight as the aquarium was ample and then the ascent, in an all-glass lift attached to the side of the tower, such that the streets of the City of London and then the rest of the capital unfurl around us. The rate of acceleration and degree of vertigo are just shy of nauseating, it being undesirable to spoil our appetite on the way to the rooftop restaurant. But there is still a mild test of nerve, appropriate to the risk-taking financial capital of the world.

On reaching the top we privileged homunculi pass through some tortuous corridors before entering a bar with a view of a terrace occupied by a tree aflame with an electric autumn of orange light. To the right stairs rise to two more levels past a glass wall; there are views of the Heron's companion towers, the Gherkin and Tower 42, Vegas-lit at their tips to announce that here too are pleasure zones. A community of cocktail drinkers is created two hundred metres into the air, for which the rest of the city – the bars and clubs of Shoreditch to the north, the suburbs stretching east

towards Essex – becomes atmosphere, a background lighting effect. Some drinkers occupy the stairs, like teenagers partying in their parents' house. At the top there is another rope, defining a more exclusive area.

If you don't turn right but continue straight on you reach the restaurant, a generous volume ceiled with a geodesic-looking lattice of thick curved bamboo. There are also hints of Oscar Niemeyer: as its name suggests, Sushisamba fuses culinary influences from Japan and Brazil, so the décor follows suit. A would-be enchanting space is formed by fragments of different sorts of nature – twigs, a crystal forest, the bamboo, the contents of plate and glass wherein slivers of flavour and texture have been sourced and combined from across the world to deliver tiny empires of experience, synaesthetic micro-symphonies of look, taste, feel, scent and even, in the surprising crunches that detonate amid smoother sensations, sound. There are clouds. A sculptural object in the ceiling resembles crystallized vapour, lights gather in cumuli, and puffs of foam, elBulli-style, float over the food. A dish of opaque fluid invites you to fish in it, as in a delicate swamp.

This is a place where City people are rewarded for their hard hours of screen-based labour, for being in effect call-centre workers with high incomes, with affirmations of status and delights of the senses (albeit one that got middling praise from the restaurant critics) in these celestial spaces. I do, however, experience some disappointment that the place is not more flagrant, more strutting, more of a coke-and-hookers inferno in the sky. Rather there is a peaceable round table of large-wristwatched young Africans and Arabs; elsewhere are seated Caucasian diners, who if loaded are discreetly so. In the bar City workers display the assertive nodding and wary bonhomie that passes for sociability when rivalrous business colleagues go out to drink and eat. There might be more overt excess beyond the rope at the top of the stairs and as the evening wears on the black skirts and heels arriving in the lift grow shorter and higher. But there is a well-behaved normality, relatively speaking, among most of the guests.

In London, as in other major cities, the arts of distraction have reached an unprecedented level of sophistication. If a cataclysm were to hit now, future generations would marvel – as we might over Petronius' descriptions of Roman excess – at our own time's range and ingenuity of food, drink, art, design and performance, of spas, bars, shops and clubs. Some are aimed at the rich, such as the 24K Cryogenic Diamond Mask facial (using diamond dust and real gold) offered by OROGOLD of Kensington High Street, Chelsea and Mayfair. Some are available to the reasonably well-off or to the large number of childless professionals with disposable income. Some, thanks to public art galleries and sponsored events, are free.

In a few weeks in 2014, for example, it was possible for a newspaper journalist to sample the following:

a visit to the London Coliseum, a stucco bubble in which fictive marble and fictive drapery coalesce in a fabric of ambiguous mass, originally the biggest of the many Edwardian music halls designed by the genius of such things Frank Matcham. There they are screening *River of Fundament*, a 6-hour film by the artist Matthew Barney, with orchestral score by Jonathan Bepler, on themes of life, death, rebirth, excrement, cars, ancient Egypt, Norman Mailer's worst novel and the suicide of Ernest Hemingway. Spa treatment at the Ironmonger Row Turkish Baths (established in 1931 by the London Borough of Finsbury, now run by the charitable social enterprise GLL). Delectable dim sum and artful multicultural cocktails in the darkly soothing basement bar of the Michelin-starred Hakkasan restaurant, restricting the budgetary impact by not permitting oneself expectations of a hearty meal. A trip outside London to see the louche eighteenth-century garden of Rousham, and the

Owens and Radić

Lido and Oto

more upright landscapes of Stowe. Walks in Wanstead Park, Epping Forest, Victoria Park. Swimming in the Olympic Aquatic Centre, designed by Zaha Hadid, and in the open-air lido in London Fields. Seeing some movies, some rented from an art-house DVD shop in Brick Lane. Watching famous footballers in a north London stadium. Turkish, Pakistani, Szechuan, Vietnamese and Persian meals, all good, none expensive, most with a fresh, invigorating pungency that could be called authentic, in Stoke Newington, Dalston, Whitechapel and Green Street. Eat in a rooftop pop-up Italian restaurant in Hackney, an actor from *Friends* on the next table. Hear music at the experimental venue Café Oto, in a space created by the young architectural collective Assemble. Experience interactions with the Belgrade-born performance artist Marina Abramović at the Serpentine Gallery, Kensington Gardens, one of them involving the counting of grains of rice. Also at the Serpentine, visit the gallery's temporary annual pavilion, designed by the architect Smiljan Radić (Chilean, of Croat descent), a heavy/light, Palaeolithic/space-age combination of rocks and fibreglass. Standing in a crowd, in the early hours of the morning, outside the car park of Selfridge's store in Oxford Street, amid men with Edward VII beards, George V trims and Henry V haircuts, until admitted past two white horses mounted by skinny long-haired riders, body-painted white, to a misty concrete deck with half-naked barmen and trans women strutting in beams of light, the whole being a Fashion Week party for the Californian-Parisian designer Rick Owens.

Not all these experiences will be to everyone's taste – not all, indeed, were to the journalist's – but they are a sample of the diversity and invention with which London daily and nightly strives to de-jade the appetites of its inhabitants. Some are built on the inheritance of past benefactions, some occupy spaces intended for other purposes. Some – the pungent meals – exemplify ways in which immigration has enriched London. Some are works of love, of cooks or artists who want to do their best with their media, others of calculation, some of both. There is both brilliance and pretension in the list. Many of these diversions consume references, memories and ideas, intellectual and physical material, with greedy promiscuity.

Peter Rees, for twenty-eight years the chief planner of the City of London, under whom projects like the Heron Tower were encouraged and approved, started late in his career to tell stories of his experiences visiting leather bars in east London. On one occasion he left a bar to find a group of Bengali teenagers fascinated with his street-parked Porsche. Some tension might be thought present in this situation – poor area, posh car, gay man, Muslim boys – but in Rees's telling he let the teenagers photograph themselves with the car and in the driving seat, which delighted them, before the parties went their separate ways. For Rees, this sort of encounter is the essence of London:

> it has always been a place where a minority could find succour; whether it was gay or religious or whatever it might be you could come into the East End of London and the East End of London would tolerate almost anything, within a very limited set of local rules which were community-run. If you think of the way that has produced a London that is the world's best party – the railway arches from Battersea to Bermondsey are full of gay saunas, discos, bars, all sorts of weird and wonderful things going on in those railway arches because there are enough people of any particular persuasion or interest in London to take a marginal space and come together in it. That then attracts more people. Twenty-, thirty-somethings come for the party. They only get the job to pay for the party.

In this eroto-economic theory of town planning, pleasure is an end in itself, a source of personal identity and freedom and an engine of the city's prosperity. The theory combines social and economic liberalism, both individual choice and competitive exploitation, in a way that is not in the end so surprising from a planner who promoted the growth of the City of London's towers:

> that's how Shoreditch came about, that's how Vauxhall came about, that's how Soho existed for many years until the degree of control started to become oppressive. Or Shepherd Market in Mayfair. You can go right back in history. There are the centres of doing naughty things or doing things that aren't the family norm which are very much part of a great city and the degree of tolerance and provision for alternative lifestyles actually determine the degree of creativity and adaptability and futureproofing that a city will have.

So central, indeed, is the pursuit of pleasure to the city that Rees believes families with children should live away from the centre of London.

To know better the economic driver he describes I find myself in a pleasant garden in the area celebrated by the poet John Betjeman as Metro-Land, the north-western corridor of suburbia that grew up along what is now the Metropolitan Underground line. Close by are the steep, bucolic slopes of Gladstone Park (opened 1901) and Dollis Hill synagogue, all concrete, with Stars of David and menorahs abstracted into hexagons and inverted arches, a quirky work of 1936–8 by the engineer-architect Owen Williams (the black glass Daily Express building in Fleet Street; Empire Pool Wembley; Pioneer Health Centre in Peckham; some clunky bridges over an early motorway, the M1, phase one).

I am talking to Edward, a retired professional about to hit seventy, a pillar of the local Jewish community, born in South Africa to Russian parents ('my father worked with Trotsky'). On Wednesdays and Sundays, he says, 'there are SBN nights. That's Stark Bollock Naked. They start at 2.30 p.m. so it's very convenient if you don't want to stay up late on Sunday night.'

Edward and his fiancé like to go to the sex clubs that Rees was talking about, of which the best known are in Vauxhall. They are often in railway arches, because the space is large, cheap, windowless, anonymous and contains noise, and it doesn't matter when a train goes overhead. They also give the sense of 'going into the darker side of life'. The outside will be discreet although with a special enclosure to deal with the fact that the law requires smoking to take place outside, but the clubbers don't want to be seen from the street naked or nearly so. One club might have four arches: 'one for getting changed, one for drinking and chatting and two for sex'. There might in the low light be 'four hundred, five hundred guys all looking the same all dressing the same: well built, a bit of leather and beard, a harness or something. Fashions change.' Some clubs

have lounge areas to change in. You can see what's there and what you fancy. People walk by with nothing on. You don't present yourself, you just walk in and go dancing . . . You start eyeing one another up and start touching and kissing or they're already busy and you join in. You're part of a big society. If you see someone you know you might just walk past and give them a stroke. The music is too loud to talk. At my age I'm hard of hearing.

Sometimes they have shows

naked, perhaps a bit of leather. One or two people. The innovation is to have orgasms on stage. Sometimes they have a hard time getting there, but usually people are enjoying themselves too much to notice . . . People are celebrating whatever turns them on. It's nothing to be ashamed of. You do what you want. You don't have to do what you don't want. You can be experimental. You can build your self-esteem if nobody likes you . . . you're enjoying yourself but there can be an undercurrent of desperation that comes from growing up gay and suffering for it . . . You have sexual urges. You're open. That's the best thing of all.

Edward says that gay sex clubs are more peaceful than the atmosphere that can grow up around straight clubs: 'Nobody's drunk, nobody fights, nobody has a cross word. It's safe as houses. There's no aggro. People are friendly. The only problem is overdoses. Clubs search you for GHB. The last thing they want is ambulances being called round.' He doesn't see much BDSM. There are other clubs for that, frequented by both gay and straight, 'multisexual', often coming in couples, for 'a little bit of torture and whipping'. There is, though, a corporal punishment night at one of the gay clubs, piss fun at another.

And, when the time comes to put clothes back on and go back into the outside world, they are 'Morris dancers to a man, or computer programmers, or bankers. It's a complete leveller – income level, social background don't matter . . . although you might sometimes get a bit of attitude, when gorgeous people don't want to be touched by less gorgeous people.'

All this is nothing new, to a degree. He cites the molly houses of the eighteenth century, the effects of the wartime city filled with British and American servicemen, the places described by Joe Orton. But there wasn't the same array of sex clubs when Edward – married, in the closet, leading a double life – first explored the gay scene 'just before AIDS started'. There was Subway in Leicester Square – 'you heard that you go to this club and you can get something that kills you'. There were bars, but more discreet. There was the Royal Vauxhall Tavern, perhaps the most venerable of gay pubs, into which legend has it Princess Diana was once smuggled, dressed as a man, with the help of Freddie Mercury and Kenny Everett. There were public toilets and Hampstead Heath, in all weathers, including snow.

At some point, he's not sure when, official attitudes began to change. One night he met a policeman on the Heath whose job was not to deter the gay men, but to protect them from violence by others. Sex clubs started in 'out-of-the-way places – Peckham, Mile End, Southwark, Dalston – often in pubs taken over, with black paint on the windows. Quiet. You don't want the self-righteous-indignation crowd to notice too much.' Local authorities became more tolerant, some more than others.

Now, he says, the clubbing and bar scenes feed on one another. The more people come, the more attractive these places become. London is a world leader. 'People fly in from all over. Paris is less tolerant. Amsterdam doesn't have the critical mass. Rome has got the Pope in the Vatican. Los Angeles and San Francisco? America doesn't allow as much as the English do. They have their Bible Belt.' He sees it as part of the city's wider cultural and economic attrac-tiveness and openness – fashion, art, food, investment – that come from a 'stable society and a free society'. 'London belongs to the foreigners,' he says. 'We the foreigners feel at home. It's our city, it's not yours.'

Edward, in short, is describing a world of deregulated interna-tional exchange much like London's banking and property sectors. In the gathering of delights from all nations and the striving for inno-vation in stimulation, a Vauxhall sex club is not unlike a Sushisamba cocktail. It is different in one respect, however, which is that it is 'not exploitative'. Someone must be making good money out of these clubs, but in Edward's telling more than Rees's they form an almost utopian republic where wealth and status fade, apart from the aristocracy of looks. A night, with a free drink, costs fifteen pounds or ten pounds to members. It costs less than going to the movies or the pub, or a single cocktail.

Elsewhere in London's contemporary hedonism industry commercial calculation is more apparent. In restaurants and bars beautifully conceived and executed, offering concoctions of sublime craft, and in plenty that do not reach these heights, you can taste the PowerPoint presentations that were made to the investors without whom such things cannot happen – defining the clientele, the differentiation from competitors, the slicing and layering of the world's cuisines into a seam rich enough for a new venture to mine, the communications strategy. 'I ate a concept last Thursday', wrote Aditya Chakrabortty in the *Guardian*, in 2014, 'not just any old abstraction, but a "heavily concepted restaurant trend", in publicist-speak. No kidding: at the new Lobster Kitchen, the name is the menu is the business model. Here you can have whatever you like so long as it's pink: lobster tails, lobster rolls, lobster with macaroni cheese . . . Just like central London homes,' he observed, 'the capital's eateries are becoming a global asset class.' The Lobster Kitchen was co-founded by Abigail Tan, 'the twenty-nine-year-old heiress to one of the wealthiest real-estate dynasties in south-east Asia, IGB of Malaysia'.

The more heterosexual sex clubs have also become professionalized businesses. The most publicized is Killing Kittens, founded in 2005. Dedicated to 'the relentless pursuit of female desire', it has been well explored by adventurous young feature writers – to whom I am grateful for sparing me this duty – whose copy usually feels the need to mention that its founder, the 'sextrepreneur' Emma Sayle, is a friend of Kate Middleton, Duchess of Cambridge. (They briefly went to the same school and were once photographed in the same dragon-boat crew.)

Much is made of the club's elite eliteness. 'We are very elitist, but that's what it's all about,' Sayle told *Time Out*. 'True, not everyone's a supermodel but all members are attractive, aspirational, successful professionals aged 20–45.' Its parties are held in 'smart venues. The rooms are candlelit, we play the right kind of music and it's black tie, so people are dressed-up. There's often a champagne and oyster reception too, rather than cheese straws . . . It's the little things that make a difference.' Now Killing Kittens is going global, to 'New York penthouses, St Tropez super-yachts and über-exclusive luxury locations the world over'. Not a railway arch in Vauxhall, then, ten pounds to enter, with five hundred heaving bodies. More like a Conran Shop for sex.

The contemporary approach to leisure and pleasure contrasts with the early 1960s pubs described by B. S. Johnson in his novel *Albert Angelo*. Albert, an architect with fading hopes of greatness, who works as a supply teacher in a brutal school to finance his modest existence, distracts himself from working on an entry for a competition to design an arts centre for a town of half a million, which might transform his life – 'it is the only way to become known, to break out of this destructive teaching' – but which he will never finish. Just after noon on a hopeful Whitsun Bank Holiday ('how marvellous, a whole free day to work') he wanders in and around Chapel Market, near the Angel, Islington. He considers

> the Chapel House, good beer, comic tile murals in passage, *Death of Cleopatra*, Act V, Sc II, the muse of Music, smearedflesh children playing fairly underneath, waiting for their parents drinking inside,

before entering

> the pub with the flowers, pots and pots on the tables, flowers, the Red House some call it because of its long name, The Agricultural, which was too long for semi-literates to cope with, so they called it the Red House, the guvnor says, because of the facing brick, which is fairly unusual in a predominance of stocks.
>
> A good guvnor, he is, one cannot choose too carefully the guvnor of one's pub.

Anyone I know here? Yes, several by sight, one by name, that's how it is. Ah, you know you're a regular when they pull your usual without having to ask.

THANKS, SID.

A pro in the public, at lunchtime, too. I thought they would sleep all day. A bourgeois concept, no doubt. Perhaps she's on days this week. Teeth like child's milk teeth, small, parallel edges, gap in the middle. Is it possible to retain milk teeth undeveloped? No good you smiling at me, anyway, dolly. I'm not a potential customer. Why aren't I?

He hears the landlord's dirty jokes, converses with the regulars and eats 'lovely raw crisp onion, with lovely raw underdone forerib of beef'. 'Pity Georgie isn't here lunchtimes,' he reflects,

for the piano. Great he is, so in control, found his way in this way, playing the songs of forty years ago with such dedication, interest, sheer interest. That's the thing about the Angel, all the pubs have something going on in them, singing and dancing, life, you never feel alone, in one sense, compared with the insufferable suburbs like Worcester Park or Sutton, where the pubs are like mausoleums, museums with stuffed people and not a sound but the cash register and the slurping of gargle.

He goes back into Chapel Market – 'it's full, of people, stalls, cabbage, boxes, purple packingpaper, bruised fruit – my Chap'. His free day having evaporated, he heads back towards his flat in Percy Circus, 'decadent and decaying, decrepit, like my state, London's state, England's state, man's state, the human condition'. On the way, outside the theatre at Sadler's Wells, he passes

The Shakespeare's Head. New pub. Old one fell down. Ten minutes after closing time one night, just as all the operagoers were wending their uplifted ways homeward, the front of the pub fell out. Just

fell out into the road. Wallop. An act of god, they concluded, a most irresponsible sort of god, evidently.

If this world inspires nostalgia, there are limits to it. It is sociable, offering simple pleasures, a place where a lonely man might feel at home, and it is torpid and sordid. It has slackness, the feeling that there is space and time to spare: there is not the sense that every minute and square foot has to pay its way. There is room for chance and the unprogrammed, including the possibility that a building might collapse. It is taken for granted that things will fall apart, and that that is part of being human.

It is in any event different from the Islington of later decades. In the 1990s the area became the home turf of a young and dynamic prime-minister-in-waiting. It had a restaurant called Granita, not at all like the beef-and-onions Red House, but the purveyor at high prices of sophisticated reinventions of Italian peasant cuisine. The décor was the white minimalism of John Pawson, also not cheap, *architettura povera* whose luxury was in its apparent absence of luxury. Its artful evocation of the simple life of working people – the appearance without the reality – made it the perfect setting for the conception of New Labour, when Tony Blair and Gordon Brown agreed in what order they would rule the country.

> A shudder in the loins engenders there
> The broken wall, the burning roof and tower
> And Agamemnon dead.

By the new millennium Islington's prosperity was middle-aged. Its attractions included a celebrity dry cleaner, which does a good job, but where a modest consignment of clothes costs more to clean than a flight to Marrakesh. The Chapel House and The Agricultural had gone. Chapel Market remained resilient, as markets can be, still a place of bruised fruit and soggy paper. The Shakespeare's Head also survived, inoculated against gentrification by its utilitarian

1950s rebuild, which allowed it to remain more pubby than more charmingly pub-like places. It did get a surprise visit from Kylie Minogue, but she had to leave when the regulars failed to keep calm and pretend they hadn't noticed. 'I almost dropped my pint when she walked in,' said one.

For livelier entertainment you would want to head down the hill of City Road, past the rising Canaletto tower ('an award-winning masterpiece', one-bedroom apartments start at £890,000) and the feckless urbanism of a McDonald's, a Texaco, some good student housing by the architects Lifschutz Davidson Sandilands and a hotel that tries to convert the angst-laden style of Daniel Libeskind into the setting for a good night's sleep.

You are now approaching the overlapping territories of Silicon Roundabout, the largest cluster of start-up companies in Europe, and Shoreditch, home of the hipster, land of the beard. I am indebted to the writing of Will Self for alerting me to the YouTube classic and unauthorized anthem of this district, 'Being a Dickhead's Cool':

> Oi, Oi, Oi, Oi
> Got on the train from Cambridgeshire
> Moved down to an east London flat
> Got a moustache and a low cut vest
> Some purple leggings and a sailor tat
> Just one gear on my fixie bike
> Got a +1 here for my gig tonight
> I play synth . . .
> We *all* play synth!
> 20–20 vision, just a pair of empty frames
> Dressing like a nerd although I never got the grades
> I remember when the kids at school would call me names
> Now we're taking over their estates!
> Woo-oo-oooo!
>
> I love my life as a dickhead . . .

Up and down the City Road

In daytime you can see that this area has perfected the art of re-presenting good, everyday things as objects of desire. On the Boundary Estate, early council housing built on the site of the atrocious Old Nichol slum, is Leila's, a grocery. With church-like murmur, incense of produce, the glimmering bloom of fruit, a reredos of goods, it is made into a shrine of food. The selection and presentation is flawless, down to the scattering of earth around the potatoes and carrots, the bread, cheese and vegetables wonderful, the atmosphere gently intoxicating. In the window is an idealized ancestor, a framed black-and-white photograph of a shop of long ago. Then the card reader whirrs out your offertory, an amount for your small bag of delights that would have paid the old shop's rent for a year.

Labour and Wait, in Redchurch Street, does something similar with domestic hardware, brooms and buckets of pre-war proletarian origin, curated like works in a gallery. In the same street the tendency becomes parody – a blanket (cashmere, but even so) for £2,800 – and in nearby Brick Lane there is Cereal Killer, where you can buy bowls of Corn Flakes, Coco Pops and Golden Grahams for £3.50 (large portion) with a choice of thirty different kinds of milk (premium milk 40p extra). In 2015 Cereal Killer had to be protected by riot police from protestors against gentrification. Survivors from a previous age show what simple places ought to be, twin competing bagel shops that now do well serving early morning clubbers: tang of salt beef, zip of mustard, yielding dough, balm of tea, the release of fruity sweetness beneath the flakes of an Eccles cake.

Also nearby is Shoreditch House, a club with a swimming pool and playfully soothing interiors for media and creative people, and until recently Les Trois Garçons, a restaurant founded in days when the area felt harsher, that bravely displayed its camp crystalline interior behind large sheets of glass. Smash me, it seemed to say, if you dare. Across the road, just north of the preserved viaduct of the defunct Bishopsgate railway station, is a strip which a writer of 1950,

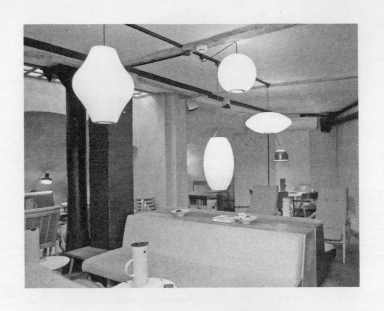

Robert Sinclair, called 'London's great dust-bin market'. It was, he said, a place where 'I would be ashamed to take a West African villager ... I could not face his laughter at the sight of one of the oldest corners of our civilisation filled with hundreds of human beings staring at rubbish. I could not admit that we still had in our midst masses of these dumb and disfigured people.'

It is now occupied by Boxpark, a 'pop-up' shopping centre made of shipping containers, 'a unique shopping and dining destination', according to its self-description, that 'places local and global brands side-by-side'. It is designed to harvest the footfall of this area until replaced by a phalanx of sun-blocking towers of a new development by the property companies Hammerson and Ballymore.

You can walk from here to the base of Great Eastern Street, where a stair redolent of old-time London dives takes you down to the basement housing Lounge Bohemia, a bar themed on the brown modernism of Cold War Prague, which nonetheless serves cocktails beyond the ken of the politburo, which in their elaboration make Sushisamba's efforts look like cans of Carling: concoctions of cardamom tequila, frankincense, patchouli, 'camomile air', that are served with effects of light and smoke from a bonsai Indiana Jones movie. If you stay on the pavement you can get a view, south down Bishopsgate, of the Heron Tower, which calls itself a set of 'villages' of 'boutique offices'. It is one of the earliest and handsomest projects in the millennial London tower boom, a rehabilitation project for the tycoon and ex-con Gerald Ronson, designed when tall buildings had to be on their best architectural behaviour if they wanted to pass a still-sceptical planning regime. It is silvery and well proportioned, its scale articulated and its mass variegated with exposed trusses and lift shafts. By day it doesn't give much hint of the pleasures at the top. After dark the lurid lighting of the lift shaft gives a clue.

At night Shoreditch is taken over by clubbers. Traffic jams, of both people and cars, form after midnight – kids from state schools and public schools, office workers, dental hygienists, reception teachers, tourists, gay men going to the area's equivalents of the Vauxhall clubs. The built environment doesn't lend much encouragement, being old workshops and back offices, with unyielding, treeless streets, but this kind of life doesn't mind much, indeed enjoys taking over space intended for something else. Good, clean fun, or at least Reesian 'naughty things', is kept within managed limits, once-transgressive attitudes to sex, drugs or music refracted into lifestyle choices. Free society and the free market combine to make an industry of distraction. The import–export businesses of the city of trade extend to transactions of pleasure.

As Rees says, people come to London for its delights and tolerate its inconveniences. In particular they put up with its expensive and restricted supply of housing, the price of which is increased by the desirability of the city. Edward says that there are many people in their late thirties who, unable to afford a house, prefer to flat-share and carry on clubbing when they might otherwise settle down. So there is a circular and addictive aspect: people come for the partying, which helps put up the price of homes, which means they have little by way of domestic space, so they keep on partying.

If you contemplate only London's buzz and dazzle, you will see that it thrives as never before. This had been a popular narrative among the city's boosters since the mid-1990s, when a spate of 'Cool Britannia' magazine features was converted into political rhetoric by the government of Tony Blair. But to wonder uncritically at these phenomena is to overlook some significant issues. One is the question whether, as it is governed more and more by the logics of investment, hedonism will stop being fun. If music and desire have something to do with realizing yourself, and if eating in a restaurant and drinking in a bar might imply a relationship with the people who make and serve the food and drink, there is much to be lost if such things become pure commodities and we passive consumers.

And, if London's pleasure industries look like triumphs of entrepreneurial city-making, they are of no use to people without the money or interest to enjoy them. They are not enough in themselves to make an urban society that is enriching and including. They also rely on the great public works of the past. Modern London dances on the engineering of its ancestors.

THE PUBLIC GOOD

4: Water

Below the last seconds of the north-easterly descent into Stansted, among the punctured bucolia of the airport hinterland, close to the thatched Three Horseshoes pub (dog-friendly, alleged connections with the highwayman Dick Turpin and King Edward VII, a bouncy castle in summer), also the premises of Perry Pallet Storage and BMS car body repairers, rises the River Roding. It flows from there, past green-belt fields and woods, business parks and golf courses, under the M25 and alongside the M11 and the North Circular Road, until it reaches Wanstead Park in east London, where it feeds the begrottoed Ornamental Waters of the fragmentary eighteenth-century landscape that once served the colossal now-ghost mansion of Wanstead House, the definitive work of English Palladianism, demolished in 1825 so that the sale of its building materials could pay off the debts of the dissolute William Pole-Tylney-Long-Wellesley, whom the heiress of Wanstead, the richest in England, had haplessly married. The river then continues past Barking Abbey (founded by St Erkenwald in AD 666), where William the Conqueror spent his first winter as King of England.

By the time the Roding joins the Thames at Barking Creek its history is erased by the fact that it is almost literally the arse of London. Here are the 250 acres of the Beckton Sewage Treatment Works, the largest in Europe, where rotating arms scrape the waste of 3.4 million inhabitants of north London around ranks of circular settlement tanks, while pumps in aeration lanes bubble air through

muck. Wastewater, cleaner than the Thames itself, is then discharged into the river. Until 1998 solid matter was removed by the SS *Bazalgette* and her sister sludge vessels, also called Bovril boats, which would dump their dark load in the Black Deep, a trench in the North Sea. European Union rules now require it to be burned to generate electricity.

One reason why the works are by Barking Creek is that in the nineteenth century it was considered far enough downriver that sewage deposited there – less meticulously treated than now – would not flow back on the flood tide as far as the Houses of Parliament. For, as the story of the Great Stink has it, it required the stench in the Palace of Westminster to become unbearable before politicians would do something to alleviate the abominably polluted Thames, which led to the creation of the sewage system which exits at the Beckton works. It would have defeated the object of the exercise if Westminster had still been contaminated.

Drains and death

This story, one of the foundation legends of modern London, has been told a few times, for example in Stephen Halliday's 1999 book *The Great Stink of London*. In the hot June of 1858, when the Gothic-Tudor rebuilding of the Palace after its fire of 1834 was still incomplete, the Thames smell forced Members of Parliament to abandon their waterside terraces and river-facing rooms such as the library, even though they placed handkerchiefs over their mouths and the windows were hung with drapes soaked in chloride of lime to cleanse the atmosphere. As serious disease was then thought to spread through miasma, or contaminated air, the stench was thought life-threatening as well as revolting. It was suggested that Parliament should leave London for Henley, on the upper Thames.

Instead it passed, in August, the Metropolis Local Management Amendment Act, proposed by the then Leader of the House Benjamin Disraeli, which created the funding and powers necessary to address the problem.

It was not news that the Thames smelt. London's population and therefore its evacuations had doubled between 1801 and 1841. At the same time the old, itself imperfect, practice of using cesspools – of which there were 200,000 by 1810 – whose contents would then be taken by cart to fertilize nearby fields, was giving way to drains emptying into the river. (And the growth of the city both made farms more distant and increased the volume of manure, which combined with the import from 1847 of cheap South American guano made the economics of human fertilizer barely viable.) The rising popularity of water closets added to the volume of fluid and the efficiency with which sewage reached the Thames, which meant that it became filthier as streets and houses became cleaner. In 1855 the great scientist Michael Faraday had stated what was by then obvious, that 'the whole of the river was an opaque, pale brown fluid' and that 'near the bridges the feculence rolled up in clouds so dense that they were visible at the surface'. He demanded that 'those exercising power' find a way to stop the river becoming 'a fermenting sewer'.

That the river was the source of drinking water for many Londoners made the pollution lethal. From the 1830s to the 1860s there were four cholera outbreaks in the city, which collectively killed tens of thousands. Over the same period and until late in the century the causes of the spread of cholera were debated, with the persistent but false idea that it was airborne slowly giving way to the realization that it was transmitted through contaminated water. In the 1850s Dr John Snow presented convincing evidence for the waterborne theory, based on his studies of outbreaks around a polluted pump in Soho, but Florence Nightingale (for example) believed until her death in 1910 that it was carried by miasma. In 1890 the social reformer Edwin Chadwick proposed a system of Eiffel-tower like structures that would bring fresh air down from higher levels. These misunderstandings slowed constructive response: it was only the supposedly fatal smell of the Thames that prompted action.

There was a history of proposals for improvement of the filthy and by now fish-less Thames. In the 1820s Parliament considered plans by the painter John Martin, better known for his storm-thick canvasses of Sodom, Pompeii, Babylon and other apocalypses. In 1839 a parliamentary Bill had proposed a Metropolitan Court of Sewers to manage better the city's drainage; it failed, it seems, because the City of London disliked losing some of its powers to the court. Between 1847 and 1855 six commissions were formed, which made some progress in assessing the problem and proposing solutions, though lacking the means to put them into practice. Frank Forster, engineer to the third of them, died from stress.

One obstacle was lack of money. Another was that, as *The Times* put it in 1855, 'there is no such place as London at all'. It was 'rent into an infinity of divisions, districts and areas' where 'local administration is carried on by no fewer than three hundred different bodies, deriving powers from about two hundred and fifty local Acts'. Simple matters such as the care of streets were, in other words, so Balkanized that coherent action was impossible across a city of over two million. The only official definition of London as a single unit had come with the creation of the Metropolitan Police in 1829 (from which, even in this case, the City of London opted out).

A necessary step in cleansing the Thames was the creation in 1855 of a city-wide body, the Metropolitan Board of Works, as a successor to the six commissions. Disraeli's Bill, in the aftermath of the Great Stink, gave the board the ability to borrow £3m, raise rates to repay it and decide where it thought the new sewers should run.

Political engineering was necessary before the constructional kind, directed by Joseph Bazalgette, could proceed.

Bazalgette, assistant to the hapless Forster, had succeeded him as chief engineer to what became the Metropolitan Board of Works, a post he held for more than three decades. In this time he developed and realized a version of plans that Forster had conceived for solving the sewage problem, which also had some similarities with those of the painter Martin, thirty years earlier. Its principal idea was the creation of two intercepting sewers running on each bank of the Thames, which would receive the waste from the north and south parts of London and direct them downriver. On the north side it headed to the Byzanto-Moorish pumping station at Abbey Mills, near Stratford, which would raise the sewage twelve metres to a point whence it could continue its slow fall to Beckton. On the south side it went to the neo-Romanesque pumping station at Crossness. Other main sewers were constructed further from the river, to form a network of converging ducts something like the veins on a hand.

Construction started within months of the 1858 Act. The project was formally opened by the Prince of Wales in 1865 and was essentially complete ten years later. It involved the building of drains sometimes the width of houses across distances of twenty miles, with temporary railways and concrete mills to serve the works. It took 300 million bricks and the excavation of 3.5 million cubic yards of earth to build the eighty-two miles of intercepting sewers, and Bazalgette had to devise and manage building contracts that would enable the project to be realized efficiently. All was achieved within the crowded, complex and in places ancient fabric of what was then the largest city of the world. Nothing similar had been done before.

It worked. The river was cleansed, the smell went, fish returned. Even though the project had started in ignorance of the causes of cholera, it and other waterborne diseases were eradicated. London's last outbreak, in 1866, was confined to an area of east London that

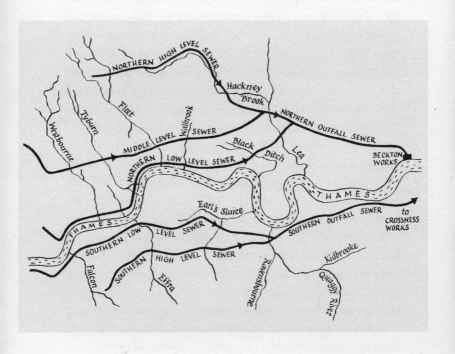

had not yet been reached by Bazalgette's drains. It continued to work: the city's population would more than double from its level when Bazalgette designed the system, and water consumption per head would also multiply, but he sized the sewers to cope with expansion. It was not until the twenty-first century that it was felt necessary to make major improvements to his system, to cope with the volume of storm water which in exceptional weather over-loads it.

There were obstacles, difficulties and revisions. It cost more and took longer than first hoped. The scale of the works changed the economic weather of British construction, pushing up the prices of bricks and labour. In 1863 Bazalgette was challenged over a conflict of interest relating to his consultancy on works in Odessa, Ukraine, for which he was reprimanded and financially penalized. By the 1880s it was decided that it was no longer acceptable to pour raw sewage into the lower Thames, by Barking Creek, which led to the enhancement of the works at Beckton and Crossness.

The rescue of London from filth and disease had happened in the face of opposition from vested interests, defenders of turf and private business. They obstructed, misinformed and delayed in a way that is common now among deniers of climate change. The City of London had successfully opposed reforming legislation in 1839 and obstructed it again in 1848. In 1847 its lord mayor stated that 'there could be no improvement in the sanitary condition of the City', as it was 'perfect'. The next year cholera broke out. The year after that an inspection was made – despite the City's refusal to fund it – which found that out of 15,010 homes inspected, 2,524 had 'offensive smells from bad drainage or other causes', 1,120 had privies 'in a very offensive state' and twenty-one had 'cellars used as cesspools'.

When cholera reappeared in east London in 1866 the East London Water Company, in the tradition of corner-cutting monopol-istic corporations and despite the fact that 4,061 of the 4,363 deaths in July and August had been in areas supplied wholly or partly by the company, rushed to assert their complete commitment to upholding standards, maintaining quality and to what would now be called customer care. 'Not a drop of unfiltered water', they said, got into their supply pipes through their flawless filtration systems, a claim damaged by the discovery that entire live eels could. It was found that a carpenter had allowed water to pass from an open, contaminated reservoir to one used for drinking water. This contravened the relevant law but, also in the tradition of corner-cutting monopolistic corporations and despite causing more deaths than (for example) the terrorists of 9/11, the company escaped heavy punishment. The maximum fine was £200.

Opponents of clean water, as with climate-change deniers, had their useful idiots in the educated press to enlist principles of philosophy to make a bogus case. Thus the *Economist* in 1848, invoking 'nature' to sustain as distilled a form of laissez-faire theology as you could wish to read: 'Suffering and evil are nature's admonitions; they cannot be got rid of; and the impatient attempts of benevolence to banish them from the world by legislation, before benevolence has learned their object and their end, have always been more productive of evil than good.' Which could be summarized as: Die now and learn why later.

Others cited Magna Carta as a reason not to save the lives of Londoners, and an Anti-Centralization Union was founded to oppose 'novel theories' and 'sweeping experimental legislation'. The prime minister, Lord John Russell, said in 1850 that 'in this city there is very naturally and properly great jealousy of any interference either with local rights or individual will and freedom from control'. Commercial interest also helps explain the persistence of the theory of miasma, in the face of John Snow's evidence that cholera was transmitted through water. The epidemiologist and campaigner William Farr observed in 1867:

As the air of London is not supplied like water to its inhabitants by companies the air has had the worst of it both before Parliamentary Committees and Royal Commissions. For air no scientific witnesses have been retained, no learned counsel has pleaded; so the atmosphere has been freely charged with the propagation and the illicit diffusion of plagues of all kinds; while Father Thames ... and the water gods of London, have been loudly proclaimed immaculate and innocent.

Yet for all this opposition there was almost no trace of it once the works were complete. No one wished them undone or argued that they should never have been attempted. Not even the most ardent believers in free enterprise have, in the century and a half since, questioned this major government intervention which not only saved tens of thousands of lives but also helped the city's businesses prosper. It is hard to imagine London being the World Class City that its boosters proclaim, if it were knee-deep in sewage.

Drains and democracy

Bazalgette's interventions in London were not just about sewers. Under his leadership the Metropolitan Board of Works built roads and bridges and abolished the tolls that had been levied on all but three of the river crossings. It initiated what became Tower Bridge and the Blackwall Tunnel. It swept through what would later be the Monopoly board, improving Park Lane, remaking Leicester Square and forming Coventry Street and Northumberland Avenue. It managed 2,603 acres of park. It demolished substandard homes and built new ones, rehousing nearly 40,000 slum dwellers. In doing all this it created the prototype of London's metropolitan government:

in 1889 the board, whose members were nominated by the city's smaller units of local government, was turned into the directly elected London County Council.

Bazalgette and his board made the Victoria, Albert and Chelsea Embankments, replacing the muddy, intricate, sometimes ramshackle edges of the Thames with walls of granite. If their primary function was to manage water and sewage, they did more. The Victoria Embankment, running on the north side from the Houses of Parliament to the City, contained both the intercepting sewer and the subterranean railway tunnel that would later house the District Line. On the fifty-two acres that they reclaimed from the Thames the embankments created new thoroughfares and – not without struggle – public gardens. In 1870 the prime minister, William Gladstone, in pursuit of his dream of abolishing income tax, wanted to raise money by building office blocks on the newly created land; he was thwarted only by a sustained campaign by the bookseller and Conservative MP W. H. Smith.

The result was described by the diarist Arthur Munby, best known for his obsessions with work-soiled charwomen, kitchen maids and she-miners, who saw in the new work an image of cleanliness that contrasted not only with his mysophilia, but also with the buried world of sewerage. 'The bright morning sun,' wrote Mundy, 'shone on the broad bright river and on the white walls of the Embankment, which stretch away as a noble curve to Westminster, under the dark contrasting masses of the bridges.'

The Victoria Embankment was what 1960s architectural dreamers would call a megastructure, an extruded multilayered construction that performed technical and social purposes simultaneously. But it was achieved and real. It was a platform for modernity, albeit framed with conservative masonry and ornamental cast-iron, its importance recognized by a royal, military and popular opening ceremony. It became the location of London's first electric street

lights. There was some democracy to it: embanked river terraces had previously been properties of privileged places such as Somerset House and the Adelphi development, but now they belonged to everybody.

Bazalgette's works changed London's relation to the river in ways that are still being interpreted and explored. They made it less intimate, ending the small interactions of wharves, steps and yards that had taken place along a tide-blurred boundary of land and water. They made the Thames flow faster and more precisely. Never again freezing, it could no longer carry, as it had for at least two centuries, occasional frost fairs. If it remained a working river it also became something more to be looked at than experienced.

The embankments were stages awaiting actors, who started to appear. Work began on a never-completed opera house close to the Palace of Westminster, the site instead becoming the headquarters of the Metropolitan Police known as New Scotland Yard. The Victoria Embankment now also includes the Ministry of Defence's defensive building, a multipinnacled apartment block called Whitehall Court, the Shell-Mex headquarters in transatlantic deco, the Savoy Hotel. St Thomas's Hospital went up on the Albert Embankment, built according to principles of segregation and ventilation set out by Florence Nightingale.

A comparison can be made with the network of boulevards that Baron Haussmann was laying across Paris at about the same time for Napoleon III. Upgraded sewerage was among their aims, but more the desire to make the city grander. Also to create wide straight streets which it would be difficult for revolutionaries to barricade and within which loyal troops could manoeuvre and charge. With their straight lines drawn across the city, often indifferent to the pre-existing, Haussmann's streets are the production of an authoritarian emperor.

Bazalgette's more adaptive approach reflects a different regime.

Part of his intention was also to clear troublesome areas and re-inforce official order, but he had to fit his plans more to natural features, property ownerships and other existing conditions. The creation of Northumberland Avenue, for example, required a battle with the Percy family, the aristocratic owners of Northumberland House and its gardens, a Jacobean palace that stood in the way. The high price at which they were bought out had to be recovered from the commercial value of development along the new avenue, to maximize which value required the bloating of the buildings, which gave this truncated fist at Haussmannian urban space less grace than it might have had.

Among the pantheon of Victorian engineers – Brunel, Paxton, Stephenson – Bazalgette is the least mythologized, the least glamorous, probably because drains are less thrilling than suspension bridges and palaces of crystal. His character and personal life are little remembered, beyond that he was restrained, meticulous, calm, persistent, hard-working and the father of many children. But he was effective. Brunel's inventions were beautiful and spectacular but, like his ship the *Great Eastern*, sometimes courted disaster. Bazalgette's creations did what they were supposed to do. Brunel was partly an entrepreneur and salesman, who had to talk up his schemes to investors. Bazalgette was a civil servant, for whom efficiency and quiet influence were the most useful virtues.

If in Haussmann's project the beautification of public spaces was more important than the drains, for Bazalgette the reverse was true. Some of his urban spaces, such as Southwark Street or Queen Victoria Street, are still subtly sterile, creations of the mindset of a plumber. Jerry White, in *London in the Nineteenth Century*, says that commercial factors led to 'particular meanness' in the major streets laid out by the Metropolitan Board of Works: they were 'shabby, narrow and undistinguished'. When Bazalgette's projects required what might officially be called architecture, as with the pumping stations, their best quality was engaging eccentricity, their worst fussiness. The suspension structures of his Hammersmith and Albert bridges are charming, but lack the epoch-defining nobility of Brunel's at Clifton, Bristol. Yet his impact on London was not just functional: above all with the embankments, he reconfigured the city itself.

The Thames reinvented

The embankments gave new forms to an old ambivalence, still not resolved, that London has about the Thames. Before Bazalgette the river was an open sewer, an industrial zone and a transport facility, upon which it was natural that the more desirable areas would turn their backs, at the same time that city life flowed easily into and across it and that grand buildings like Chelsea Hospital and the Houses of Parliament would face it. The new embankments formed both sharp edges and river-facing gardens, which suggested that the river was something to be enjoyed. It was more desirable but less accessible. It is uncertain whether it is a front or a back, the 'heart of London', as the architect Richard Rogers has called it, or the gap between two edges, of the northern and southern halves of the city. It is magnificent, but also quiet and sometimes neglected, with the more intense life of the city taking place a few blocks inland. It has a redundancy that comes from London's not quite knowing what to do with it, which may be its greatest asset: it gives openness, the sense of possibility, the quality of a place that has not been fully defined, codified and appropriated, properties that also make it vulnerable to exploitation.

In places that the Board of Works did not itself embank the reinvention of the river was continued and interpreted by others, of which the post-war cultural enrichment of the South Bank, started by the Festival of Britain of 1951, was the most sustained and inventive. The festival itself, an exhibition of British science and arts held in jolly modernist structures, is remembered now as an expression of national relief after years of war and post-war shortages. It was an affirmation of benign public works, of the values of the welfare state and of the Labour government that had commissioned it, and a celebration of modernity and progress. Its structures, the levitating vertical cigarillo called the Skylon and the shallow meniscus of the Dome of Discovery, presented the architecture of the time as cheerful waterside attractions.

Over the next quarter-century the festival's legacy was the creation of the South Bank arts centre on and around its site. The Royal Festival Hall, a 2,500-seat concert hall built at the time, was later extended. In 1967 and 1968 two more music venues, the Queen Elizabeth Hall and the Purcell Room, were completed, and the Hayward art gallery. In 1976 the National Theatre opened on a site further downriver. All can be called modernist, but they exhibit changing attitudes in architecture. The Royal Festival Hall was in the light, Scandinavian-influenced style of the festival, an unthreatening version of the modern movement for a nation sceptical of it. Younger architects found this style tepid, effete, too pretty, and advocated something rougher and they hoped less elitist. In practice this meant raw concrete, often marked with the grain of its timber shuttering, and spaces which were supposed to serve the everyday dramas of modern cities. The approach came to be called brutalism: because it derives from the French for rough concrete, which is *béton brut*, because a leading protagonist, Peter Smithson, was nicknamed Brutus, and because it sounded tough.

By the 1960s the Angry Young Architects had seized the levers. The Queen Elizabeth Hall, Purcell Room and Hayward Gallery are officially credited to the architects' department, led by Hubert Bennett, of the Greater London Council, which the London County Council

Royal Festival Hall

Hayward Gallery

**Undercroft of
Queen Elizabeth Hall**

became in 1965. But much of the creative energy came from young men working in the department, Dennis Crompton, Warren Chalk and Ron Herron. All three were part of Archigram, an avant-garde group who had started speculating that technology might liberate mankind from the need for fixed buildings, that the future could be one of adaptable, flexible, pleasurable, electronically serviced environments. For Archigram, who traded in hypothetical projects more than completed buildings, the music spaces and gallery on the South Bank are their main built monuments.

Here they were unable to abolish fixed architecture – far from it: the buildings are in immobile reinforced concrete. But they avoid the symmetries and compositional niceties of the Royal Festival Hall, in which a ghostly classicism lingers, in favour of a looser assemblage of blocks and terraces. It is hard to distinguish one building from another, or from the external decks. Outside and inside are considered as a continuous tissue of structures and hard landscape, within which it was hoped that spontaneous events – happenings – would take place. A drawing by Ron Herron, published in a 1972 issue of Archigram's magazine, makes this clear: the ubiquitous grey of the buildings is populated with colour, blondes, tents, TV screens, signs. Above, in wavy LP-cover lettering, it says:

TURN OFF THE CULTURE – CHANGE THE LABELS – ASTROTURF THE DECKS – CLIP ON THE SHOPS – CHEER UP.

Then, bafflingly:

ENVIRO POLE INFO NODE CRENATE THE HARD GROUND.

(I don't know what he means by this.)

Denys Lasdun, architect of the National Theatre, was neither a member of Archigram nor a brutalist, but he was also interested in creating rough concrete platforms for social interaction. His design is more composed and articulated than that of Crompton and Co.,

but it centres on the idea of the theatre made by the audience themselves as they move about the internal and external balconies and terraces. In all the cultural buildings on the South Bank, from the 1950s, 60s and 70s, the presence of the river is crucial. It becomes a place of release and festivity, a displaced seaside where different rules apply.

The Festival of Britain was conceived as the revival of another memorable moment of Victorian engineering, the 1851 Great Exhibition inside Joseph Paxton's Crystal Palace, but it and the subsequent South Bank are also continuations of Bazalgette's works. They took forward the concept pioneered in the embankments of building platforms for city life next to a cleaned river. They were built in the belief that city-wide authority, working with national government, could deliver major works for the benefit of everyone. They were created with the help of the institutions which grew from the Metropolitan Board of Works. If making space for culture and happenings seems dilettante next to removing cholera, it is still a vital part of the success of a city.

The New River

The sewage treatment works at Beckton are set out like a Roman army camp, in gridded rows of concrete circles and troughs. They are almost invisible, except from satellite or plane, or on one of the rare occasions that they are opened to public tours. Not even from the summit of the nearby Beckton Alps, a heap of toxic gas-works waste, can you get much of a view. To the casual visitor, approaching via discouraging roads, it presents only berms, fences, security notices and a faint whiff, a much-diluted whisper of the Great Stink, which might not even be sewage at all, but to do with the industrial zone on the other side of Barking Creek.

It is a disjointed and forgotten part of London, edged by the noisy viaducts of the A13. There are purposeless patches of grass and wood, the odd fruit tree and other rumours of countryside, enclaves of inward-looking housing and the ballets of roundabouts and radiused roads in which transport engineers indulge when there is nothing to stop them doing otherwise. There is a retail park, where a Union flag and a McDonald's banner flutter side by side, while jackdaws squabble over the French fries that they hold like edible twigs in their beaks.

Just outside the works the ground rises in a slow ramp, which then becomes a straight, almost level line heading back towards the middle of London. It is a broad bank on which you can walk or cycle, raised about the height of the bedroom windows of the houses that it passes. This is the Northern Outfall Sewer, or the Sewerbank, rebranded as the Greenway in the 1990s, as jaunty metal signs from time to time remind you. It is faintly a catwalk, slightly a boulevard, perhaps a Hadrian's Wall or an avenue in the garden of a stately home, but in any event something whose purposeful geometry is in London found more in things of function than of pomp. It has a basic purpose, but it gives a sense of spaciousness and achievement. It was a good idea to let people stroll on it.

In time it gets to Abbey Mills, with the pumping station whose interior ironwork – again, rarely visitable – is, like its orientalizing exterior, ornate. There seems to be a desire to decorate excrement – perhaps to deodorize it by some synaesthetic magic – similar to flower patterns often found on toilet paper wrappers, or indeed the decision to call a sewer a Greenway. There used to be two minaret-like chimneys here to serve its steam-powered mechanisms, but they were demolished on suspicion of acting as navigational aids for Luftwaffe bomber pilots in the Second World War. There is also a handsome pitched-roof structure in zinc-coated aluminium, compared by its architects to both a cathedral and a temple, which from 1997 took over from Bazalgette's station the task of pumping up sewage.

From here the Northern Outfall Sewer heads on, bifurcating later into the Northern High Level sewer – which, incorporating stretches of the old river Fleet, extends to the edge of Hampstead – and the Middle Level Sewer, which reaches Paddington. The Northern Lower Level Sewer sets off left from Abbey Mills towards the City of London, the Victoria Embankment and, by way of the Chelsea Embankment, to Hammersmith. At some stage a pipe will branch off and connect through a union of nineteenth- and twenty-first-century technology with the waste systems of the Heron Tower, which then ascend forty storeys to the toilets of Sushisamba, where the products of the Fukoko Cloud cocktails and of the scallop ceviche with mandarin *leche de tigre*, pickled mandarin and *shiso* might begin their journey to the mouth of the River Roding. After which the punctilious diner might wash her hands in the water flowing from the taps, which water will have been on its own journey from the countryside north of London.

Around Sadler's Wells, about two miles uphill from the Heron Tower, unusual geometries appear – fragments of curve, a truncated brick cone in a car park behind a block of flats. In the middle of Claremont Square, which is otherwise conventional, sloped banks rise to an invisible plateau. Street signs, exciting their usual indifference, nonetheless offer clues – Amwell Street, Chadwell Street, Myddelton Square – to the significance of the place. This zone is the head of the New River, a twenty-mile-long artificial course that has been bringing water into London since the early seventeenth century. The thing in the square is a reservoir. The truncated cone is the remnant of a windmill that powered a pump. The curves are traces of a round pond.

Beyond here you can follow the river upstream, ascending at a rate of five inches per mile, using a waterside path thoughtfully

provided. In Islington it is now piped underground, with a small stream left at ground level to weave along the river's old course through a little park behind the backs of houses. Passing the home of Dickens's mistress the route then runs beneath Petherton Road, ordinary enough but of a width that would be inexplicable if you didn't know there was a watercourse below. It fills a lake in Clissold Park. A pumping station in the form of a Scottish castle, now a climbing centre, watches twin reservoirs now used for canoeing. To one side a once hopeful council estate called Woodberry Down, then written off and now rebuilt, has been repackaged and partly sold to private investors in South-East Asia, its value enhanced by views of water.

Above the reservoirs the river is mostly uncovered and takes a looping course that hugs a consistent contour of the faintly hilly land – in order to hold steady its vertical position, its horizontal path is erratic. It creates incident in suburban streets, sometimes merges with railway lands and industrial zones, sometimes edges recreation grounds and sports fields. In Enfield, birthplace of Joseph Bazalgette, a public park is formed out of a loop formed by the river that was later short-cutted by an aqueduct. Near Turkey Street it passes the £45m training ground of Tottenham Hotspur Football Club, where young millionaires come in expensive cars to their work. The river goes under the North Circular Road and the M25. Eventually, if you follow the riverside path, you pass green-belt fields and woods, business parks and golf courses, until you get to the village of Amwell and soon after it the New River's source in Chadwell Spring, a circular basin near Ware in Hertfordshire, which lies below the last minute or so of the south-westerly descent into Stansted.

The New River was remarkable in its time as Bazalgette's sewerage was in his. It was conceived in about 1600 by someone called Edmund Coulthurst, who proved unable to fund it, and realized by the Welsh-born businessman Hugh Myddelton, who, himself

William Hogarth, *Evening*, 1738, showing Sadler's Wells

needing financial and political support, formed a joint venture with James I. The King was useful in suppressing competing projects, overruling objecting landowners and encouraging the only some-times supportive City of London. It was therefore both a public work and a commercial business, with the New River Company remaining a private concern, sometimes self-serving and dishonest, until it was taken into public ownership in 1904 as part of the Metropolitan Water Board.

Like Bazalgette's works, Myddelton's had effects that went beyond the functional. The New River encouraged angling and suicide, then the world's first lifesaving society, The Institution for Affording Immediate Relief to Persons Apparently Dead from Drown-ing, renamed in an outbreak of pith the Royal Humane Society. The watercourse irrigated the social life of its neighbourhoods. Around Sadler's Wells grew up pleasure gardens, spas and tea houses along with the prostitution and thieving usually found in the city's fringes of leisure. An aquatic theatre was founded there in 1804, which used the abundant supplies of the river to recreate naval battles, but was closed for non-payment of its water bill. The leading dance theatre, called Sadler's Wells, now stands there.

Myddelton's water supply and Bazalgette's sewer system were bold interventions for the public good that still serve London. They were both imaginative, requiring the invention of engineering, polit-ical and financial structures that had not previously existed. Both were opposed by vested interests. Both went beyond the functional and, by accident and design, had social, cultural and civic effects. Neither was purely public-spirited, but included such motives as Myddelton's desire for profit and the MPs' wish for a deodorized library.

Myddleton's and Bazalgette's projects are also different from each other, the New River being more entrepreneurial and oppor-tunistic. They were expedient as well as ambitious, adaptive to physical and political landscapes, responses to the conditions of their time which in other circumstances could not be repeated in the same way. What can be repeated is the spirit of both, the determination to find a way to meet an urgent need.

5: Fire, Air, Nature

The first thing you see about Percy Circus is that it stands most of the way up a hill, sideways, leaning upright against the slope like a practised seaman. And then the next thing is that half of it is not there. There are trees in the circular railinged area in the middle: planes mostly, but one or two oaks and a long, hanging willow, oddly twisted like a one-legged circus tumbler. There is a little grass there, too, and rubbish of various kinds littered around – bicycle wheels, bottomless enamel buckets, tins, rotting cardboard. Some of the houses have patches where new London stocks show up yellow against the older blackened ones; then you know what happened to the rest of the Circus. New flats abut at an angle, awkwardly. A blue plaque tells you that Lenin once lived at number sixteen.

Percy Circus can be dated early Victorian by the windows, which have stucco surrounds as wide as the reveals are deep, with a scroll-bracket on either side at the top. The proportions are quite good, though the move away from Georgian is obvious except in the top and leadflashed dormers. There is stucco channelled jointing up to the bottom of the first-floor windows, which have little cast-iron balconies swelling enceintely. Each house is subtly different in its detail from each of its neighbours. The paintwork is everywhere brown and old and peeling.

B. S. Johnson *Albert Angelo*, 1964

At the time that B. S. Johnson described Percy Circus it was at the bottom of its fortunes. Bombing (the 'what' that had 'happened to the rest of the Circus') had made it into another of the broken circles in the area around the New River Head. The houses, built for well-off families, had long been divided into multiple lodgings for transient populations, places where an indigent Russian revolutionary might live early in the century or, later, the failing architect of Johnson's novel. It is the address of an alcoholic dancer in the 1958 Max Bygraves film *A Cry from the Streets*, about poverty-stricken orphans in one of London's hard neighbourhoods. It is also a microcosm of the ways in which the perils of fire and bad air have shaped the fabric of London.

In 1964 Percy Circus was the property of the New River Company, which, since the Metropolitan Water Board had taken over its function of supplying water in 1904, had survived for the purpose of running its holdings of real estate. The shrunken company's offices were in no. 18 Percy Circus, just along from one of Lenin's lodgings. They marked their property with a livery of what one writer calls 'drab chocolate', which is the same paint that Johnson calls 'brown and old and peeling'. In the year of *Albert Angelo*'s publication the company applied for permission to destroy most of the classical streets and squares in their ownership and replace them with towers and slabs, a plan narrowly defeated by the introduction of conservation areas, a designation that protects the qualities of neighbourhoods rather than individual historic buildings. What the company hadn't appreciated was that its run-down property was an example of one of London's most admired and successful urban inventions, the estate of speculatively built terraces of houses. Rasmussen called the type 'a refined industrial product brought to perfection through constant selection during repeated serial construction'. Another writer, Dan Cruickshank, calls it 'England's most consistent contribution to European architecture'.

'Leaning upright against the slope like a practised seaman'

In the early nineteenth century these were cow-strewn fields, owned by the New River Company so that they could lay a web of elm-wood pipes under them, which needed to be dug up often for repairs. They were kept free of buildings until the introduction of efficient and durable cast-iron pipes and a need for money led the company, from 1811 to 1853, to develop their land with housing. It was built to the plans of William Chadwell Mylne, who had succeeded his father, Robert, as surveyor to the company (a post that father and son would between them hold for nearly a century, from 1767 to 1861: they might be called company men, especially as the older would give the younger the New River's source as his middle name). William Chadwell would build the fantasy of a Scottish castle that enclosed the pumping station near Clissold Park, but for the residential estate he took an approach that the *Survey of London* calls 'sustained coherence and stylistic conservatism'. It followed eighteenth-century patterns, but with details as B. S. Johnson says of the nineteenth; it has some ornamental plasterwork of a type that Rasmussen calls a 'vulgarization' of Georgian simplicity.

The development proceeded in increments of a few houses at a time, built by grocers, glassmakers, tea merchants and other businessmen who tried to enlarge their commercial successes with property speculation, but often went bankrupt. The New River Company did not build these houses itself: its role was to grant leases and ensure the architectural uniformity on which Mylne insisted, the slight differences in detail that Johnson notes being due to the hands of different builders. As the company retained the freehold, the houses reverted to it when their long leases expired, which is why it remained the owner in the 1960s. In these respects it followed the standard practice of the areas into which London expanded: the unified districts of Bloomsbury or Marylebone were built by multiple speculators following guidelines laid down by large landowners like the Dukes of Bedford, Portland and Grafton.

The consistency and elegance of houses built on the great estates come from both speculation and regulation. According to Rasmussen,

> the whole form of the houses is an adequate expression of the taste of the period. Just because they were executed as refined industrial products made for sale their aesthetic appearance was specially considered. In order to be sold they had to satisfy the prevailing ideas of beauty. People would choose a house as they would nowadays choose a car.

At least since the early eighteenth century, when with the help of Wanstead House English Palladianism was launched, the predominant taste had been for external restraint, although it is a feature of this form of housebuilding that it enables flourishes and variations of fashion while staying basically the same. Nash for example would start facing his houses in oil-painted render, rather than the exposed or painted brick that had been standard. Different styles of doorcase and metalwork, various treatments of brickwork and in Victorian times eclectic ornament could be added to the same chassis.

The seventeenth-century prototypes of London's speculative domestic urbanism were formed with active public and state intervention. When in the 1630s the Earl of Bedford built the Piazza in Covent Garden on what had been land belonging to Westminster Abbey, a condition of his permission to build was that he work to the designs of the King's architect, Inigo Jones. When Lincoln's Inn Fields was laid out a few years later the developer had to reach a compromise with those who used the area for sport and recreation, with the result that a large green space was formed in its middle. These two developments, both large, orderly rectangles about a central open space, were the models for the many London squares of the next 250 years.

The standard London house was formed by laws, especially

Georgian houses in Bloomsbury and Spitalfields

those following the Great Fire of 1666, when an overcrowded, poorly built, largely timber city was destroyed. From 1667 onwards a series of Acts demanded brick or stone construction, restrictions on over-hangs, windows set a minimum distance from their neighbours, parapets instead of eaves on front elevations and window frames set within recessed reveals. Ratios were set of house size to width of street. If the most urgent need was to design against fire, there was also a concern about quality of construction, as the leasehold terms under which speculators built on other people's land gave them no incentive to design for the long term.

In the mid-eighteenth century the architect Isaac Ware wrote: 'It is certain the present methods of running up houses in London, not only disgraces us in the eyes of strangers, but threatens contin-ual disasters. Till such a control shall be laid upon bad builders by public authority, those who have more skill and integrity should distinguish themselves from them by their work.'

The Building Act of 1774, drafted by the architects Robert Taylor and George Dance, responded to these issues by consolidating pre-vious laws, improving methods of inspection and establishing types of house quality and size, from 'First Rate' to 'Fourth Rate', related to the size of streets on which they might be built. A set of standards for each rate was set out that builders had to follow. It was called the 'Black Act' because of what were seen as its intolerable levels of control, but it was the basis on which the largest city in the world, including the houses of the New River Estate, would be built over the following century.

Health through housing

The new flats that 'abut at an angle awkwardly' are Holford House, a small introductory building, like the gatehouse before a stately home, to what was going to be called Lenin Court. Vladimir Ilych had lived his migrant life not only in Percy Circus but also in its neighbour Holford Square, on the bombed site of which the court was built. As the 1940s wore on, however, and relations with the Soviet Union chilled, it was renamed Bevin Court after the foreign secretary in the post-war Labour government. With admirable economy, only two letters needed to be changed.

Bevin Court is an eight-storey block of council flats, completed in 1954, which responds to the radiating geometry of Percy Circus with three blocks attached like the blades of a propeller to a central hub. It sets up an affinity with Mylne's plan but also antagonism: where the older construction creates a void within a solid form, the new is a solid form in the centre of open space. Through the front entrance are two miraculous events: a lively mural of London signs and symbols by the artist Peter Yates and an exhilarating central staircase which takes the shapes of circle and triangle – those of the old Circus and the new Court – and reconciles them as a vertical ballet that rises the height of the building. Myth has it that a bust of Lenin is buried beneath this stair, from a memorial which, erected around here in 1942, was attacked, required a police guard and was finally removed.

The architects of Bevin Court were Berthold Lubetkin and his practice Tecton, who had designed the ill-fated memorial, and whose helical ramps in the London Zoo Penguin Pool can be seen as a prototype of the dynamic stair. The housing block was one of several that they designed for what were then the London Boroughs of Finsbury, Bethnal Green and Paddington, as part of the wave of social housing promoted by the government of which the eponymous Ernest Bevin was part. The court derives from Le Corbusier's *Ville Radieuse*, a vision of free-standing blocks, their wings projecting from central cores to catch sunlight and air, set in open gardens and parks where citizens could engage in sport and other healthy

activities. In the 1930s Lubetkin had built Highpoints 1 and 2, private housing blocks that realized Le Corbusier's ideas as fully as anyone had then achieved. Bevin Court applies similar ideas to public housing; with its 120-degree geometry it adds some of the constructivism with which, as a young architect in Russia, Lubetkin had professionally grown up.

The stair and the mural are signs of his idea that 'nothing is too good for ordinary people'. The exterior is enlivened by distinctive chequered rhythms of brick, concrete and glass which, while following the rules of the same building legislation that governs Percy Circus, are also inspired by the Caucasian rugs of Lubetkin's native Georgia. The patterning caused some teeth-sucking among modernist architects of the time, who saw it as an impure corruption of their rationalist aesthetic. For Lubetkin it was a way of humanizing what might otherwise be stark and barren.

Bevin Court has antecedents. One is the tradition of council housing going back to the London County Council's Boundary Estate in Shoreditch, of the 1890s, in its centre another circus, this one called Arnold. Another is Tecton's Finsbury Health Centre, built half a mile south of Percy Circus in 1938. Here Lubetkin was invited by Dr Chuni Lal Katial to design a new type of health building, where multiple facilities – children's and women's clinics, dentistry, podiatry, a flat for displaced families, a solarium, a mortuary – were provided under one roof. It also had an educational aim, with a lecture theatre for promoting better health and murals that delivered messages in the reception area: FRESH AIR NIGHT AND DAY; LIVE OUT OF DOORS AS MUCH AS YOU CAN. In these ways the centre was a harbinger of the not-yet-conceived National Health Service; Lubetkin's biographer John Allan calls it the 'architectural birthplace of the British Welfare State'.

Katial, a Punjabi-born man who had once introduced Mahatma Gandhi to Charlie Chaplin in his Canning Town house, was the chairman of Finsbury Council's Public Health Committee and later the borough's mayor. The centre was the start of his Finsbury Plan, a health and housing programme that was interrupted by the war. That the two subjects should be linked in one set of policies and that housing should be directed by a health committee indicates the thinking of the times: the quality of living environments was seen as a matter of public hygiene. Until 1951, for example, housing in Britain as a whole was the responsibility of the Ministry of Health.

As with the *Ville Radieuse* and Bevin Court, the design of the centre is preoccupied with the health-giving properties of light and air. Its wings splay to catch the most of both, with the help of plenty of glass, and the building stands as an isolated object, both as an emissary of a hoped-for future and as if to avoid infection by its neighbours. Hygienic white and cream finishes predominate. Here there are echoes of the Victorian preoccupation with miasma, although with a better medical base: the recession of cholera from European cities had left tuberculosis as the most feared urban disease, for which exposure to fresh air was, before the discovery of antibiotics, the least useless treatment.

The association of the light and airy with health and of dank old cities with illness was a central idea of the early modern movement; a health centre in the phlegmy streets of Finsbury was a good place to put it into practice. The building's guiding concept is stated by a wartime morale-boosting poster: designed by the master of such things, Abram Games, it showed the centre transcendent with solar yellow and placed before a skulking ruin of scabrous brickwork, the word 'disease' scribbled on the wall and a rachitic child lurking in the brown murk. Winston Churchill banned the image for showing too negative a version of Britain, but the purpose of the poster was to show a better country which would make the war worthwhile. YOUR **BRITAIN**, it said, FIGHT FOR IT **NOW**.

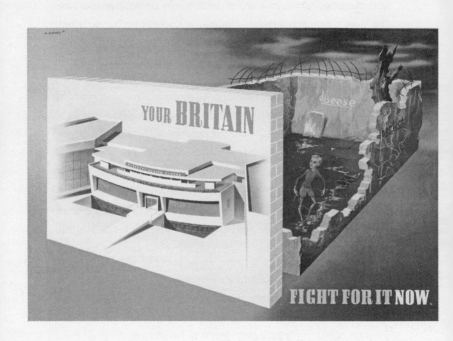

It is an amazing idea to ask people to die for modern architecture but, such was the faith that it could change the world for the better, this was at least part of the message. The bombing and burning of London in the war gave hope that a better world could be built on the ruins; as an ally of medicine, modernism might even save lives. Given the antithesis shown in Games's poster of bright modern life to raddled brickwork, it is not surprising that there is an edgy relation between Bevin Court and the Victorian houses, then decrepit, of Percy Circus.

But Lubetkin was more than a hygienist. The generosity and magnificence of the Bevin Court stair, as if the spirit of a baroque palace had been donated to workers' housing, was part of a belief in elevating the everyday. Finsbury Health Centre also brings ceremony to its entry: its symmetrical wings open in welcome and an upward sloping bridge leads to a light-filled reception area, enriched with Gordon Cullen's mural. The Indian doctor and his Georgian architect wanted the atmosphere to be that of a non-exclusive club, without a reception desk, where nurses would appear and ask you how they could help. Its intent is to be social as well as medical, and beautifully so.

Greek bodies and Christian souls

If white modernism was one response to bad air an older one was the creation and preservation of green space.

Visitors often notice London's verdure. Thus Henry James:

> The congregation of the parks . . . constitute an ornament not elsewhere to be matched and give the place a superiority that none of its uglinesses overcome. They spread themselves with such a luxury of space in the centre of the town that they form a part of

the impression of every walk, of almost any view, and, with an audacity altogether their own, make a pastoral landscape under the smoky sky.

Or Rasmussen:

London has changed and developed an emancipated outdoor life, to which all classes have access. No one is nowadays too good to play with balls or to kick a football, and nobody is too poor to disport himself in one of the numerous parks. The number of recreation grounds in the central parts of London has increased during the last century while it has diminished considerably in other great cities (especially in Paris).

For Rasmussen, London parks grew from an English love of sport, which in turn accounted for the admirable 'Englishman of today', who was 'a well-balanced and self-controlled person under all conditions'. He believed that 'if the modern Englishman is always to exercise considerable control over himself he must of necessity, now and then, give way to his natural instincts. The less moderate will take to drinking and gambling, but the more cultivated man will find a way out of the difficulty in some sort of sport.'

He described the development by Victorian educationalists of sporting ideals, of physical fitness, team spirit and fair play, which he summarized as the idea that 'sport was to give youth a body like that of a Greek . . . and a soul like that of a Christian knight'. He produced a striking theory: 'It is said that prostitution is unknown in Oxford and Cambridge, where thousands of well-to-do young people live. It can only be explained by the fact, that physical training has become the ideal of the students.'

Rasmussen also noted the English tradition of nonsense literature, of Lewis Carroll and Edward Lear, and stated 'how valuable it is to have access to the wonderland of an unrestrained imagination'.

London's parks, he believed, offered similar escapism, spiritual and unfettered, from the hard streets. He liked them for being unmanicured, muddy and worn by human use, and was enraptured by the fact that, in his day, the grass of Hyde Park and Lincoln's Inn Fields was kept short by sheep. He felt that the English, rightly, had chosen 'the park constructed for the sake of men' over one 'constructed for the sake of plants'.

He loved Hampstead Heath, a place formed by nature, quarrying and other human exploitations, on whose rural-seeming slopes John Constable had painted clouds and John Keats mused. Here, said Rasmussen,

> you will find beauty in all seasons. The undulating country is so full of variation that you will find nearly all the artistic effects that European painters have depicted . . . But those thousands who enjoy Hampstead Heath do not look at it this way. Their view has not been determined by art, they feel a much more primitive relation to Nature . . . They walk with delight in the high grass when they escape from the streets. They do not only see, they feel the forms of the land when they wearily plod up the hill. Here they are rewarded by the splendid view . . . All the sports which are practised on Hampstead Heath may be looked upon as an attempt to perceive Nature in a more intensive way. Like Prospero in *The Tempest* the English want to know all the spirits of Nature, to understand them and to master them . . . The English love the raw sensation of the elements, to feel the wind and the moisture in their faces. That is why they swim in the lakes, dive down to muddy depths – becoming fishes in the coolness of the water . . .
>
> Everybody who walks here has some object or other, something to do, either kicking at a ball or diving into the lake or flying a kite, and thereby keeps his own nature pure and unspoiled. He is not moved by second hand emotions, he does not love the

A hot day at Highgate Ponds (August 1930)

If you tell a Londoner what a fine park Hampstead Heath is he will look at you astonished and ask: 'Do you consider Hampstead Heath a park?' In fact he has never realized what Hampstead Heath is at all. To him it is a piece of uncultivated land which — for some unexplained reason — still lies there untouched in spite of the development of the town. He lives

333

place because it reminds him of something which he knows is considered refined and civilized. In Hampstead we have in the middle of the great city an instance of the right preservation of Nature – *the human nature*.

The London park was for Rasmussen wholesome, liberating, democratic, available, shared, restorative, nourishing of the soul, invigorating of the body and a means for making physical, sensory connection between humanity and nature. His account is supported by monochrome photographs, now dreamy and evocative, of lost sun-dappled inter-war afternoons, with the white triangles of toy yachts and the black silhouettes of hat-wearing fathers defining themselves against smudgy shadows.

They show a distant universe, and his vision of the English character, always idealized, is now dated. Grecian bodies, gym-honed, might still be found in the Heath's cruising grounds, but the behaviours are not those attributed at least in the official accounts to Christian knights. Yet the Heath of Rasmussen's moving description is still there. It and Hyde Park and the more obscure green spaces around the city's suburbs still have their qualities of multiplicity, escape and openness. It remains one of the city's miracles that even its drab districts open up into zones of mature trees, fresh air and free space, decorated with well-made architectural embellishments. The city's changing populations have given new purposes: huge Lebanese picnics, hookah-assisted, in Hyde Park, curried goat in Burgess Park, Southwark.

They contribute too, Hampstead Heath in particular, to the evolution of the whole city. The Heath's powers of stimulating the imagination, its combinations of boskiness, water and wide views of London, have inspired writers, visionaries, intellectuals and dreamers. They have made it a place of sudden inspirations and slow study that prompts people and ideas that change the entire city, from the American tycoon who created much of the Underground network to pioneers of modernist architecture. This is a vital part of London's being.

The preservation of the commons

The joys and liberties of green space were not won without struggles, such as those against Thomas Maryon-Wilson, who had inherited ancient rights over Hampstead Heath and wanted to maximize his profits. In the mid-nineteenth century he sold land to the Midland Railway Company, so that they could quarry materials for the lines north out of St Pancras. In 1865 he started building houses on prominent locations on the Heath, to establish a precedent for further development. It was his bad luck his efforts coincided with a rising feeling that open spaces around London were precious and should be protected. 'The people of this country should have some interest in the land of this country', was how the Commons Preservation Society put it, and 'the amenities of everyday life should be placed within the reach of rich and poor alike'.

The society was set up in 1865 by George Shaw Lefevre, later Lord Eversley, a Liberal MP who would devote a half-century of his working life to championing public access to green space. He was assisted by Philip Henry Lawrence, a lawyer motivated by the fact that he lived near Wimbledon Common, which had also been threatened by development. Other supporters included the philosopher John Stuart Mill and the bookseller W. H. Smith, who would successfully oppose Gladstone's plans for building office blocks on the new Thames embankments. The Tory Smith and the Liberal Mill fought each other in the 1865 and 1868 parliamentary elections for the constituency of Westminster, with the thinker winning the first time and the shopkeeper the second, but on the subject of the commons they were united.

Between them Shaw Lefevre and Lawrence ran a political, legal and press campaign that relied on the Saxon concept of common land, which had as Shaw Lefevre said, 'been burdened from time immemorial with the rights of numerous adjoining owners and occupiers to turn out cattle or sheep on them, and to dig turf, or cut gorse, bracken, or heather for fuel, litter, or thatching'. On the other side of the argument were the nominal owners of such land, with the feudal title of lords of the manor, who had both duties and rights relating to it. Over centuries, sometimes with support of legislation, they often tried to enclose it with barriers and make it wholly theirs.

In Victorian London, with cheap coal, slate roofs and disappearing farms, the needs for cow-grazing, turf-digging, gorse-gathering and thatch-making had dwindled, at the same time that, as the value of building land increased, so did the incentive to develop commons. But by now the rights-holding commoners were not all yeoman farmers, but suburban professionals like Lawrence – prototype nimbies – with the means and the will to defend the continued public use of such land. And so Maryon-Wilson, who was lord of the manor of Hampstead, found himself confronting the society, who supported the locals with whom he had been wrestling since the 1830s. 'By the outcry that has been raised against me,' he moaned, 'I have been deprived of £50,000 a year.' He argued that as the old uses had disappeared, so had the rights; the society's case was that access for whatever purposes should be maintained.

Maryon-Wilson died in 1868, before the lawsuit against him finished, and his heir reached an agreement whereby the Metropolitan Board of Works, for a ninth of the price sought by Sir Thomas, bought the Heath for public benefit. Over following decades there would be successful efforts to enlarge it and head off other development plans, for example by the aristocratic owners of the adjoining house and gardens of Kenwood. The Heath, Shaw Lefevre said later, 'was perhaps the most important of all the London Commons, not by reason of its extent, but from its position and its natural beauties and salubrity, which make it more popular and frequented than any other'.

The society, which is now called the Open Spaces Society, went on to fight battles for public access all over England. Their biggest, and the lords of the manor's Götterdämmerung, was fought over the forests of Epping and Hainault, on the north-east edge of London, woodlands and fields contested between several property-owners and rights-holders. Epping was also a royal hunting forest, which gave the Crown the benefit of an intricate tissue of some-times vicious laws aimed at the well-being of deer, such that they could then be slaughtered by sporting monarchs. No fence could be built too high, for example, for a doe and her young to leap over. Branches had to be preserved at the height at which the animals could browse them. Dogs had to be 'expeditated', which means the removal of claws or parts of the balls of their feet, to stop them chasing the precious beasts.

The battle was fought on several fronts. Lords of the manor who started enclosing land and cutting down trees were opposed by locals trying to protect their freedom to gather firewood. The society campaigned in Parliament to make the Crown assert its rights, orig-inally for hunting, for the public good. At one point a compromise was proposed, which would have kept access to one fifth of the then-unenclosed area. The society considered it, but after a speech by Mill it was rejected by a margin of one vote. 'It is a most interest-ing fact', wrote Shaw Lefevre, that Epping Forest was saved from the improvident and discreditable bargain . . . which would have resulted in its being lost to the people of London, by the motion of the great philosopher, Mr. John Stuart Mill, at a meeting of the Society.'

The Corporation of London joined on the side of the public, being anxious to build their reputation at a time when they feared losing powers to what would become the London County Council. They happened to have bought land on the edge of the forest for use as a cemetery, which gave them rights to common land, on which basis they fought in court the thirteen lords of the manor who were trying to enclose the forest and, in 1874, won. They took on responsibility for managing it for the public benefit, which they still do.

In these struggles there were villains. Mr Maitland, Rector of Loughton, close to Epping, being also lord of the manor chose to show his Christian love for his parishioners by enclosing 1,300 acres and leaving them nine for their continued enjoyment. Shaw Lefevre cites William Pole-Tylney-Long-Wellesley, the rake and wrecker of Wanstead House, who 'in lieu of maintaining the Forest, as he was bound in duty to do, led the way to its destruction, by inclosing and appropriating a great part within his own Manors'. His stunts included the appointment of his own solicitor to run the court, supposedly independent, that was charged with looking after the forest.

There were heroes, around Epping and elsewhere. A tree-lopper called Willingdale and his two sons asserted wood-cutting rights in the land enclosed by Mr Maitland: for this they were imprisoned with hard labour by a magistrate with financial interests in the property, which led to the death from pneumonia of one of the boys. Augustus Smith, banker and MP, paid for 120 navvies to travel at midnight from London to Berkhamsted Common in Hertfordshire and take down a two-mile iron fence that had been wrongly erected. In 1897 several thousand rioters stormed and burned a golf course formed by enclosing One Tree Hill in Honor Oak; their repulse prompted *Golf* magazine to report that 'we are not likely to hear anything more of the alleged right-of-way over One Tree Hill, which nature evidently intended for a golf course', but the protestors' actions eventually led to its being made into a public open space in 1905. Shaw Lefevre himself, now almost forgotten, was a giant of patience, persistence and public spirit. Most of those parks celebrated by Rasmussen and essential to the spirit and success of the modern city, would not have existed without him.

The book he wrote of his campaigns, *Commons, Forests and Footpaths*, is as gripping a work as can be, for one that describes medieval property law and Victorian parliamentary procedure. In this he states his belief that

> where such Metropolitan or Suburban Commons exist it is difficult to exaggerate their value to the public. They are natural parks, over which every one may roam freely . . . They are reservoirs of fresh air and health, whence fresh breezes blow into the adjoining town. They bring home to the poorest something of the sense and beauty of nature.

In the particular stress on fresh air there may still be a hint of miasmatic anxiety. Otherwise this is as pure a statement of nature-loving democracy as you could wish for.

Wonderlands of unrestrained imagination

As well as the fields and woods rescued by the society, other forms of public green space were enabled in nineteenth-century London. Old graveyards in the centre were made into public gardens, after burials were moved to the suburbs. Leicester Square was converted from a dump for rubbish and manure into public gardens. Deprived East-Enders, always the subject of fear and pity, were given Victoria Park, designed by Nash's pupil James Pennethorne as a Regent's Park for the proletariat. Gladstone Park was created in Dollis Hill, in the face of opposition from the editor of the *Willesden Chronicle*, who thought it a waste of public money.

In *London in the Nineteenth Century* Jerry White tells how

> in suburban London the parks had to be rescued, plucked bodily from developers' grasp. The heroes were various. There were plutocratic landlords who forfeited the profit they might have made, donating or selling land at low value to public authorities. There were committees of local worthies who agitated, raised funds and won a county or vestry contribution to buy up a country house garden ... There were local authorities who mortgaged the rates to take over a threatened beauty spot. There was the City Corporation, which had no need to mortgage anything but used its wealth to buy 6,500 acres for the benefit of Londoners. And there was the enterprising Metropolitan Board of Works and its successor, which laid out great parks and preserved commons at Battersea, Blackheath, Bostall and Plumstead Heaths, Brockwell Park, Clapham Common, Finsbury Park, Hackney Marshes, Hampstead Heath and Parliament Hill, each over 100 acres in extent and some much more.

The result is that ordinary and obscure suburbs can find themselves blessed with ancient woodland, the aristocratic landscape of a grand house, biodiverse marshes, plains of sport, topographic wonders, pockets of mystery, unique conjunctions of buildings, woods and water. In 1891 the same Maryon-Wilson family who had owned Hampstead Heath donated Charlton sandpits in south-east London to the Greater London Council. Becoming Maryon Park, it would enrich London's filmography by acting, in 1966, as the key location of Antonioni's *Blow-Up*.

The philosophies of the preservers of the commons had a later resurgence, from the 1970s on, with the 'wilding' of spare space – the preservation and enhancement of the spontaneous outbreaks

Blow-Up

of nature that had occurred on bomb sites and industrial residue, copses, ponds and hillocks that would retain some of the dishevelled and weedy character they had had when abandoned. They tended to an ad hoc and homemade quality that reflected the methods of the volunteer groups who created them, often gaining curious topographies from the man-made works they overlay and retaining the element of surprise that comes with sudden sproutings among hard streets. An early example was the William Curtis Ecological Park, 1976–85, the first of its kind in Britain, which grew next to Tower Bridge on land later occupied by the headquarters of the mayor of London, City Hall.

In 1981 a conference on Nature in London was held in Stoke Newington Secondary School, an event nourished with carrot cake and chickpea soup, five pounds to attend, at which four hundred people turned up, and in the same year the London Wildlife Trust held their inaugural gathering on Primrose Hill. Here they tried to plant a single symbolic primrose, but were denied permission by officers of the Department of the Environment and the Royal Parks Department. They did manage to issue the Primrose Hill Declaration. Dodgily typeset, it proclaimed:

> Through a renaissance of care for the environment, London's countryside can be recovered; nature and wildlife will reclaim yet the smallest open space on the street or on window ledges.

> We, the London Wildlife Trust, therefore affirm the rights of London's people to:
> — clean air
> — unpolluted water
> — the integrity of our ecological world for our children and theirs
> — ample open space as in the best of the countryside
> — live and plan in harmony with wildlife
> — determine the reasonable use of our land and resources.

It sounds dreamy and utopian, but the trust and the movement it represents have been successful. They gained the support of the nature-loving, newt-fancying Ken Livingstone, who became leader of the Greater London Council in 1981 and set up an Ecology Unit in 1982. The unit's director David Goode now recalls how, thanks to his leader's backing, council officers would be exceptionally obliging of his requests. Mathew Frith, the Wildlife Trust's director of conservation, says that they changed the way the GLC's parks were managed, which had been 'parlous for wildlife', dominated by sports pitches and overdone horticulture. In 1984–5 the whole of London was surveyed 'by a team of six armed with coloured pencils and maps' in order to identify places important to wildlife, whether ancient woods and meadows or newly colonized wastelands. 'Sites of Importance to Nature Conservation' were identified, of which by January 2015 there were 1,571, 'from Richmond Park to tiny community gardens'.

The trust's main aim was to preserve sites, of which it now manages over forty. Many more have been saved with its help. Early successes included:

Gunnersbury Triangle, a damp tangle of willows and birch in the crotch of three west London railway lines, where campaigners thwarted plans to build a business park.

Sydenham Hill, an area of what had once been the county of Surrey's Great North Wood, historically a source of charcoal for London and ships' timber for the Royal Navy, on which large Victorian houses had been built as a result of the railway line laid to serve the locally re-erected Crystal Palace, which burned down in 1936, which caused the railway line to close, which caused the houses to be abandoned as too inconvenient and big to maintain, which led to nature reclaiming the hill as a hybrid of the original wood, the planting of the houses' gardens and opportunistic growth. From such sequences of unfortunate and fortunate events may a city's assets be made.

Camley Street Natural Park, two acres of an old coal yard in King's Cross, which manages in its small space to contain meadow, wood, marsh and ponds, a fecund mirage between railway viaduct and canal. It opened to the public in 1985, thanks to an alliance between volunteers from the local community, Ken Livingstone and the London Borough of Camden. Within a few years the area was subject to plans for comprehensive redevelopment, with the proposed Channel Tunnel Rail Link set to obliterate the park, and it became a focal point of resistance, an eloquent statement of natural and social life to counter the emblanding proposals of the property companies. When a more touchy-feely rebuilding of the area eventually took place, Camley Street became one of its jewels and prime attractions.

The concept of wilding, like allied movements to create city farms and adventure playgrounds on oddments of land, was a response to a part-abandoned city, its population and economy declining. It flourished at a time when the city's government was more left wing than before or since, and when an anarchistic faith in small-scale community actions was at its peak. Most of these tendencies have been reversed in the three decades since, yet the ideas of promoting nature within the city have continued to grow.

One manifestation is the rise of guerrilla gardening, the practice of unlawful planting on pieces of public land neglected by its official owners. The best-known practitioner, Richard Reynolds, has since 2004 been nurturing plots around his flat in Elephant and Castle, in particular on the area's large traffic gyratory. The spirit is opportunistic and all-embracing: rather than specify planting he encourages people to use whatever seeds and cuttings they can lay their hands on. Guerrilla gardening might be considered the revenge of the banned Primrose Hill primrose against officialdom.

As with the preservation of the commons the movement has grown from community action into public policy. Livingstone, in his second political coming as mayor of London, saved Rainham Marshes, 1,184 acres of wetland on the eastern edge of the city, a former military test-firing range, where Universal Studios had been thinking of building a European outpost. Livingstone also started the process which led, under his successor Boris Johnson, to the creation of the All London Green Grid, a concept which joins together and gives value to the often neglected fragments of nature across the city. Johnson has declared his aim of increasing London's green cover, through living roofs and other means, by 5 per cent by 2030.

A perception that unites these movements, which in the 1970s was radical, is that its history of close interaction with humanity makes nature in London exceptional. Frith says that it is 'arguably the most biodiverse part of the United Kingdom', with 13,100 species recorded. Its 3.2 million private gardens contribute, as does 'a multi-cultural ecology' created by trade and migration. Flora and fauna arrive in the holds and bilge-water of boats, in the baggage of trav-ellers, with consignments of imports: the horse-chestnut leaf miner moth from the Balkans, the Chinese mitten crab, the zebra mussel from South-East Asia. Foreign imports most often prompt bad news reports about invasive species, but Frith opposes the 'fundamental-ists' who 'say that everything that wasn't in this country before shouldn't be there. Britain has long been one of the most disturbed and managed islands in the world. We have what we have. The majority that come in are fairly benign.'

Another essential idea is that the ultimate aim of nature conser-vation is the benefit of people, not just flora and fauna, that habitats and species should be protected not only for their own sake, but also for the enjoyment and fulfilment they give to humans. It is a social as well as an environmental movement that draws on the power of land and the life that grows on it to give identity, bring people together and nourish individuals. 'We are animals after all,' as the landscape architect Jo Gibbons puts it, 'and the sense of the seasons, of sensual contact with nature, is something that we all need. Sticking our fingers into the soil and smelling it. I don't believe that we can survive without it.'

Here we are getting back towards Rasmussen's 'park constructed for the sake of men' and his wonderlands of unrestrained imagination, the spirit of Carroll and Lear. He, the preservers of the commons, the pioneers of wilding, guerrilla gardeners and even the mayors of London have this much in common, that they believe nature is good for the soul.

A supply service of hygienic importance

They share a view that goes back at least to 1708 and the 3rd Earl of Shaftesbury's reflection that

> I shall no longer resist the Passion growing in me for Things of a natural kind; where neither Art nor the Conceit or Caprice of man has spoil'd their genuine Order, by breaking in upon that primitive State. Even the rude Rocks, the mossy Caverns, the irregular unwrought Grotto's and broken Falls of Waters, with all the horrid Graces of the Wilderness it-self, as representing NATURE more, will be the more engaging and appear with a Magnificence far beyond the formal Mockery of Princely Gardens.

It was a formative text for the landscape gardens of stately homes whose combination of regular architecture and loose nature was translated, as aristocratic forms were made bourgeois, into the gardens enclosed by the squares of Georgian, Regency and Victorian

London. Recharged by the Romantic movement and finding new expression in Regent's Park, the Shaftesbury dream, democratized, then guided the preservers of the commons. The Victorian parks created a powerful vision of residential neighbourhoods penetrated by green and with it the assumption that the most important force in the well-being of a city was fresh air and contact with nature, which developed into an urban philosophy. But political matters of this scale are not won by dreams alone: it is also necessary to make a hard practical case.

In 1898 the Londoner Ebenezer Howard published *To-Morrow: A Peaceful Path to Real Reform*, later renamed *Garden Cities of To-morrow*, which proposed the 'Garden City' as a fusion of the best of town and country. London itself, in Howard's vision, was to be depopulated, resulting in lowered prices, larger homes and abandoned slum areas that would then be returned to nature. He believed that London's population should be reduced by four-fifths. (At which point he lost sight of something important about places like Hampstead Heath: they have power precisely because they are surrounded by well-populated city.)

Howard inspired prototype garden cities outside London, in Letchworth and Welwyn, which in turn prompted similar towns and suburbs in (for example) Goiânia, Brazil, Greendale, Wisconsin and Svit, Slovakia. Hampstead Garden Suburb was created under his influence on the edge of the now-enlarged Heath, as a way of building on green space while keeping its best qualities. In the early twentieth century a 'green girdle', inspired by both Howard and the example of Epping Forest, was persistently proposed by architects and planners. Later called a 'green belt', its advocates said it was to be 'a great communal estate', 'a healthful zone of pleasure, civic interest and enlightenment'. It should 'protect its inhabitants from disease, by providing fresh air, fresh fruit and vegetables, space for recreation and contact with and knowledge of nature'.

These campaigns were more successful than anyone might have imagined, thanks to the Greater London Plan drawn up by the planner Patrick Abercrombie in 1944. Following Howard, he proposed a ring of garden cities, now called 'new towns', depopulation – although less drastic than Howard's 80 per cent – and the green belt. All came to pass, although the population stopped declining and started growing again in the 1980s. London's green belt, originally proposed as 'a beautiful sylvan line' about a quarter of a mile wide, is in places thirty-five miles across. Officially designated green belts now cover 13 per cent of the land area of England and form one of the country's most powerful social and geographical ideas. The new towns are there: for example Milton Keynes, Stevenage, Basildon, Bracknell, and, lying between the sources of the New River and the Roding, Harlow.

There is also a lot of Howard in Le Corbusier's verdant *Ville Radieuse*, even if the Swiss-French architect's towers are very different from the cottage-like dwellings of the English garden cities. And so Howard, and before him the Commons Preservation Society, stand behind each of the many Corbusian estates built across the world. Their influence is enormous.

Throughout the many campaigns for urban green space, the importance of fresh air is stressed. It became common to call parks 'green lungs', a respiratory and quasi-medical term still in use. Howard listed 'foul air and murky sky' among the vices of the city, compared with the garden city's 'pure air and water . . . good drainage . . . no smoke . . . no slums'. He quoted an 1884 article on 'The Housing of the London Poor': 'whatever reforms be introduced into the dwellings of the London poor, it will remain true that the whole area of London is insufficient to supply its population with fresh air and the free space that is wanted for wholesome recreation'.

Here green space was seen less as a reflection of Shaftesburian musings, but as a sanitary necessity, an extension of the Metropolitan Board of Works' central concern with sewerage. Early advocates of the green belt spoke in the same terms, motivated in part by the discovery that high numbers of potential military recruits, coming from urban areas, were found unfit for service. As Rasmussen put it, parks 'might be regarded as some sort of supply service of hygienic importance just as water supply, common sewers, etc.'

Smoke and fog

In the preoccupations with air the Ghost of Miasma Past lingers. The more realistic concern about TB was also there, but for Howard the main airborne menace was not the smell of sewage but the smoke of coal fires: 'the sunlight is more and more being shut out', he wrote, 'while the air is so vitiated that the fine public buildings, like the sparrows, rapidly become covered in soot and the very statues are in despair'. His observation wasn't new. Shakespeare had noticed it, as had the seventeenth-century diarist John Evelyn. London fog, mixed with smoke to make smog, was one of the city's mythic attributes; its buildings would be embraced like Io by a dark cloud, conceiving prodigies. Dickens saw 'chance people on bridges peeping over the parapets into a nether sky of fog, with fog all round them, as if they were up in a balloon and hanging in the misty clouds.' Rimbaud described 'sheets of fog spread out in ghastly layers in the sky . . . formed by the most treacherous black smoke that the Ocean in mourning can produce'. T. S. Eliot, poet and cat-lover, wrote of fog rubbing its back upon window panes and licking its tongue into the corners of the evening. It would become the cinematic signature of the city, with the happy side effect for studio-made movies that, if streets were forever disappearing into murk, it required less money to be spent on building sets.

Fogs could last for months. Smog caused the middle classes to flee to suburbs, with the help of unhelpfully coal-powered trains. It killed. In December 1952 it caused 4,000 human deaths (or, by later estimates, 12,000). Daytime visibility could go down to three feet, theatres closed because the audience couldn't see the stage and people fell into a river they didn't know was there. Cattle at the Smithfield Agricultural Show suffered and in at least one case died, which possibly caused more outrage among the animal-loving British public than the human toll. Reluctant to legislate on the grounds of expense, the government eventually passed the 1956 Clean Air Act, which banned the burning of smoke-producing fuel in urban areas. The Act, which has been called 'the first successful air pollution law in the world', ended smogs and raised public health. It also allowed the possibility that the centre of the city might again be a desirable place to inhabit. This change, slowly but profoundly, would realign London's social fabric.

The Percy Circus that B. S. Johnson describes is formed by the intersection of society, law and atmospherics. Its bricks are governed by air, smoke and fire. The openings and details of its houses are directed by the Acts that followed the Great Fire, its part-ruined state is due to wartime incineration and the form of neighbouring Bevin Court is driven by the belief that, in the better world built on bombed-out ruins, workers' housing should have the maximum of light and air. The trees in the middle of the circus descend via eighteenth-century stately homes from the Earl of Shaftesbury's thoughts. The court stands in gardens that are a fragment of the landscape of the *Ville Radieuse*, inspired by the smoke-fearing Howard, who was inspired by the Victorian opening-up of urban parks. The circus's London stock bricks are blackened with pollution. The New River Company's ubiquitous brown paint was, one imagines, chosen for its ability to make soot less conspicuous and so reduce the expense of cleaning and repainting.

That the circus had fallen from the genteel aspirations of its builders in the early nineteenth century was largely due to filthy air. By B. S. Johnson's time the Clean Air Act would have made redundant the houses' infrastructure of chimneys, fireplaces and coal-holes, but its implications for the desirability of property had not yet been felt. In 1974 the remnants of Hugh Myddelton's company sold its estate of several hundred houses to the London Borough of Islington for just over £4m. By 2015 a single flat in Percy Circus might sell for a million. Without the Clean Air Act, it would not.

6: Darkness

One bounty which Ebenezer Howard allowed to cities was 'well-lit streets'.

He made this concession at a time when London was reaching a new peak in the slow improvement of its public lighting, that had progressed from the 5,000 oil lamps provided by the City of London in the 1730s, to the installation of gaslights in Pall Mall in 1807, of arc lamps on Bazalgette's Embankment in 1878, to Thomas Edison's 1882 switching-on of the world's first steam-generated power station at Holborn Viaduct. In the same year the Electricity Lighting Act allowed companies to install cables in streets, following which private companies and municipal suppliers, power stations and networks, often with different voltages, proliferated, leading to attempts to unify the system, which were finally successful with the nationalization of electricity supply by the Labour government of 1945–51.

In 1881 Robert Louis Stevenson foresaw that

> our tame stars are to come out in future, not one by one, but all in a body and at once. A sedate electrician somewhere in a back office touches a spring – and behold! From one end to another of the city, from east to west, from the Alexandra to the Crystal Palace, there is light! *Fiat Lux*, says the sedate electrician. What a spectacle, on some clear, dark nightfall, from the edge of Hampstead Hill, when in a moment, in the twinkling of an eye, the design of the

monstrous city flashes into vision – a glittering hieroglyph many square miles in extent.

This change, in which London was a pioneer, had profound effects on urban life, indeed human life generally. It altered, writes Roger Ekirch in his 2005 book *At Day's Close*, 'Circadian rhythms as old as man himself'. Poets had commented on the limited uses of night time: to 'sleepe, feed and fart' (Thomas Middleton) or 'love and fornication' (Dryden). But, as Stevenson put it:

> when gas first spread along a city, mapping it forth about evenfall for the eye of observant birds, a new age had begun for sociality and corporate pleasure-seeking . . . The work of Prometheus had advanced by another stride . . . and the day was lengthened to every man's fancy. The city-folk had stars of their own; biddable, domesticated stars.

Or, in 1861, in an article in Charles Dickens' magazine *All the Year Round*, on the laying of the first gas pipe:

> the landing of Julius Cesar, the signing of the Magna Carta and the death of Harold furnish more romantic groupings for historical painters, but no one can say they were of more historical importance. Civilisation took a vast stride on that eventful occasion – the living outdoor life of man was lengthened more than half . . . The Battle of Waterloo was a mere puff of smoke in comparison.

There were obvious benefits for law and order and public safety, for reducing crime and prostitution. Artificial light, meanwhile, expanded the possibilities for licit shopping, as in this 1829 description: 'The display of the shops, lighted up with peculiar brilliancy, and filled with valuable merchandise, which to decoy the customer, are rendered oftentimes more brilliant by the reflections of numerous mirrors, is most striking in effect.'

It was seen as a tool and emblem of scientific progress. 'Put an undeveloped human being,' said Edison, 'into an environment where there is artificial light and he will improve'. But there were also costs and losses. A writer on Berlin in 1868 described the 'accelerated, nervous excitation' induced by artificial light and we can infer the same for London. Stevenson regretted the switch to electricity, 'a new sort of urban star' he said, that 'now shines out nightly, horrible, unearthly, obnoxious to the human eye; a lamp for a nightmare! Such a light as this should shine only on murders and public crime, or along the corridors of lunatic asylums, a horror to heighten horror.'

Ekirch argues that humanity lost 'a sanctuary from ordinary existence', a time 'of liberation and renewal', and were 'disannulled of our first sleep and cheated of our dreams and fantasies'. He observes that 'personal conduct in public grew more repressed'. In European cities street lighting 'was a friend of the established order', for which reason rebels like Victor Hugo's urchin Gavroche would set about smashing lamps. In the early years of London's street lighting, says Ekirch, it was a means of social differentiation and segregation:

> the lower orders found themselves in ill-lit warrens segregated from major thoroughfares and wealthier residential areas. Whereas their forebears had once roamed cities and towns at will, exerting nocturnal authority over a vast domain, the indigent were increasingly confined to zones of darkness riddled by extensive crime, as captured by Gustave Doré in his prints of London slums.

Yet when electrification reached the whole city, this effect would be modified. In the nineteenth century it was common to refer to London's poorest areas, especially the East End, as a 'Dark Continent', as unknowable and 'uncivilized' as Britain's possessions in Africa. Once lit, these areas could be perceived differently. Old mythologies would linger, but it became possible to see (as in fact it should have been all along) that the East End was made up of comprehensible streets and houses and inhabited by human beings, as rational or not as anyone else.

Electric light made London more practical, safer, more available, more governable, more exploitable, more graspable, less mysterious, less oneirically enriching, less intimate, possibly more neurotic and intense. It is now, of course, something taken for granted, without which city life is inconceivable.

The Underground

At the same time that nights grew brighter, days became darker. This was partly an effect of smog. It was also a result of choice, when Londoners started using the underground railways which, from the completion of the first stretch of the Metropolitan Railway in 1863, served the city.

By then there was an extensive network of above-ground railways which, both vital to growth and devastating in its social and environmental effects, epitomized technology's Kali-like powers of creation and destruction. Railways were typically pushed through poorer areas that were less able to mobilize opposition, but were also more densely populated. Many tens of thousands were displaced, without compensation, amplifying London's already atrocious problems of overcrowded housing. 'You pass above lines of railway,' said the novelist George Gissing of the area north of King's Cross, 'which cleave the region with black-breathing fissure . . . the valley of the shadow of vilest servitude.' 'From the very core of this dire disaster,' wrote Dickens of wreckage wreaked by building a railway, it 'trailed smoothly away, upon its mighty course of civilization and improvement.'

As David Welsh says in *Underground Writing*, steam engines

PROPOSED STATION AT BAKER STREET.

were seen as demonic, as fire-breathing dragons, as man-killing monsters. They were more so when placed underground where, despite devices for extracting fumes, their smoke, dirt, smell, noise and danger would intensify. The American journalist R. D. Blumenfeld, in 1887, wrote:

> I had my first experience of Hades to-day, and if the real thing is to be like that I shall never again do anything wrong. I got into the Underground railway at Baker Street. I wanted to go to Moorgate Street in the City ... The compartment in which I sat was filled with passengers who were smoking pipes, as is the British habit, and as the smoke and sulphur from the engine filled the tunnel, all the windows have to be closed. The atmosphere was a mixture of sulphur, coal dust and foul fumes from the oil lamp above; so that by the time we reached Moorgate Street I was near dead of asphyxiation and heat. I should think these Underground railways must soon be discontinued, for they are a menace to health.

If Victorian writers liked to apply Dantean images of the Inferno to London, the underground railways supplied the realization of their metaphors. To which was added the extra hell of commercial exploitation of the system's inner surfaces, in Gissing's description:

> high and low, on every available yard of wall, advertisements clamoured to the eye: theatres, journals, soaps, medicines, concerts, furniture, wines, prayer-meetings – all the produce and refuse of civilisation announced in staring letters, in daubed effigies, base, paltry, grotesque. A battle-ground of advertisements, fitly chosen amid subterranean din and reek.

When Lewis Carroll proposed a novel called *Alice's Adventures Under Ground*, just after the Metropolitan Railway opened, he was warned against the negative associations of the last two words, which he changed to *in Wonderland*.

As later with electricity generation, the early development of underground railways was in the hands of competing private enterprises who, obstructing each other's efforts, created a duplicating, disconnected and incomplete network, a 'muddle', said Arthur Munby, 'in all directions possible and impossible, with no general public scheme, no general public supervision, enormous waste of money, no fixed accountability'. Although they received public subsidies from the Corporation of London and the Metropolitan Board of Works, the companies' failure to cooperate could hold up vital connections for twenty years. Trains would sometimes arrive three hours late. As each company refused to produce maps showing their rivals' lines, it was impossible to get an overview of the system.

Despite their operational failings and their sensory assaults, the underground railways were adopted by London's middle classes – they did, after all, provide a useful service. Above-ground hierarchies were recreated below, with three classes of passenger whose segregation was policed by staff. The very poorest could not afford to travel and the slightly less poor could do so only third class and with the help of special off-peak 'workmen's fares'. The main users were office workers and shoppers, and in Gissing's later novels the underground railways become more a purgatory than an inferno, a constant struggle for his characters to sustain themselves with pointless jobs, 'trapped in a whirlpool of urban modernity', according to Welsh, 'in which they are figuratively locked to endure endless journeys around the system'.

At the same time that they made central London hellish the railways offered escape to rural paradises, in the form of either day-trips or permanent relocation to new suburbs such as the Eastbury Estate near Northwood, which the *Watford Observer* called:

> A rare opportunity for small capitalists and speculators. Yet only a few minutes away is a charming landscape . . . tiny hills and

hollows . . . pools of water, brambly wildernesses, where in spring nightingales sing and the air is sweet with the smell of violets, primroses and hawthorn, and in autumn the district is rich with crimson and gold leaves and hedges.

In 1843 the solicitor and campaigner Charles Pearson had suggested a prototype of Howard's Garden City, in which model settlements of artisans' housing would be built in the countryside, their streets radiating from a central station and connected to inner London by train. His proposal, called *Suburban Residences for London Mechanics*, came to nothing, but Pearson's influence did contribute to the creation of the Metropolitan Line which, extending westward, would fertilize new suburbs such as Westbourne Park and the Ladbroke Estate in what had been green space. Like Percy Circus, these districts would in turn lose their desirability to the further expansion of the underground railways in the twentieth century, accompanied by new housing further out.

To the contrast in space between centre and suburb can be added one in time, between the 1890s and the 1930s. When Rasmussen came to write about the Underground, it was no longer the iniquitous, sulphurous, exploitative and bewildering pandemonium described by Gissing. In *London, the Unique City* the Dane expresses distaste for the 'shallow and conventional' above-ground buildings of Piccadilly Circus, now 'repeated mechanically to suit the taste of some mercantile magnate', before descending into 'another and more modern world literally beneath all this stale architecture – that is the London Underground Railway'. He continues:

> At Piccadilly Circus there is an excellent illustration of what the Underground has done for modern civilisation . . . It is planned as a large oval with exits and entrances all round it leading to the street . . . The subterranean station is a thoroughfare with splendid show-windows along the sides of it and is always filled with

people ... The architects who have designed it have done the right thing in the right way. Everything is made of a smooth material easy to clean and always looking neat and orderly ... It is all carried out in the same sober style. The tunnels have no ornamentation or decorated mouldings. The walls are covered with glazed tiles as easy to clean as those of a bathroom . . . Here, there and everywhere, posters and signboards are the only decoration. And the signboards are many. It is never necessary to ask the way, the stranger finds his way about the Underground as easily as the Londoner.

The old opposition of civilization above and filth below is inverted. Now it is the ground-level buildings that are 'stale', the subterranean world that is clean and orderly. The poet John Betjeman would recall that in the 1920s and 30s the Central Line was 'regarded as a sort of health resort' because filtered, ozonized air was pumped into it, 'which was meant to smell like the sea and certainly did smell of something'.

Rasmussen shows the inside of a carriage, an image of perspectival balance like the nave of a Brunelleschi basilica. It is all one class now. He praises the lettering used for all the signs, created by Edward Johnston in 1916. 'It was to be so simple that there could be no possible doubt of the meaning and it must be legible from a distance'. It is 'so soberly executed' that 'it does not date itself ... one can look after it year after year without growing tired of it.' He admires the informative posters that announce fares and suggest excursions, often to leafy or watery retreats, and which, designed by 'the best artists', provide 'an exhibition that is constantly being re-hung'. By 'an indirect method of advertising it is impressed upon the public that a company of their standing always keeps its advertising boards in perfect order'.

'The impression of unity,' says the Dane, 'felt everywhere, is impressive.' It can be found in the designs of the new stations on the suburban extensions to the Piccadilly Line and the District Line, stripped but occasionally playful works in brick, steel-framed glazing and concrete by the architect Charles Holden, and in the impressive white tower, at the time the tallest office building in London, that Holden designed for the company's headquarters above St James's Park station. Rasmussen still uses a demonic image – 'the trains themselves, with their long, red, cylindrical bodies, rush through the "tubes" like a serpent shooting through the earth' – but it jars with the dominant impression of calm modernity.

He does not mention the Underground's two most powerful and enduring visual creations, the red circle penetrated by a blue bar that identifies the system wherever it is found, and its map, invented in his spare time by the engineering draughtsman Harry Beck and since emulated all over the world. First published in 1933, the map sacrificed geographic precision in order to focus on the connections and relationships of the lines and stations, in the style of an electrical circuit diagram, thereby bringing to near-perfect lucidity the opaque tangle of rival lines bequeathed by the nineteenth century. It is democratic and accessible, showing with almost equal dispassion rich places and poor, East End and West End, south of the river and north. There is no Dark Continent here. It makes into everyday reality Robert Louis Stevenson's dream that the 'design of the monstrous city flashes into vision', that electricity would make visible what was inchoate.

This transformation of the once satanic system was due to science, financial piracy, administrative genius and state intervention. It started with the first electrified lines, from 1890 on, which not only removed smoke and fire but also, thanks to the reduced need for ventilation, allowed deeper tunnels, which did not have to contend with issues of property ownership closer to ground level. It continued thanks to the American businessman and ex-convict

Charles Tyson Yerkes, who, with help of bribes, bullying and financial instruments of head-scrambling complexity, had taken over much of Chicago's transit system. The investors he lured to his schemes tended not to see much of their money again, but in the early twentieth century he merged some of London's fractious railway companies, and in a few years he created most of the deep lines that serve the centre of the city now. He was reportedly inspired to these actions by contemplating the huge city from Hampstead Heath – like Constable, Keats and Stevenson, he used the Heath as a place to dream – and deciding he could do something to transform it.

A less drastic but as effective figure was Albert Stanley, later Lord Ashfield, the general manager, then managing director and finally chairman of the company founded by Yerkes, the United Electric Railways Company of London. Over more than three decades he wielded charm, patience and political skill to drive the slow unification of the system into a single organization. In 1907 it was agreed that all stations, in whatever ownership, would be identified with the same UNDERGROUND sign. By the outbreak of the First World War most of the system was run by a single company, and Ashfield started integrating buses with trains. In the 1920s multiple private bus operators were creating chaos in London's streets, causing accidents by racing to grab passengers, and failing to coordinate with each other or the railways. In the early 1930s the Labour Transport Minister Herbert Morrison addressed both this problem and the continuing disconnections in the tube network, by unifying the Underground and the city's trams and buses under the London Passenger Transport Board. This admirable organization, brought into being with the help of Lord Ashfield's influence and chaired by Lord Ashfield, was independent but answerable to government. Competition between departments was, according to Rasmussen, 'a point of honour and not a question of private gain'.

If electricity was the Holy Spirit in the redemption of the Underground and the Father was Ashfield, the Son was a man from Lincolnshire called Frank Pick. He was the chief executive officer and vice chairman of the new board, having worked his way up the United Electric Railways Company of London and its successors since 1906. He had a passion for design. Inspired by the writings of John Ruskin and William Morris, he believed that 'the test of the goodness of a thing is its fitness for use. If it fails on this first test, no amount of ornamentation or finish will make it any better; it will only make it more expensive, more foolish.' Like good modernists, he wanted to create designs and buildings that would speak of the spirit of their own time.

During his careers at UERL and the LPTB Pick introduced the roundel motif and commissioned the typeface from Edward Johnston that Rasmussen admired. He also brought order to the riot of commercial advertisements hated by Gissing, by standardizing their sizes and defining their locations. He chose a smaller size for the Underground's own posters which, with their well-chosen designs, nonetheless stood out. He commissioned Holden and with him toured Europe's modern architecture to find models for new stations: he disliked the 'extravagant revolt of the new architecture in Germany', preferring instead the 'restraint and sanity' of Willem Dudok, City Architect for the Dutch town of Hilversum, and the 'orderly planning which . . . has nowhere been permitted to become mechanical or dehumanized'.

Holden's suburban stations tended to look like pared-down town halls, sometimes with bell-less campaniles, and in some ways they were. They were at least central landmarks, gathering places, hopeful signs of a town before it had quite arrived. But Pick's modernism was not just a question of look. He was passionate about connection, communication, coherence and the avoidance of waste, an attitude that ran from his conception of London as a whole and the rationalization of inefficient lines, to signage in stations, the

design of bus stops and of the posts supporting the power lines for trolleybuses.

In person, connection and communication were not his strong points. Pick was 'prickly', says one writer, 'a rather Spartan low-church northerner . . . a mixture of shyness and arrogance, of self-confidence and timidity'. He was perfectionist and dictatorial, honourable and loyal, but a workaholic bad at delegating, traits which seem to have contributed to his unexpected retirement from the LPTB in 1940 and his death from a cerebral haemorrhage the following year. Yet the same traits helped him create what remains a powerful expression of London as a whole, modern and available city.

'The great appalling fact of these millions cast down'

At a certain moment in the afternoon of Wednesday, 6 June 1894, it would have been possible to observe that Lord Rosebery's primrose-and-rose silks were handily positioned on the descent towards Tattenham Corner. In the area of downland enclosed by the horseshoe-shaped racetrack were perhaps half a million people, believed to be the largest of the large crowds that ever attended the Derby, at that time the greatest horse race in the world. The place was Epsom Downs, an area of common land where the lord of the manor's attempts at enclosure were then being contested by commoners; it is fifteen miles from Westminster, which on a good day is visible from the Downs, outside London but in its orbit. In the nineteenth century the building of three train stations had made Epsom accessible to those working Londoners not too poor for the fare, for whom Derby Day became a secular festival. A significant proportion of the city's population would extract themselves to these Surrey slopes, eat, drink, watch sideshows and take funfair rides, and in many cases barely glimpse a racing horse. The industrial technology of railways had combined with the survival of Saxon customs of common land to enable a popular invasion of the aristocratic sport of horse racing, a temporary reinvention of a huge city as a rural fair and a tableau of contemporary social structures and masquerades. It was a self-celebration of the urban crowd at an unprecedented scale.

On the other side of the finishing straight from the central throng were a series of enclosures and stands of ascending social status. In the most exclusive was Archibald Primrose, fifth earl of Rosebery, a famous and galvanizing orator at a time when political speechmaking was a path to celebrity, and by now prime minister, if with limited success and happiness. Thanks to his marriage to Hannah, the daughter of the banker Baron Mayer de Rothschild, and offensively described by Henry James as 'large, coarse, Hebrew-looking . . . and personally unattractive', he was the wealthiest prime minister Britain has ever had. Although he overcame anti-Semitic taboos to marry Hannah, and praised her sweetness of character, Rosebery possibly enjoyed sex with men: at least the Marquess of Queensberry, who while not a pleasant man had an efficient gaydar, thought so. The father of Lord Alfred Douglas, it was the marquess who destroyed Oscar Wilde over the writer's relationship with the young aristocrat. He also believed that the earl had 'corrupted' another of his sons – for which reason, armed with a dog whip, Queensberry stalked Rosebery when the latter was on holiday with the Prince of Wales in the German resort of Bad Homburg.

As a young man Rosebery had reportedly announced three ambitions: to marry an heiress, become prime minister and own the winner of the Derby. The first two accomplished, he now watched as his jockey, gaily clad in pink and yellow hoops, surged to the front, held off a late challenge from another and, to a vast roar from the crowd, crossed the line one length and a half ahead. Rosebery remains the only prime minister to own a Derby winner while in office, but he found that 'politics and racing were inconsistent, which seemed a good reason to give up politics'. The earl would win the race two more times and die in Epsom in 1929, in one of the many houses he owned from the Firth of Forth to the Bay of Naples, to the sound of a gramophone playing, at his request, the 'Eton Boating Song'.

This singular and florally named nobleman was formed by many of the freedoms, ideals, pretences and prejudices of his class and time. If he were gay, he had to hide it. To marry a Jew was awkward, but it helped if she were rich. He could enjoy vast privileges, but was also propelled by conscience and duty to public speaking and high office, which could then be relinquished in order to enjoy those privileges to the full. On his rise to the top Rosebery had been the first chairman of the London County Council. Which makes it striking that he should have said, in a speech quoted by Ebenezer Howard in the first pages of *Garden Cities of Tomorrow*, that

> there is no thought of pride associated in my mind with the idea of London. I am always haunted by the awfulness of London: by the great appalling fact of these millions cast down, as it would appear by hazard, on the banks of this noble stream, working each in their own groove and their own cell, without regard or knowledge of each other, without heeding each other, without having the slightest idea how the other lives – the heedless casualty of unnumbered thousands of men. Sixty years ago a great Englishman, Cobbett, called it a wen. If it was a wen then, what is it now? A tumour, an elephantiasis sucking into its gorged system half the life and the blood and the bone of the rural districts.

Here is the head of a city who regards it as an unmitigated disaster, as a disease to be cured, a cancer which by implication must be removed. He speaks with sympathy for its nameless masses but not with intimacy, assuming on uncertain evidence a social incompetence which is at odds with later observations of gregarious Cockney solidarity. And which assumption, perhaps, he ought to have challenged by observing the partying people on the other side of the racetrack at Epsom. He does not speak as a Londoner – one of his houses, for sure, was in Berkeley Square, but he was as likely to be found in Scotland, Buckinghamshire, Surrey or Campania. His voice is that of a landed patrician, concerned but distant, as worried about the depopulation of villages as about the overcrowding of the city. He speaks with well-founded horror at the compound miseries of London, but fails to see its strengths and hopes.

Much of Howard's career was spent recording political, legal and religious speeches and his stenographic spirit hovers over the text as he quotes Rosebery and other authorities at length. They beat the same drum, that the urbanization of Britain is 'evil', that flight from the countryside is the 'greatest danger to modern existence', that 'great cities tend more and more to become the graveyards of the physique of our race', on account of the 'houses so foul, so squalid, so ill-drained, so vitiated by neglect and dirt'.

Charged with these kryptonite statements, Howard then sheds his clerical bonds and takes flight. He quotes the lines from William Blake's 'Jerusalem', about England's green and pleasant land, that have been repeated ever since whenever there is a threat to landscape from development. His tone becomes patriotic, messianic and moralistic:

> Yes, the key to the problem of how to restore the people to the land – that beautiful land of ours, with its canopy of sky, the air that blows upon it, the sun that warms it, the rain and dew that moisten it – the very embodiment of Divine love for man – is indeed a *MasterKey*, for it is the key to the portal through which, even when scarce ajar, will be seen to pour a flood of light on the problems of

intemperance, of excessive toil, of restless anxiety, of grinding poverty – the true limits of Governmental interference, ay, and even the relations of man to the Supreme Power.

His 'MasterKey' was the Garden City. Welwyn and Letchworth would be emissaries of divine love for the world, or at least for Hertfordshire.

Implicit and explicit is the idea that London is not only an unpleasant place to live, but also spiritually corrupt. Immoral behaviour (intemperance) is conflated with misfortune (grinding poverty) as if there were no real difference between the active choices of city dwellers and the situations in which they passively found themselves. For Rosebery, Howard and the others whom Howard quotes, the city inspired not only outrage but also incomprehension and fear. In which mindset it was easy for disgust at living conditions to blur with disgust at those living among them and for the removal of one to be confused with the removal of the other.

Robin Evans, a writer on architecture of some wisdom, described in his 1978 essay *Rookeries and Model Dwellings* how 'these two words, physical and moral, were as good as welded together in the literature of improvement'. He cited as typical a Victorian reformer's view that 'filthy habits of life were never far from moral filthiness'. Another spoke of 'the miasma of moral disease', stating clearly and with as little science the belief that, just as cholera could be spread through bad air, so could vice. In his essay Evans reproduced 'The Disease Mist', an 1847 map of Bethnal Green purporting to show a noxious cloud that thickens around the notorious area called Old Nichol. He describes the 1887 'Descriptive Map of London Poverty' by the businessman and social researcher Charles Booth, in which every street is categorized according to the wealth of its inhabitants. Six of the seven levels are given neutral descriptions – 'Fairly comfortable. Good ordinary earnings' – but the lowest, coloured black on his maps, is given a moral value: 'Lowest-class. Vicious, semi-criminal.'

In *Sanitary Ramblings*, the publication that contained 'The Disease Mist', there was also a three-level cutaway drawing of a fictional slum, in which the cellar was full of sewage, the ground floor crowded with drunks and the attic packed with sleeping bodies, male and female, adults and children. 'This was the spectre behind philanthropy,' wrote Evans, 'these three types of interior stood for certain specific evils. The cellar flooded with effluent was regarded as the source of zymotic diseases; the day-room (or common kitchen) was characteristically portrayed as the scene of daylight dissipation, drunkenness and criminal conspiracy; the dormitory as a nest of sexual promiscuity.'

Evans observed that visitors to the worst slums, called 'rookeries', found them mysterious and bewildering. Like other London houses they generally had simple plans and often indeed were quite large and well-built houses that had become slums only through multiple occupation and poor upkeep, but moral campaigners could see only a confusion of spaces, indistinct boundaries and a proliferation of exits and entrances.

In contrast to these miasmic labyrinths of the reformers' imagination the notion of the 'decent home' grew up, a term which, with its moral content faded, is still with us. Also called 'model dwellings', their design stressed everything that the rookeries were thought to lack: separation of families into separate units, separate rooms within the home, three bedrooms, such that parents and male and female children could all sleep apart, a single entrance, open landings on shared staircases for inhaling fresh air. 'Model houses, in their fixity,' wrote Evans, 'stood in stark contrast to the confused, overlapping territories teeming with family life in the slum.' Early estates of philanthropic housing were built along these lines, along with strict rules about drinking, ball games, hanging

laundry and such like, to improve behaviour further. According to Evans, slum dwellers sometimes proved reluctant to move into their sanitary new homes, or if they did they might continue to share a single bedroom and leave the others empty. This phenomenon was attributed at the time to 'wilful and ignorant contempt for the means of health and comfort' which 'causes mingled feelings of vexation and pity'. Evans argues that these people were not attracted to filth and squalor but, feeling that they were being pushed into a model of segregated family life that was not their own, resisted.

This is the context in which soon after its formation the London County Council pioneered council housing by building the Boundary Estate. It was on the site of Old Nichol, by then made famous by a novel about its miseries, *A Child of the Jago*. ('Old Jago Street lay black and close under the quivering red sky,' it reads, stressing as so often in literature on poverty its unlitness, 'and slinking forms, as of great rats, followed one another quickly between the posts in the gut by the High Street and scattered'.) Moving on from the housing projects of philanthropic charities and the Metropolitan Board of Works, the Boundary Estate is a faintly Flemish development of dense, five-storey apartment blocks, gabled, their walls in red brick, London stocks and soot-proof glazed bricks, striated with bands of salmon pink, set off with pale stone trimmings and white-painted sash windows. Oriented to catch the best light, its blocks radiate from Arnold Circus, in the centre of which is a mound formed from the rubble of the Jago's old houses, surmounted by a bandstand.

Despite its density it feels fresh, bright and airy, with handsome trees between its blocks. Earlier philanthropic housing, for example that built by the Peabody Trust, had had a penal and reformatory quality. The Boundary Estate is humane and civilized and respectful of its residents. It was a remarkable achievement and vast in its influence, but, as Lynsey Hanley pointed out in her book *Estates*, it

did little for the 5,719 inhabitants of the Jago, who, apart from eleven who were rehoused on the new estate, were removed without compensation and left to find shelter elsewhere. The beneficiaries of the Boundary Estate were the better-paid working people who could afford its three-shillings-per-week rent.

The Jago-dwellers, in other words, were seen not as victims of the disease of slum housing, but the disease itself, and the response to poverty was less to address it than to move it somewhere less visible. In which respect the Boundary Estate was not alone. As Jerry White says in *London in the Nineteenth Century*, over 12,000 were made homeless between 1879 and 1897 by street improvements whose aim was not only easing traffic but also what White calls 'the apparent social gains of demolishing old housing – removing the causes of disease, scattering expensive paupers and breaking up districts where police found it hard to penetrate and crime could flourish'.

One of these new roads, called Rosebery Avenue after the earl, winds uphill past the New River Head and Sadler's Wells with, now, on its southern side, Tecton's Spa Green Estate. As Charles Booth said at the time, 'a double object was kept in view: to provide, in the first place, a good and direct thoroughfare ... and secondly, to effect a clearance in some of the poorer streets and courts of Clerkenwell. Both objects have been realised.' When combined with the mass evictions that accompanied the building of the major railways, White believes that these clearances amounted to 'a class war of attrition, a social cleansing of inner London'.

The fear of moral contagion was accompanied by that of revolution, the suspicion that the poor would find their living conditions too abominable and resort to violence (and why wouldn't they?), the terror of a tribe which Charles Kingsley had described, in 1857, as having 'nothing to lose and everything to gain by anarchy'. A subject of political debate was the concessions that might pacify this threat. The same anxiety can be read into the title that Ebenezer Howard gave his book in its first edition: *To-morrow: A Peaceful Path to Real Reform*. In the 1920s Le Corbusier would echo the Victorian conflation of good behaviour and hygiene when he called for houses that would be 'healthy (and morally so, too) and beautiful', before ending his most influential book, *Toward an Architecture*, with the lines:

Architecture or Revolution
Revolution can be avoided.

Le Corbusier's urban ideas, followed in London and elsewhere after the Second World War, were among other things prophylactics against violent uprising, means to control the mob.

Given the ambivalences that governed Victorian reform – between compassion and fear, charity and self-interest, and between seeing the very poor as both patients and agents of disease – it is not surprising that its built works could be benign and unsympathetic at once. Equally, the main complaint about the twentieth-century council housing that followed both the precedent of the Boundary Estate and Corbusian teaching, would be that it destroyed community spirit, that it was 'soulless'. Jonathan Raban, writing about a Southampton council estate in the 1970s, described 'the neurotic privacy behind which so many of the place's inhabitants have taken to hiding. The stay-at-home mother in a tower-block flat can be as alone as an astronaut marooned in space.' If it had its origins in moral and physical hygiene, if housing were an extension of a sanitation programme, it was liable to disinfect not only harmful bacteria but also the mulch in which grew the social cultures of the people it was supposed to help.

There are two main points here. The first is the enduring power of the London-hate, the fear of cities, the astyphobia articulated by Rosebery, Howard and others. The second is the presence of mixed motives in social change, the fact that reforming actions are never perfectly disinterested, impartial, enlightened, unprejudiced, clear-sighted or well-informed. Such matters are always contested. Progress is always bumpy.

This is not to invalidate the works of Bazalgette, Shaw Lefevre or the London County Council. They left their city better than they found it and addressed urgent and vast problems. They established structures and precedents whereby, eventually, even the grandchildren of the Jago might be well housed, and a narrow definition of moral improvement would no longer be a precondition of material help. Nor does it follow that every heir of nineteenth-century philanthropy should share its attitudes, or every successor of Lord Rosebery his aristocratic distance. Lubetkin and Tecton, for example, had a vision of housing that went beyond social sanitation.

The Victorian reformers created the physical and administrative infrastructure that still underpins the city. They set in motion ideas about the relations of public and private which, while never fixed, remain. In the 1930s Rasmussen praised London as an airy, green model of civilized life. That he could do this forty years after Rosebery and Howard had declared it an abomination is a tribute to those who fought to right its wrongs.

DAS ENGLISCHE HAUS

7: Exile

'You can have whatever you want', says Robert Holden, happiness expert, founder of The Happiness Project and Success Intelligence, author of *Happiness NOW!*, *Shift Happens!* and *Loveability*, whose website tells us that he is a consultant to Unilever, IBM, Dove and the Royal National Theatre. That he has a PhD is also stressed, though in what and from where is vague, and repeated enquiries to his press officer on the subject are blanked. In a video-recorded presentation he tells his enraptured off-screen audience that he learned the secret of happiness at the age of twenty-five from an Indian guru: it is 'to get past your idea of who you think you are . . . to get even more to the truth of who you are'.

Some residents of the Heygate Estate in Elephant and Castle weren't trying hard enough to get past their idea of who they were. What other explanation could there be? The 'whatever' that they wanted was to stay in their homes among neighbours whom they knew and trusted. They wouldn't have minded, either, if the London Borough of Southwark would keep some of their promises rather than oversee the estate's decline over a fifteen-year process of delay, false starts and obfuscation. Try as they might, they didn't get their wishes, despite the fact that in 2008 Southwark offered to pay Holden's company to provide a bit of Happiness Therapy to such residents as might want it.

The Heygate was planned from 1968–9 and built from 1970–74, a late and large descendant of the Boundary Estate that on its twenty-five acres provided 1,212 council homes, reduced to 1,033 by the sale of 179 to their tenants. Designed by Tim Tinker, Rick Mather and John Kesteven, three young members of the architects' department of the London Borough of Southwark, it consisted of five concrete slab blocks, up to twelve storeys in height, within whose wall-like shelter was a lush enclave of low houses and gardens. It was built using the Jespersen industrialized building system, meaning it employed repetitive concrete panels prefabricated in a factory. The estate replaced a treeless tissue of tenements that Tinker recalls as 'a rat run, terrible, really horrible, like Naples'.

Subconsciously reflecting the area's quaint name, the Heygate was the colour of elephants and looked like a castle. On one face the blocks presented the pronounced repeating horizontals of their access balconies in a way that was abstractly beautiful. Residents praised their spacious and light-filled flats, but you could also call the estate forbidding, not helped by the fact that a cost-cutting exercise removed balconies proposed for the inner faces of the blocks. 'I bitterly regret it,' says Tinker now, 'it was a decision from on high. If you cut something like that you can never put it back.' Movement was elevated onto walkways one or two storeys above the large roads built around it, following a functionalist belief in the separation of different modes of transport. Next to the estate was a linked pair of large traffic roundabouts, together with a system of pedestrian underpasses and a shopping centre. 'Planners laid it down and we did it,' says Tinker. 'All they wanted was housing. The political parties were outbidding each other to build the most housing. There was a shortage of bricklayers so they were obliged to build a proportion in system building. There were absolute fixes. Flexibility was very limited. The system tended to dominate, therefore they tended to build on large sites.'

The Highways Department stipulated the separation of cars and pedestrians, because their 'aim in life was to keep traffic running at

30 mph'. The architects then had to make sense of these demands. Tinker denies the common charge against architects of his generation, that they were trying to create a brave new world, as cliché puts it, that reflected more their theoretical fantasies than real life:

> No, we never set out to build a utopia. That's a nonsense; we were trying to do the best we could. The fundamentals in my book were correct. People would give their right arm for these sort of living conditions. It was a place near to the centre where you can park your car, it was quiet – it was unbelievable. You could walk to school or workplace without being hit by a car. That actually worked.

The estate is Corbusian in its concentration of units in high structures, so as to liberate the ground for trees and transport, although it also reflects the more recent ideas of the architect Leslie Martin in favour of courts and perimeter buildings rather than point blocks. Astyphobic assumptions linger – the ideas that old streets have to be erased to allow for the new, that people should be lifted high above the miasmatic ground and turned to face the light, that the street-level contamination of multiple uses and of people and cars, should be subjected to hygienic separation. But, as architects were by the 1960s and 70s talking about the joys of street life, it was also hoped that community spirit could be recreated by the protected interior and the raised walkways.

The Heygate was a companion to an earlier huge estate to the south, the Aylesbury. They both came towards the end of the post-war surge in large-scale council housing, just as the backlash was starting to attack its architectural and social defects, real and perceived. Thus one judgement, in *The Architecture of London* of 1983:

> In the twentieth century, as a result of heavy bombing and the Second World War, the LCC and subsequently the London Borough of Southwark replaced much of this nineteenth century housing

stock. The resulting urban picture is sad – at best a piecemeal catalogue of local authority housing fashions. The most unfortunate
developments are to be found south of the Elephant and Castle:
the Heygate Estate and the Aylesbury Estate.

In Bridget Cherry and Nikolaus Pevsner's *Buildings of England*
guide to south London, also of 1983, the Heygate's slabs 'make an
impressive sight from a distance . . . but that is all one can say in their
favour'. The twin roundabouts, just outside the estate but part of the
same grand 1960s planning, were voted by readers of the *Evening
Standard* as one of the places they would most like to see removed
by the year 2000.

It became axiomatic that such estates were inhumane and
out of scale in their design, from which it followed that their residents would be alienated and miserable, their walls covered with
graffiti, their immobile lifts puddled with piss. They attracted ritual-
ized epithets – concrete monstrosity, mugger's paradise, no-go area,
windswept walkway. They would leak and fail, as when in 1968 four
people were killed by the partial collapse of Ronan Point, a twenty-
two-storey tower in east London. The architects of these schemes
were accused of social engineering, of a naive belief that enlightened modern design would create enlightened modern people.
Then, with opposite but equal determinism, critics of such projects
asserted that their design caused crime and deprivation.

Like much received wisdom, these views were based on reality,
but oversimplified. They overlooked the extent to which factors
other than architecture, such as housing policy, contributed to the
success or failure of estates. They failed to discriminate between
better and worse examples, or to notice when modern blocks were
successful, or when traditionally designed projects were dysfunc-
tional. When riots took place on the Victorian streets of Brixton,
nobody blamed the architecture, but when on the Broadwater Farm

Estate in Tottenham, they did. Throughout the 1980s and 90s it was an unchallenged truth that modernist mass housing had failed.

In 1997, on the day after his first election victory, a dewy Tony Blair chose the Aylesbury as the setting for his first speech as prime minister. 'There will be no forgotten people in the Britain I want to build,' he said. These sombre blocks were chosen as symbols of the exclusion and deprivation he would banish. By then plans had already started to transform Southwark, which would lead to ambitious plans for eliminating the gigantic mistake, as it was seen to be, of the Heygate.

They were led by Southwark's director of regeneration and planning, Fred Manson, who was a new type of bureaucrat in a new type of job. As his title suggests, his role was not just to be a planner who said no to things, but one who would positively encourage regeneration. Manson was smart, articulate, energetic, engaging, design-aware, imaginative, unafraid of challenging convention.

With Manson's encouragement the Tate's new gallery of modern art came to the borough, and the Millennium Bridge would link his borough to the riches of the City of London. He would help bring to Southwark the Renzo Piano-designed Shard, the tallest building in western Europe, and the headquarters of London's new mayor, City Hall. He also ran a programme of public space interventions by interesting young architects, which were partly implemented.

In Manson's view the problem with places like the Heygate was that they were insufficiently middle class:

> we need to have a wider range of people in the borough. Because social housing generates people on low incomes coming in and that generates poor school performances, middle-class people stay away . . . we have to believe we can change attitudes. We're trying to move people from a benefit-dependency culture to an enterprise culture. If you have 25 to 30 per cent of the population in need,

things can still work reasonably well. But above 30 per cent it becomes pathological.

The point was abrasively made, without giving much impression of love for the poor, but it was in the name of the common good. Nobody, well off or not, went the argument, benefited from social ghettos. Better if people of different incomes could live together. If ambitious middle-class parents raised the standards of schools, everyone would benefit. The borough of Southwark, whose housing was at the time 60 per cent social rented, would no longer be stigmatized as 'Councilville'. 'The borough's simply got more than it wants for local needs,' said an anonymous planner. 'It just sucks in refugees and other people with problems.' Manson's ambitions matched Tony Blair's aim 'to bridge the gap between the poorest neighbourhoods and the rest of Britain'. Southwark, with its vast council estates, represented the failures of the Old Labour policies from which Blair wanted to escape.

In 1998, as chronicled on the website heygatewashome.org, Southwark council started a survey of their stock of 40,000 homes. In the same year their Strategic Committee agreed that there should be 'substantial change' to Elephant and Castle – its hated roundabouts, the shopping centre, the Heygate. The area was well placed, close to the centre of London and well connected by transport. It had a 'strong potential for wealth creation uses' and could be 'a model of high quality urban living'. It was recognized that 'the Council cannot on its own raise money to finance the project' and that therefore 'it is essential that the majority of the funding is from the private sector. The major asset that the Council has is significant landholding in the area. Better use of this land is key to the development of this project.'

'Benefits of the new projects' were to 'assist all residents in the borough'. The importance of consultation was stressed, although it was noted that repairs to the Heygate were already being deferred, owing to uncertainty about its future. It seems that the council already had demolition in mind, although they hadn't discussed this with those who lived there. These residents fell into two main groups: those holding secure tenancies from Southwark, whom the council were obliged to rehouse, and those who had bought long leaseholds. There would be a growing third category, of council tenants who came to the estate once redevelopment plans had been conceived, who were not given rights of tenure.

In 1999 the council selected the developers SLR Ltd as their partners in a scheme intended to provide a new public square, a public park, replacement homes for residents of the Heygate, and about £250m in cash to the council. In 2002 the deal collapsed, with Southwark accused by both developers and residents of killing it by asking for unreasonable levels of profit for themselves. The *Estates Gazette*, an organ of the property business, blamed 'council stupidity and greed, plus developer overoptimism'. Manson, speaking in 2015, puts a different view: SLR 'didn't believe that the Local Authority would walk away, so they just kept pushing and pushing and pushing.' He had left Southwark by the time the deal broke down, but he believes the council did the right thing.

In 2004 the council published a new framework which would establish Elephant and Castle as 'a new cultural entertainment/ creative business focus'. Under the scheme, 4,200 new homes would be created, of which 1,200, or 28.6 per cent would be 'social rented' – that is, at levels of rent that enable people on low incomes to live in the area – to replace those lost by demolition of the Heygate. The development would be a pioneer of carbon neutral design, with a biomass boiler and a water supply from a chalk aquifer borehole. Bill Clinton came to pay tribute.

In 2005 the council promised fifteen 'early housing' sites in the surrounding neighbourhoods, to where holders of secure tenancies could move when the Heygate blocks were demolished. In a 'groundbreaking and revolutionary' programme, some residents were involved in choosing the architects and specifying the layouts and decoration of their new homes.

In 2007 a consortium led by the Australian property company Lend Lease became the council's new development partners. Later in the same year the 'decant' of residents was brought forward, in order to 'provide symbolic and tangible evidence to the people of Southwark that the Council is driving ahead with the regeneration of the Borough'. This came as a shock to the people who were to be moved out. They had received no warning and as the homes they had helped design did not yet exist, they would not be getting them. They were offered a 'right to return', but one valid for only seven years. By 2008 the estate would be half empty, with most of the remaining residents elderly. Hundreds of others, often forced out with eviction notices, were tipped into a borough where they had to bid for one of the thirty-five void properties available per fortnight.

It was about now that the offer of Happiness Therapy was made, followed in 2009 by the announcement that six of the proposed fifteen 'early housing' developments – only one of which had been built – would be scrapped. Remaining tenants were instead offered guided tours 'to find out more about what different areas of the borough have to offer'. In 2010 the estate's supplies of heating and hot water stopped working and were not restarted; residents were offered portable electric heaters instead. In 2013 the last lease-holders – those who had bought homes there and were not renting them from the council – were evicted and obliged to pay £7,000 for the costs involved. It was found that the council was going to be paid £50m, plus an uncertain promise of jam tomorrow, for a site on which they had spent £65m and had described as a 'major asset'. Meanwhile the number of social rented units on the Heygate site had shrunk to about eighty. (The precise number will not be fixed until what are known as 'reserved matters' are decided.)

The replacement of the Heygate was sustained by assumptions and myth. Both the council and media had called the estate 'infamous', 'crime ridden', a 'mugger's paradise'. According to the *Independent*, 'this crime-racked labyrinth of grey high-rise blocks and small terraced houses, linked by raised foot bridges and stone stairwells, stands as a monument to the failure of post-war mass housing'. The actor Michael Caine, who grew up nearby and whose vigilante movie *Harry Brown* was shot on the Heygate, said it was a 'rotten place . . . which fortunately is being pulled down. It should never have been built.'

Yet the same article quotes Laura Cross, a resident, saying that this had been a safe, happy place to live: 'Every morning you'd come out of your door and there'd be people on the balcony and you'd chat,' she said. Also Kevin Watson: 'this wasn't a bad place to live. There was a sense of belonging. We'd all meet up at the bingo. It's important for the older people to have that friendship network.' According to a study by the Metropolitan Police the estate had half the crime rate for the borough as a whole, from 1998 to 2003, when it was still fully occupied.

Objectors to the demolition have gathered a portfolio of testimonials from former residents:

- I am fed up of reading that the estate was a hotbed of crime and deprivation by the media and local politicians.
- I feel quite angry when people call the estate a slum. It's not a slum and it never has been. It was run down because of the regeneration. What we were told once is that they are trying to 'introduce a better class of people to the Elephant and Castle'; well I said, 'You can't get a better class of people than us.'

- It was one of the strongest and friendliest communities in the borough.

Among the oversimplifications was that all mass housing blocks were the same. In fact the team who designed the Heygate, learning from the experience of the Aylesbury, improved on it. 'We went to a great deal of trouble to avoid muggers,' says Tinker. 'I was always conscious of these issues.' Another exaggeration was that it was a maintenance nightmare. An anonymous council source, speaking in 2010, said 'it was a crap building in the first place and it became too costly to maintain'. Yet according to the council's survey of its buildings in 1998–9, the thirty-year cost of upkeep on the Heygate would have been below the average of the council's stock. Tinker suspects that 'politicians confused the Heygate with the Aylesbury'.

It was ignored that there was lush and diverse vegetation in the central area sheltered by the slabs, with 450 mature trees mostly put there by Tinker and his colleagues – planes, a huge silver maple, hydrangeas, bay trees and a three-storey-high loquat. Campaigners used methods approved by the Forestry Commission to put the trees' combined value at £15m. Early regeneration proposals didn't seem to notice they were there, preferring to obliterate and replace them with saplings that would take decades to match what would be lost; only under pressure were plans revised to include at least some of the existing trees.

There was also some piquancy in the fact that Lend Lease eventually sent delegations to inspect The Curve, a public garden created on railway lands in Dalston by the landscape architect Jo Gibbons and the architects muf, so that they could learn from it for their new landscape. They did so four times. It was piquant because The Curve's beauty was based on what Gibbons calls 'the hidden ruderal' ecology that grows on part-neglected land, and it inspired the last survivors of the Heygate to create something similar in the estate's final years, which was then wiped out by Lend Lease even as they were coming to Dalston to see how they could do something like the thing they were wiping out.

It was claimed from the beginning that residents supported the plans. A MORI poll in 1999 found that '70% of Heygate residents expressed a wish to move to a new home on the site of the Heygate Estate', which the council later reported as saying '70% of Heygate residents expressed a wish to move to a new home'. The point, which the council's truncation concealed, was not that anyone loved every aspect of the existing estate, but they wanted to stay together in one place. Overwhelming support for change was claimed on the basis of another survey, in which 5 per cent of residents responded. Jerry Flynn, a former resident, says that consultations consisted of

> a few tick boxes with very general questions. They were confined to soft areas, like 'What do you think of the design?' They didn't ask 'What do you feel about the amount of social housing?' or 'How do you feel about developers making a lot of money out of the site?' The next thing you know is that answers are collated and they say, 'Look, everyone agrees with the scheme.'

The council also went back on a promise to ballot residents on the proposals. Asked about this in a filmed interview, Manson is uncomfortable:

> You're getting straight into the political questions and politicians have to speak about what they said about those areas and what they were bringing ballots to.

> A lot of other issues have come up and it is all those factors in combination which is going to determine what the council does.

> I didn't understand the question. You can't ask me that question.

Heygate was accused of horrors it didn't cause because it looked the part. It was big and concrete and had walkways, therefore it had to be a hell of crime and bad maintenance. It was conflated with the nearby roundabouts and their threatening subways, which were not part of the estate. If residents offered different or more nuanced views, they were ignored or misrepresented. The upshot of the demonization and the half-truths is that many former residents felt brutalized and mugged, not by criminals but by their local authority. One, Ian Redpath, accused the council of 'systematically' running down the estate. Another, Angela Ampomah, said, 'We have been here for so long; we have had our children here and now you want to just throw us out like an empty bag of crisps? This regeneration has been a crime against the people who lived here; it has killed their livelihoods, their morale and their spirit.'

On Oprah Winfrey's show the happiness expert Robert Holden told his hostess that his philosophy 'is based on some very timeless principles and it starts with a very wild idea which is actually that the physical world doesn't really exist'. We inhabit, he said, 'a mental world and actually we project ourselves onto the world. This is the key. We project what we think we deserve onto the world.' Here could be another explanation for the failure of Heygatians to be happy with their treatment by Southwark: perhaps the estate never existed, it was all a state of mind and all that is necessary to find inner peace is to realize this truth. It would make as much sense as many of the other fantasies spun about the place in the last two decades.

By early 2015 it had gone, leaving an expanse of mud and such trees as were retained. In one corner was an odd fragment of Tinker's original design with its own stub of now purposeless walkway attached, the Crossway United Reformed Church. This expanse is the site of Lend Lease's future development of 2,500 homes. The gains and losses in public benefit can be summarized as follows:

Twenty-five acres of publicly owned land transferred to the private sector.

Expenditure by the London Borough of Southwark of £65m.

Payment to Southwark by Lend Lease of £50m, plus the promise of 'overage' – a share of future additional profits on the development. However, this depends on a negotiation with Lend Lease in which there is every reason to suppose that they will use their superior legal firepower to push as hard as they can to pay little or nothing. We can suppose this (a) because this is how property companies usually behave in such circumstances and (b) because Lend Lease have previous when it comes to squeezing public authorities, in New York and in Barangaroo, New South Wales. Overage will not in any case be paid before 2025.

The 1,033 social rented flats of the unregenerated Heygate replaced by (according to the best available estimate) 82. There will also be 198 'affordable' and 316 'shared ownership', which are intermediate levels between social rented and market properties.

Two decades of disruption and uncertainty.

The break-up of established communities. Holders of secure tenancies were rehoused at other locations in the borough. Leaseholders were often unable to buy replacement homes nearby, and were scattered in a fifty-mile-wide diaspora around London.

'Central London's largest park in over seventy years', according to Lend Lease, a claim which ignores the previous existence of a large, tree-filled area in the centre of the estate, that was designated as Metropolitan Open Space.

The new park will not have this protection, and will be privately owned and managed.

The development will not be zero-carbon as previously promised – that is to cause no net release of carbon dioxide – but zero-carbon-growth, which means that it will not release more carbon dioxide than the former estate. As is usual in such calculations, the enormous cost in energy and carbon of demolition and rebuilding is not taken into consideration.

'It's a tragedy it's been lost,' says Tinker. 'By all means knock it down if you can do better. I'm actually livid that they didn't. The whole idea was that they were going to sell the site so they could move social housing elsewhere. They did no such thing. It has been municipal gentrification on a grand scale. The people who bought into it have been ripped off.'

There were other changes to the area, not funded by the redevelopment of the Heygate. A private residential tower, Strata SE1, which would win the 2010 Carbuncle Cup for Britain's ugliest building, was built. The wind turbines at its summit, installed as a gesture of eco-friendliness, but which stopped turning after complaints about their noise, became objects of ridicule. Another tower, One The Elephant, started construction in 2014. The southern of the two roundabouts was reconfigured into a different traffic layout, but not to the extent that it became nice. Plans were also made for improving the larger northern roundabout, possibly with more positive effect, although multilane roads will still dominate. Blocks of flats were proposed and built in nearby locations. The rebuilding of the shopping centre was proposed – the new one will be less tatty, but is unlikely to serve the needs of local people as well as the small shops and cafes of the older one did.

There are some good things here, some of them subsidized by

several other large developments that are planned in addition to the Heygate replacement, although objectors argue that the council drove poor bargains to get them. On balance Elephant and Castle will be a physically more pleasant place than it was before. Some of the new architecture will be better, some worse: a plain shoddy block called Flamingo Court, for example, or a twenty-seven-storey tower by the developers Delancey that has many of the bad aspects of 1960s council housing and not all the good. Peter John, the leader of Southwark Council, says that he has met ex-residents of the Heygate who are happy with their new homes; it is in fact impossible to judge the balance of satisfaction and dissatisfaction among those affected, as the relevant research has not been carried out.

Those involved were not all or entirely fools or rogues. The way things looked in the mid-1990s, Manson's ideas seemed to make sense. John defends the actions of his Labour administration, which came to power in 2010, on the basis that they got the best deal they could. He says that the borough's previous Liberal Democrat rulers had failed to stipulate any level of affordable housing in their agreement with Lend Lease, but were going to leave it to the processes of granting planning permission to achieve this goal. He argues that the property market was weak in 2010, that he faced the prospect of the project not proceeding at all, which, as it had already been delayed by years, was politically unacceptable. 'Sometimes pragmatic choices are necessary to get housing. We could have pushed for 35 per cent affordable, but ended up with nothing. And 35 per cent of nothing is nothing.' He also likes to point out how much affordable housing the council is achieving elsewhere in the borough. He has a point, but it doesn't alter the arguments around the Heygate.

The deeper issue is that, in order to realize projects like this, local authorities are obliged to enter unequal partnerships with multi-national developers. The latter, for whom deal-making is their principal business, have bargaining skills and resources that councils find hard to match. Councils, as developers are well aware, are subject to political winds, changes of administration and public pressures that can weaken their position at a given moment. The good intentions of the project are therefore progressively reduced. 'When the council encounters a problem it takes the easy route,' says Flynn. 'Who at the table is in the weakest position? The commu-nity. We are nothing compared to developers. They are hard-nosed. They question everything and they don't question nicely. They do it very aggressively.'

Fred Manson expresses sympathy with those who would have kept more of the old estate – 'it was gorgeous, really well laid out' – but argues that the means and resources available to the council made incremental changes impossible. There were other factors, such as needing to convince London's new mayor that Elephant and Castle could be a 'strategic centre', which would mean more infra-structure money being directed its way. 'At the time', he says, 'a lot of people didn't think that the Elephant had any credibility at all.' The only option, he says, was to do a deal with a big property com-pany for the replacement of the whole estate, which was why there was no ballot of the residents ('there was no point in asking people because that decision had been made'.) But 'a really interesting lesson that I have now learned is that if you hand something over to a single developer you lose control over everything'.

Under different administrations the council has been played by developers. It has had its tummy tickled, arm twisted and arse kicked. It has got a poor deal in return for its considerable assets, multiple promises have been broken and violence done to the lives of many who lived there. If the original vision had been of Blairite inclusiveness, of all incomes living together, of smart middle-class people helping poor people to raise their aspirations, many of these residents, in whose name the regeneration project had started, would not be part of it. A predominantly working-class place near the centre of London is being made into a zone of expensive apartments into which some people on low incomes will be admitted.

Paul Barker, one of the young men who wrote *Non-Plan* in 1969, studied Southwark in the late 1990s. The council, he wrote,

> needs to remember its history, as well as gazing into its future. Estates . . . were built by councillors who also believed they were building a brighter tomorrow. The trouble came when a good idea was pursued too doggedly, on too large a scale. As I buy a bag of oranges in East Street market, I hope we're not going that way again.

Going that way again, in a different form, is what the council did. In the 1950s and 60s politicians looked at overcrowded and insanitary Victorian streets and saw only slums. So they swept them away, overlooking the social structures that they contained, the qualities of the houses and the possibility that they might be renovated. In the 1990s they starting looking at towers and slabs like the Heygate in a similar way, with similar prejudices and exclusions. It may not have been necessary to eliminate the entire estate. Perhaps it could have been partly rebuilt and partly renovated, which would have been less disruptive to those living there. We will never know for sure, but if you listen carefully you might hear the soft disheartening thuds of babies being thrown out with bathwater.

Troublingly, the redevelopment of the Heygate was in 2015 held up as model by both the Conservative housing minister Brandon Lewis and the Labour politician Lord Adonis. The most charitable view of the project should be that it was a well-intentioned plan flawed in execution and undermined by circumstances beyond the council's control, from whose mistakes lessons might be learned.

But no such qualifications were expressed by Lewis or Adonis. For them it is the future.

The right to **** off and die

The Heygate would become a pioneer of a tendency whereby central London and not-so-central London became less and less available to people on low or medium incomes. In the north-west of the city, for example, the borough of Barnet decided to rebuild the West Hendon Estate – described by the council leader as 'grotty' – in a Heygate-like partnership with the developers Barratt. As at the Heygate, the number of social rented units went down, non-secure tenants faced an uncertain future and leaseholders were threatened with eviction by compulsory purchase orders. They were offered £175,000 for a two-bedroom flat, compared with the £415,000 at which new units were expected to sell. Both leaseholders and non-secure tenants faced the possibility of ending up far from London. Residents of all kinds complained about the break-up of communities and the loss of mutual support. According to the website mappinglondonshous-ingstruggles.wordpress.com, seventy to eighty estates were, in 2015, being made over in this way, affecting 160,000 people. Some of these will be the useful and reasonable upgrading of run-down estates. Many are about building new homes mostly for sale at market rates, with a much smaller number at rents that the former residents could afford.

The process was assisted by changes in rules on the benefits paid to people on low incomes, brought in as part of the austerity drive launched by the coalition government of 2010–15. A cap was put in place such that a family with children could claim benefits – including assistance with housing – totalling no more than £500 per week. In Greater London, where average rents were well over £1,000 per week, this had the effect of forcing people to move out of the city, in many cases abandoning employment, schools, friends and family. The coalition also introduced the under-occupancy charge, unofficially known as the bedroom tax, which reduced benefits in cases where residents were deemed to have more space than necessary in their homes. This obliged old people to move out of homes where they had been for years and hit disabled people hard, in situations where they required a spare bedroom for equipment or a carer, or were unable to find accommodation both smaller and suitable to their needs. According to a group of seven charities 420,000 disabled people across the country might be affected by the bedroom tax.

At the same time the government continued Right to Buy, the policy introduced by Margaret Thatcher that allowed tenants of council housing to buy their homes at subsidized prices, which has the effect of reducing the number of homes available for social rent. Indeed, it enhanced Right to Buy by increasing the size of the subsidy. Following the 2015 election the Conservative government set about extending it to include homes owned by housing associations, which are private, not-for-profit organizations dedicated to providing affordable housing. It also planned to oblige councils to sell off homes in more valuable areas when they became vacant. The eventual effect, in terms of excluding people on low or middle incomes from central London, is likely to be enormous. It is not the policy of a government that cares about meeting the city's housing needs. 'Starter homes' were introduced, where public subsidy helped people to buy homes at 20 per cent discounts, but these were of limited use in a city where prices were as far beyond the reach of average incomes as they are in London.

Another factor, from the 1990s onwards, was the practice of Buy to Let, of individuals buying homes as investments which they could then rent out at market rents. Combined, in what might be called

Right to Buy to Let, these policies had a perverse effect: a home belonging to a council might be bought by its tenant, who might then sell it to an investor, who would charge market rents. The council, obliged to find homes for its homeless, would then have to place some of them in such a flat, paying several times the original rent for the use of a flat it had once owned. According to Tom Copley, a Labour member of the London Assembly, 52,000 homes were being paid for in this way, which he called 'incredibly poor value for money to taxpayers'.

The concept of planning gain, which had become the principal way of providing affordable housing, was weakened. It is the mechanism whereby, in return for receiving planning permission for a residential development, property companies are required to provide a certain number of homes at affordable prices. 'Affordable' was redefined as meaning anything up to 80 per cent of market rates, which in much of London puts homes beyond the reach of all but a few. In 2014 the coalition government invented 'vacant building credit', whereby developers could reduce their contributions to affordable housing when bringing vacant buildings back into use. One of the first beneficiaries was Abu Dhabi's investment fund, who reduced their payment on a luxury block in Mayfair by £9m; politicians of all main parties denounced the measure for its 'far-reaching and potentially catastrophic effects, both for jobs and for the provision of affordable homes in London' and even major property companies attacked it.

David Cameron's government also gave special authority to commercial viability assessments. These were procedures that allowed property companies to argue that their projects would be made unviable if local authorities asked too much of them in terms of affordable housing or other public benefits, or limited their height or bulk, 'viability' being defined as a profit of 20 or 25 per cent.

The premise behind such assessments begs a large question:

if the requirements of local authorities, known at the time that the site was bought by a given developer, were onerous, why did the buyer not pay less for the site? Their main effect was to increase the leverage of the developers, as councils would struggle to fund the evidence that might prove applicants' claims wrong. As this is an inexact subject any evidence will be fuzzy and contestable by lawyers, while the consultants who produce and scrutinize such assessments tend to earn most of their living from property companies, so are unlikely to do anything to upset them even when commissioned by councils. 'All these developers' equations are in my view suspect,' says Fred Manson, 'but councils aren't in a good position to argue them.'

Obvious tricks were pulled to talk up costs and talk down values. As Oliver Wainwright reported in the *Guardian*, costs were sometimes based on estimates set in the future, whereas values were based on those current at the time of the assessment. On the Greenwich Peninsula the Hong Kong-based developer Knight Dragon stressed the costs of remediating contaminated land, even though this had already been done at public expense. George Turner, a campaigner against overdevelopment in Waterloo and Vauxhall, presented evidence in his case at the Court of Appeal that different stories on value were told simultaneously. This was a dense, light-blocking £1.2bn plan around the 1960s Shell Centre, led by the Canary Wharf Group and Qatari Diar; the local authority was told that the average sales value would be £1,275 per sq ft, but potential investors were told it would be £1,641. The difference, added up across the scheme's approximately 900 flats, would be £274m. Viability assessments contributed (for example) to the large-scale reduction or elimination of affordable housing in the large redevelopments of the exhibition centre in Earls Court, the plans for the Royal Mail's sorting office at Mount Pleasant in Islington and on the Heygate Estate, as well as in Greenwich and at the Shell Centre.

The combined effects of benefit cuts, the selling of council housing, the failures to build more in sufficient numbers and the continuing inflation in house prices were captured by James Meek in his book *Private Island*, when he described the experience of Pat Quinn, a sixty-something widow who was struggling to stay in her two-bedroom flat on the Tecton-designed Cranbrook Estate in Bethnal Green, where she had lived for forty years. Her benefits were being cut on the basis that she no longer needed the second bedroom, which as Meek said 'wouldn't be so tough' if there were one-bedroom flats available to her, but there were not. At the same time the incapacity benefit she received for several ailments was removed, as due to a change of the rules she was deemed no longer ill enough for them. Yet, as Meek said, 'the government would love to give her £100,000', which is the maximum discount that a council tenant can get under Right to Buy, but, because she can't raise a mortgage, 'she's not in a position to qualify for it'. She 'never got rich enough to get richer'.

Or there is the case of Nikola Gardner: her mother died, which meant there was no longer anyone to look after her children, which obliged her to give up her job and depend on benefits. With successive benefit cuts she had to move five times in four years, with consequent disruption of her children's schooling, from the relatively central borough of Islington to the outer area of Enfield and thence possibly out of London altogether. She said that Grimsby, two hundred miles north, had been mentioned as a possibility.

In all such cases it can be and is asked why the state should pay large sums to these individuals so that they can live in London. This is the wrong question – what should be challenged is why living in London has become a luxury item, even for modest homes in unglamorous areas and for people who have spent their lives in the city. It can also be said that, in times of austerity, painful sacrifices have to be made, but this argument is undermined by the government's willingness to continue to subsidize Right to Buy and the waste caused by Right to Buy to Let.

What is overlooked, both in the pitiless calculations of benefit and in the grand erasures of old council estates, is the value of the mutual support than can come with settled communities, with people living near their friends and members of their family. Its value is social and personal but also – if this is to be the measure that counts – financial. If people help each other with things like childcare and disability, they are less likely to call on the state to provide it. But such considerations have almost disappeared from political decision-making.

By the end of 2014 there were signs of resistance to the logics of displacement. In the borough of Newham, home of the 2012 Olympics, a group of twenty-nine single mothers were told that they had to move out of their hostel to the distant towns of Birmingham, Manchester and Hastings. Which somehow grated with the borough's claim that it is 'a place where people choose to live, work and stay'. Like the Victorian campaigners for common land in Berkhamsted, the young women took direct action; with the support of the Revolutionary Communist Group, they took over a block in the Carpenters Estate, an empty council property awaiting redevelopment, redecorated it and moved in. The mayor of Newham, Robin Wales, called them 'despicable'. 'If you can't afford to live in Newham,' he told them, 'you can't afford to live in Newham.' He later apologized and pleaded that the real problem was 'the lack of housing supply, the Conservative government's barbaric benefit bashing and the private rented sector's spiralling rents and declining standards'. The council agreed to create temporary accommodation on some of the estate. The women moved out voluntarily and started to help others with the legal and political struggles necessary to stay in their homes.

If you can't afford to live in Newham . . .

On the New Era Estate in Hoxton, a place close to but little touched by the world's most intense concentration of hipsters, residents found themselves facing a trebling or near quadrupling of their rent, after it was bought by the American investment company Westbrook Partners. The estate had been built in the 1930s by a charitable trust so that working people could live there at affordable rents, but now its new owners wanted to maximize their revenues. Lyndsey Garratt, for example, a care coordinator for the National Health Service and a single mother, found that her monthly payments would be going from £640 to £2,400, which would be more than her entire income. But the residents resisted and protested. They pressured the MP Richard Benyon into withdrawing his shareholding from Westbrook, who for their part sold the estate to the Dolphin Square Charitable Foundation, who promised to protect existing rents and tenancies.

These were small victories in a large fight. If a fundamental quality of London is its availability, its multiplicity, the chance it offers to almost anyone to find a niche somewhere, that quality is threatened by the conversion of more and more of its fabric to high-value residential property. If the nineteenth and twentieth centuries saw long and imperfect struggles to achieve decent living standards for Londoners at every level, their achievements are now being reversed.

8. At Home in London

Here are some good places to live in London.

Lillington Gardens Estate, Pimlico, City of Westminster

Built in three phases from 1964 to 1972, this estate borrows the DNA of the high Victorian church of St James-the-Less (1858–61, designed by George Street) and multiplies it into a linked series of fourteen blocks, from three to eight storeys in height and containing 540 flats, that run a good chunk of the mile between Vauxhall Bridge and Victoria Station. The church is eventful, receding and advancing, rising and falling; so is the housing. The church has decorative trimmings and pale horizontal bands which the housing reinterprets as the exposed edges of its concrete slabs. The estate, like the church, is made mostly of red bricks, very, very many red bricks.

Its craggy blocks wrap around lush shared gardens that, although the estate lines one side of Vauxhall Bridge Road, which is long, straight and busy, create bubbles of peace. Its broken-up shapes were intended to humanize its scale. Its density is high, but the design aims to encourage intimacy and community. The complex has some oddnesses and awkwardnesses but, to judge by testimonies of residents, it succeeded.

It was designed by the architect John Darbourne, who, when aged twenty-six, won the commission in a competition, and

Geoffrey Darke, whom he invited to work with him. It is a land-mark of the reaction against earlier, more mechanistic forms of modernism. It showed how to achieve density without towers and how to make 'streets in the air' that worked. (The approach earned the ugly name of Ratrad, which stood for rationalized traditional architecture.)

The bricks were a reaction against machine-age materials, but also practical. As the blog Municipal Dreams records, Darbourne said that rendering would have been expensive to replace and good-looking concrete would have cost 'a fortune', whereas 'with brick you can get the mortar over the face and the joint out of place, but even done poorly it is just about acceptable. That is not the case with concrete.'

All this – low-income housing, homes for the elderly, thought-ful architecture, peaceful enclaves – was achieved in the heart of London, within earshot of Big Ben. Many Members of Parliament now like to have their London flats here.

Trellick Tower, North Kensington, Royal Borough of Kensington and Chelsea

Seen from the Westway, the 1960s elevated highway that heads outwards towards Oxford or inwards to Marylebone, the Trellick Tower is a poem of mass and motion. This thirty-one-storey stela, broad on its flanks and narrow at its ends, in the approximate proportions of a book or a cigarette packet, seems to passing motorists to turn slowly. It is a frozen up-pouring of concrete, as if forced from a vast hidden reservoir which has also formed the viaducts on which you are driving. Complex rhythms of balconies and windows, informed by studies of the Golden Section, animate its broad sides. Its lift tower stands apart, linking to the block with covered bridges, which capture oblongs of sky in the spaces between them.

Which sublimity and art was not much consolation to its residents when, in the years after its completion in 1972, it became known as the Tower of Terror or Colditz in the Sky, a place of rape, assault, suicide, drug abuse, non-functioning lifts, vandalism, broken glass, old syringes, used condoms, graffiti, rough sleeping, misplaced bodily evacuations. It was said that the tales of tribal welfare in J. G. Ballard's *High Rise*, although the book is set in another part of London, were inspired by the Trellick. If so its architect, Ernö Goldfinger, would have inspired two fictional villains: James Bond's adversary and Ballard's Anthony Royal.

But, in a way that became famous, the tower's fortunes changed when the local authority altered its housing policies. In 1986 it decided that no one should live there unless they wanted to do so. Because the tower is well placed on the fringes of Notting Hill, and because it gives marvellous views, and because of the finishes and details of Goldfinger's design – the marble and stained glass in its lobby, its cedar-clad balconies – and because of its proportions and light, it started attracting design-aware pioneers. A concierge was

installed, who should have been there all along. In 1987 the *London Daily News* said it was 'terrifying but now fashionable'. In 1999 the *Guardian* called it 'the height of fashion'. By 2013 the *Evening Standard* could report on Redemption, a 'mocktail' bar and veggie cafe in the Trellick, run by 'entrepreneur with a conscience' Catherine Salway, and on the Goldfinger Factory, a design studio and shop created by 'eco-preneur Oliver Waddington-Ball'. Interior designer Bella Huddart, a resident, said of the Trellick that 'it's über-chic and feels the way Portobello did before it became Kurt Geigered'.

Dawson's Heights, East Dulwich, London Borough of Southwark

A suburban hilltop made more dramatic with mountainous blocks of up to twelve storeys. Powerful and romantic, a magnificent amplification of the south London landscape, but also intimate and protective, with private balconies and shared open space. Its twenty-eight-year-old architect Kate Macintosh was seeking an alternative to 'the anonymous grid expression of the exteriors' of much London housing of the time, which she found 'repellent'. It was built between 1968 and 1972 and contains 296 homes.

Ted Hollamby's Lambeth

Ted Hollamby was director of architecture, planning and development for the London Borough of Lambeth from 1969 to 1981; according to Ken Livingstone, he 'passionately believed that council housing should be as good if not better than private housing'. Across the borough's large territory, which extends from the south bank of the Thames to the foothills of Crystal Palace, he encouraged a group of able and committed architects to create beautiful, thoughtful and imaginative places to live. An example is 269 Leigham Court Road, which Kate Macintosh designed after she moved to Lambeth from Southwark, a series of two-storey blocks for the elderly grouped around courts and gardens. 'I like the silence,' a resident says. 'You're surrounded by all this green. The fresh air makes you feel so good. I am one of those people who likes solitude, but you can relate to others as much as you like. You can choose.'

Others include Lambeth Towers, an eventful and sociable cluster near the Imperial War Museum, by Macintosh's husband George Finch, and Central Hill, in the far south of the borough. Designed by Rosemary Stjernstedt (who was English-born, worked in Sweden and took the surname of a Swede to whom she was married for a while) the latter drapes 470 well-designed homes over the steep slopes of what was once a fragment of the Great North Wood, creating a wonderful range of courts and gardens, mature trees interspersed with buildings, terraces turned to face magnificent views and extensive car-free areas where children play and neighbours meet.

Golden Lane Estate, City of London

Designed by Chamberlain Powell and Bon, a practice formed in 1952 after the thirty-two-year-old Geoffry Powell won the commission in a competition, and completed in phases from 1957 to 1962. On the northern edge of the City of London, it consists of medium-height blocks around a loose network of peaceful courts, with sunken areas formed by the retained basements of bombed-out buildings. Panels in primary colours animate the blocks, as if the estate were a three-dimensional abstract painting. The sixteen-storey yellow-panelled Great Arthur House rises to an eccentric, pagoda-like roof for the lift machinery, whose soffit would be animated by light bouncing from the pools of its communal roof garden. The detail is light and glassy, creating transparencies between inside and out and a rapport between the interiors of the homes, within which privacy is nonetheless maintained. A notable feature is the open-tread terrazzo stair in each maisonette which, descending towards a glass wall that faces other flats, introduces an element of self-

consciousness or theatre to the descent to breakfast. (Optional: curtains or blinds may be employed by residents not wishing to take part in this experience.) There is some strangeness in the circulation, with inexplicable changes of level, a quirk of these architects that will be familiar to anyone who knows their later Barbican complex, which is just to the south of Golden Lane.

Spa Green Estate, Sadler's Wells, London Borough of Islington

The very best of Tecton's estates for what was then the Borough of Finsbury. Opposite the head of the New River. One sinuous block and two oblong, up to eight storeys high, providing 126 flats, set in sloping gardens. An aerofoil roof was supposed to accelerate airflow through the clothes-drying areas beneath it. Completed in 1950.

Alton Estate, Roehampton, London Borough of Wandsworth

The garden city dream realized in the 1950s as Corbusian blocks set in green landscape, with towers and little houses dotted about. For Nikolaus Pevsner, 'a synthesis of buildings and nature was bound to become an English task. It was taken up brilliantly by the then architect to the county of London, J. Leslie Martin, and his Roehampton Estate . . . is aesthetically the best housing estate to date.' The great architectural writer Ian Nairn liked it less: 'the eye of technique and elegance in individual buildings is wide open; the eye of understanding and feeling for a total place is firmly shut.'

Alexandra and Ainsworth Estate, St John's Wood, London Borough of Camden

Praise for this estate has to be qualified by the fact that its construction budget was blown and its heating systems failed. It suffered from problems of concrete maintenance and soundproofing and is a forbidding place to approach by car or on foot.

What's good about it is that it creates a sheltered, social place on a site next to the main railway lines out of Euston, that it has well considered, well-lit flats with generous balconies, that it is domestic and noble at once, that it is part of London but also a place of its own, like nowhere else. Its form and geometry are strong, but it accepts inhabitation and change. It fits 520 homes onto its site at high density, without feeling overcrowded and without going above six storeys.

Seen from a passing train, its long cantilevered flank looks like the back of a stadium, 985 feet of industrial/Roman engineering, but like an extruded hand it holds sweeping crescents of homes which, stepping back from each other, open towards the sky. When it was finished in 1979, terraced, pristine and bright, it was called the Costa del Alexandra. Its weathered concrete is now more Hebridean than Mediterranean.

A 2010 film, *One Below the Queen*, records residents' reactions:

— One of my neighbours said 'Oh my God it's like Alcatraz', but
  I don't think it's like Alcatraz. I love it, I really love it. I think it's
  a very beautiful piece of architecture.
— It's like a family house. It's like a big family house.
— An enormous concrete crocodile that had been in an accident.
  It was horrendous.
— I certainly can hear my neighbour, my neighbour can hear me,
  and you can see the neighbours from across the road so to some
  degree we start participating in each other's lives.

— The way it steps back like this, you always feel the sky, I never feel
  shut in, ever.
— [Addressed to another resident, evidently quite young, out of shot]
  I'm sure I remember going up the estate one day and it was
  summer, and I think you lot were out and – correct me if I'm wrong
  but have you done Irish dancing? Anyway you and your sisters were
  out on the street and there's kids who live near you and I think
  they're Asian kids and there are other kids who I think are Somali.
  So they were really dark and the Asian kids are brown and then
  there were you London Irish I presume, yeah, and you were teaching
  them how to do Irish dancing and it was the funniest most brilliant
  thing I've ever seen. It was a real kind of London scene on the estate,
  am I right? I haven't made that up? So thanks for that, it was a
  great memory.
— It just seemed impossibly nice to stick it out [said the estate's
  architect Neave Brown, talking about a balcony that projects from
  the end wall of the crescent] . . . it's entirely wilful, not functional

in any way at all. I remember a meeting we had ... and the builder
saying at the end 'now I know what that's for. It's for the architect
to jump off of when the building is finished.'

Churchill Gardens, Pimlico, City of Westminster

Elegant riverside living for the common people. Mass housing
humanely realized. About 5,000 people living in 1,661 homes, in
thirty-six blocks, on a site of thirty acres. Competition-winning
modern design of 1946 by Philip Powell, aged twenty-four, and
Hidalgo Moya, aged twenty-five, who would later design the much-
loved Skylon at the Festival of Britain. Nine- to eleven-storey blocks
mostly set end-on to the Thames. Shared garden spaces in between.

The leader of the London County Council said it would 'certainly
cost a great deal, but not more than unplanned building and a lot

less than war. In a way, you know, this is London's war, against decay and dirt and inefficiency.' 'The Estate', says the blog Municipal Dreams 'was intended to accommodate a balanced cross-section' of the population. Rather than 'cater only for the working class [it] captures post-war visions of a classless society.'

Municipal Dreams also records that residents of Dolphin Square, a nearby luxury block, complained that 'many of the flats are not as nice as those put up by the council in Churchill Gardens opposite'. Early residents said that 'it was like moving into heaven' and 'it seemed endless and full of variety . . . there was nothing like it anywhere else in London'.

All these are council estates, products of the post-war surge in local-authority housing that reached its maximum extent in the late 1960s and was ended by Margaret Thatcher's government in the early 1980s. Some were built by Labour councils, some by Conservative, but all accept the idea that housing for working-class and low-income residents should be built all over the capital, including in places like Westminster and the City of London.

All were designed by architects motivated by the idea of creating the best housing for everyone. They considered homes not in isolation but as part of a greater whole and paid as much attention to shared spaces as to individual units. Some suffer from an excessive wish to make an architectural statement and an associated tendency to employ ambitious and insufficiently tested construction methods. Many are serious and successful attempts make dignified and sociable places on low budgets. They were built, as was private housing of the time, to space standards set by law, known as Parker Morris, which determined minimum acceptable dimensions for individual rooms and for flats and houses as a whole.

They are now part of the tissue of London. Through Right to Buy, many were bought by their tenants, many of whom sold them on, such that they entered the housing market, such that Members of Parliament, interior designers and eco-preneurs could end up owning them.

To learn something of another widespread housing type, of different origins and intentions, you can first look at the map of the Underground. It has a significant distortion, which is that the distances between the outer stations are under-represented, compared with those at the centre. This is practical, giving more space where the lines are more crowded, but also affects the perception of the city. It makes it look more unified and less straggling. (It now causes an unpleasant dream-like sensation, if you are late for a plane at Heathrow, on the extremity of the map, that the distances expand the nearer you are to your destination.)

By underplaying the distances to the outer edge of the underground railways' domain the maps served their role as agents of urban growth. Following, consciously or not, Charles Pearson's 1843 ideas in *Suburban Residences for London Mechanics*, the railways aimed not only to serve existing demand but also to anticipate and create future needs. New lines were projected into almost pure verdure or to small rural settlements about which new suburbs would then form, which accommodated much of London's continued considerable expansion between the wars. In these ways a public transport business changed both the perception and reality of London in ways that are still with us.

An example in the early twentieth century was the formation of Hampstead Garden Suburb around the extension of the Northern Line to Golders Green, where Henrietta Barnett and the architect Raymond Unwin achieved one of the first realizations of the ideas of

Ebenezer Howard. Henrietta Barnett was a social reformer who had worked for the education, health and welfare of poor East Enders and with her vicar husband she helped start the Whitechapel Art Gallery. She was an ally of George Shaw Lefevre in his campaigns to protect green space and helped fight off the rapacious designs of Eton College, which wanted to develop for profit some land it happened to own in Hampstead. She then set up trusts to acquire 243 acres and build a model community planned by Unwin, in which two-storey, cottage-like houses were scattered about leafy roads and closes. It had educational institutions for children and adults, religious buildings for different dominations and an open-air theatre.

Her dream, as Rasmussen put it,

> was to create a new and better quarter with better homes for the poorer members of the community . . . Instead of entire and widespread quarters for the poor alone and others only for the rich, the city was to be broken up into nothing but small units, all equally well laid-out. In such town cells the single individual need not feel utterly lost in an immense and disjointed quarter, rich and poor together making a well defined little community . . . an ideal town, with recreation grounds, civic centre and with finer roads than had ever then been known.

Rasmussen then describes a walk around the green spaces of Hampstead where, like Stevenson and Yerkes on the same heath, he has a vision of the future: 'After one has . . . gazed at the sunset over the wide stretches of the country, hardly distinguishable through the evening haze, one tries to imagine the whole of it covered with such towns. It is evident that the harmonious city is not a Utopia. We have experienced the reality of it.'

In fact the precise model of Hampstead Garden Suburb was not widely followed and Barnett's dreams of a socially mixed community would largely fail. The Suburb just proved too nice for the better off to resist and it is now a place where the average price of a home is about £2.7 million. As Owen Hatherley has pointed out, you have to go to the munitions workers' homes built on the Well Hall Estate in south-east London to see a truer fulfilment. But Rasmussen was more accurate when he added that Barnett and Unwin's 'wholesome ideals . . . are also shared by the man in the street. It is the lesson of London. One look at the advertisements of the building speculators in the English newspapers is sufficient to show that Englishmen want to live in a cottage.'

That hazy landscape is indeed covered with settlements. They are less high-minded than Barnett's, built by the 'building speculators' that Rasmussen mentions, which nonetheless continue the dream of living in a quasi-rustic setting within reach of the centre of London. These are the outer suburbs built between the wars around the stations of the expanding railway network that, though still called the Underground, tends to surface when it leaves the crowded centre. Their growth was also assisted by government loans and grants aimed at boosting building, for example the £75 per house offered to builders by the Conservative government of 1923, and by the low cost of building labour during economic depression.

The generic type of these suburbs is the semi-detached two-storey house, usually in a style derived from arts-and-crafts architecture of the early twentieth century, in turn inspired by traditional cottages. Certain details – front doors, touches of stained glass and ornamental metalwork, paint, alternative styles such as mock-Tudor or moderne – could be chosen to taste. The semi-detached house economically allowed an idea of individuality within a much-repeated model. It also allowed room for front and back gardens which gave further scope for conformity or personal expression. Twentieth-century architects often fantasized about building houses like cars – mass-produced, economical, possible to customize.

Hampstead Garden Suburb and Northwood

They didn't notice that the semi-detached, although its construction is essentially low-technology, is as close as anyone got to achieving this dream.

Such houses, said J. B. Priestley in 1933, came with 'their little garages, their wireless sets, their periodicals about film stars, their swimming costumes and tennis rackets and dancing shoes' and were part of an England of 'giant cinemas and dance-halls and cafes, bungalows with tiny garages, cocktail bars, Woolworths, motor coaches, wireless, hiking, factory girls looking like actresses, grey-hound racing and dirt tracks, swimming pools and everything given away for cigarette coupons'. In a tripartite stylistic alliance their arts-and-crafts nostalgia sat alongside art deco cinemas and, in those places lucky enough to have one, the modernity of Charles Holden's stations.

Suburbs like this accounted for most of the doubling of London's area between 1921 and 1939, and of the increase of its population by 1,228,000. At a cost of £400–500 in the mid-1930s, they made the owning of homes affordable for people on relatively modest incomes. Although commercially driven, they retained some of the idealism of Howard and others, as in this advertisement by the British Freehold Land Company:

> Try to own a suburban home; it will make you a better citizen and help your family. The suburbs have fresh air, sunlight, roomy houses, green lawns and social advantages.

To their residents they were exciting, pioneering, even modernistic, as for this homeowner in Northwood Hills:

> I was to find that residing in a suburb adds a thrill and a zest to life. It is an experience in having no traditions to live up to.

The developer-built suburbs did not, however, do much for the very poorest, the slum dwellers, who were still far off the bottom rung of the suburban property ladder. If suburban council estates were sometimes built for people on low incomes to rent, they might not be welcomed by the owner-occupiers. In 1926 the 'Downham Wall' – brick, seven feet high and topped with broken glass – was built to stop the 'vulgar people' of the London County Council's Downham Estate from walking down the private road of Alexandra Crescent on their way to Bromley town centre. It stood until 1950.

As Jerry White records, the suburbs were themselves looked down on by such as the Kensington-dwelling writer Rachel Ferguson:

> Which of us [she wrote in 1939], on hearing that a person is 'suburban', does not instantly conjure up an over-eager half-sir who talks of 'the wife', and . . . mows a ridiculous lawn on Saturday afternoons, while his wife, saying 'pleased to meet you', sets out 'the preserves' on a d'oyley before her whist party.

Before her, in 1907, a Liberal politician had condemned the emerging suburban classes as 'clerks . . . adding up other men's accounts, writing other men's letters'. Suburbia would later be the place that made the playwright and Angry Young Man John Osborne, who grew up in a stultifying part of Surrey, angry.

Henrietta Barnett's dream for the suburbs, that the 'poor shall teach the rich and . . . the rich, let us hope, shall help the poor to help themselves', was not coming true. But if the suburbs could be divisive, this was at least hardly new. The private residential estate of Moor Park, built between the wars around a magnificent eighteenth-century country house towards the outer end of the Metropolitan Line, is sometimes called the first gated community, but the Georgian estates of Bloomsbury and Marylebone were, when first built, effectively such things.

By 1973, in a celebrated television documentary, the architectural writer and poet John Betjeman could convert snobbery into affection, if with patronizing notes. He travelled the stretch of the Metropolitan Line that extends north-west from Baker Street, through inner and outer suburbs to the green belt town of Amersham, which is no longer in London at all. Around it grew 'Metro-Land', the collective word for the new residential districts built around the line, 'child of the First War', as Betjeman put it, 'forgotten by the Second, where a city clerk turned countryman again'. 'Metro-Land' was first coined to name the estates that the Metropolitan Railway built on its own land, but for Betjeman it describes a wider territory fertilized by its transport links; it is now used to describe London suburbia in general.

Betjeman met a man who had made himself an expert on the wildlife of Gladstone Park, Dollis Hill, as others might of the Serengeti or the Great Barrier Reef. He visited The Orchards in Chorley Wood, the house that the arts-and-crafts architect C. F. A. Voysey built for himself in 1899–1900, whose gables and roughcast walls made a prototype for millions of imitative semi-detacheds. He admired the trompe l'oeil frescoes of Moor Park, lightly mocked the golfers on the course outside it and observed the creepy flirtatiousness of the man who controlled the gate to the gated estate. He found someone who had acquired the vast cinema organ of the Empire, Leicester Square – made redundant with the passing of silent movies – and assembled it, fully functioning but in a new arrangement, around his little house, such that it became as much a giant musical instrument as a home.

He visited the castle-like residences in Kingsbury designed by the vegetarian Swedenborgian architect Ernest George Trobridge (who, as taking insulin contravened his beliefs, would die of diabetes). Betjeman remembered the vain attempt to build a rival to the Eiffel Tower in Wembley, on the site of which its stadium was then built. He watched a medieval-style annual pageant in Pinner, that had been invented in the 1950s. Metro-Land for him had

Trobridge in Kingsbury

Mandir in Neasden

Dollis Hill Synagogue

pretensions and follies, but he saw in it 'bastions of individual taste'. He noted the 'variety created in each façade and in the colour of the trees'. It offered in his view both simple contentment and the opportunity to be yourself, however normal or eccentric you might be.

In Betjeman's film almost everyone is white, but since then London's suburbia has become a place that absorbs ethnic minorities, as long as they achieve the financial entry level to buy a property. The facades of the semi-detached houses, whose samplings of old English styles were intended for Anglo-Saxon tastes, can as well house Sikhs, Jews and Muslims. Some have been knocked together and expanded to accommodate the large families favoured by some communities; others have been divided into flats. If Betjeman were making his film now, he would include the BAPS Shri Swaminarayan Mandir, built in Neasden by 1,000 volunteers out of Bulgarian limestone and Italian marble, which when it was completed in 1995 was the largest Hindu temple outside India.

Pre-war suburbia and post-war council estates between them created hundreds of thousands of homes at high speed. They are opposites, in that the suburbs were mostly built for private sale by private developers, albeit assisted by government handouts and investment in transport, whereas the estates were built for subsidized rental under local government ownership. One is found more in outer, the other more in inner London. Their preferred architecture, typology and construction could hardly be more different, even though you can find modernist blocks of private flats and council estates made up of semi-detached houses.

Both have been accused of being monotonous, dull, unimaginative, devoid of character, shoddily built and socially divisive, their residents stigmatized in different ways. Sometimes the accusations are true. But they perform vital roles in providing housing without which the city would not exist in its current form. They enrich the stock of ways in which to live in the city. They offer multiple choices of greater or lesser contact with nature, with other people, with the centre or the periphery, of anonymity, privacy or expression, of transience and permanence.

It is more common to praise the terraces and formal spaces of Georgian and early Victorian London – Percy Circus, for example – and they deserve it. Also built to house large numbers with efficiency and speed, they attain an external cohesiveness and order which permit limitless inner lives and adaptations. They have a certain quality that comes with being hand-made but mass-produced. There is something pleasing about their proportions and their interiors' quality of light. They can have their faults – dank basements, dry rot, narrowness – and received opinion in the nineteenth century was that they were, as Benjamin Disraeli put it, 'flat, dull spiritless streets all resembling each other, like a large family of plain children'. Dickens, in *Dombey and Son*, saw them as soulless and vulgar. But almost everything is now forgiven by virtue of their inherent qualities and their cachet in the property market.

The point is that there is no single or perfect form of housing in London, but that there are many good ones (as well as the OK, the just-about-bearable and downright-horrible). A beauty of London is its variety of versions of home and the vast range of lives and identities they encourage or allow. It is not just a city of Georgian/Victorian terraces, or inter-war semis, or post-war council estates. For example:

Self-build

In the 1970s the Swiss-born architect Walter Segal devised a simple way of building houses, using standard timber sizes and other elements obtainable from a builders' merchant, such that people could build them themselves with a minimum of professional help.

It saved money, it was personally rewarding for those involved, and it created delightful, faintly Japanese, faintly Tudor constructions. He persuaded the London Borough of Lewisham to release two awkward scraps of sloping land for his purposes, which came to be named in the architect's honour: Segal Close and Walters Way. The residents loved them and almost everyone agreed how out-standing was Segal's idea. But it was not followed up and there are few successors to the twenty-seven houses built in Lewisham.

Posh brutalism

Textured concrete and raised walkways are found not only in council estates like the Heygate, but also in more expensive developments such as the 2,000-home Barbican in the City of London, by the same architects as the neighbouring Golden Lane Estate. Has become more appreciated and fashionable in recent decades. Sociable and peaceful and amazingly quiet at night. At times, for example when viewed across its central lake in the evening, breathtaking.

Early philanthropic

In the 1860s the American entrepreneur George Peabody started building blocks of housing for the London poor that were intended to be more physically and morally healthy than the slums. They are still there, enclaves within central areas that have long since gentrified. Their basic decency endures, but so does a hard, reforma-tory quality that was noticed and disliked when they were first built.

Mansion block

The British are sometimes said to be a nation of house-dwellers, for whom flats are an alien concept. A series of successful apart-ment buildings, especially from the 1870s to the 1930s, argues otherwise. They are effective ways of achieving urban living at high

Walters Way

Barbican

Peabody

Albert Hall Mansions

Pulman Court

Du Cane Court

densities with good quality homes and shared facilities. See for example:

Albert Hall Mansions, Kensington, 1879–86. Rising up to nine storeys high, red brick with Flemish gables, their curving shapes echo, like the reverberations of a giant drum, the cylinder of the Albert Hall, which they surround.

Pulman Court, Streatham, 1935. Bright modernist blocks, white painted and balconied, racy, with a swimming pool and a landscape of lawns and mature trees. Designed by Frederick Gibberd, later responsible for Liverpool's Roman Catholic cathedral and Harlow New Town.

Du Cane Court, Balham, 1938. Brick, art deco, with strong horizontals, curved corners and Crittall steel window frames. 676 flats. Roof gardens, a club, a bar, a 'stylish' restaurant. Popular with actors, comedians and mid-level sports stars, such as the table-tennis ace Ernest Bubley, now inexplicably forgotten. Striking enough to generate urban myths, for example that Hitler intended to use it as his London headquarters.

Two-storey terrace

One of the most common and effective types in London, from the late nineteenth and early twentieth century, usually with bay windows. Generally built for people on modest incomes, in what were then outer suburbs.

Becontree

With 120,000 people in 27,000 homes, this was the largest council estate in the world. The most tangible outcome of the promise made by the Prime Minister David Lloyd George in 1919 to provide 'Homes fit for Heroes' – that soldiers who had fought in the First World War deserved something better than slums. It followed Hampstead Garden Suburb's ideal that working families should live among green space in cottage-like houses and, while it is less beautiful than Hampstead, it was more successful in benefiting actual poor people. It suffered from a shortage of schools, garages (because it was never imagined that its residents might own cars) and – in order to encourage them to live more wholesome lives – pubs.

Inter-war LCC

Council flats in medium-height blocks (six storeys or so) with open-access balconies. Approximately Georgian detailing adapted to a larger scale: brick (usually red), slate or tile roofs, hipped and steep-pitched, flat arches over white painted timber-framed sash windows, which have now almost all been replaced by uPVC (that is, plastic). Decent, effective. Typically come with hard but practicable courtyards, sometimes improved by trees and grass.

Span

Well-detailed, light-filled two-storey houses in a gentle modernist style built in the post-war decades by the architect Eric Lyons and the developer Geoffrey Townsend, arranged around car-free shared gardens to engender a sense of community. Which they do.

Lofts

Term imported from Manhattan in the 1980s to describe conversions of warehouses, factories, schools and other redundant buildings into blocks of spacious, open apartments. Common in the former dock areas of east London.

'Lofts'

1990s estate agents' term to describe flats which pretend to the free-and-easy quality of converted warehouses, but aren't spacious.

1970s 'vernacular'

With a dawning sense that modernist mass housing had problems,

Two-storey
terrace

Becontree

LCC

Span

Lofts

1970s
vernacular

but with council homes still being built in large numbers, architects turned to modernized versions of traditional styles, even in places where they weren't traditional. See the Setchell Estate, by Neylan and Ungless, 1972–8, which bizarrely but pleasantly brings the low-eaved pitched roofs of rustic architecture into the dense heart of Bermondsey.

1980s PTSD

By the 1980s architects were feeling even worse about their recent past and designed blocks of flats for housing associations with jolly brickwork and coloured woodwork. Developer-built houses were similar. There is sometimes attention to such things as the sub-cills to the windows, which, as this minor art has now disappeared from construction, is to be appreciated.

Docklands exuberant

A high-walled circus in blue glazed brick. The Einstein Tower, Potsdam, a masterpiece of German expressionism, reworked as waterside apartments in bright red. Unexpected spikes, lugs, logs. The most enjoyable part of the 1980s redevelopment of the old docks, delivered by the architects CZWG and their most conspicuous partner Piers Gough. The best examples are around Butlers Wharf, near the south end of Tower Bridge.

Student housing

At some point in the first decade of the new millennium it was discovered that the provision of small units at high rents to (mostly) overseas students made an attractive investment proposition. The results range from 465 Caledonian Road, Islington, which the Carbuncle Cup jury 'struggled to see as remotely fit for human habitation', to Scape East, Mile End Road, a reasonably handsome work of modernized Georgian simplicity.

PTSD

Docklands exuberant

Scape East

Willow Road

**Straw Bale
House**

**The Blue
House**

The modern one-off

Designing singular houses with as much artistry as if they were novels or musical compositions was something that modern movement architects were good at, from Paris suburbs in the 1920s to California in the 1960s. Often, though not always, designed for the architects' own use. London examples include:

1–3 Willow Road, Hampstead: 1939. A row designed by the Hungarian-born Ernö Goldfinger, which includes his own house. Disliked and opposed when it was built by many Hampstead residents, including Ian Fleming, which is why he later named a Bond villain after the architect. Now owned by the National Trust, better known for preserving stately homes and ancient landscapes.

Straw Bale House, Islington: 2000. Home and office created by the architects Sarah Wigglesworth and Jeremy Till for themselves, with a pioneering use of sustainable materials and techniques: gabions full of recycled concrete, sandbags and walls made of straw bales. Also ideas and shapes spilling out in every direction. Inspirations include the vernacular architecture of the Iranian plateau.

The Blue House, Hackney: 2002. A house, coloured blue, designed by and for Sean Griffiths of the practice FAT. It sets out to break as many architectural taboos as possible, for example by reviving the officially dead style of postmodernism. Described as a billboard, a cartoon and a dolls' house, it also shows a mastery of scale, detail and the organization of plan and section that is beyond many more restrained architects.

Brick House, Paddington: 2005. Inserted into the sort of complicated leftover space that high land values make viable, this house by Caruso St John is barely visible outside. It is all interior, but in an external material, brick, used to the point of relentlessness. The client could afford luxury but, in another reversal of expectations, the mood is of studied austerity. It is serene, with animation supplied by the appearance of light from unexpected directions.

Hopkins House, Hampstead: 1976. A short walk from the Goldfinger House. Inspired by the Case Study Houses – exemplary modern homes in southern California – the design applies industrial construction to domestic use. Light, delicate and glassy, it seems more transient than the trees around. It is un-greedy in its use of land: now, in order to make the most out of the valuable plot on which it stands, it would have at least two more storeys. Designed by Michael and Patty Hopkins, architects of the Mound Stand at Lord's Cricket Ground, for themselves.

Houses for artists

Houses built for artists inject healthy mutations into the DNA of a city's housing. Their studios demand altered proportions and particular ways of catching light and, being artists, they like to do things differently. At certain periods, such as the late nineteenth and late twentieth centuries, some artists have been rich enough to commission handsome architecture. Examples include Lord Leighton's part-Moorish mini-palace in Holland Park and David Adjaye's Dirty House in Shoreditch, for Tim Noble and Sue Webster, a rough/smooth, heavy/light, scumbled/precise work which combines the hefty, worn walls of an old warehouse, painted black, with sharp planes of mirror glass. There is also, on the main route out to Heathrow, an 1891 row of house/studios built for 'bachelor artists', whose high round-headed studio windows now look too fragile to survive the thunderous traffic outside.

Bonnington Square, Vauxhall

A Victorian Square like many others, but made special by the fact that it was occupied by squatters in the 1970s and 80s to prevent its planned demolition. In time they formed a housing cooperative, leased the houses and brought them back to life. A riotous garden now occupies its centre. The collaborative history of its resurrection

Brick House

Hopkins House

Dirty House

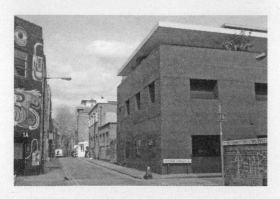

Bonnington square

Rural residue

Athletes' village

can be felt in the ways that space is occupied: boundaries between public and private territories are blurred, pavements are populated by tables and flower pots, vegetation reaches out from the houses towards the central garden and back again.

Rural residue

In outer areas there are sometimes survivors from the time when these places were country towns and villages not yet absorbed by the city – cottages, manors, a stately home in Bexley, a timber-clad dispensary in the Romford Road, oblivious to the fire-proofing requirements of the London Building Acts. Sometimes charming, sometimes forlorn, always curious.

The Athletes' Village

Now rebranded as East Village, the housing created for the athletes in the 2012 Olympic Games is a weird mixture of good intentions and brute function. It had to be built for an immoveable deadline and the contractors/developers Bovis Lend Lease knew how they wanted to build it. It was therefore system-built, standardized and prefabricated to a degree rarely seen in housing since the days of the Heygate Estate. There was also a desire to combine a continental urbanism of blocks and courts with the communal gardens of the late Victorian housing of Maida Vale. This could have aligned well with the regular construction system but, with their rectangularities multiplying and their scale inflating, the blocks headed off in the direction of Khrushchev's Moscow or Ceaușescu's Bucharest. Numerous talented architects were hired to enliven the elevations but, with all the critical decisions predetermined, their effect was limited. Now owned by the ruling family of Qatar, it has open space and some degree of quality in its construction, but it hasn't shed all of its Warsaw Pact aura. It is nothing like a 'village'. It is very little like Maida Vale.

Peabody contemporary

In recent times the Trust founded by George Peabody has made a point of commissioning intelligent and handsome architecture. Examples include Mint Street in Bethnal Green, designed by Pitman Tozer, where an unpromising location next to an elevated railway was the occasion for a delightful block that matches the curve of the viaduct, creates winter gardens to buffer the noise and with a combination of green-glazed and blue brick makes an industrial setting and industrial materials into something delightful and humane. Another is Darbishire Place, Whitechapel, where the architect Niall McLaughlin reinvented the nineteenth-century Peabody dwellings – plain, somewhat barrack-like – as more generous, humane and better lit versions of themselves.

Pocket Living

Pocket Living is a property company that, through intelligent use of design, construction and the planning process, sells homes to local people at 20 per cent below market rates, without the help of public subsidy. Their properties are tight, neat, simple and considered, with importance given to such things as cycle storage and shared space. They have identified a need that is hard to meet: they have 20,000 people on their waiting list, but in 2015 were producing about 250 homes per year, with the hope of increasing the rate to 400.

New towns

Although not within London, the post-war new towns built thirty or so miles from the city's centre were responses to its housing needs. They realize Howard's ideas of the Garden City with modernized architectural styles, car-based transport and low-density houses with gardens. Much mocked and capable of improvement, but successful in their main aims of creating new communities, affordable homes and relieving pressure on the capital.

Mint Street

Pocket living

**Harlow
new town**

Design Guide Housing

Since 2010, there have appeared apartment buildings that are different from their immediate predecessors. The most obvious outward sign is that they have more generous balconies, but they also have such features as better ceiling heights and room sizes, improved use of daylight and orientation, more considered relationships between outside and inside, provision for storage, bicycles and accessibility and more pleasant shared access. These are the products of the *London Housing Design Guide*, an unexpectedly thoughtful document from the mayoralty of Boris Johnson.

Like the London Building Acts, the guide is simple and clear and in focussing on straightforward and often measurable qualities has prompted not only a raising of standards but also a changed culture of housing. The simple facts of the balconies and well-sized window openings gives even the most average new buildings a more generous relationship to the street. The experience of public as well as private space is made subtly more pleasant. The guide tends to encourage (although does not demand) a simpler, plainer kind of architecture than some of the trashier works of the boom time.

It is quietly radical. It demonstrates that it is still possible for public authorities to direct city-building for the better. The guide was pushed through, with some compromises, in the face of opposition from developers, who argued that it would suffocate the building of houses. It has not. Such costs as it adds would be reflected in a lowering of land values which, their being enormous, would barely register.

9. The Values of Value

And yet.

This abundance of types of homes, this smorgasbord, this – at the very least – well-stocked grocery of nutritious items and occasional delicacies – is for large numbers of Londoners, more every day, an impossible dream, a story told from another time. A home is no longer an expression of who you are or want to be, or a fulfilment of a dream, but the least unacceptable unit of floor space that – by extorting as much money from yourself as possible in mortgage payments – you can lay your hands on. If you can get a mortgage at all.

In 2015 a two-bedroom flat in Churchill Gardens cost £500,000. A three-bedroom flat in the Lillington Gardens Estate cost £825,000. If you wanted to hear birdsong in Metro-Land, you might have had to pay £500,000 (or more, depending on location) for one of those two-bedroom semis which in the 1930s made home ownership so accessible. In 2014 the average London home cost £458,000, or thirteen times the median full-time income. Younger buyers, who tend to earn less, would be even more remote from owning something. And some homes were much more expensive: £140m for a penthouse in the One Hyde Park development, £300m for a house in Prince's Gate. Of course, there will be crashes, but the overall trend will be upward.

The reasons are multiple, starting with elementary principles of supply and demand. Between 1988 and 2015 London's population increased at a rate of 74,000 per year, which is predicted to continue and accelerate. Between 1921 and 1939 London's population increased at about 60,000 per year but at the same time the city doubled in geographical area. As London is now surrounded by a green belt, in which new development is restricted, this population must be absorbed within its existing boundaries. Land has to be used more efficiently and densely, which is a more slow, complex and expensive business than building on open fields. Between the wars about 43,000 new homes were constructed per year in Greater London; in the decade up to 2015 the rate bumped about between 12,000 and 22,000.

It is also a global trend that cities like London – or New York or San Francisco – are becoming more desirable, including to people on high incomes, which pushes the prices up. London appeals to investors from other countries, in part because it is seen as politically and economically stable and legally trustworthy, which means that people with wealth in countries that are less so want to transfer it to London property. A significant amount of the money – no one knows how much – is criminal. As was shown by a Channel 4 TV programme, *From Russia with Cash*, in which a journalist posed as a corrupt government official seeking to launder his illegal earnings, some of the city's estate agents seem willing to help with such requests. According to the *Financial Times* more than a hundred billion pounds of property in England and Wales is owned by off-shore companies. Much or most of this property will be in London; many of the ultimate owners will use such companies for the anonymity they offer, some to conceal the dubious sources of their wealth.

These multipliers, working together, push prices up, which then creates another multiplier. London residential property becomes a speculative investment with a good return, which encourages more people to invest, which pushes the prices up further. At this point

London homes could be diamonds or Impressionist paintings or pork-belly futures, but they happened to be more attractive than any of these commodities. Or, as the lawyers Norton Rose Fulbright put it, 'it seems clear that the residential sector will become a mainstream asset class for domestic and international companies, whether they be large scale developers or institutions whose interest lies principally in the long term deployment of significant amounts of capital'.

As the twenty-first century progressed the forces of investment took on striking forms. One was the iceberg house, where several levels of basement would be inserted beneath an existing residence, usually Victorian or Georgian, in a desirable part of town. The new and the old together might add up to a house nine storeys high. Being underground, the new spaces lent themselves to private cinemas, art galleries, saunas, swimming pools, wine cellars, car museums, tennis courts, climbing walls, gyms, bowling alleys and servants' quarters. In 2015 the *New Yorker* reported on Witanhurst, an already huge house in north London, which was to be multiplied by basements to 'about ninety thousand square feet of interior space, making it the second-largest mansion in the city, after Buckingham Palace.' It included a garage for twenty-five cars. The magazine penetrated layers of secrecy to identify the house's owner as the oligarch Andrey Guryev, for whom the property would when finished play 'three roles: refuge, showroom, deposit box. Witanhurst may still look like a grand English estate, but, with so many of its riches buried below the surface, its design is distinctly modern – the architectural embodiment of an offshore account.'

The iceberg house was invented when some architects, called Volume 3, who were working on a house for the founder of London's most voracious estate agents, spotted loopholes in policy and law. The basements were typically built in areas deemed historic, meaning that there are careful controls on changes to external appearance

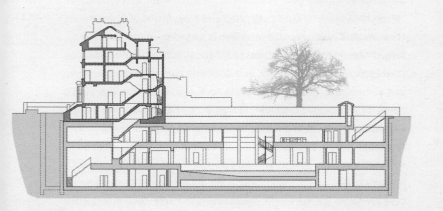

and increases in height, but not on invisible downward extension, which could also extend below gardens to the boundaries of the property. 'We analysed the planning laws,' said Ademir Volic of Volume 3, 'and realized that they cover everything above the surface of the ground, but nothing beneath it. There was nothing whatsoever that could stop us from drilling all the way down to the South Pole.'

Given a choice, few would want to build into the earth rather than sideways or upwards, into the light. Propping an old house such that tons of earth might be extracted and tons of concrete put in, which earth and concrete has to be shipped from and to the site through city traffic, is expensive and risky. There is little intrinsically pleasant about the lightless spaces created – without the bodily delights of private spas and gyms it would be like living in a bank vault. They can be explained partly by simple arithmetic – 'the economics are compelling when the cost of above-ground space in all the best areas is well above £2,000 per sq ft,' said the *Financial Times* in 2012, 'and the cost of digging down is only £500 per sq ft.' They are also a matter of status. 'Houses in this part of London are trophy asset purchases,' said an estate agent, 'people don't want to move out, so they have to find a way of bringing everything they want into their homes.'

Another phenomenon was the ghost street. In areas like Kensington and Knightsbridge the nomadic super-rich would buy homes as part of an international portfolio that might also include New York, Mumbai, Monte Carlo, St Moritz, the Caribbean or Miami. They would visit their London homes seasonally, for example when it's too hot in the Gulf or too cold in Russia, leaving them maintained but empty for nine or more months out of twelve. The very best parts of the city, the ones with the finest streets, the best access to both parks and the pleasures of the centre – or at least those considered so – would become lifeless, the lights out at night, the streets lacking people, the shops established to serve the tastes of the neighbourhood struggling to survive for lack of custom. As these were the same districts where iceberg houses were built, there was a bizarre double effect: more and more space was created to contain less and less humanity.

A luxury development in Knightsbridge, at 8 o'clock last night

The third response to property inflation was to build high. This is not permitted in much of the centre of the city, designated as a series of conservation areas for their history and beauty, and there are further restrictions on tall buildings in places where they might interrupt specific views of St Paul's Cathedral or the Palace of Westminster, which controls increase pressure on the zones that they do not cover. Areas along the south side of the Thames were susceptible, especially formerly industrial sites that contained nothing much thought worthy of protection. So, in Vauxhall, Waterloo, Blackfriars and Bermondsey, towers and plans for towers started sprouting. Inland spots too: City Road, just north of the City of London, for example, or Shoreditch to its east.

With a tower it's easier to see the attraction for the buyer – view, light, a sense of spaciousness – but there is little else delightful about London's new homes in the sky: for example Strata SE1, the 148m-high tower built near the Heygate Estate. Flanked by a brick railway viaduct and by Draper House, a decent if worn-out tower with an expressed concrete structure, Strata is approached across a busy road junction to which perfunctory improvements have been made. The tower itself, an extruded part-ellipse with a sawn-off top, whose strident black-on-white vertical stripes jigger about with mannered offsets, whose wide-jointed aluminium panels look cheap and whose rooftop trinity of non-rotating fans is plain absurd, only adds to the cacophony. It expresses only aggression to its surroundings. There is no reason to hope that, together with its present and future neighbours, the Strata might create an external space that would make you feel good. It offers no sense of welcome or shelter at ground level – just another harsh slash in the cladding panels.

Inside are the usual sort of lifts and lift lobbies, neutral, a-sensual, something to be got through in order to get somewhere else, like entering credit-card details on a flight booking, but when you get to the somewhere else – a flat – you find that tower's external geometries make awkward angles and ugly junctions inside. The windows are sometimes narrow vertical strips, because the architect thought that would look good on the outside. They don't open. Unlike the council flats in the Draper House, these don't have balconies. You are in the fuselage of a plane that will never reach its destination, an experience, in the form of a two-bedroom flat, that costs £625,000. It is what happens when flats' function as units of investment outruns their character as homes, when they become what the planner Peter Rees calls 'safety deposit boxes in the sky'.

If the actual joys of these units were limited there was the compensating rhetoric of marketing. Developments were branded with names like aftershaves, patisseries, estate cars and white wines: Essence, Mettle & Poise, Lexicon, Canaletto. There was escalating sexiness in the publicity materials. Buy This and Get Laid was the message, communicated with decreasing subtlety. Some developments contented with themselves with the ever-popular imagery of tight white dress, sparkling wine and skyline-at-dusk viewed from timber-boarded, glass-balustraded balcony. One Commercial Street in Aldgate, which for some years had been a recession-frozen concrete frame, decorated itself with a giant image of a City lad and another of a vaguely bohemian Shoreditch lady of a kind he might hope to meet in the local bars. 'DECADENT ON EVERY LEVEL, Sophisticated and unashamedly indulgent', boasted Eagle Black in City Road, '. . . redefines decadence with extravagant, open-plan entertaining space made for showing off and inspired little luxuries that make every day a pleasure.' The genre reached a climax early in 2015, with a video about One Commercial Street that was so derided that the developers Redrow took it down:

> They say nothing comes easy and looking back it's hard to disagree [*says gimlet-eyed, firm-jawed, suited and somewhat ferrety man*]. The mornings that felt like night. The days that melted into months and years. [*Scenes of jostling with fellow commuters on bridges and tube trains, walking through urban grot*] The missed opportunities. [*Catches eye of hot girl in office lift, doesn't press his advantage; clutches early noughties Nokia following a failed deal*] The doubts. The need to be different. To define yourself. To be more than an

Redrow psycho

individual. [I don't know what this means.] To stay true to what you believe. [*Row with red-haired girlfriend, one guesses on the theme of career vs. relationship*] To make the impossible possible. [*Arrives in taxi outside apartment building, enters lobby. It is night, so you can't see the mediocrity of the external architecture*] To rise. And rise. [*Takes lift. Enters apartment. New girlfriend, or possibly the same, but presumably more compliant on career vs. relationship issues, possibly encouraged into this compliance by chance to live in luxury apartment, asleep. Gimlet eyes smirk*] Yes, they say nothing comes easy but if it was easy then it wouldn't feel as good. [*Camera scans apartment: German kitchen, artistic objects, a book on design, receptacles for alcohol*] To look out on the city that could have swallowed you whole and say I Did This. [*View of Gherkin, Cheesegrater*] To stand with the world at your feet. [*Close. Title*]

Unfortunate similarities to *American Psycho*, with its gimlet-eyed, firmed-jawed and suited hero, were highlighted by the architect Sam Jacob, who spliced the Redrow advert with dialogue from the movie:

there is an idea of a Patrick Bateman, some kind of abstraction, but there is no real me. Only an entity, something illusory, and though I can hide my cold gaze and you can shake my hand and feel flesh gripping yours and maybe you can even sense our lifestyles are probably comparable I simply ... am ... not ... there. I like to dissect girls. Did you know I am utterly insane ...

What these types have in common – the iceberg house, the ghost street, the ugly tower – is the forgetting of the qualities that make a house or a neighbourhood most worth inhabiting. It is strange of the rich to want to live like Morlocks, or in streets without street life, or to pay high prices for shoddy successors to the tower blocks which, when built for local authorities in the 1960s, became the most derided housing type of modern times. But then their purpose as places or as homes has been outrun by their function as units of investment. Homes bring together with special power two meanings of one word – they ideally embody personal and social values, some notion of what a good life might be, but they are also objects of property value, the most expensive asset many people might own. The latter, when overinflated, tends to corrupt the former.

At the other end of the market there was a complementary development of new types. There were the beds-in-sheds, where property-owners would maximize their returns on their back gardens by illegally housing immigrants in structures intended for garden tools and disused play equipment. There was the slice-up or hidden favela, where a two-bedroom flat might be made into four tiny bedsits. In June 2015 twenty-five adults and a child were found to be living in a three-bedroom house in East Ham, seven of them in a windowless basement. And there was the Zone Z home, a flat in Luton, Hastings, Stoke or some other town fifty or a hundred miles or more from London, where people would be moved by boroughs unable to house them on their own territories.

Property, and the price of property, became a fixation and a mythology. It was a narrative with no clear end, except the ever-increasing sacrifice of ideas of domesticity and community to absurdities of price. It was one of the principal preoccupations of the *Evening Standard*, to go with its insatiable fascination with the model Cara Delevingne and the goings-on at a celebrity hang-out – 'the hotel that lit a match under London' – called the Chiltern Firehouse. On a single day in January 2015, for example:

> 'Council treats homeless like cattle by moving them
> out of the capital'

How 26 people lived in a three-bedroom house

First floor

Back room – no access
Rear room – no access
Front room – one
bunk bed and three
single beds

Ground floor

Front room – occupied
by two adults and
one child
Ground floor rear
room – occupied by
one adult

Basement

Three bunk beds all
with bedding and in
recent use and a
double bed

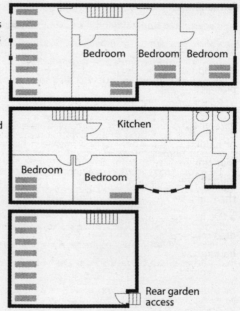

First floor: Bedroom, Bedroom, Bedroom

Ground floor: Kitchen, Bedroom, Bedroom

Basement: Rear garden access

> Balham is capital's hottest property spot
>
> Raid on Lottery winner 'with bed in shed property'
>
> Tycoon's flats plan for barracks site 'will ruin memory of military past'

But the price of homes in London and desirable parts of Britain is not an act of nature. It is not an economic inevitability dictated by the laws of the market. It is not pure fate, as the mayor of Newham seemed to imply when he said that 'if you can't afford to live in Newham, you can't afford to live in Newham'. Yes, it has a lot to do with supply and demand and with phenomena that can be seen in other affluent countries. But it is also something both willed by the policies of Conservative and Labour governments from the 1980s on and encouraged by their inactions.

Inflation, so feared in any other commodity, was exalted when it came to homes. Increases would be celebrated on the front pages of tabloids. From Margaret Thatcher onwards, owner-occupation was presented as the most desirable way of having a home, far beyond any other. When she allowed council tenants to buy their own homes at subsidized prices, she forbade local authorities to replenish supply by building more. Easy credit was encouraged such that people could borrow 95 per cent or more of the value of their homes. Non-domiciled tax status, whereby people can pay less tax by living in the UK but registering as a foreign national, has long encouraged people to invest in London property. The introduction of council tax in the early 1990s, a local property tax which is gentle on expensive homes, also encouraged prices to rise.

Margaret Thatcher's government introduced the Assured Shorthold Tenancy which made it easier for landlords to eject tenants. Combined with the willingness of banks to lend money on what they liked to call 'innovative mortgage products', an accommodating tax regime and with continuing house price inflation, this led in the

1990s to the rise of Buy to Let, the acquisition of homes by individuals to act as investments. Some became tycoons, like a couple in Kent called Judith and Fergus Wilson who announced in December 2015 that they were selling their entire portfolio 'for a figure exceeding £250m'. In the twenty-first century developers started building housing blocks aimed at this market.

The fall in house prices that followed the 2008 crash was not seen as a healthy correction of an overheating market, but as a calamity to be averted. The Coalition government that came to power in 2010 tried to encourage banks to lend some of the finance released by quantitative easing to house buyers. They changed pension rules such that, on reaching fifty-five, people could have greater freedom to access the funds they had gathered with the help of tax breaks through their working lives. Some of this money will be invested in property and further push up its price.

They introduced Help to Buy, its name a nostalgic echo of Thatcher's Right to Buy, which was intended to support first-time buyers unable to raise a large enough deposit to get a mortgage. The government would guarantee an additional loan to bridge the gap, taking on the risk at which banks were baulking. Some buyers, who got their timing right, indeed benefited, and the measure helped to boost the rate of house building. But an effect of this and other incentives to buy homes is to put prices up, which puts homes further out of reach; the main beneficiaries are those who already own property. It is a subsidy to landowners and developers which also encourages first-time buyers to take on possibly unsustainable debts and exposes government – us, taxpayers – to risk if they default. It gives the government a stake in continuing inflation: if prices start falling, they (we) lose. The *Financial Times* called it 'economically illiterate'.

The attitude of government to housing has, since Thatcher, mostly been that the market will provide. If it fails to do so it must be because it is inadequately stimulated and that it is held back by pesky regulations and controls. Therefore, goes the logic, more inducements have to be invented and regulations and planning departments weakened. So they reduced local authorities' powers to oppose damaging new developments and to insist on such things as targets for sustainability.

But the market does not provide. It never has, at least for many decades. A figure often given for Britain's annual need for new homes is about 240,000, which has never been attained by private homebuilders since before the Second World War. From the 1950s the private sector built at a steady rate of about 150,000 to 200,000 until 2008, when the number fell below 100,000. In 2012–13 a total of 107,000 new homes were built.

The numbers were made up by council housing, with the help of which a total of 400,000 homes per year were built in the late 1960s, until it was stopped in the 1980s. Some were built, and continue to be built, by housing associations, not-for-profit organizations dedicated to providing affordable homes, but never in the same numbers as local authorities had done, and the magic total of 240,000 has never been achieved since the 1970s. London followed the national trend, in that numbers peaked at the same time. House price inflation gathered speed in the 1970s as council housing reduced and started rocketing in the 1980s, when it ended altogether.

One reason why private housebuilders will not build enough houses is a phenomenon known as absorption. They will only build at the rate at which they can sell quickly, so that they are not left holding on to empty properties for any length of time. They will not flood their own market to the point where they reduce the price of their product. They do this not because they are evil, but because it is good business.

Another reason is that planning and regulation will always be there – it is a fantasy to imagine their reduction sufficient on its own

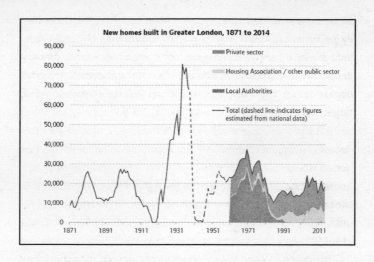

New homes built in Greater London, 1871 to 2014

- Private sector
- Housing Association / other public sector
- Local Authorities
- Total (dashed line indicates figures estimated from national data)

to make a real impact on supply and price. The last time that the housing market did a reasonable job of meeting demand was in the 1930s, before the introduction of the green belt restricted the use of land. Almost no one would now want the removal of all protections on rural areas, least of all the conservative residents of south-east England who helped vote David Cameron's governments into power. Housing in Britain is impaled on the contradiction inherent in the meanings of 'conservative': the word describes both believers in the free market, who oppose state intervention, and people who want to conserve things, which, if the thing to be conserved is an undeveloped green belt, requires state intervention.

There is also a confusion of aims. The problems of London housing are of both quantity and price. Too few are being built and those that exist are too expensive – issues which are linked, but not identical. In relying so much on private property companies to deliver more homes, the government finds itself incentivizing them by encouraging higher prices. Which defeats at least half of the object.

There are alternatives. Government can stop pushing prices up.

It could conceivably set targets for stable or slowly deflating prices, in the same way that targets are set for other forms of inflation. In this way property would gradually come within reach of more people and the heat would be taken out of the speculative market. Options other than ownership, such as privately renting, would become more attractive – there would be less of the desperate desire to get into the property market before it rises still further. Households would have greater freedom to move between one type and another.

Given that the government is involved in planning, it could be in a more constructive way. Planning in Britain tends to be about restriction – dams are created to development which are then allowed to leak to a greater or lesser extent, with energy expended by developers and planners in trying to push more through or hold more back. Development is treated as pollution, with the result that it is. The possibility of creating positive ideas of future neighbourhoods, in which all concerned could benefit, is almost absent. Yet there are British precedents for such positive models, in the garden cities of the early twentieth century and the new towns built from the 1950s to the 1980s, both of which were admired and imitated around the world.

There are many ways to create more homes in and around London, which will never happen if the market is left to itself. For example:

The city is full of two-storey streets that could have three or four

There is a generic type of London street, brick, two-storeys, c.1900, sometimes pleasant, sometimes drab, never exceptional, where extra storeys could be added without harm to its character, or even improving it. Planners and neighbours rightly fear that piecemeal additions could be damaging and ugly. But it is possible to define a design applicable to a whole street, or several streets, that sets a minimum standard of quality and consistency. It might even be possible to devise ways that a portion of the profit from these extensions goes to a shared benefit. It is conceivable that some-times it might be desirable to rebuild whole terraces, larger and to a better quality than before. There are also streets of three, four and five storeys that could benefit from an extra one.

Make roads into boulevards

Western Avenue, Romford Road, Sidcup Road: these are some of the unhappiest zones in London, arteries lined with undersized houses huddled against the noise of traffic. They would be better with apartment blocks of seven or eight storeys, equal to the scale of the transport engineering and designed to mitigate the imperfect environment. It would, however, require intelligent and effective planning to ensure that the new buildings improved the ambience of the road. Recent London offers plenty of examples, such as the row of blocks along Stratford High Street, of how bad it could be otherwise.

There is room for many more homes in outer suburbs

The inter-war expansion of London, careless of the amount of land it used, was at a low density. If parts of the outer suburbs were rebuilt at the density of the Victorian streets of inner London, enor-mous quantities of homes could be created. Existing residents of suburbs would fear for the character of their areas and their quality of life: again, it would be essential that they gained clear benefits and that new developments were thoughtfully designed.

Use public land, and use it well

An unknown, partly uncharted but large amount of spare land exists in London that is owned by public bodies – the fringes of railway lines and hospital car parks, oddments owned by the Fire Service or by local authorities. This can be identified and released, but with conditions attached – for example that they are used for homes for people who might contribute something to the city, rather than for units of investment. Some of these sites will be too scrappy for large property companies to take an interest, which prompts a further point, which is that London's government should make life easier for the small and medium-sized businesses who might be able to make something of them.

Buildings can sometimes be tall

Building towers became, by 2014, a way of building homes in London that was popular among developers. Often the effects were devastating on surrounding areas. But tall buildings have been part of the city's repertory of housing types at least since Highpoint in the 1930s. There is also room for the relatively high, such as something six storeys in an area that is mostly two. It depends how it is done and where.

New towns worked quite well. Why not have more, and better?

The new towns succeeded in rehousing hundreds of thousands of people. The largest, Milton Keynes, achieved the exceptional feat of creating a city of 250,000 in forty years, which scores highly in surveys of residents' contentment and quality of life. The new towns' planners made mistakes – they tended to put cars at the centre of their transport planning and built houses at absurdly low densities, with the effect that you can hardly see where the town has gone – but there is no reason to repeat them.

Building on the green belt does not always have to be terrible

As first conceived, the Metropolitan Green Belt was to be a narrow strip whose primary purpose was the recreation of city-dwellers. It is now a band up to thirty-five miles wide which mostly serves the people who live in it. Some of it is inaccessible, some less than beautiful, some not even green. In 2014 the planning consultancy URBED proposed ways in which new communities could be built on parts of British green belts, in such a way that, as well as providing more homes, more people would have access to the beauties of nature. Their plans envisaged well-considered settlements with such things as sustainable transport systems. There is a well-founded fear that any relaxation of current restrictions would release an exploitative and destructive rampage of development but, if Britain could rediscover its former ability for constructive planning, it would not have to be like that.

Council estates

Post-war estates tend to be at low densities, even when their buildings are tall, because of the large amounts of open space in which they stand. In principle more homes can be created on at least some of them, although the Heygate shows that caution is needed. The important thing is to recognize that whatever is already there might have value to residents, which should be respected.

None of these options is easy. All typically need skill in planning and design and respect for the reasonable wishes of people who already live in places that might be changed. They require government, local and national, to do more than tickle and nudge the private sector, or plead and cajole. It has to propose, plan and drive forward.

Councils can contribute by building new homes, as in recent years they have again been allowed to do. This does not have to mean a return to making the inhumane ghettoes for which they were attacked, sometimes with justification, in the past. It is possible for local authorities to build for people at several levels of income, as they do in (for example) Singapore, where 85 per cent

of the population live in state-owned homes. Government will still
make mistakes, but then so do private developers.

The English House

Early in the last century the German architect Hermann Muthesius
published a survey called *Das englische Haus*, because he believed
that the England of garden cities and arts-and-crafts design led the
world in domestic architecture and that his own country should
learn from it. He wouldn't do this now. As well as the highest
prices, new British homes have the meanest dimensions and among
the poorest designs to be found in Europe. Rather, planners, architects, developers and sometimes even politicians go to Germany
to see exemplary housing – well designed, cohesive, supportive of
community life, sustainable – in places like Vauban in Freiburg and
HafenCity in Hamburg.

Rasmussen also admired London housing. 'We have a great deal
to learn from that form of civilization in which London has taken the
lead,' he wrote – by which he meant qualities such as tolerance,
empirical science, economic and intellectual freedom, 'a highly
developed form of local government' – before explaining that 'the
one-family house, open-air life and all that we others admire and
are fain to imitate, is inseparable from the English mode of thought
and life'. He went on to dream of a 'town of the future' based on
Hampstead Garden Suburb, where

> the houses are modest compared with the buildings of many of
> the old monumental cities, but there is no home without a garden
> in which children can be out of doors and enjoy the sun and air
> as soon as they can notice anything at all. They crawl about in the
> grass, stand up and try to touch the flowers, birds and insects, make

unintelligible remarks to them, and try their strength in a hundred harmless ways . . .

Here he is romanticizing and simplistic. London housing was never all single-family houses, nor should it have been. Not everyone wants or needs to live like this and the idea that apartment living is un-English is exaggerated. But he is also repeating a common and well-founded view of visitors to London, that one of its beauties is its greenery, the possibilities it offers for contact with nature in the middle of a big city. It is an idea that has faded from new housing developments. The newly built house with a garden is virtually extinct and minimal attention is applied to creating substitutes in blocks of flats.

It has fallen victim to the flesh-eating bug of house price inflation, which consumes ideals, invention, generosity, communal life. A central part of Margaret Thatcher's vision, exalted in her first speech as leader of the Conservative Party, was the 'property-owning democracy': she argued that people who owned their homes would become better citizens, by virtue of owning a share in the national economy. One of her ministers, sounding like Rasmussen, said that 'home-ownership stimulates the attitudes of independence and self-reliance that are the bedrock of a free society'.

High house prices and the shortage of good alternatives to ownership have instead created a class of mortgage slaves, chained to debts they can barely afford, restricted in their choices, fearful of losing the means to hold on to their home and of the home itself losing value. It distorts their choices in life – when to have children, whether to change career, whether to continue or end a relationship. Inflation makes people into gamblers on the property market so that they can have shelter. It corrodes public spirit: people are more likely to oppose a school for children with learning difficulties, or social housing, or a workshop that creates jobs, or a drugs rehabilitation centre, if they think it will affect the price of their house. The value of property skews human values.

House price inflation is a tax on the young by the old and by the haves on the have-nots, but it has also created a financial environment in which most people don't benefit. The most obvious losers are people who don't own a home and will never afford a decent one, followed by those who have one but can hardly keep their repayments afloat. But even those lucky enough to buy one early enough have little to show for their paper profit. If they bought twenty years ago, they might have a 1000 per cent uplift on the amount they paid, but they have no access to this wealth unless they sell their house, in which case they remove themselves or their children from the all-important property ladder. The real winners are those who own more property than they live in, as an investment.

In London, bars and restaurants have closed, because people who moved in nearby, in the full knowledge that these places existed, have then used licensing laws to demand that their opening hours are restricted. The Wapping Project, a magnificent cultural centre and restaurant in an old power station, was one. Pauline Forster, landlady of the George Tavern in Stepney, has battled to stop a block of flats being built next door, for fear the same thing might happen to her pub. Even the mighty Tate Modern has found that residents of neighbouring blocks of flats, built to exploit the rising values that came with the gallery's arrival, are trying to limit its evening events. If you pay seven-figure sums for your patch of floor space, you are more likely to feel a sense of entitlement about what happens around you.

Assisted by relaxations in planning rules, places of employment such as workshops and offices are made into residential property, because their value goes up several times if they do. So are local shops. The pressure on care homes, charities, religious orders and cultural institutions becomes impossible to resist, to cash in on the uplift in property values that comes with building residential units. Those who still live in social housing in valuable areas (which now includes most of central and not-so-central London) receive in effect huge hidden subsidies, which gives rise to the question whether they can be justified. But what should be asked is how we came to accept the absurdity of these prices as normal.

The necrotizing fasciitis of residential value consumes the things that make London work and give it life. Anything good or interesting – an area with a colourful market, a place colonized by artists, a neighbourhood made more accessible by new transport – acquires a price tag. The most obviously desirable places, of the kind that creates London's international identity as a good place to live – like Primrose Hill or Notting Hill – become distant galaxies to the vast majority of Londoners, in ways in which they were not a generation ago.

London's property market will fluctuate, fall and sometimes even crash, but to address the city's current housing deficiencies it would have to do so at a scale that would be both improbable and cataclysmic. Crashes bring their own problems, such as destroying blameless individuals who are suckered in to the market at the wrong time, and stopping the supply even of the inadequate amounts that the boom times create. The market therefore offers the choice between homes that are too few and expensive in the good times, and almost none in the bad.

It is also true that London has always had expensive houses and zones of wealth, but it was possible for those on low and middle incomes to live close and enjoy the common pleasures of such amenities as the great parks – if you couldn't afford Kensington or Knightsbridge you might still live near enough to share in their splendours of culture, nature and consumption. This availability is disappearing, which would matter less if the art of making new areas that are enjoyable and affordable was flourishing. But when it comes to decent homes built at reasonably high densities, with some leafiness, open space and sense of community, some pleasant architecture and some variety in the local shops, which are the things that people like about central London's residential streets, they don't make them like they used to.

And property inflation creates the Redrow Psycho. This figure, of the lone suited man who, like the Wanderer Above a Sea of Fog, looks down from his glass box on a huddled city, has become an emblem of aspiration for the sales literature of luxury apartments. It is an image of success, of someone who has climbed his way to the top, but also of isolation, of someone above and apart from his city, whose contact with his neighbourhood is limited to the pavement between a car and the tower's lobby. His crystal cocoon is as different and as removed as can be from the brick streets around, and the only contact between one and the other is through wordless looking. Is this – whether for the Redrow Psycho or for everyone else – the best, most desirable, most rewarding way of living in a city like London?

SMART CITY, DUMB CITY

Note on Planning

At this point it is helpful to provide a brief outline of London's planning system. If you are reading this on a beach, while nursing your young, operating heavy machinery or in other circumstances of impaired concentration, I apologize. You may also skip this note. However, it may be helpful to refer to it in the some of the following chapters.

In London planning applications for new buildings are submitted for approval to the planning committees of the boroughs in which the projects are to be built. There are thirty-two boroughs plus the City of London, which is technically a different entity but performs similar functions. (The City of Westminster is called a 'city', but is a borough.) The committees are made up of councillors. The councillors are elected by residents, except in the City of London, where they are called common councilmen and where businesses as well as residents have votes. The committees are advised by planning officers, who are paid employees. Sometimes officers can make decisions themselves, in cases not considered too controversial or significant.

Since 2000 the mayor of London has had the ability to refuse projects approved by boroughs, in cases of potential strategic importance to London. Since 2008 the mayor has also had the power to approve projects refused by boroughs. The mayor is assisted in these decisions by paid advisers.

Since 1999 the design review panel of the Commission for Architecture and the Built Environment (CABE) has offered its opinions on significant projects, which opinions carry some weight in the decisions of boroughs etc. Previously a similar role was performed by the Royal Fine Art Commission (RFAC). Since 2011 CABE's status has been diminished by its merger with another body called the Design Council. Where proposals have an impact on historic buildings, the views of English Heritage were also expressed and given weight. From April 2015 this role became the responsibility of a new body, Historic England.

Applicants have the right to appeal against refusals. In contentious and significant cases a public inquiry might be held, a quasi-judicial process in which a government-appointed planning inspector hears evidence from interested parties, who are usually assisted by lawyers. The inspector will then recommend approval or refusal of the planning application to the minister in charge of the planning process, who from 2001 was called the Secretary of State for Communities and Local Government. The minister usually but not always endorses the view of the inspector.

In some cases, where there is a possibility that legal procedures have been incorrectly followed, there might be a judicial review, at the end of which a court may or may not rule previous decisions invalid, which may lead to the relevant processes being rerun. This court's decision may sometimes be appealed.

At every stage of the process decisions have to be justified with reference to government planning policy, to plans set out by the boroughs and to the London Plan issued by the mayor. These plans propose (for example) where and in what circumstances housing or any other use might be desirable, what provisions might be desirable for affordable housing, what might be a good approach to historically sensitive areas or to the arrangement of tall buildings. Policies and plans are usually stated in quite general terms and are open to interpretation. A notable exception is the View Management Framework, which sets out with some precision and with the help of diagrams zones where tall buildings cannot be built, because they would intrude on specific views of St Paul's Cathedral or the Palace of Westminster, some of these views from many miles away, or on their backdrops. Guidance on towers outside these zones, however, is vague.

An important element of the planning process is the Section 106 agreement whereby, in return for receiving planning permission, developers are required to contribute to public benefits such as affordable housing, transport improvements or upgrades to the public realm. Sometimes called 'legalized bribes', these agreements play a vital role in the development of London. British planning policy also allows payments to be raised through a Community Infrastructure Levy (CIL). In London the mayor uses CIL to help fund the Crossrail underground rail project. Developers can use viability assessments to argue for a reduction in obligations laid on them by planners, if they can show that they would make a development unviable.

It will be observed that planning in London is complex, many-layered and imprecise, with multiple opportunities for discussion and opinion. It also involves proliferating numbers of interested parties and professional players, such as:

For the client: *The clients themselves (e.g. a business, an individual or a public body), architects, agents, planning consultants (i.e. experts in planning processes), townscape consultants (who are people considered expert in aesthetics and urban design), experts in such things as Rights of Light, commercial valuers, PR consultants and lobbyists.*

For local, city and national government: *Councillors, the mayor and minister, their officers, advisers and civil servants. Advisory bodies such as Historic England (formerly English Heritage) and CABE, each with their own committees and professional staff. Inspectors and judges.*

For the interests of citizens and communities, and the protection of heritage and other amenities: *Individual objectors, voluntary local amenity groups (the Amwell Society, the Angel Association, the Balham Society . . .) preservation societies such as SAVE Britain's Heritage or the Georgian, Victorian and Twentieth Century Societies, plus their professional consultants.*

For any of the above: *Solicitors and barristers with expertise in planning, expert witnesses.*

I hope that's clear, then.

10. Mipimism

'I'm sorry I'm late,' said a well-known nasal drone, as much part of London's identity as red buses, 'I was enjoying the hotel Jacuzzi too much.' We were on a terrace washed with March sunshine, some year in the mid-noughties, with a view of a bay where, as if in a turbo-capitalist Raoul Dufy painting, fat chartered yachts swayed at anchor. On one side was the concrete Palais des Festivals. Behind was the Croisette, famous for its parades of stars during the Cannes Film Festival.

The occasion was MIPIM, Le marché international des professionnels de l'immobilier, an annual property trade fair where chunks of city are traded much like other products that have their days in Cannes, such as swimwear and luxury travel. There are food chains: property companies and local authorities are selling to investors; agents and consultants are selling to property companies; and architects are selling to everyone. Here more than in town halls and parliaments the futures of the world's cities are decided.

The environment is beautiful-ugly and the atmosphere louche-businesslike. There are palm trees, the curve of the bay, hills behind, relics of old architecture, the kitschy elegance of the Martinez and the Carlton hotels, all blessed with the balm of early spring. The Palais itself is obnoxious, its sun-proof interior not improved by the gesticulating exhibition design with which stallholders attract attention, the experience of transaction being a notch above drug-dealing in a car park. In the Vieux Port ranks of white boats are moored, selling from their sterns as if in a multimillion-pound car boot sale. Projects are promoted on the streets: one year people dressed as oranges publicized Norman Foster's Project Orange, a plan on behalf of the property-magnate wife of Moscow's then-Mayor Yury Luzhkov to replace the State Tretyakov Gallery, home of the world's finest collection of twentieth-century Russian art, with an office and residential development shaped like stacked-up orange segments.

MIPIM prides itself on its excess. There is a boast that it drinks more champagne in four days than the film festival does in two weeks. The gender ratio might be nineteen men to each woman, even counting the micro-skirted models used to decorate phalloid city plans in central Asia. The air is thick with frustrated testos-terone, some not frustrated. Men swarm women in hotel bars. A special guide to MIPIM gives advice on finding prostitutes 'if you must'. A brawl might break out on the Croisette relating to an England–France rugby game. There are excursions, by invitation, to fine restaurants in hill towns once beloved of cubists and surrealists and to Blofeltian villas in the hinterland, such as the Palais Bulles or 'bubble houses' of the Hungarian architect Antti Lovag, with their pools, fish tanks, intersecting spheres, cacti and guard dogs.

Among the sellers are mayors, local politicians and planning officers, emerging blinking from their council offices into the south-ern light, pale amid the property men's winter tans and hoping to sew up public-private regeneration projects for their problematic civic centres and social housing estates. They take care to avoid accusations back home of living the high life at taxpayers' expense, so some accept invitations from property companies – Southwark's leader Peter John, for example, who went as a guest of the Heygate developers Lend Lease. Which is no less problematic. But apparently there is no choice but to be there – if you are not at MIPIM you

are not in the game. Local democracy has to come to the court of Property to get a hearing.

In this space such things as architecture, planning and the wishes of communities become distant abstractions, notwithstanding seminars on these subjects in the bowels of the Palais by such bodies as the Commission for Architecture and the Built Environment or CABE. They are lost in the exchange of urban meat. The dominant city at MIPIM, with an impressive display built around a huge model in the centre of the Palais, is London. This is partly because the city is now as skilled in the arts of trading property as, in the Middle Ages, it was in the commerce of sheep's wool, with world-beating agents, lawyers, planning consultants, engineers, PR people and other essential wheel-oilers. It is also because London is itself a prime item of stock. It offers more extensive and enticing development opportunities than any other city.

The man with the drone, Jacuzzi-fresh, was Ken Livingstone, the first directly elected mayor of London, in office for eight years from 2000. We were meeting so that he could dispense platitudes to me in my role as a writer for a London newspaper. He was in Cannes so that he could pursue an essential part of his plan, which was to bet everything on London continuing its rise as a financial centre, with associated property development, so that he could then take a tithe from the proceeds to pay for such things as affordable housing. He stated this plan to the crowd of shirts around the model in the Palais, urging them to make as much money as possible, but to spare a share for him. This was a change of tactic from his previous existence as the leader of the Greater London Council from 1981 to 1986. Then known as Red Ken, he was a scourge of developers, a champion of minorities who infuriated Margaret Thatcher so much that, by closing down the GLC, she ended – temporarily as it turned out – London's city-wide government.

Good architecture is good business

Around the year that Livingstone became mayor London was experiencing a resurgence. British and foreign media noted its style, its music, its fashion, its design. Its restaurants, once risible, invited smug comparisons with Paris, its art world with New York. Its diversity was celebrated, the number of languages counted, its Caribbean carnivals and Indian cuisine becoming a staple subject of in-flight magazines. The prime minister of the country of which London is capital looked young, dynamic and confident. The post of mayor created by Tony Blair's government, an attempt to repair Thatcher's vandalism in abolishing the GLC, was also seen as an expression of London's new energy. Its architectural expression was the rediscovery of modernism, reinvented as popular and exciting.

The 1970s and 80s had declared the modern movement finished, its architects condemned for misguided social engineering, stained concrete, leaky roofs, condensation problems, fungal growth, arrogance, corruption, brutality, waste, family breakdown, abetting crime, destruction of the historic environment and an irritating fondness for wearing bow ties. In 1985 a competition was held for replacing a mediocre Victorian building in Trafalgar Square, which attracted many inventive entries, including ones by a thoughtful young practice called Allies and Morrison and by the also-young Zaha Hadid. Given such choice, the competition's jury could think of nothing better than a proposal to rebuild the mediocre building as a more mediocre version of its former self, which was duly realized.

During the same period Norman Foster and Richard Rogers, who were achieving international success and esteem of a kind never before achieved by British architects, were routinely snubbed in their home city. The two had met as students at Yale and had together helped form the practice of Team Four in the 1960s. Both practised what was called 'high-tech', a style which sought to turn to the benefit of society the beauties and efficiencies of industrial construction, although with different characters: Foster was calm and grey, Rogers exuberant and polychrome. Rogers designed the Lloyds building in the City in the early 1980s, but their acceptance in London and that of their style really started with the completion of Foster's Stansted Airport and his Sackler Galleries for the Royal Academy, both in 1991. As it served a modern form of transport, the choice of a modern style for the airport was uncontroversial, leaving its users free to admire the elegance of its steel structure. With the Sackler, clean-lined modernity was slipped between crumbly old walls, the two being brought together in polite but detached co-existence. It suggested that modern architects could be trusted with historic architecture.

From 1984 onwards the Broadgate development went up around and on the site of the former Broad Street station in the City of London. It was designed by a team led by Peter Foggo of Arup Associates, a practice then known for thoughtful concert halls and university buildings. Their project went beyond the usual practice of creating slabs of rentable floor area: instead the blocks were arranged around open spaces designed for public activities such as cafes, bars, musical performances and, in winter, a version of the ice rink at the Rockefeller Center in New York. Their external treatment of gridded screens in purple granite was a mannered compromise between Arup's austere instincts and the pomp preferred by 1980s commerce, but was still a step or three above the standard of most City buildings of the time.

Broadgate's developer, Stuart Lipton, liked to say that 'good architecture is good business'. A well-designed building, he argued, would be efficient, attractive to employees and easy to run. He combined this belief with the use of pioneering construction techniques whereby large sections of building – house-sized cladding panels, entire toilet blocks – would be made in factories and lifted whole

Broadgate

into place. This enabled better quality control, reduced exposure to the hazards of weather and building-site mishaps and, by cutting down the amount of manual labour, would limit the ability of the construction workers' trades unions to delay progress.

Before Broadgate, City buildings were typically designed by people known as 'commercial architects', foremost among them Colonel Richard Seifert (1910–2001), who were employed for their ability to finagle the planning system, their willingness to oblige the wishes of their clients and not let architectural ideals get in the way. Once Lipton started hiring Foggo on Broadgate, and on other projects Foster and Rogers, other developers followed suit. Arup Associates had accepted the Broadgate commission only after some soul-searching as to whether it would suit their ethos to accept the commercial shilling, but their scruples would soon look quaint, as it became common practice for architects like them to work for property companies.

In the 1990s two other events assisted London's rediscovery of modernist architecture. One was the approach of the new millennium and with it the feeling that somehow or other forward-looking ways should be found to celebrate the event. The other was the introduction by John Major's government of the National Lottery, which from 1994 generated billions of pounds to be spent on 'good causes' such as culture and sport. The rules stated that funding could only go to capital projects, which most of the time meant buildings, which meant that the Lottery became a vast and half-accidental engine of architectural patronage. It had been a common lament until then that Britain was failing to match the *grands projets*, the spectacular structures with which President Mitterrand and others were decorating French cities, but suddenly, if haphazardly, they were happening in Britain.

One product of millenarian architecture, though not funded by the National Lottery, was the London Eye, the 443ft-high Ferris wheel that introduced a giant funfair ride into the august company of the Palace of Westminster. It was created by the architects David Marks and Julia Barfield, who first entered the project in a newspaper competition to find good ideas for celebrating the millennium. Undeterred by their failure to win they pursued their plan doggedly and with energy, until they found sponsorship and a commercial leisure operator willing to build it. Like the Eiffel Tower, the Eye was first presented as a temporary structure, with permission to stand for five years, but became a permanent landmark of its city. It was less of a public project than the Eiffel Tower, more of an entrepreneurial adventure that paid off.

Meanwhile the Lottery helped produce the Foster-designed Great Court of the British Museum, where a steel structure of some engineering sophistication spans the neo-Greek stone centre of the museum. It was both a blow-up of the Sackler new-meets-old formula and an anglicization of the glass pyramid that had been inserted in the centre of the Louvre in 1989. The Lottery also led to the Foster-designed Millennium Bridge, which links the City of London with the Lottery-funded Tate Modern and which, despite wobbling soon after opening, became a popular and useful addition to London.

In the twenty-first century the agitation for what was considered good design had wider effects. It led to office buildings, such as OMA's headquarters for Rothschild Bank, with spatial intrigue and complexity absent from their 1970s or 80s equivalents. Foster (especially) and Rogers became prolific designers of office blocks and private residential developments, and were joined by others outside the rut of commercial architects: Stanton Williams and Eric Parry, for example, who had made their names with cultural and university buildings. The French Pritzker-winner Jean Nouvel designed One New Change, a shopping centre and office block that folded reflections of St Paul's into its dark glass. In the historic areas of the City of Westminster contemporary but sensitive insertions were developed, well crafted, somewhat self-satisfied, nonetheless better than traditionalist-but-clumsy. David Chipperfield, an architect long valued abroad more than in his own country, was given commissions in London, although not necessarily those that gave his talents the best chances to flourish.

A generation of British architects developed who were judicious, serious, sometimes playful, and keen to apply their abilities to schools and social housing as well as the private homes and galleries that are the traditional commissions for young talent. They tended not to be revolutionary or provocative. Their earlier years were spent in an atmosphere of scepticism about the usefulness of modern architects, so they take nothing for granted and feel the need to prove themselves again and again. But, if you look selectively and screen out the outright rank dross, you could say that contemporary London architecture became lively, varied, skilled, intelligent, with occasional outbreaks of adventure, and a significant advance on what it had been for two or three decades. Their names include Alison Brooks, de Rijke Marsh Morgan, Deborah Saunt and David Hills, Karakusevic Carson, Haworth Tompkins, Allford Hall Monaghan Morris. The main drawback was that the qualities they exemplified were not always applied to London's most conspicuous buildings.

The vibrant city

Richard Rogers long campaigned for a city renovated and re-energized by enlightened architecture. In 1986 he presented a large model at the Royal Academy, with real water, of *London As It Could Be*, with Bazalgette's embankments invigorated with enlarged parks, the roads that run along it having been buried. A new pedestrian bridge and river islands were celebrated with boisterous towers. A zone of relaxed perambulation was to be created from Trafalgar Square to the South Bank.

One New Change

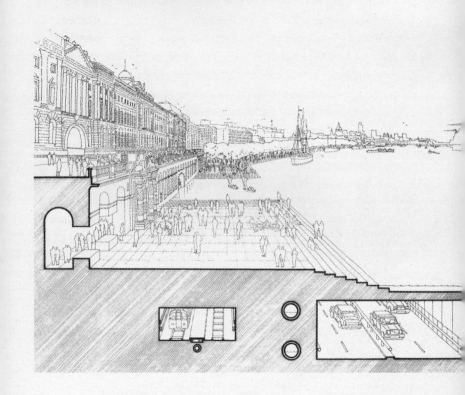

London as it could be

In the run-up to the 1992 election he published *A New London*, co-written with the Labour politician Mark Fisher, which called for 'the rebirth of London – one that involves architecture, planning and the development of London's under-used resources, such as its river'. Frustrated but not deterred by that year's Conservative election victory, he gave the 1995 Reith lectures on his urban beliefs, published them as *Cities for a Small Planet* and in due course won the ear of the new Leader of the Opposition, Tony Blair. When Blair became prime minister in 1997 Rogers was as close to political power as any British architect in decades. He was ennobled as a 'working peer' and put in charge of an Urban Task Force which produced a report called 'Towards an Urban Renaissance', which was translated into a White Paper called *Our Towns and Cities – the Future*, a government policy document which influenced the extensive redevelopment of British cities in the first decade of the new millennium.

Rogers's influence contributed among other things to the renaming of the Department of National Heritage as the more progressive Department of Culture. Trafalgar Square, in a part-realization of Rogers's 1986 proposal, was partly pedestrianized. The Commission for Architecture and the Built Environment was created, its first chair the Broadgate man Stuart Lipton, with the task of raising the standard of design in public buildings and other significant projects. CABE was an enlarged, Blairized version of the Old World institution it replaced, the Royal Fine Art Commission, which had met in clubby oak-panelled rooms in St James's and whose generally astute verdicts were sometimes undermined by a loss of judgement on projects involving royalty.

Rogers's argument was that it is good for cities to be built at high densities, so as to encourage interaction between its citizens, use land well, make transport and other public services more efficient and promote 'vibrancy'. High density, however, would require good architectural design, especially in the making of public spaces, or else the co-existence of many people at close quarters would become intolerable. His favourite model was Barcelona, a smaller but denser city than London, where the 1992 Olympics had helped stimulate some notable cultural buildings, and imaginative changes to its streets and squares.

This was a reversal of the belief in lowering inner London's population that went back to Ebenezer Howard's call for an 80 per cent reduction and Patrick Abercrombie's more gentle but practical policies for dispersal in the Greater London Plan of 1944. That London's population had in fact been rising again since the mid-1980s meant that Rogers's ideas matched reality. They suited the spirit of happy public-private synergy promoted by Blair's Third Way: if developers wanted to maximize returns on their land by packing it with flats and offices, this would also, as a contribution to making a vibrant city, be in the public interest. CABE would make sure that this land-optimization/vibrancy-production was done in the best possible way.

By the early years of Livingstone's mayoralty Rogers's relationship with Blair had chilled. In 1997 Rogers had urged on Blair the desirability of building the Rogers-designed, Lottery-funded, ultra-millennial Millennium Dome, which flopped. Blair's government wasn't showing as much commitment to good modern architecture as Rogers had hoped. Rogers and Blair would later take opposite positions on the invasion of Iraq. But Rogers stayed on good terms with John Prescott, the minister in charge of the country's planning, and he found an ally in Ken Livingstone, who liked Rogers's idea of London intensifying and flourishing within the boundary set by the green belt.

Livingstone made Rogers an adviser and set up an Architecture and Urbanism Unit to put his ideas into practice. A London Plan was published for the future development of the city, which incorporated Rogers's principles. A promise was made that a hundred public spaces would be formed or renewed, in imitation of Barcelona. An Olympic bid, also Barça-style, was contemplated and then launched.

One effect of the enthusiasm for density and modern architecture was the emergence of proposals for tall buildings. It has long been well known among architects and planners that you can achieve density without towers – courtyarded blocks of eight storeys or so, of the kind that you get in Paris, Berlin and Barcelona, can do it – but towers are a conspicuous way of raising urban intensity, or seeming to do so. For landowners, in theory, they increase return on their land, hopefully to a degree that compensates for their high construction costs. The London Plan said that tall buildings could contribute positively to London, if they were well designed and in the right place; they were especially encouraged next to transport interchanges, as this would encourage more people to use public transport.

'It might just be a masterpiece'

In April 1992, just after the Conservative Party led by John Major had won the general election, the Irish Republican Army detonated a bomb in the City of London. It killed three people and damaged the Baltic Exchange, an ornate work of Edwardian baroque that was listed as an historic building, Grade II*. Usually such a building would be repaired and restored but, after the site was sold, its new owners proposed that a tower of outstanding modern design be built in its place. Planners seemed inclined to support this idea, which annoyed the former owners, who said that they would have sold it for more if they had known that such a development would be permitted.

The planners' precedent for their argument was a project called Number One Poultry. Here Peter Palumbo, heir to a property business and lover of architecture, who at one point owned houses by

Mies van der Rohe and Le Corbusier, had strived to build a tower whose design he commissioned from Mies before the latter's death in 1969. By the time Palumbo was ready to build the tower, in the early 1980s, the stylistic wind had changed. Mies was regarded as sterile, inhumane, insensitive and his proposal a 'giant glass stump'. Towers were out. The ornate Victorian buildings on the site were listed and regarded as more precious to London than something by Mies. Palumbo's dream was rejected by planners and then by a public inquiry, whose inspector nonetheless left a door ajar. It might be acceptable to replace the Victorian buildings, he said, if its replacement were an exceptional work of architecture.

Palumbo came back with a design by James Stirling, then recognized as one of Britain's most important architects. It wasn't a tower, but filled the triangular site occupied by the Victorian buildings with a brooding, muscular compaction of cylinders and prisms, Egyptian-Hawksmoorian-nautical in influence, an unfloatable ship in hefty stone striated with the colours of rhubarb and custard. It was a cussed protest against glassy smoothness and in favour of the idea that architecture might churn and puzzle, whose best feature is its steep, tenebrous, unroofed central court, with concrete coffers and dark blue tiles punctuated by colourful window frames. It imparts an awareness of weight and weather. It makes the sky, glimpsed as you enter the bottom of the space, into something to be yearned for, such that the progression there from the ground becomes a pilgrimage for the imagining eye.

With the encouragement of the City of London's chief planner, Peter Rees, it offered a 'public space' on top, a roof garden which, while serving an expensive restaurant, would be accessible to any member of the public who wanted to go there. A pair of pert balconies flanked the building's prow, projecting like diving boards, as if inviting despairing speculators to take their final plunge, an invitation which sadly would be taken up more than once after

the 2008 crash. They have now been modified to deter further attempts.

Stirling's design went to another public inquiry, whose inspector said that 'it might just be a masterpiece' and recommended that it be given permission. After delays caused by the recession of the early 1990s, Number One Poultry was completed in 1997, by which time Stirling had died and his postmodernism had fallen as far out of fashion as, in the 1980s, had Mies's modernism. Fashion, however, can be expected to change and the building did create that roof garden which, if you get past the discouraging elevator journey to get there – you feel that the building's owners don't want you to know that this is a 'public space' – is a remarkable spot for experiencing the changing panoramas of the City.

Number One Poultry established the principle that a listed building might be demolished, or other planning policies relaxed, if a new work of outstanding quality were proposed. In 1996 the developers of the Baltic Exchange site hired Norman Foster to create just such outstandingness and, harnessing the rhetoric of pre-millennial excitement, proposed the London Millennium Tower. It was to be 1,265 feet high, which at the time would have made it the sixth tallest in the world. They argued that it was vital to the competitiveness of the City of London: as financial institutions expanded through mergers and acquisitions they needed colossal buildings. The Foster tower was considered big enough to house two mega-banks.

It was refused permission, partly out of concern that it would be an obstacle to air traffic, but not before its curving projections had earned it the nickname of 'erotic gherkin'. Then a new proposal came forward, lower but still conspicuous, for the headquarters of the insurance company Swiss Re. This version was circular in plan, in profile swelling and then tapering to a blunt point. It was wrapped in a diamond grid of steel structure, with upward swirls indicating the presence behind the glass surface of a ventilation system which,

while innovative, didn't in the end work as hoped. The idea was that each floor would have a number of small atria cut into them which, placed above each other and slightly offset, would create spiral shafts for drawing through cooling air.

The name Gherkin attached itself to this proposal and, to the chagrin of its owners, stuck. They would rather it were called 30 St Mary Axe, Swiss Re having by now decided that it would not be its corporate headquarters after all. It was approved in 2000 and, with the remains of the Baltic Exchange demolished, completed in 2003. It became a popular and famous landmark of the new London, an emblem of its thrust and nerve. Being circular, like the dome of St Paul's, it has the knack of looking the same in whichever distant view it is glimpsed. It is an extravagant building, complex to build and carefree in its donating of valuable floor space to its pocket atria, which thanks to the generosity of its planning permission it could afford.

There were other significant approvals, such as Montevetro, a Thames-side residential tower set among small-scale houses in Battersea, designed by Richard Rogers, the seductive model of which helped persuade the relevant minister at the time, John Gummer, to support it. The Heron Tower in Bishopsgate in the City of London, designed by the American practice KPF, was opposed by English Heritage on the grounds that it affected the settings of historic buildings. This was an unwise fight to pick, as the tower falls outside the designated protected views of St Paul's Cathedral, and they lost. In 2002 another Rogers tower was conceived for the City of London, the Leadenhall Building, otherwise the Cheesegrater, a tall wedge that receded at the top so as to reduce its impact on views of St Paul's down Fleet Street. It included a high wall-less space at ground level above which the substance of the tower would hover. This space, promised for public use, was an important part of its successful case for gaining planning permission.

In 2000 the developer Irvine Sellar revealed a plan to build the tallest building in Europe on a site next to London Bridge station, in the borough of Southwark. Sellar, who had started out with market stalls in Essex and the East End, made his first fortune in Carnaby Street in the 1960s, with Mates by Irvine Sellar, a pioneer unisex fashion store. He went into property, crashed with a reported debt of £28m in 1991 and resurrected himself with modest projects that were nothing like the ambitious one that he was now taking on. He was not always taken seriously by his peers in the London property business. His first choice of architect for his tower was Broadway Malyan, a practice without the design reputation of Foster or Rogers; their St George Wharf development in Vauxhall was twice voted worst building in the world in the *Architects' Journal*'s annual poll of their profession.

Sellar responded to suggestions that such a prominent project required a more eminent architect, and, while retaining Broadway Malyan in an assistant role, hired Renzo Piano, who, like Foster, was a former partner of Richard Rogers. In the 1970s Piano had worked with Rogers to create the Pompidou Centre in Paris and had since developed a reputation as a refined and cultivated exponent of the high-tech school of architecture practised by all three architects.

Piano proposed a fractured pyramid, much-elongated, 'a shard of crystal' as he called it that grew from a thick base to a sharp point. It was inspired, he said, by old views of the area populated with church spires and the masts of ships: his building would be similar, if bigger. It was also conceived as a vertical surge of the linear energy of the area's clusters of railway tracks. With the help of a special kind of glass, which would catch the changing light, it would 'have a nice light presence'; at the bottom it would 'melt into the city' and at the top it would 'come almost to nothing'. 'Towers belong to our imagination,' he said, 'and if a new one can fit with the dream of people it will be a success.' It would be a 'vertical village', combining apartments, a hotel, restaurants, bars and a viewing gallery as well as its twenty-seven floors of office space.

It would be 1,017 feet high. Ever since 1920s Manhattan, when skyscrapers competed to be the tallest, architects have used different devices to extend them. The simplest is the functionless spike, but here Piano proposed a 'radiator', a multistorey device which, by catching the high-level winds, could use them as part of the cooling system of the building. As, in the end, it never performed this role, it became a large redundant sculpture, but at least it was integrated into the overall form, rather than looking like an add-on.

Like other conspicuous projects the Shard, as it was now called, required a public inquiry. Unlike the Heron it would feature in a protected view: when seen from Parliament Hill on Hampstead Heath, it would clash or jostle with the dome of St Paul's or, as Piano put it, 'when together, the two buildings will kiss each other'. In its favour was its fulfilment of the policy of the London Plan that endorsed high densities near railway stations and, under what might be called the Palumbo principle or the Poultry pretext, the architect's prestige helped win the argument. John Prescott declared himself 'satisfied that the proposed tower is of the highest architectural quality'.

The Shard still took a while to build, despite being backed by Southwark's director of regeneration Fred Manson and by Mayor Livingstone. At one point the mayor gave it a nudge by promising to locate the offices of Transport for London inside it (which never in fact came to pass). But it wasn't an easy commercial proposition and when the economy worsened many assumed it would never happen. Then Sellar announced that the Shangri-La hotel group would be running the Shard's hotel and then that Qatari Diar, the property arm of the sovereign wealth fund of the State of Qatar, would be taking on the Shard as part of its series of acquisitions of trophy assets in London. It was opened in 2012, in a lurid pre-Olympic show

'A nice light presence'

The Gherkin hits the ground

of lights and lasers which only increased its resemblance to an invading alien machine. It was a triumph for Sellar, who had proved his snobbish doubters wrong. 'We can kick sand in the face of the Eiffel Tower,' he said.

These towers, Montevetro, the Gherkin, the Heron, the Cheesegrater and the Shard, designed by Rogers, his former partners and by KPF, set a pattern for the future. After a pause of more than two decades, towers could be built again in central London – even when, as with the Shard, some aspects of policy suggested they couldn't. It helped if there were some gestures to the public (the open space at the bottom of the Cheesegrater, the promise of a viewing gallery, albeit with entrance charges at £25, in the Shard) and to sustainability (the Gherkin's ventilating spirals, the Shard's radiator). The architecture had to be 'outstanding' or 'world class'.

This begged the question of what good design might be. For Lipton at Broadgate it had been to do with making a business run more smoothly, making staff happier, building more efficiently and creating a unified, well-considered environment that included external spaces as well as individual office buildings. In the 1990s an additional idea developed, that it was good to be 'iconic'. With Frank Gehry's Guggenheim in Bilbao as the prime example, it was believed that architectural flourishes were good for a city. They could lift the spirits of the public in some indefinable way, while also raising a city's profile to international investors – enormous marketing devices, in effect, which had the benefit of selling both individual developments and the urban zones in which they were placed. In the sozzled blur of MIPIM, it's the stranger-looking projects that stand out.

John Prescott endorsed the idea of the icon, which he called 'wow factor.' It eclipsed other definitions of good design, in particular that places in cities are formed not by single buildings, but by several working together. If the Gherkin has a certain confident presence on the skyline, its vigorous diagonal geometry disintegrates into a series of painful clashes when it hits the pavement. It leaves the ends of neighbouring buildings exposed and unregarded; it considers not at all a building across the street, the beautiful and subtle Holland House, which was completed in 1916 to the designs of the Dutch proto-modernist H. P. Berlage. The Shard fails to be part of a coherent vision for its neighbourhood: in another time and another place such a drastic addition might have been considered within a greater whole. Here a gap opened in the planning system and Sellar and his allies were smart enough to exploit it. The surrounding street remains rugged and inchoate, and subject to incoherent and ill-considered proposals, one an as yet unbuilt tower of special ugliness.

The idea of iconic architecture also relies on the real or imagined genius of its creators, for who would want an artistic statement by a bad artist? In its purer form it is practised by architects who have earned a level of reputation and critical esteem, often validated by the Pritzker Prize. The early examples of London's millennial wave of towers conformed to this pattern, being designed by Foster and Piano (Pritzker winners in 1998 and 1999) and Rogers, who would win it in 2007. But they set a bar below which other tall building projects would fall.

It's not what you know, but who you know

The idea of the icon excludes the complexities (spatial, social, constructional) that make architecture what it is, and replace them with look. The look is both a distraction and a sales tool. Being subjective, it is negotiable.

Iconic buildings are coalitions of brands – the architect's, the city's, the developer's – but are based on a friable concept, which is the supposed talent of the architect. For if through some sort of consensus some names rise above others, on what substance is this based? It is always possible to find dissenting voices; brilliance is a hard thing to define in terms of policy and law. In new-millennium London reliance was placed on 'design review' committees set up by CABE and local authorities, made up of architects and others who might have a valid opinion. They sometimes did good work, but, however scrupulous their procedures and personnel, such matters are susceptible to pressure and influence and to accusations of favouritism and prejudice. Thus CABE's design review committee included architects who designed tall buildings, who would decorously declare an interest and withdraw while their projects were being endorsed, for example as 'a bold addition to the London skyline', but return at a later date to back schemes by their colleagues.

In London much is determined by the power of networks, the overlapping schemata of politics, institutions, development, architecture, consultancies, fixers, academe, media, and marketing. Boundaries, as between information, selling and decision-making, can be blurred. Sometimes several roles might be combined in a single person or institution. In such ways marketing and influence blur with information and debate and no one objects. Controversy is neutralized. Access is privileged. Interests conflict. Success comes to those who can navigate these structures; the grand schmooze of MIPIM is a perfect supplement and stimulant. In such a world meaningful assessment of architectural quality is apt to be difficult.

In the projects that came after the Shard, whatever architectural ambition it had was diluted. It proved possible to claim quality and iconicity without a Pritzker in your pocket. The Gherkin generated diffusion lines, with various former Foster employees claiming their share of the credit for it. Some of them designed Strata SE1 in Elephant and Castle, which was said by CABE to be an 'appropriate proposition' and a 'strong' concept, albeit one where 'the cladding and energy strategy have not yet come together into a successful whole'. Their reservations were not enough to stop the tower going up; after completion its Carbuncle Cup citation spoke more pithily of its 'Philishave stylings', its 'grim stridency exacerbated by its sporty livery of alternating black and white stripes, configured in voguish barcode distribution' and its 'breakfast-extracting ugliness'. It shared the Gherkin's indifference to its surroundings, its clumsiness in hitting the ground but not, partly because it was built to a lower budget, its stylishness.

Dubai-on-Thames

A critical moment was reached with the Vauxhall Tower, a 594ft-tall residential building on a conspicuous site on the south side of the Thames. The proposed project featured in something classed as an 'important view', one looking upstream from Westminster Bridge, with the Houses of Parliament on the right. It was designed by Broadway Malyan, the architects whom Sellar had deemed not eminent enough for the Shard, and was to stand right next to the St George Wharf development, also by Broadway Malyan, that the *Architect's Journal* poll had twice condemned. The same developer, St George, was responsible for both the tower and the earlier development.

When CABE had criticisms the architects, who had an office in the same building as the commission, came back to them with modifications, until in the end the verdict was cautiously approving, praising the scheme's 'well-worked-out, clear and attractive plan'. But the design's fundamentals remained similar throughout: a conspicuous cylinder whose outline was elegant enough, but whose elements failed to cohere. Its shaft was one thing, its base another, its top – surmounted like the Shard and Strata SE1 by a gestural ecological wind-exploiting thingy – something else again. The 'public realm' at ground level was desultory and ill formed. The cladding, it would turn out when built, would look cheap. The best features of a Renzo Piano – consistency, attention to detail, confidence – were absent.

The London Borough of Lambeth refused permission and it went to a public inquiry where, although Mayor Livingstone spent taxpayers' money supporting the proposed tower, the inspector dismissed it. Secretary of State Prescott then exercised his prerogative to overturn the inspector and approve the project. His civil servants advised that he shouldn't do this: it 'could set a precedent for the indiscriminate scattering of very tall buildings across London', they said. But, once it had become clear that Prescott was not a man to be put off by quibbles, the civil servants then advised him how to spin his decision so as to reduce outrage. People who worked on the planning of London's boroughs later recalled their despair that a project that had gone through all the due procedures and been found wanting, could then be passed on a whim. 'If this could get through,' said one, 'then anything could.'

Anything, indeed, would, albeit slowed by the financial crisis. By 2015 more than 250 towers over twenty storeys were under construction or planned for London. Many were in prominent places, dominating stretches of the Thames, popping up in conservation areas and casting long, deep shadows over homes. In many cases pretences to architectural quality were nugatory to the point of non-existence. The Vauxhall Tower, now called St George Wharf Tower, was complete. If the planning inspector had felt its impact unacceptable it was now part of a thicket of taller, bulkier and not necessarily prettier towers that were proposed and approved around it.

By now developers' hands had been further strengthened by

the rise of commercial viability assessments, which allowed them to challenge not only requirements for affordable housing, but also restrictions on height and bulk. The use of assessments added another layer of consultancy, where property experts were hired to produce quasi-scientific reports on the values and costs of individual projects. A government that professed its intention of removing red tape and procedural obfuscation from the planning process found enthusiasm for such things when they could be wielded by developers.

Meanwhile local authorities found their budgets cut by austerity measures, which made them less able to fund the planning departments whose job is to oppose damaging proposals and guide applications towards better outcomes. They struggled to afford the lawyers and consultants to counter those on the applicants' side. They found it hard to challenge the claims made, the campaigner George Turner revealed, by developers' paid experts on overshadowing and rights of light. A gross disparity arose of resources and expertise.

The same cuts made councils more desperate for the donations (or planning gain) that come with developments, the effects being felt with special violence on the Thames. As Tony Travers of the London School of Economics points out, the river acts as a boundary for the boroughs along its banks which, as it is a fact of political life that local authorities care about their centres and neglect their edges, makes it a ribbon of casual decisions. Asset that it is for London as a whole, the river is cared for by no one in particular.

The sprouting of towers along the Thames might have been surprising to followers of the 2008 mayoral election campaign, when Boris Johnson had attacked Ken Livingstone's fondness for tall buildings. He announced his opposition to creating a 'Dubai-on-Thames'. But this was before he took office, became a mipimist convert to tall buildings, and overruled boroughs to push through

'If this could get through, then anything could'

contentious schemes. Wordsmith that he is, Johnson could not have found a more perfect description of the cityscape which, by the end of the second term of his mayoralty, he was creating.

In his 2000 novel *Super-Cannes*, J. G. Ballard describes Eden-Olympia, an 'intelligent city' and 'suburb of paradise' in the hills above Cannes. Here 'the most highly paid professional caste in Europe, a new elite of administrators, *énarques* and scientific entre-preneurs' work and live in 'a vision of glass and titanium straight from the drawing boards of Richard Neutra and Frank Gehry, but softened by landscaped parks and artificial lakes, a humane version of Le Corbusier's radiant city'. Unfortunately this gives rise to fatal boredom, 'a kind of waiting madness, like a state of undeclared war', which requires the intervention of the omnipotent psychiatrist Wilder Penrose. 'Psychopathy', believes the doctor, 'is its own most potent cure, and always has been. At times, it grasps entire nations in its grip and sends them through vast therapeutic spasms. No drug in the world is that powerful.'

He encourages 'bowling clubs', gangs of Eden-Olympia residents who get in touch with their dark side by descending into the town and attacking with random violence North African pimps and drug dealers, and Russian criminals. Escalating, these *ratissages* lose their flimsy pretext of cleaning the streets of undesirables. In due course they go to the Pierre Cardin Foundation, in one of Lovag's Palais Bulles, and assault blameless members of a Japanese fashion shoot:

> A huge melee had engulfed the terrace. Groups of technicians and make-up assistants cowered against the balustrade, watching as vicious fist-fights erupted among the camera crew and the guards near the pantechnicon. A second group … had appeared within the museum, and lashed out with their clubs like warriors in a battle scene from a Kurosawa epic.

Many in the property business are not like this, but responsible people trying to do a good job. But so, at first, were some of the occupants of Eden-Olympia. Looking at the London skyline, it appears to be suffering a Cannes-born beating-up from the pages of Ballard.

11. Public and Publoid

In June 1855 the London correspondent for the Breslau publication *Neue Oder Zeitung* reported that posters had gone up around the city. They announced that 'an open-air meeting of artisans, workers and "the lower orders" generally of the capital will take place in Hyde Park on Sunday afternoon to see how religiously the aristocracy is observing the Sabbath'. These protestors were provoked by a Sunday Trading Bill, which would stop workers shopping and drinking on what was then their only day off, their mood not improved by the pleas of Lord Robert Grosvenor, sponsor of the Bill. It was fair to restrict working people in this way, he said, given that 'the aristocracy was largely refraining from employing its servants and horses on Sundays'.

'200,000 people', continued Karl Marx (for the correspondent was he), then went to the place where 'the English high society . . . parade their magnificent horses and carriages with all their trappings, followed by swarms of lackeys'. There were three hours of speeches and creative abuse-hurling, after which the event ended with fighting. A week later a similar protest was dispersed when stave-wielding policemen, in the words of a later parliamentary inquiry, 'acted with violence, inflicting severe injuries on several persons who were not shown to have been guilty of any violence'.

A decade later class conflict broke out again in the same place. In the Hyde Park Railings Affair of 1866 a demonstration in favour of universal male suffrage, locked out of the park, forced down its surrounding fence and, overwhelming the police 'like flies before the waiter's napkin', surged inside. The crowd then held a peaceful meeting and left at nightfall. *The Times* complained that 'it is against all reason and all justice that motley crowds from all parts of the metropolis should take possession of Hyde Park and interfere with the enjoyments of those to whom the Park more particularly belongs'. But the outcome of the affair was that from 1872 Parliament granted the right of protest there, if restricted to the north-eastern point that came to be called Speaker's Corner.

These two events accelerated the democratization of the park. Unlike the commons, it was not threatened with development: the issue was not the preservation of greenery but how and by whom it was to be enjoyed. It is a royal park, originally for hunting, taken by Henry VIII from the monks of Westminster Abbey. Charles II put a brick wall around it and from his reign until Queen Victoria's its primary function was as a place of display and socializing by actual and aspirant nobility. Rotten Row, originally *route de roi*, ran through it to Kensington Palace, serving as a catwalk for fashion shows on horseback.

In 1851 the holding of the Great Exhibition brought six million mostly not-posh people to Hyde Park. In *London in the Nineteenth Century*, Jerry White quotes the complaints of the ancient dandy Captain Rees Gronow that 'democracy' had invaded the park with 'a "Brummagem society", with shabby-genteel carriages and servants'. This was in 1860; in his heyday fifty years earlier there had been 'regions which, with a sort of tacit understanding, were then given up exclusively to persons of rank and fashion'.

Had he lived until the First World War Gronow would have been appalled by further appropriations. Mike Harman, in the Libertarian Communist blog libcom.org, records that on one August night, two patrolwomen and a male police constable 'observed a corporal in the London regiment having sexual intercourse with a lady clerk from Harrods'. The corporal was subsequently fined; his friend got off with a warning. On another occasion, according to a police memo, 'two male persons are in Hyde Park; a youth of seventeen years is seen lying on his back and a man of forty-two years had the younger man's person in his mouth'. The men pleaded guilty to gross indecency.

Gronow's horror would have been at the social not the sexual elements of these incidents: in his day the performance of such acts in the park was reserved for people like himself, for example in the interiors of carriages.

Harman also notes that in the twentieth century the park was contested by the rallies of suffragettes, anti-fascists, campaigners for gay rights and the Campaign for Nuclear Disarmament. A love-in was held in 1967, which the co-editor of the hippie magazine *Oz*, Richard Neville, described as 'a field of fluorescent flower children, dancing, hugging and swapping colossal joints. Allen Ginsberg sat cross-legged on the grass playing a Tibetan squeeze box and chanting Om Mane Padme Hum, Om Mane Padme Hum . . .'

In 1969 the Rolling Stones gave a free concert which, taking place a few days after the swimming pool drowning of founding Stone Brian Jones, turned into a memorial event. In 1994 there was the Revolt of the Ravers, a protest against laws designed to end illicit raves. It featured an ingenious use of a small electric vehicle called the Sinclair C5, otherwise best known as a comical dead end of technological evolution, here used to carry sound systems about the park.

Karl Marx and the *Daily Telegraph* as comrades-in-arms; their legacy under threat

The accumulation of these occupations, by the Great Exhibition, the Sunday trading protestors and the railings-uprooters, by the suffragettes and flower children, and by the khaki Romeo and the unknown fellationist, made the park into a place where it is taken for granted that anyone can, within or just beyond the reasonable limits of the law, do what they like. If *The Times* of 1866 could speak of 'those to whom the Park more particularly belongs', it in principle now belongs to everybody. In this the effects of popular action have been assisted or managed by judicious legislative retreats, such as the creation of Speaker's Corner. In Hyde Park and elsewhere, it has not happened naturally or without struggle.

Regent's Park was originally exclusive: although it was complete by 1828, the general public were only allowed in from 1835 for two days per week, and from 1841 more widely. The streets and squares of the Georgian great estates, admired as the park was by Rasmussen as examples of civilized and humane city-building, were, as Anna Minton writes in *Ground Control*,

> fortified by hundreds of gates, bars and posts. Now some of the most open and public parts of the city, great efforts used to be made by the landlords to protect those inside the gates from the outside world. The estates employed their own private-security forces and, in one particularly well-guarded patch on the boundary of the Bedford Estate and disreputable Camden Town, there were five sentry boxes. The Bedford Estate used uniformed ex-prison officers to patrol their enclave and when a fight over entry into the area broke out, leading to a death, the coroner is recorded as saying that government conduct was 'disgraceful in allowing these squares and places to be closed to the public'.

Minton describes how public opposition and the rise of local government led to the removal of these barriers:

> By 1864–5, after two major parliamentary inquiries, 163 miles of road were passed over to local-authority control, and 140 toll bars were removed. By the 1880s, anger at the remaining restrictions caused the *Daily Telegraph* to denounce the 'persistence on the part of a few great landowners in a selfish and tyrannical policy' and proclaim that 'the noble obstructors of the queen's highway have enjoyed that fantastically feudal privilege for quite long enough'.

As a result of this surge of indignation, it became common practice for local authorities to 'adopt' streets and squares, meaning that they manage and maintain them, whether or not they own them.

From the 1980s onwards the freedoms for which Marx's protestors and the *Telegraph* had both fought went discreetly into reverse. There was a return to creating privately owned open spaces which, if not as ferociously policed as the Bedford Estate, still placed limits on what could be done in them and who could go there: no political protest, no photography with tripods, no picnics, no chaining-up of bikes, no rough sleeping, no playing of music, no ball games. Many local authorities, relieved to be relieved of the responsibilities and costs of maintenance, were happy to reverse the nineteenth-century tendency to adopt spaces. Broadgate and Canary Wharf were early examples, although with the alibi that their sites had earlier been private, or incompletely public: a station once built for a private railway company in one case, a walled dock in the other.

Canary Wharf and Broadgate pioneered what became the standard way of creating shared places in cities – developer-led, with the public invited in – which can be found in large-scale development projects across London. One is More London, the place close to the southern end of Tower Bridge where London's city government is located, which means that anyone wishing to protest against the actions of the mayor might be moved on by private security. Another is Paternoster Square, next to St Paul's Cathedral, where a modernist 1960s precinct was after protracted debate replaced by a more classical-ish and more densely packed development. Stratford City in east London was also planned as a variant on the Canary Wharf theme, but skewed towards retail by the Olympically fuelled intervention of the Australian shopping-mall company Westfield.

Such places are presented as attractions and civic gifts by the backers of proposed developments. They can be attractive and popular and play their part in the degrees of publicness and privateness of which a city is made. But it becomes a problem when they become the dominant type of new space, when they take over from common territory, and when they start to occupy the most desirable and significant locations in a given area. It also matters that they are called 'public spaces' which, since they are privately owned and managed, they are not.

This became clear in 2011, when the Occupy movement went searching for something in the City of London that might resemble a public square. Paternoster looked the part, but was not, and the management erected barriers and notices. In the long planning discussions leading to the creation of this development, the square had been described by its architects and developers as a 'public space'. Now, as a sign said,

> Paternoster Square is private land. Any licence to the public
> to enter or cross this land is revoked forthwith. There is
> no implied or express permission to enter the premises
> or any part. Any such entry will constitute a trespass.

So Occupy pitched its tents around the skirts of the cathedral instead.

Shrubs in the sky

Misuse of the phrase 'public space' multiplied. It was applied to the area at the base of the Cheesegrater which, with escalators driving through it, is more like a wall-less if magnificent office lobby – you could not imagine an Allen Ginsberg performance or a suffragette protest happening here.

Such misuse reached absurdity with 20 Fenchurch Street, the thirty-seven-storey, £500m tower that was also called the Walkie-Talkie, due to its resemblance to outdated telecommunications equipment. Its big idea was to swell upwards as it rose higher, such that more floor area was created in the places where it was more valuable, which made it above all a celebration of the price of office space; its form and surfaces were enlivened with swooshy curves denoting iconicity, which related awkwardly to the tendency of office buildings and their constructional elements to be rectangular. Early versions of the design showed something relatively svelte, but commercial considerations caused the final version to thicken and bloat like a retired boxer.

The Walkie-Talkie was of the generation of towers that followed the consenting of the Gherkin and the Shard. Its architect, Rafael Viñoly, was born in Montevideo, built his practice in Argentina in the 1960s and 70s and then moved to New York. He has not and may never win the Pritzker Prize, but he carries a Pritzker-y aura about with him. Profiles note his ability as a pianist, the two Steinways he keeps in his office and the nine pianos he owns in total: 'architecture is essentially a score', he has said, 'and what happens with it depends on the people who play it, enjoy it, use it or hate it'. He had a striking habit of wearing three pairs of glasses on his head at once. 'I am an individual', the multiple spectacles seemed to say, 'a free spirit.'

'A very special public space'

Planning in London, with the weight it gives to 'quality architecture' or outstanding or 'world-class' design, leans on opinions: on those of planners in boroughs, of the mayor and his advisers, of CABE, ultimately of the inspector who decides on planning enquiries and of the minister who may or may not endorse the inspector. In this case Viñoly convinced not only his clients and their consultants of the brilliance of his scheme, but also the City's planner, Peter Rees, and CABE. 'One of the strengths of the architectural experience in the City,' said the latter, 'comes from the excitement of dramatic contrasts and changes in scale. We believe this design would enhance the experience of a world city, driven by the character and dynamism of a thriving commercial economy.'

This support was important, as there was concern from English Heritage and others that the tower would have an unacceptable impact on the UNESCO World Heritage Site of the Tower of London. The proposal also violated what Rees had set out as an important principle of planning tall buildings in the City, that they should be grouped in a 'cluster', an imaginary approximate cone centred somewhere near the Bank of England. The Walkie-Talkie stands outside this cone, a fact that Rees would attempt to explain: 'we came to think of it as the figurehead at the prow of our ship,' he said, 'a viewing platform where you could look back to the vibrancy of the City's engine room behind you.'

Being contentious, the proposal went to a public inquiry, where the inspector in charge of proceedings also fell under the spell of Viñoly's design. 'The quality of the design would make a significant contribution to London's architecture,' he said. But the clinching argument was that the tower would create what CABE called 'a very special public space' at the top, a 'sky garden' where anyone could go for free. Cluster or no cluster, UNESCO-schmunesco, this gift to the people of London justified the creation of the tower.

While under construction the tower became an object of hilarity when its concave glass facade focussed the sun's rays with sufficient intensity to start melting a Jaguar parked nearby. Completed, it became clear that, whatever magic mushrooms had been consumed by the experts who declared the design masterful had not been shared by many members of the public. For example: 'a monumental planning mistake', 'reminds me of the monster from Looney Tunes cartoons', 'it brings new meaning to the words "just because you can, doesn't mean you should"', 'bulbous stack of s**te', 'it's a tumour!'

It was also obvious, as it should have been all along, that the Sky Garden was in no meaningful sense what the official description called 'the UK's tallest public park'. Members of the public would have to book at least three days in advance to go there. Free access was for restricted hours. Photo ID required. Terms and conditions apply. It was not a place where anyone could do such park-y things as walk a dog, throw a Frisbee, jog, have a picnic, sunbathe, paddle, build a snowman, play on swings or kick a ball and, as with the Cheesegrater, no suffragettes, no Ginsbergs seemed likely. There were not even many places to sit down, unless you were a paying customer at the large expensive bar and the large expensive restaurant that hog the centre of the space ('Rhubarb Viñoly' cocktails at £14.50, Dover sole at £42.00). Rather than a friendly park keeper, perhaps wearing a uniform and cap supplied by the council, the space was managed by the events and restaurant business Rhubarb. Their self-description chose to stress not any civic role but an 'international reputation catering at the most glamorous private, corporate, sports and charity events from film premieres to royal celebrations'. Greenery, which for the wilders and the preservers of the commons had been identified with equality and freedom, was now camouflage for exploitation.

There was not as much vegetation as might be expected. The restaurant and bar, which had been in the plans approved by the planning inspector, were later quietly enlarged, at the expense of the planting, with the consent of the City of London. On its north side the garden became an expanse of floor, empty but for some moveable pot plants, the better to hold corporate functions there. This left two banks of subtropical fuzz flanking the big box of the restaurant, like sideburns on a glam rock guitarist or a Victorian railway magnate. The clearest explanation of the de-gardening of the Sky Garden was given by Peter Rees, for whom it was an extension of his eroto-economic approach to planning: 'we are taking every opportunity to create the party city in the sky. It's very important to our business offer that people can party as close to their desks as possible.' The point, then, was less to create a park than to add to the glowing heads of the new City towers, along with the Heron, the Gherkin and the revamped Tower 42, that collectively form, high above the ground and for the benefit of financial workers more than the general public, a Krug-fuelled Magaluf.

It is still good to have a place where people can look at impressive views of London, for no charge, even though it would be easier to enjoy them if the assertive angled struts of Viñoly's design did not get in the way. Better to have such a thing than not. But it was questionable whether this not-quite-as-promised asset justified the thumping impact of the tower on its surroundings.

It is also a significant abuse of language to call something 'public' when it is not. It reveals an understanding of the word atrophied to the point of non-existence.

Life in public

A public space should enrich possibilities and expand freedoms. It is more than a zone where people who may not know each other can be together in certain numbers. It should allow the possibility of being in a crowd, solitary, in a couple or a small group. It includes the opportunity for you to inhabit it in your own way, to make it temporarily your own, through your actions and imagination.

There should be the chance that emotions and perceptions, in all their power and complexity, might be experienced as fully but differently from their manifestations in private. They might include surprise, risk, adventure, anger, uncertainty, paradox, delight – to a greater degree than the buzz of a view at the end of an elevator ride – as public life is not just bovine, not just grazing. Such potentials cannot all be designed into a space. Architecture can mostly offer hints, inspirations, provocations and cues, and settings that resonate rather than discourage and obstruct. Occasionally its role is to be extraordinary in its own right, more often to be conducive to whatever it might contain, for example through providing a background of dignity, a foil, a representation of order to which life can react, and through the choice of registers of sensuality in its materials and lighting. Much of the time the main task is to avoid designing out the possibilities of a place.

The already-there is important, as it offers an unauthored source of enrichment for which architectural genius is rarely an adequate substitute. Strangeness is invaluable. Although contemporary planners of public spaces tend to conformity and to the established forms of squares and circuses, the most potent places have unexpected features often bequeathed by accidents of history or topology – the facts that the Piazza Navona was a racetrack, that Venice is full of water, that the Rockefeller Center has an ice-rink, or that there are exotic beasts at the foot of Primrose Hill.

Incompleteness is essential, as built spaces are completed by the actions and thoughts of their users. There has to be vacancy and the right to be bored, without which there is no possibility of discovery or reflection. The enemies of public space include the excess of vending, programming, branding and scripting, the things which, often but not always in the pursuit of profit, eliminate the spontaneous and uncalculated. There is a view of public space that defines its success by the number of people it attracts, and there are professional consultancies that employ quasi-scientific measures to assess it on these terms, which exalts to a dangerous degree quantity over quality. Sometimes you want some emptiness, too.

It is not that every shared space in a city can or should always be equally available to all people and all actions. There are places with gradations of publicness, governed by varying rules and ownerships, some free to enter and some not: train stations, buses, museums, restaurants, markets, supermarkets, workplaces, cinemas, theatres, bars, clubs, hotel lobbies, town halls, hospitals, doctors' surgeries, churches, mosques, colleges, airports, sports grounds and stadia, historic houses open to the public, as well as the more generally recognized streets, squares and parks. Nor is there precisely such a thing as 'the public', but rather many publics with desires and identities that only sometimes overlap.

London has its own forms for life in public. It has seldom been comfortable with the piazza or public square as found in much of continental Europe, the formal space for ceremonial or theatrical enactments of public life – rituals of church or court, mass events like the Sienese Palio, or popular actions like the *passeggiata* of southern European countries. In the seventeenth century a 'piazza' was created in Covent Garden in imitation of both Italian models and the Place des Vosges in Paris, but lacking other purposes it filled up with a fruit and vegetable market. London has a similar problem with boulevards. Kingsway, a rare attempt to make a broad, straight public thoroughfare, is sterile and unconvincing. There is an uneasiness about creating places just to dwell in the presence of other people, an urge to find a use and thus a tendency for formal places to become highways, traffic roundabouts or shopping parades, to default to either engineering or retail.

London's public life takes place more in parks and on heaths and on park-like constructions like the embankments and the terraces in and around the South Bank Centre. It can occur casually and opportunistically in unintended places: the small-hours inter-club society of Shoreditch and Hoxton is as vital as any, but it gets minimal encouragement from the area's hard streets and narrow pavements. London's public life tends to be ambulatory rather than promenading, about wandering and looking more than displaying and conversing. It has also thrived indoors, in enclosed, semi-private spaces like pubs, clubs, cinemas, museums and galleries.

One of the most successful places of London's Lottery-funded public works is the Turbine Hall of the former Bankside Power Station, after it was converted into the art museum Tate Modern. The hall is big and free to enter while also enclosed; it is locked up outside visiting hours. While it is open to everyone it is in practice more likely to attract people for whom modern art has some appeal. It combines a recognizable purpose, as a foyer and gathering point for an art museum, with some openness: as it is bigger than it needs to be, it has a sense of potential, of something beyond its stated purpose.

It helps that it is a found space more than a designed one, and Tate Modern a found building. When conceived in 1947 Bankside Power Station had a clear practical function, but its siting across the Thames from St Paul's Cathedral meant that some mitigation was felt to be needed to the fact – amazing, outrageous, negligent – of putting smoky industry so close to the Portland stone of the Established Church. So a respected architect, Giles Gilbert Scott, was hired to give it dignity, symmetry and an unusually tall chimney to take its pollution to a less damaging height.

Tate Modern, which opened in 2000, was partly the realization at a huge scale of the familiar type of industrial premises turned into arts space, but the power station's design history had also given

it a latent civic quality which, at the time of its unforeseen transformation into a national institution, came into its own. This was
not any old factory, but one whose axiality and proportions made
it into an alternative, industrialized version of St Paul's itself.
The Turbine Hall, the scale of a cathedral nave, owes its proportions
to the practicalities of the large machines it used to contain, but
the exterior's spirit of cultural importance colours the experience
of the interior.

Tate's architects, Herzog and de Meuron, chose to amplify the
power of the hall by removing its ground floor and thus adding its
basement to its total height. It was a giveaway of space that might
in theory have been useful, which prodigality would hardly be
noticed by Tate Modern's five million visitors a year. Only students of
the power station's history would know that there had once been a
separate basement. What they do experience is a wide ramp that,
going down into the hall, inverts the ascent up broad steps that
more usually prefaces art museums. The slope imparts a sense of
occasion and an altered awareness that entering on the level would
lack. It engages your body in a way that the horizontal does not. The
height of the hall unfolds as you descend. All of which effects may
not sound like much, but they take the space out of the realms of
the predictable and the prosaic.

If the Turbine Hall had been the all-new creation of a celebrated
architect, it would have been unbearable and bombastic. It would
have been a statement of the prestige and authority of Tate expressed through the signature of its designer. Other interpretations
and imaginings would have been stifled. Instead, the museum and
its architects allowed the chances of time to give them a space with
the properties of superfluity, redundancy, strangeness, obliqueness,
a refusal to prescribe and incompleteness. By including accidents
of the past the space made itself open to unpredictabilities of the
future; if the hall had not existed, you could not have made it up.

Tate then presented a series of special commissions in the hall of a kind that could not have been created anywhere else, and ranged from the crowd-pleasing to the subtle. Olafur Eliasson installed a sun-like disc on the end wall and a mirrored ceiling, such that visitors would splay themselves on the ground, as if in a Druidic-hippy rite, and watch their and their neighbours' celestial reflections. Carsten Höller built helter-skelters that descended the full height of the hall. Doris Salcedo put a crack 548 feet long, harder to achieve than it looked, in the floor. Bruce Nauman made spaces out of sound. The hall is a shared space, where the things shared, at their best, alter your view of the world, move or provoke you, and are unforgettable. This is important, it being too often assumed that publicly accessible places should be realms of the already known and the commonplace. When there are no installations, the hall can be experienced as a place that is not exploited to its last square inch, or programmed so intensively that there is nothing left for your imagination to inhabit. In this condition it can be glum, which is partly because Herzog and de Meuron's intentions for its finishes were reduced to a bare minimum by budget considerations, but its under-exploited void is still a thing to treasure.

The parts defeat the whole

If you exit Tate Modern, you don't find the same resonances that you can inside. This is not for want of trying. The decision to move Tate's collection of modern art to the area, taken in the mid-1990s, was accompanied by the desire to transform what was then a zone sleepy and overlooked, at least by those who didn't live or work there. The Millennium Bridge was built, designed by Foster in collaboration with the artist Anthony Caro and the engineering practice that still bore the name of the great calculator and enabler of the

Penguin Pool ramps, Ove Arup. Gunther Vogt, a subtle Swiss landscape architect, was hired to create the immediate environs of Tate Modern.

A short distance downstream a replica of Shakespeare's Globe theatre was taking shape, authentically oak-framed and thatch-roofed, in approximately its original location, the result of a decades-long effort by the American actor and director Sam Wanamaker. Then, as Tate Modern progressed, the area did indeed start changing. Harry Handelsman, a developer who had done much to make desirable the idea of living in modern apartments, commissioned a striking tower, yellow and cylindrical, from the striking architect Piers Gough. A high-density apartment complex called Neo Bankside later went up nearby, to the designs of Richard Rogers's practice Rogers Stirk Harbour and Partners. To the south of Tate Modern the developers Land Securities built a hefty block whose elevations were animated by blue glass fins, called the Blue Fin Building. In another direction towers of fifty-two and forty-eight storeys were approved around the southern approach to Blackfriars Bridge.

Tate itself expanded. In the initial conversion of the power station Herzog and de Meuron had been discreet to a degree baffling to those British architects who felt that a modern art gallery needed to be housed in a statement of modern architecture. The Swiss proceeded with cuts and edits and understatements of their substantial changes to the fabric of the building. For their extension to the southern, landward side of the museum, nearing completion in 2015, they ditched their modesty and designed a mountain of brick, with twisting and sloping geometries that ran the gamut of the material's expressive powers.

Bankside, in short, has been charged with intense levels of cultural, financial and architectural energy, and some exceptionally smart people have contributed to the area's immense change. Three Pritzker-winning architects, Foster, Rogers and Herzog and

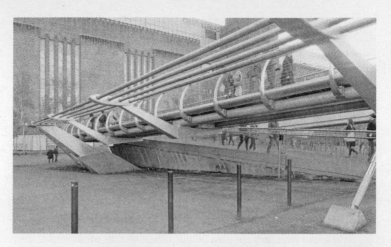

de Meuron, have worked there, as well as the well-respected Allies and Morrison and the rarely boring Piers Gough. Crowds have come. Memorable exhibitions and installations have been displayed. The bridge has opened up a much-used connection between the north and south sides of the river, and the Turbine Hall is a potent addition to London's stock of almost-public spaces. The Globe, which could have been a touristic waxwork, has brought new dimensions to the performance of drama – especially but not exclusively Shakespearean. The city's zones of stimulation and revelation have been expanded and enhanced.

It should be and in some ways is one of the greatest places in London, but, if you were to walk around its open spaces, you wouldn't know it. They are disjointed and lack the positive qualities that make city spaces memorable. The Foster bridge is elegant, even with the alterations necessary to stop it wobbling, except when it gets close to Tate Modern, where it proffers an aggressive cantilever and a ramp that awkwardly doubles back on itself. The Rogers blocks of flats, with exposed steel cross-bracing and sharply detailed glass, have a handsome if misplaced muscliness – torsos with too much gym-work – but they show no interest in relating to anything around them. They use a 45/135 degree geometry that is as antithetic as could be to anything that might be built nearby. Herzog and de Meuron's tower at least refers back to the old power station by using a similar material, and it aims to form a landscape and piazzas at ground level, but its reaction to its noisy neighbours is to shout too.

A consequence of hiring world-famous architects in this area has been an outbreak of braying and snorting, of competitive ground-pawing by their eminent hooves, which landscape architects must try to tame. Vogt's groves of silver birches are pleasant, but feel underfunded and unequal to their task. At the bases of the Rogers blocks agreeable shrubberies gather to which the public have access, although conspicuous security staff and glass gates are discouraging presences. But these plantings of birches and bushes do not feel part of any larger idea of what all the new developments might make together. The spaces between them, where you might hope for some interplay with the various publics of gallery goers, residents and office workers and some pleasure in the multiplicity of the area, are haphazard and joyless.

The design energy expended on individual buildings is not given to the spaces that they collectively make, which are more important to the enjoyment of the city. This is partly an effect of architecture in the high-tech tradition of Rogers and Foster, which tends towards a fixation with machine-like objects, and overrates contrast as a way of relating a new building to an old one. It undervalues the uses of rapport, affinity and the ability to operate in different registers, to be both alike and different at once.

Mostly the discombobulation of Bankside reflects the role of entrepreneurial players in shaping London and the relative weakness of public authorities in managing and directing them. Sam Wanamaker, Harry Handelsman and other developers made their cultural and commercial punts; the London Borough of Southwark could encourage or (as it did in the early, pre-Manson, years of the Globe's planning) thwart them. The London mayor and national government might play a part. But the public bodies are incapable of suggesting what kind of public realm might be constructed by cumulative actions and guiding the individual players to work together to achieve it.

These players included Tate (not, due to its branding strategy's banning of the definite article, 'the Tate'). Lottery funding required that institutions had to bid for it, and find funding from multiple sources to match the 50 to 75 per cent that the Lottery might offer. Tate therefore had to hustle and promote, to excite donors and generate a buzz. Its energies were focused more on its own territory than its surroundings, although the regeneration of Bankside was always an important part of its promise. Then, when its presence started attracting property speculation around it, it had to argue and lever to ensure that development was less harmful and more beneficial than it might otherwise have been. Tate's new brick tower, which was not driven by overwhelming artistic demands, was in part the staking of a claim and a device for attracting benefits that might arise from the commercial projects. The places between the museum and the apartment and office blocks are therefore not so much the willed and desired forms of an idea of the public good, as the residue of haggles and punts.

Terms and conditions apply

If you want contemporary examples of coherent open space, it's easier to find examples built by private property companies, such as Broadgate, Canary Wharf and the More London development around the mayoral headquarters at City Hall. The unstated deal is this: you can have quality (good paving, high levels of management and maintenance, desirable waterside locations) or you can have places that are available to the public without the terms and conditions applied by private ownership, but you will decreasingly find both in the same place.

There is also the redevelopment of sixty-seven acres of old railway lands near King's Cross station with offices, restaurants, housing both luxury and affordable, schools, a swimming pool and other public benefits. This was of similar scale and ambition to Canary Wharf but tried to do things differently: it accumulated a wider and more surprising range of uses, was more willing to incorporate the accidents of history found on the site, and aimed to blur the boundary of the new estate with its surrounding neighbourhoods.

The developers Argent brought to the site the University of the Arts, an amalgamation of some of London's best art and performance colleges, thereby animating the not-yet completed development with thousands of energetic and good-looking young people. They preserved and restored industrial remnants, such as a Victorian grain-handling facility, canals and gas-holders. They maintained Camley Street Natural Park. Children come from nearby housing estates to play in the fountains in its central square, in a way you don't see at Canary Wharf.

Argent hired notable architects like David Chipperfield and Allies and Morrison to design their office buildings and encouraged inventive restaurants and food stalls. They backed Shrimpy's, the temporary conversion of an old petrol station into a Peruvian-Mexican-Californian-Deep-South restaurant, designed by the promising architects Carmody Groarke. Argent were rewarded for their creativity by the decision of Google, attracted by all this liveliness and the central location, to locate their United Kingdom headquarters, a proposed 'campus within a building', one million square feet, and as long as the Shard is tall, in King's Cross.

It was not all Argent's own work. The London Borough of Camden, which worked with the developers to achieve some of the public benefits, played a part. Above all there were the local campaigners who had fought fierce battles for years against more destructive, more excluding and cruder plans and for the preservation of those fragments, the granary included, on which the development's claims for character now depend. Most of the site is covered by protected views of St Paul's from Hampstead which, preventing towers being built, pushed the developers into more creative ways of achieving high densities. The whole project was prompted by a public investment, the bringing of the terminus for Channel Tunnel trains to the nearby St Pancras station.

Camley
Street

Granary
Square

Chipperfield

King's Cross takes far the idea that a property company might act as a de facto municipality and, as a piece of developer-led city building, it is the best of its kind. But it has limitations. The local artist Richard Wentworth calls the new district 'Insipidia'. It is comfy, frictionless, normalizing, a physical cousin of the Google universe in which all things are given equal weight or lack thereof, filleted of their power to move, shock or surprise the emotions – and in truth it is hard to imagine a property company ever being the best organ for realizing such things. King's Cross is highly managed and with sophistication, the more so to achieve its degrees of permissiveness and inclusion. It cannot entirely escape the feeling that it is made by developers for developers' clientele, into which the rest of the public is invited – with however much friendliness and creativity – which invitation could be restricted in the future by a change of management policy.

It might be hoped that King's Cross would be an experience from which ever better approaches might be learned, a base camp for new heights of city-making, but it is more probably as good as it gets, a model which few if any comparable developments are matching or are likely to match. The powers and resources of local authorities have been lowered since the days when the Borough of Camden used them to influence King's Cross. Instead, London is offered the upscale flowerpots attached to Rhubarb's catering operation and told that this is 'public'.

Public bodies lack the ability and confidence to lead, to propose areas of the city that are available, and well executed, and desirable, and resonant, where commercial development has to follow patterns set firstly by the public interest. Past examples include Bazalgette's embankments, nineteenth-century parks and the South Bank Centre. The tendency is rather to nudge and encourage property companies to offer a bit more than they might otherwise – with increasing impotence, thanks to the changing balance of power in favour of the private sector. Yet the notion of public intervention at a large scale has not disappeared. After all, London held the Olympics.

12. You've been Heatherwicked

High Street 2012

Should you leave the Redrow Psycho's apartment and take the lift back to the ground, you will find yourself in a mill of traffic around the entrances to Aldgate East Underground station. In one direction are the towers of the City. In the other is a long, straight-ish road with a number of names as it heads east: Whitechapel High Street, Whitechapel Road, Mile End Road, Bow Road, Stratford High Street.

In the run-up to the London Olympics this four-mile stretch was branded High Street 2012, as it would be the main route from the centre of London to the site of the Games. It was also an opportunity to assuage guilt about two of the deprived boroughs, Tower Hamlets and Newham, in whose name the Olympic bid had been made. While much had been made of the Games' ability to help these places there was some danger that, with the main site and its essential facilities consuming money and attention, they might be neglected. So it was promised that the culminating part of the marathon would be run along here, such that this diverse slice of London could be presented to the TV cameras of the world – an inclusive proposal later abandoned in favour of more photogenic and possibly easier-to-police locations.

There would also be a programme of enlightened improvements to its public spaces that would be assets to the locals and present a new face to international visitors. These were implemented, although with budgets that were drips of the sums spent on the Olympic project as a whole. The road became an avenue of good intentions, clumsy development, small-scale achievement and large-scale ineptitude, laid over what was already a long line of urban code that encrypts several centuries of life and aspiration in its variegated fabric.

It starts with the Redrow block and a glass stub of a companion across the road, lumps of speculation cast down from the computers of time-starved architects. At this point the street is struggling to find an identity, but it picks up a tune with some variegated elevations, quite narrow, of different periods, with small shops or ex-pubs at ground level. Somewhere around is the ghost of Blooms, a famous kosher restaurant that served the now almost-gone Jewish community. Cafes, with pistachio cupcakes, *pastéis de nata* and heart-shaped filigree on the cappuccino froth, are moving in.

Among the shops is the arresting front of the Whitechapel Art Gallery, one of Henrietta Barnett's projects to bring cultural light to the East End. It is in pollution-proof terracotta, in a style that might be called Art Nouveau or Jugendstil but is really unique to the small oeuvre of its architect, Charles Harrison Townsend. It combines plainness with intricate outbreaks of ornament, and an overlarge arch with the too-small windows. It sets up symmetry and then riffs on asymmetry. It is all facade, broad and flat, a billboard of beauty that breaks into three dimensions at its skyline and entrance. It was embellished in 2012 by a scattering of golden leaves, based on the organic decoration of the original, by the artist Rachel Whiteread. It was a daring liberty on her part, to treat this rare elevation in this way, but it works.

Next door is the Whitechapel Library, another work of civilizing Caliban, as the art historian Frances Borzello called the import of culture to the East End, also known as the 'University of the Ghetto', that nourished local authors such as Arnold Wesker and

Redrow

Whiteread's Whitechapel

Altab Ali

Isaac Rosenberg. The books now gone, the gallery has taken over the building. Obliquely across the road is Altab Ali Park, named after a teenager killed in a racist attack in the 1970s, and formed on the site of the church which, once coated in lime and chalk, was the eponymous White Chapel. The park was somewhat ragged and neglected, apart from a monument to martyrs of the Bengali Language Movement. As part of the High Street 2012 project muf architecture/art enriched the park with real and fictive archae-ology, revealing or creating the outline of the church, fragments of carving and paving, rocks and odd logs, while leaving an eighteenth-century stone tomb, approaching the size and shape of a skip, to stand proud and alone. The idea was to bring together these sug-gestive fragments, Christian, Muslim and whatever, in such a way as to animate the previously bland turf and to hint at but not pre-scribe different ways of inhabiting the space. Like the Whiteread, it works, but it would have worked better if its budget had been less palpably small.

Further along is a bell foundry, established 1570, Big Ben and the Liberty Bell among its products, followed by the East London Mosque, mostly brick, completed in 1985 with the help of a gift from King Fahd of Saudi Arabia. Then the street widens enough to sustain a market: fruit, vegetables, plastic toys, SIM cards. This area is another beneficiary of public-realm improvements, which include some dented metal patterned faintly Bengali bin stores, but they are submerged beneath the stalls, produce and footfall. Behind the dignified eighteenth-century facade of the former Royal London Hospital is its replacement – created under a Private Finance Initia-tive that as well as putting the Health Service in vast hock for a generation squeezes out architecture – an array of large blocks clad in a rash of mottled blue, as if suffering from measles and extreme cold at once. In 2015, before he was found guilty of corrupt and ille-gal electoral practices, the mayor of Tower Hamlets, Lutfur Rahman, announced a plan to turn the old hospital building into a town hall, or 'civic hub', for which it looks the part. Nearby is the ruin of one of Giles Gilbert Scott's red K6 phone boxes. Invented to make streets more orderly and harmonious, those that remain – protected as historic structures but left to rot by their privatized owners – achieve the opposite effect.

Behind a stretch of market rises the building where the Whitechapel Library was relocated, losing some books and patina in the process. The word 'library' was thought elitist or off-putting, so a branding agency called it an 'idea store', but people don't know what an idea store is, so retrofitted signs tell you that it is a library. It is an early public commission for David Adjaye, later entrusted with the Museum of African American History on the Mall in Washington DC and the Moscow School of Management. It is wrapped in glazing in dark-blue-and-green vertical stripes, prompted by the colours of the nearby market stalls, quite lovely and almost iridescent. The interior is more shabby and awkward, but well used. An external escalator was intended to attract people from the street into its upper levels of learning and it encouraged some idiot critic to call the building 'a Cockney Pompidou', but it never runs.

Around here is the scent of grotesqueries and crimes past, pursued by guided tours – Ripper sites, the Blind Beggar pub, where the south London gangster George Cornell paid the ultimate penalty for calling Ronnie Kray a 'fat poof'. The area is haunted by the memory of the deformed Joseph Merrick, the 'Elephant Man', who was exhibited in a freak show on Whitechapel Road, was cared for by Frederick Treves at the London Hospital, and died there. His hat, veil and skeleton remain. Stalin once lived a short distance to the south and Lenin used to give lectures nearby. Notoriety persists: in 2015 newspapers reported on 'secret meetings' in the basement of a 'Halal sweet shop' in the area, at which a young man called Brusthom Ziamani, who would be convicted of plotting to behead

Cockney Pompidou

Nairn's joke

**Captain Cook
was here**

a British serviceman, was mentored by a member of the 'banned terror group al-Muhajiroun'.

The road widens again to allow a magnificent double row of planes along Mile End Waste, a place so dire in the nineteenth century that it inspired the birth of the Salvation Army. There are two memorials to the army's founder, General William Booth, and one, erected in 2015, to his wife Catherine. Behind stands Trinity Green, a delightful court of tiny almshouses for retired sea captains, red brick with stone trimmings, attributed without evidence to Christopher Wren but a miniature version of Wren's Chelsea Hospital, with two wings flanking a central chapel. Stone carvings of seventeenth-century warships, miraculous in their accuracy and fragility, adorn the gables. The Waste is also muf-enhanced, 2012-assisted, with further suggestive fragments. Next there is the former Wickhams department store, an ambitious imitation of Selfridges in Oxford Street which nonetheless couldn't persuade a small jeweller's business called Spiegelhalters to get out of the way, such that the steady beat of its stone Ionic columns had to pause for the little brick shop and then start again. Ian Nairn called it the 'best architectural joke in London'. In 2015 this two-storey punchline was threatened with removal, then reprieved.

On the other side of the road there is a row of old buildings restored with High Street 2012 money. The pointing and paint colours look authentic, and the biryani houses and convenience stores in front were encouraged, assisted and indeed instructed to replace their garish plastic with hand-painted wooden signs. Some are finding ingenious ways to backslide – neon just behind glass, for example, such that it doesn't in planning terms count as part of the exterior. But you can still get a sudden draught of distant time, as if Captain Cook had, beyond the corner of your vision, just entered the house (now gone) that he had along here.

From here the road speeds up, passing Georgian houses too

Bow: church and flyover

grand for the subsequent history of the area, outbreaks of philanthropy, postmodernist speculations, pubs and ex-pubs, utilitarian council housing improved by intelligent new landscaping, places of learning, some not-bad student housing and more Georgian terraces whose handsome proportions fight for their grace amid the noise of vehicles. Eventually, you get to Bow church, which hugs its trees and gravestones close on the narrow traffic island it is allowed. There are bridges along the way. The Lottery-funded 'green bridge', designed by Piers Gough, cleverly links the north and south halves of Mile End Park by carrying vegetation over the road, although it is diminished by the fact that its trees died. A flyover rises beyond Bow church, a piece of multilevel transport engineering which takes the road above an intersection with an urban motorway.

From here things fall apart. Stratford High Street is nothing like a high street, but a grinding dual carriageway with haphazard development either side. On the right, some industrial remnants. On the left speculative residential units accumulated into blocks and towers that jostle with the near-empty council housing of the Carpenters Estate, tactlessly vivid reminders of the malfunctions in London's housing. A newish apartment block resembles the prison ship HMP Weare, that was once moored off the cost of Dorset; later is the Halo, a sealed tube in shades of purple and grey, as if in the livery of a budget airline, whose airless claustrophobia the flats replicate. There is a suspicion that, however shoddy these buildings look now, this is as good as they will get. They don't promise to age well.

Lacking is a conception of what the street might be as a whole, and how the surge of investment might help it. There is no idea of relationship between one building and another. Even a few more trees wrung from the developers' budgets would make a difference. There are the blue strips and elaborate kerbage of a 'cycle superhighway' which, however worthy the aim of promoting cycling, is an intrusive addition to the environment for pedestrians, and too

Carpenters Estate and Stratford High Street

elaborate and interrupted to be enjoyed on a bike. An unhappy number of cycling fatalities have happened along it.

Heartbreakingly, all this is taking place in sight of the Olympic zone, the place where London was to display its creative genius to the world, where committees of experts ran competitions to ensure design excellence, which games were also to re-energize their battered surroundings and did indeed give a fillip to residential development, most of the repulsive architecture along Stratford High Street having been conceived and built in the glow of Olympic expectation. Then, worse, is the belated remorse: a person or persons in authority seem to have sensed that something was lacking and commissioned designs from the infantilizing school of public-realm improvements, with blobs of light in changing colours strung from strings, as if east London streets needed more than anything else to resemble a children's birthday party, but sans jelly, sans fun.

As in the film genre where the protagonist loses girlfriend, job, home and then finds that his vintage car has been filled with cement, or in the Book of Job, this is not, even now, all. The road sweeps left then right as part of an unpleasant mid-century gyratory system. There are manifestations from different decades of the upbeat swooshes with which public authorities, having helped to make a place a dump, try to assert that it is no such thing, but end up drawing attention to its dumpness. There is a bouquet of curving steel tracks that reference the area's history as a railway centre, and a bus station with a grove of inverted Hopkins hats. Behind it is Wilkinson Eyre's Jubilee Line station of 1999, whose relative calm and elegance failed to set a precedent for further development in the area. Then, on the left, a grand stair leads to the shopping mall through which the Olympic Park is accessed. On the right are a humbler shopping centre, car park and mud-coloured office tower from the same era as the gyratory, which have not sucked at the energy drink of Olympic optimism.

Anchored by fish

Again, the off-message architecture was spotted, so an artwork called The Shoal was installed, a screen of puffy rhomboids ('leaves') in shining green/gold/blue/mauve, that are supported on bunches of dirt-gathering metal *bucatini*. In the official explanation, epic in its mixing of metaphors, the leaves

> playfully raise the spirits of its onlookers, rising and falling with the choreographic elegance of a shoal of fish ... The Shoal allows the emerging plans for Stratford to take shape with a new titanium veil in the foreground, like a grandiose shimmering palisade, the Shoal plays a positive role in anchoring this place as it re-emerges confidently after the Olympics.

Perhaps the first time fish have been used to anchor something. I can't see the elegance and spirit-lifting myself; it seems more to say Ohmigod This Place Isn't Very 2012 Let's Do Something Quick and Whatever You Do Don't Look Over Here at the Ugly Old Stuff Behind This Somewhat Inadequate Screen. Which, of course, has the effect of making you look over here at the ugly old stuff.

And then, if you are in the area on a Saturday, you might find the Revolutionary Communist/Focus E15 stall, over by a neo-Gothic 1834 structure described by Ian Nairn as 'one of the hungriest-looking churches in London'. Here you might meet Afham Ismail, an asylum-seeker who, on the street and later on the top floor of a small tower block, tells his story, which gives an idea of some of the lives lived around here. His account, in shortened form, goes like this:

> He has scars on his face and leg and a limp, from the time when Sri Lankan police blindfolded him, beat him with gun butts or similar and slammed his leg in the door of an armoured vehicle. He has lived in London since 2004, for much of which time he has been engaged in complex struggles with immigration and housing agencies, with inaccurate reporting of his case by the *Sun*

newspaper, and with the continued hostility of the Sri Lankan government. He is epileptic and contracted tuberculosis while in London. He is a computer engineer and has worked as a teacher; his wife, Nazrah, from Mauritius, is also a teacher. Since 2010 they have been forbidden to work.

In 2012 he and his family were evicted from the key-worker housing which as teachers they had been able to occupy. They challenged their landlords, and lost, were temporarily rehoused by Newham, and then offered a move to Birmingham. They refused, as it would mean changing their children's school and losing their networks of support in London. The first attempt by Newham's bailiffs to evict them was thwarted by a crowd of eighty supporters, who had been alerted by Focus E15's use of social media, but at 6.30 a.m. on 18 December 2014 their door was broken open by The Sheriffs Office, a company specializing in enforcement and eviction, and the Ismails and their three children were evicted. The children might then have been taken into care and the parents left to fend for themselves, but Focus E15 had spread the word of their plight. A stranger offered them the use of her house, free of charge, for a few weeks. 'She didn't know us,' says Ismail, 'and her computer, TV, books, everything was there, but she just gave us the keys.'

Since then they have been borrowing space in friends' flats, Nazrah and the children in a single room, with Afham sleeping on the floor in the corridor. Shortly after the eviction, a Twitter account called BritishBorn1 started denouncing him: 'AfhamIsmail could be a Terrorist FocusE15 are trying to house him which is dangerous putting peeps lives at risk'.

In 2013 Ismail posted a photograph of his father, senior guard at the British High Commission in Colombo, receiving an honorary MBE from Prince Charles. According to BritishBorn1 (apparently confusing father and son) 'you have mocked The Price of Walse [sic] in that pic shaking hands as a FAILED ASYLUM SEEKER!!!'

In the summer of 2015 the Ismails were still fighting to stay in Britain, to recover their ability to work and get a place to live. They were also using their experience to help, through Focus E15, other people facing relocation and eviction.

Faster, higher, stronger

There is, at last, the Olympic zone itself, a new park scattered with sporting structures and criss-crossed by old waterways. Here London did a good job of achieving the flawed concept intrinsic to the Games, which is to build a vast and expensive infrastructure for a brief sporting event. Intelligence was applied to the question of which venues would have lives after the Games and which should be temporary, and there were mostly successful attempts to avoid the scrapyards of follies that were left in other Olympic cities after the crowds had left. There were some good buildings, some less so, the best being the taut Velodrome by Hopkins Architects. There was the above-average residential development of the Athletes' Village, if with its Comecon flavour.

Zaha Hadid, London's biggest if locally frustrated architectural superstar, got to build in her home city. Her Aquatic Centre is magnificent for the way its vast mass swoops, but its majesty requires some excuses: for its colossal cost, the fact that its roof used thirty times as much steel as the Velodrome's, the awkwardness with which temporary additional seating was tacked on during the Games, the difficulty of finding the entrance. A while after the Centre's post-Games reopening an ugly slather of blue plastic filled its glass wall, to allow 'greater control of the light . . . improving conditions, particularly for TV coverage of international diving and swimming events, but also for divers and spectators'. But it was better than the ArcelorMittal Orbit, the 376-foot sculpture in

writhing red steel by the artist Anish Kapoor, the engineer Cecil Balmond and the architect Kathryn Findlay, sponsored by the steel billionaire Lakshmi Mittal and backed by Boris Johnson. In the beginning it looked like a pointless vanity project and three years after its opening it continued to look like a pointless vanity project. To no great surprise it struggled to attract the hoped-for numbers of visitors, so in 2015 it was decided to jolly it up by attaching a slide.

The 2012 news management was deft: the inevitable cost over-runs were dealt with early, in 2007, with the cool announcement that the budget would not be £2.4bn as previously hoped, but £9.29bn. When the final cost was announced as £8.77bn, it was presented as a triumph of management, not as the more-than-tripling of the original figure. There were fudging, sleight of hand and compromise. The building of a Westfield shopping centre was portrayed as evidence of the Games' regenerative power, even though it was planned before London won the Olympic bid. It also so happened that the main route to and from the Games and to the Olympic Park ran through the retail: like a very big version of Anne Hathaway's cottage and other English tourist traps, you were obliged to exit through the shop.

During the Games the park absorbed the crowds well and cre-ated a good-natured, festive arena. Renamed after Queen Elizabeth, it would afterwards be divided into a more wild northern area for wandering and relaxation, with high aspirations of biodiversity and access, and a southern zone for more programmed and sometimes ticketed activities (Where's Wally? at the top of the ArcelorMittal Orbit; a Mandeville Place Wassail Party). In its current form it gets its combinations of consistency and diversity the wrong way round: on one hand it lays the clammy hand of its self-conscious Olympic exemplariness on places that already had their own charms, for example on the canalized river along the edge of Hackney Wick; on the other it suffers from an excess of gestures, too many ideas of what a seat or a handrail might be, the multiple assuaging of anxieties. It is a landscape of boxes ticked – sustainability, ecology, diversity, access, children, revenue, sponsors, innovation, art, regeneration. But for all that, the basic premises work and it is popular. Fears that it would become abandoned and sinister have proved unfounded.

The stadium was a spare and quite elegant structure, justly proud of its economy of materials, designed around the sensible-sounding idea that it could be partly dismantled after the Games, on the basis that its 80,000 capacity was too large for any athletics event except the World Championships and the Olympics themselves. But such dismantling was opposed by the chairman of the 2012 organizing committee and former runner Sebastian Coe, who wanted it preserved as a temple to his sport. The outcome was that the building had to be clumsily and expensively adapted to accommodate football as well as athletics, with West Ham United Football Club becoming tenants on favourable terms. A club from the richest league in the world, owned by two pornography magnates, was in effect given a huge subsidy from the public purse. As the total cost would exceed £700 million, the stadium was economical only in appearance.

Despite its follies and absurdities, the London Olympics achieved what they set out to do. The 2012 Games were said to be among the best ever, British public opinion was largely won over, and an area of east London was improved, all with some professionalism and quality and few of the catastrophes that often accompany such projects. Two conclusions might be drawn from the experience:

> that it is possible for public authorities to carry out major urban projects if they put their mind to it;

> that politicians can erect futile and extravagant monuments and get away with it.

Queen Elizabeth Olympic Park, south and north

The future health of London depends on which of these precedents is followed.

Have a go

The pattern from Aldgate to Stratford is of a failure to invest in the not-great cost of architectural intelligence that might guide new development, or to address the more challenging but not impossible question of housing needs, followed by the panic-buying of gestures to retrieve the irretrievable. They act in the seeming hope that the undirected destructiveness of the Redrow block or the Halo is invisible: just look at these coloured blobs or leaves/fish, they say, and have your spirits lifted. Design is seen as something applied to singular events, frozen photo opportunities that have little to do with each other or their surroundings. Accumulated, they create the aesthetic wreckage of the centre of Stratford.

In these respects High Street 2012 offered a truthful vision of contemporary London to its Olympic visitors. Over the previous decades a declining ability to plan had coincided with the rise in entrepreneurial interventions of art or architecture, some of them beautiful or effective, usually calculated to attract attention in the media. The London Eye was a pioneering example. From 2000 onwards the Serpentine Gallery started building its annual temporary pavilion, with which brilliant architects from around the world were invited to make their debuts in London. In the late 1990s the cookery expert Prue Leith declared that it was a scandal that a plinth in Trafalgar Square was empty – it had once been intended for an equestrian statue of the little-loved King William IV, but no one had got round to putting one up. Most people wouldn't have noticed the absence that appalled Leith, but it didn't matter. She prompted a programme of enjoyable and provocative temporary artworks on

the plinth that punctured the torpor of indifference that had fallen on the square's monuments.

There is also street art of growing scale and complexity, following the precedent of the anonymous celebrity Banksy, which now populates the walls of Shoreditch with creatures, ships, superheroes, faces, jokes and slogans. They have generated a tourist industry of their own. Although bottom-up and unofficial, like Prue Leith and the makers of the London Eye they regard public space as a canvas on which to project their ideas.

The attitude behind the promotion and acceptance of these projects was not unlike that behind the Gherkin or the Shard. In all cases there was a desire to attract attention, to put faith in things contemporary and creative and to liven up London, plus a why-not spirit of giving something a go. If they succeeded in offering morsels of delight or at least distraction, it was only unfortunate that they created the impression that such things are the main and best use of design or architecture. Politicians became enthusiastic adopters of their gestural power and, being hungry for sponsorship, such projects also tended to invite corporations into the public space of the city. The London Eye, for example, having first carried British Airways' unobtrusive branding, became in 2015 the Coca-Cola London Eye and was lit Coke-can red at night. It was far from the intentions of the Eye's inventors that it should be the world's biggest advert for fizzy tooth-rot, but that is what it became, as it did so resembling less the Parisian structure with which it was often compared: there is not, not yet at least, a Coca-Cola Eiffel Tower.

The privileging of gesture matched the office of London mayor, whose limited powers and fundraising abilities are outrun by his or her celebrity and public profile. The first, Ken Livingstone, wasn't bad at this game. The second, Boris Johnson, took it to a new level. In person he had a penchant for memorable actions in front of cameras – punching a trainer in a boxing ring, getting stuck in a zip wire, aiming a rifle in Kurdistan, riding a bike with ungainly enthusiasm. His favoured projects tended to share characteristics – the promise of private funding, brand prominence and other benefits for the sponsor, metaphorical more than actual usefulness, the slow revelation that the work would cost the public purse more than first suggested, a spectacular quality, a preference for being on or over water. The Orbit has some of these qualities. The Emirates Air Line has all of them, a cable car over the Thames from Nowhere in Particular to Nothing Much, costing an estimated £24m to the London taxpayer, which by 2013 was carrying 10 per cent of its capacity, of whom the number of users classified as regular commuters was four. This 'howling success', as Johnson called it, enabled Emirates, the airline based in Dubai, to have its name printed on the London Underground Map. The sponsorship contract, until changed after a press outcry, restricted Transport for London's ability to deal with Israeli companies and of either TfL or the mayor to criticize the government and royal family of the United Arab Emirates.

'A tiara on the head of our fabulous city'

Johnson also threw his weight behind the Garden Bridge, which was first conceived by the actress Joanna Lumley soon after the death of Princess Diana, as a memorial. Lumley wanted to create 'a chance to walk through woodlands over one of the greatest rivers in the world . . . For commuters, it will provide a quick and beautiful route . . . for dreamers a quiet place to linger among trees and grasses to look at the views.' In time she found a site, the unencumbered stretch of river between Waterloo and Blackfriars bridges. She chose a designer, Thomas Heatherwick, called by the retailer and entrepreneur Terence Conran the 'Leonardo da Vinci of our times'.

Heatherwick is a product designer by training who likes to

venture into sculpture and architecture (in which he is helped by his associate director Fred Manson, the former Southwark regenerator). His forte is in making materials and structures do unlikely things – a pavilion that looks hairy, a footbridge that curls up like an armadillo, a bench made by squeezing hot aluminium through a die, 'like toothpaste from a tube'. He performs these feats with skill and flair, like a conjuror, and carries an aura of creative magic that has earned him more adulation than any of his profession for many decades. For the Olympic opening ceremony he captured the imagination of watching billions with a cauldron made up of 'petals' carried by children from each competing nation. He also designed a new, jazzed-up version of the classic double-decker Routemaster bus. Together, Heatherwick and Lumley generated irresistible levels of lovability and enthusiasm.

> Dear Boris, dear Mayor, [wrote the actress in 2012]
>
> a thousand congratulations on being re-elected Mayor of London
> – our cheers + shouts reached the rafters, soared over the Shard . . .
> wonderful news for London!
> Thomas Heatherwick and I would very much like to meet you in the
> near future to talk earnestly about the idea of a BRIDGE, a green
> pedestrian bridge, with cycle tracks alongside, with container-grown
> trees: & beauty
> + practicality
> in equal measure.
> We have done a lot of groundwork, as we had this idea several years
> ago – will you let us come to explain to you how it could be
> accomplished? It will be a boon for Londoners and visitors alike and
> will add to the great loveliness of the Thames.
> Please say yes.
> with warmest good wishes
> and salaams

yours ever,

Joanna.

P. S. I think now is the time for this.

P. P. S. Many thanks for the tulips and Fourth plinth photographs.

The letter was effective. In June 2013 the bridge was unveiled with the promise that, with its £60 million budget paid for by private sponsorship, it would cost the taxpayer almost nothing. In December it was announced that, actually, £30 million would be coming from national government for a project now being put at £120–150 million. Johnson praised the relevant Treasury minister for 'wielding his gigantic chequebook in favour of the Garden Bridge'. The next month it slipped out that another £30 million would come from the budget of Transport for London (of which £20m was later re-packaged, in an effort to deflect public criticism, as a loan on easy terms), which is overseen by the mayor. By the summer of 2014 the budget was £175 million. It later emerged that the Chancellor of the Exchequer, George Osborne, keen on cutting funding to the homeless and the disabled in the name of austerity, backed this extravagance more vigorously even than Johnson.

In December 2014 the mayor was asked whether he would be underwriting the running costs of £3.5 million per year. 'I can confirm that no such agreement has been made,' he said, 'and nor will I make any undertaking to do so.' He repeated this point in a radio interview in February 2015. In March it emerged that he had made just such a guarantee. He blustered on the subject to the Greater London Assembly. A judge, in considering an application for judicial review of the project, said that the mayor's excuses made sense 'neither in terms of English, nor of what Mr Johnson intended'.

Doubts accumulated. It turned out that, rather than being a public garden, it would be privately managed, would close at midnight and also twelve times a year for corporate fundraising events. At busy times people would have to queue to get on. A list of thirty prohibitions was released. It would not, as Lumley had promised in her breathy letter, be open to cycling. The amount of green space on the bridge would be equivalent to less than half a football pitch. For all the project's apparent green-ness, its steel structure and copper-nickel cladding were likely to be greedy of embodied energy, which is that required to create a permanent structure rather than expended through its use. Whichever sponsors might come up with the tens of millions still required – the government of Qatar? Banks? – would surely not be wholly altruistic, but like the Emirates would want some kind of influence or consideration in return. There would be no free lunch.

Heatherwick claimed the bridge would be a form of 'guerrilla gardening', a quite offensive appropriation of a concept opposite in spirit to the bridge. Guerrilla gardening is a bottom-up, spontaneous activity. The bridge is a top-down imposition. Real practitioners hated it: 'I would ask whether this is an honest piece of design, or a valuable commercial commodity disguising itself as art,' said one. Another attacked

> flagship, headline-grabbing, 'place-making' marketing initiatives aimed at boosting London's brand image and of course the Boris legacy, too. If TfL has money to spend on green infrastructure, they should be investing it in increasing the diversity of our city's flora and fauna by creating new pavement gardens, green roofs and bucolic station platforms – not by creating a garden in the air over water.

The people in charge of St Paul's Cathedral objected to the effect it would have on views of their building. The Royal Society for the Protection of Birds said that it 'falls short for wildlife' and that they could 'suggest much easier and cheaper ways to make life more pleasant for Londoners and urban wildlife'. The business group

'Beauty and practicality in equal measure'

London First said that other proposed crossings of the Thames should have a higher priority. According to the bridge engineer Simon Bourne it was not good value: you could build ten bridges or forty times as much garden for the same price, he said. The lawyers of the Middle Temple believed that there was an 'unacceptable uncertainty of income stream' and that it might be 'unlawful to grant permission when there are so many uncertainties about crucial issues'. The Ramblers' Association, the Metropolitan Public Gardens Association, the Green Party, the Liberal Democrats and the Taxpayers' Alliance also opposed. Local residents objected that thirty existing trees would have to be cut down to make room for its landing on the South Bank and that it would cause serious over-crowding: 'they're dropping a tourist attraction, with projected visitor figures second only to Disneyland Paris, into an area that already sees 25 million people a year.' The Garden Bridge Trust com-missioned a poll that showed 78 per cent of Londoners liking the idea – who wouldn't? – but needless to say the costs and doubts weren't spelt out to respondents.

Despite the promise that it would be a place to 'linger and enjoy the river and all of its attributes in a peaceful and tranquil environ-ment', Transport for London estimated that the crowds around its landing point would sometimes have a Pedestrian Comfort Level of 'D', the second worst of five categories. It means 'very uncomfort-able'. There were also objections that, in the process of selecting a designer for the bridge, Heatherwick's 'relevant design experience' had been ranked over that of architects who had designed many more bridges than him. The mayor's response capped Conran's da Vinci comparison: 'Michelangelo probably never built a Duomo before he did the Sistine Chapel, so it's a ludicrous argument,' said Johnson, ludicrously.

Behind the objections lay a flaw in the bridge's concept, which is that its ambitions were incompatible. It wanted to be a 'haven of peace', an addition to the city's transport infrastructure and a tourist attraction, but it couldn't be peaceful if its 35,520 square feet of paved area were packed to its maximum capacity of 2,500 and it couldn't be useful if commuters would have to queue to get on it.

Back to Bazalgette?

At this point we should introduce the Thames Tideway Tunnel, which will run along the bottom of the river that the Garden Bridge is planned to cross. It sounds sensible: as Bazalgette's system is at last unable to cope with the demands of modern London a vast additional sewer will increase its capacity. The problem arises from the fact that the original network handles sewage and rainwater at once, which means that the volume of fluid surges with storms and heavy rainfall and overflows into the river.

Sadly, many people who know about such things think that the Thames Tideway Tunnel is not a necessary, effective or desirable way of addressing this issue. Professor Chris Binnie, who chaired the Thames Tideway Strategic Study that initially supported the project, said in 2014 that the project 'is almost certainly a stupendous waste of money for very limited benefit'. His argument was that, in the ten years since he and others had approved the tunnel, the technology of more sophisticated and less drastic methods had developed to a degree that made it excessive. Binnie was part of a group of academics, environmentalists and engineers who said that the project would 'be of significant detriment to London's future growth, international reputation and prosperity'. 'I haven't a clue – apart from it being a great big infrastructure project – why on earth we are going ahead with it,' said Margaret Hodge MP, chair of the parliamentary Public Accounts Committee.

An alternative proposition is to use 'green infrastructure' to reduce the amount of rainwater that reaches the sewage system and to slow the rate at which it arrives. It can do this through living roofs, rainwater gardens, porous pavements, and domestic water butts and planters. Such a system of incremental improvements would make the city a cooler and a more pleasant place, and would create local jobs. Green infrastructure is not fantasy, but is being developed by (for example) the city of Philadelphia.

The construction of the Thames Tideway Tunnel will have devastating effects for many years on people who live near its work sites. As the government's planning inspectorate acknowledged, 'we do not consider that the proposals meet the first aim of [the relevant policy] to avoid significant adverse impacts on health and quality of life from noise.' Its official £4.2 billion cost is high, a large increase on earlier estimates of £1.7 billion and likely to go up further. It will be paid for by domestic (but not business) users of Thames Water's supplies, with a compulsory addition to their water bills for several years. As the London Stock Exchange points out to investors, the government has also offered a 'support package which provides significant mitigation to the risks of construction', which means that taxpayers will underwrite the project to an unlimited degree if it goes wrong.

Confidence is not increased by the nature of Thames Water itself. It is a privatized monopoly partly owned in the tax haven of Luxembourg, with a number of unnecessary corporate layers between the UK licensed company and its shareholders. It has debt in the Cayman Islands of such magnitude that in 2013 it paid £328.2 million interest on 'inter-company loans' via a Cayman Islands funding vehicle. 'Given the extraordinary secrecy surrounding such tax havens,' say objectors, 'there is no way of knowing [where] this money has come from.' The company paid no UK corporation tax in 2014/15 – and said in 2013, 'It will be seven to ten years until we pay tax' – but they have paid approximately £1.8 billion in dividends to their shareholders between 2007 and 2015. In 2014/15, Thames Water's CEO and Financial Director received remuneration increases of 60 and 80 per cent respectively, to £2.06 million and £1.41 million.

These arrangements suggest that Thames Water's primary motivation is not to serve the best interests of the London public. They also make it harder to improve the system with green infrastructure. This would require a level of integration with the public authorities responsible for the city's streets and open spaces, which is less likely to happen if the water company is autonomous, privately owned and lacking any brief for the wider benefits of the city.

As the sites for the Garden Bridge and the Thames Tideway Tunnel intersect, the bridge's backers say they have to start building quickly so that the two projects don't get in each other's way; taken together, this pair might be viewed as an updating of the Metropolitan Board of Works' combination of drains with the public spaces of the embankments. In reality their version of public spirit is a parody of the Bazalgette works. The main way in which the tunnel is Victorian is that its promoters can think of no better way to deal with overflows, a century and a half later, than to build a whacking great pipe, with the opportunity to be a world leader given up to Philadelphia. What the tunnel and the bridge have in common is that they favour the logic of big money, of contractors, investors and sponsors, over the particular, the specific and the local, not to mention common sense.

Complexity and contradiction

At the time of writing it is unknown whether the bridge's backers will get the funding they need, although they are proceeding as if they will: it may join the ranks of London's unbuilt follies, or it may come to pass. Whatever happens, the plan symbolized several good things at once, without being any of them, in which lies its significance. The proposal took to an extreme the concept of the gestural project, something that makes it look as if a city's leaders are addressing its needs and desires with ambition and daring, while creating a stage for the aggrandizement of the main players and a space for the trading of influence. It was Potemkin infrastructure, pantomime planning, costume-drama problem-solving. It was a weapon of mass distraction: the same mayor who did little to stop the *ratissage* of London's airspace with mipimist towers could cast himself as one casting flowers on the Thames, the bestower of what Lumley called 'a tiara on the head of our fabulous city'.

Such projects abuse architecture. Architecture is about complexities and contradictions, and their reconciliation and co-existence. It might start with practical matters – the serving of certain needs within constraints of budget and land area, combined with the managing of weather and gravity. An arch is architecture: it occurs when the need for a wall to stand up, which would prefer uninterrupted solidity, encounters the competing need for a window or a door, which requires an opening.

It tends to take on questions of value and significance. A room might have one set of dimensions, materials and lighting conditions that are adequate to its function, but another that give pleasure or dignity to that function, which then might take on connotations of status or social relationships. The placing and specification of a kitchen, for example, whether of porcelain and lead in the servants' quarters in a Victorian basement, or of stainless steel and marble in the middle of an open-plan apartment, embody the relative roles of those who cook and eat. So it is with a city's relationships of shared and private spaces, of commercial, domestic, cultural, educational and governmental, of new investment and inherited form, of the histories preserved and erased, of spaces for cars, bicycles, buses and pedestrians, of trees, sky and water and the people who might enjoy them.

Durability, use and appearance, to rename Vitruvius' *firmitas*, *utilitas* and *venustas*, are cultural and social. If a building is built to last, something is implied about the prosperity of its makers and their confidence in a stable or secure future. If temporary, as in a shanty town, it reveals something else. Embellishment, form and finish, or the distribution of luxury or squalor between public and private spaces, make material the intentions and social structures of the people who made them. Building elements and styles carry significances: Gothic spires, Moorish domes, Classical columns, mipimist glazing. Different methods of construction can be more or less exploitative of building workers, or engaging of their skills and knowledge.

Architecture brings with it tendencies to fantasy and aspiration, the desire to suggest futures better than the present; city buildings collectively create spaces for the imagination to inhabit. For all its apparent fixity and solidity, architecture is also subject to illusion, evanescence and perceptual change. A building can look like one thing and be another, or change its significance from one generation to the next. The hard, heavy, expensive stuff of which it is made is secondary to the spaces it forms, which in turn serve both practical uses and what the Brazilian architect Lina Bo Bardi called 'subtle substances' – air, light, nature and art – to which might be added the effects of time, atmosphere, the movements of people.

If architecture is a matter of both use and imagination, it is important whose use and whose imagination it serves; who owns its illusive and elusive qualities. Architecture is typically made by one group of people – clients, architects, builders – and remade by those who use and experience it. It is the mineral interval between the thoughts and actions that make it and the thoughts and actions that inhabit it. It is a powerful but clumsy form of communication between people who may not know each other or even live at the same time. At the end of its construction period a building is still unfinished – it is completed by the lives in and around it. Nor does it act alone: the spaces of cities are not made by single magic objects, but by several buildings acting together and by man-made fabric working with climate and nature.

If a building is too prescriptive both functionally and imaginatively, and allows you to act or think in only one way, it is a form of control, the exerting of power by its makers or users. A theme park, for example, encourages the narrowing of ways of thinking, the better to sell programmed experiences to its consumers. But there is also tyranny in neutrality, in permitting everything and nothing. Architects and others involved in making buildings cannot dissemble the fact that they are exercising power in doing so, that they are adjusting a fragment of the world in a way that will make different aspects of living more or less likely – the art is in handling the extent and limits of this power. Good architecture is not a prescription or a prediction, but a proposition and sometimes a provocation: a suggestion of future life that carries its own awareness that it will be imperfectly followed. A good proposition may be hard won and unobvious and require bloody-mindedness and struggle – we should sometimes be grateful for a demanding architect. Though how can these be told from arrogance and ego? There is no infallible way: just a series of judgements of what seems right at the time.

Take the National Theatre, completed in 1976 to the designs of Denys Lasdun on an outcrop of the south embankment of the Thames. Its elements are its location, the fact that it is a theatre with three auditoria offering different types of dramatic space, that it is publicly funded and 'National' and therefore in some way different from commercial theatre. It comes at the end of a period of

high-minded belief in the value of artistic culture, and of making it democratic, and it has the serious modernist architecture that went with this belief. The theatre concludes the making of this stretch of embankment into platforms for art and performance, a process that started with the Festival of Britain of 1951.

The first thing a child might notice about the building is its material. It is concrete, inside and out, and bears the imprint of the grain of the timber moulds in which it was formed, such that it seems to be two materials at once, like the Doric Order masonry with a memory of wood. Concrete has other protean qualities, being a fluid that hardens into something stone-like but can also hover and vault in ways that stone does not. It can be mouldable like clay and precise like steel. It can give a building, as it does at the National Theatre, the feeling of being made all of one stuff, jointlessly, in one go, a property more often found in antique temples than in everyday architecture. It denotes something out of the ordinary.

It can also lend the quality of terrain to architecture, as was Lasdun's intention. He conceived the building as a set of geological 'strata' which repeat the platform of the embankment as a series of ascending layers that carry the life of the theatre. In this way he wanted to translate the ancient open-air theatre of Epidaurus, and the way it sets drama in landscape, to a roofed building in a colder climate. The rocky concrete is softened internally by a purplish carpet that was intended to recollect the heather that sprouts around the Greek theatre.

Rather than the hills of Argolis that surround Epidaurus, the National Theatre's setting is the Thames and its buildings – the low bounce of the arches of Waterloo Bridge, the dignified stone wall-paper of the long elevation of Somerset House, on the other side of the river, and the drum and dome of St Paul's, which gains power from being seen from the elbow in the river on which the theatre stands. It means the cathedral is seen across water, elevated on a rise, against a clear sky. The theatre responds: Somerset House becomes a backdrop to the interiors, a deferred wall seen through a layer of glass; the strata multiply the horizontals of the bridge and of the embankment, and mediate the descent from one to the other. When seen from the bridge, the cathedral is put into a calculated composition with the newer building, with horizontals and verticals in balance and contrast.

At the centre of Lasdun's thinking was the idea of the 'fourth theatre', in addition to the three auditoria, made by the inhabitation by audiences and their circulation. Rather than the poky rococo of West End foyers, they are here the noblest spaces, with stairs and balconies for looking and being looked at, a place of society and expectation played out against glimpses of the river and the illuminated city. This notion of the theatre of theatre-goers goes back to the grand staircase of the Paris Opera and beyond, but here with a different mood. There is grandeur in the National Theatre but also an informality that comes from its democratizing ambitions. It was remarked when it opened that it was a place where you felt comfortable sitting on the floor.

The theatre's subtle substances include light, shadow, the night, electricity, performance, movement, anticipation and different registers of time. There is the aspiration to timelessness that comes with its Greek yearnings, the time of construction remembered in the boards' grain, the ephemera of stage sets, lighting and the daily flux of audiences. There is the enigma of the fossilized timber of which it is made: concrete might seem too factual a material for the make-believe world of theatre, and Victorian architects like Frank Matcham favoured the honest fakery – architectural greasepaint – of papier mâché and gilt, but Lasdun gives concrete an illusionary as well as physical force. For Le Corbusier and other modernists the glory of the material was to be naked in bright sunlight, but at the

Matcham's architectural greasepaint

National Theatre it takes on another existence, levitated by lighting, at night.

The National Theatre is a matter of relationships, between audience, performance and city. The building mediates them, but not neutrally. It is a vigorous presence that revels in its weight, composed according to fierce geometries inscrutable to the casual visitor. It takes from the English baroque architect Nicholas Hawksmoor – a hero of Lasdun's – a love of compression and release, brooding mass, occasional perversity, denial and welcome. A limited palette – concrete, carpet, dark hardwood, blue engineering brick, aluminium glass and stainless steel – is wielded with rigorous consistency, the better to bring out the richness of the spaces. There are hierarchies of detail, such as a change in ceiling coffering from the more to the less formal spaces, that can for years escape the notice even of experts.

Architects after Lasdun would worship transparency; their reaction to a view out to a riverscape or inwards to crowds would be to install as large a plane of glass as possible. Visitors to the theatre, indeed, sometimes question why the architecture interposes, such that the views are not 360 degree Panavision. There are places where the building gets in the way too much and it suffers from confusing circulation. But more often it intensifies. It brings resonance to the relationships. The subtle substances are more palpable for the embrace of monolithic concrete.

The B of banality

And then – splat! – the Garden Bridge would squirt into the space between the theatre and the cathedral. It is a cartoon of architecture, which converts the medium's properties into parody. It has what looks like complexity – it's a garden AND a bridge – and the illusion of function: it helps you cross the river. It has a notable form, with sprouting mushroom-like piers and serrated edges, denoting the genius of the maker. It has a striking choice of material – the copper-nickel cladding whose expense would be reduced by the support of Glencore, the international mining conglomerate who deny accusations of involvement in environmental and human rights abuses. It requires the struggle – with budget, fundraising, objectors, planning law – that is the lot of artists.

What this digital jism lacks are considered relationships to the surrounding city, to the spaces and buildings around its landings, or between its own elements. Its twin mushrooms are solipsistic sculptures indifferent to their setting, and would also shout down whatever poetry there might be in the idea of putting plants over water. There is little sense of scale – the form looks as if it could be enlarged or reduced without being significantly different – scale being a means by which relationships are formed between the spaces of a city and the people who inhabit them. It looks as if it has not downloaded fully from the computers in which it was conceived. Without such connections the design is an assertion rather than a conversation, a dance for one, the notes of a nice tune in the wrong order.

If one were to take seriously for a moment the comparisons with Michelangelo or Leonardo, it would become clear how empty they are. The Laurentian Library, the Medici tombs or the Virgin of the Rocks are reflections on humanity whose richness approaches infinity, that reward contemplation with the revelation of harmonies, resonances, turbulences and emotions. They unfold through space, imagery and technique. They engage and involve. To stand in front of a Heatherwick is not like this – let's say his B of the Bang sculpture erected for the 2002 Commonwealth Games in Manchester, the representation in bursting metal of the noise of a starter's pistol in a race. It gave, before its habit of shedding spikes caused it to be removed, a depthless buzz, a sugar-rush, instantaneity of comprehension, logo-like inanity. There was nothing to be gained from lingering in front of it.

The question, then, is why Heatherwick, beyond his undoubted skills as a designer, should, along with purveyors of 'iconic' architecture, have such a prominent role in shaping and symbolizing contemporary London. Especially as many of his projects are afflicted by glitches: his bus, for example, was renamed the Roastmaster for its habit of overheating inside. Responsibility for such flaws tends to be a complex matter involving parties other than or additional to the designer, but Heatherwick was afforded more forgiveness than many architects linked to famous malfunctions.

The answer is that these works squeeze architecture into such a narrow definition that it becomes detached from the actual complexities of making the places of a city. They promise the abolition of friction, freedom from real difficulty, and turn shared space into an amnesiac void that can be more easily exploited by sponsors and other interests. Politicians are absolved of solving problems. Look! We have hired Leonardangelo. What more could you want?

CITY OF TEN MILLION

13. Subtle Substances

'At present, people see fogs,' says Vivian in Oscar Wilde's *The Decay of Lying*, 'not because there are fogs, but because poets and painters have taught them the mysterious loveliness of such effects.'

Oscar Wilde's London

Atmosphere – fog, wind, temperature, light – is part of the space of a city, and the ability to inhabit its spaces with imagination is part of living in a city. Wilde brings both together as imaginary meteorology. Neither atmosphere nor imagination can be designed, but the hard substance of buildings creates conditions for both. A paradoxical task of architecture is to serve these elusive properties with means that are measured, solid and difficult to achieve, and as well as framing intangibles architecture grows out of them – politics,

economics, private and public desires. Buildings are physical inter-
ludes between these intangibles, the forces that precede and follow
them, but architects and other makers of buildings have to work
with the minority that can be seen and touched. As in cosmology,
there is more dark matter than matter. Architects often don't understand this; bad architecture comes from the belief that the building
is the final product.

Atmosphere and imagination are political and social. London's
government descends from the Metropolitan Board of Works, which
was prompted into being by the effect of the Great Stink on Members of Parliament. Fog can give rise both to poetry and to fear of
crime. Tall buildings provoke contests over daylight and over views
of the sky. It matters who owns the shared spaces of a city and for
whose benefit, who writes the scripts and whether there are scripts
at all. This was at the centre of the debate about the Garden Bridge:
whether the new structure would enlarge the experiences of this
part of London, or commandeer, commodify and overprogramme
what was already freely available.

Illusion and fiction are essential to the fabric of a city. The
generic type of housing in Victorian and Georgian London was the
terrace, classical in inspiration, which combined an orderly front
with a rear that was open to adaptation and modification. The interior proposed ideas of respectability and hierarchy but was also
capable of reinterpretation. It could be crowded or empty and house
people of almost any social class, cultural identity or personal moral-
ity. The front was therefore a mask, which might give some clues to
the inner life, while also concealing it behind an image of propriety.
No one can live their lives with perfect transparency or nakedness,
which makes necessary these masks, costumes or stage sets.

Fiction eases the coexistence of differences on which cities
depend. Regent's Park, for example, became both the people's park
of which Rasmussen wrote and the setting of homes of extraordi-

nary expense, a combination which could have been jarring, if it were not managed by the relative discretion of the homes and by their incorporation into their shared space of the park: the terraces become an enclosing backdrop, the villas points of interest in the landscape.

At the same time appearance can be abused. It can assist the pretence that drastic social change, such as the conversion of central London into an exclusive luxury product, is not really happening. Paternoster Square and Canary Wharf take the outward form of public space, while filleting it of some essential qualities. Heatherwick's History Wall absolves HSBC of its dark histories. The Walkie-Talkie is justified with reference to theories of composition that require the City's 'cluster' of tall buildings to be contemplated from a 'viewing platform'. These are the politics of the picturesque that includes among its ancestors the eighteenth-century creation of ideal landscapes out of agricultural expropriations. It uses the visually charming or striking to hide the socially ugly.

Marketing the Elephant

There is a difference between theatre and marketing. In theatre the makers of the illusion invite the audience to take part and interpret it in their own way. In marketing there is no such reciprocity: the aim is to deliver messages that the consumer passively receives. One could take for example the video *Elephant Creative Vision*, whose aim was to portray the redevelopment of the Heygate Estate and the Elephant and Castle shopping centre as a gift to the area's vibrant communities.

To a modern jazz soundtrack as grating as squeaking chalk, artistic hands smear multicoloured paint over images of the grey old estate. Angst-less abstract expressionism erases the homes of thousands. 'This is going to be an opportunity,' says a husky Latina voice, 'for us to create our vision as artists for Elephant and Castle and to influence policy.' Fun facts on diversity pop up:

> The largest Latin American festival in Europe begins in Elephant and Castle
>
> Elephant and Castle has the largest Sierra Leonean population outside the country itself

and worthy statements of intent:

> It should be new, greener, safe
> and a place to live and enjoy . . .
> . . . to learn, to make money, to visit or to stay
> creativity and culture can be at the heart of this regeneration
> Let's see a creative vision of the future
> It's not enough to create buildings
> Let them grow from what the community has to offer.
> Imagine public spaces where people can come together, share ideas
> . . . dip into different cultures . . .
> . . . *spaces for people to make a living.*

A mipimy voice (developers or council? it makes no difference) joins in. It has the easy confidence of one who is calling the shots:

> Regeneration is not really about buildings, it's about people. It's about changing ideas of what's possible in people's minds.
>
> What I am not looking for is a gentrification process. What we like about Elephant and Castle — what is interesting about it — is this very rich kind of cultural mix. It's this quirky quality which is very difficult to kind of put down but there are qualities about the Elephant and Castle which make it a specific part of London.

Also a south London accent, matriarchal:

> I think it would be nice if there was a young persons' space, if that space were able to be shared that could be a useful way of a social opportunity and a leisure opportunity being combined with a creative opportunity in a space and linking up with other parts of the local community that might not usually link up.

This video is a small dollop of grease in the great mechanism whereby – as we know – almost all that was already there was wiped out, to be replaced by luxury housing and a shopping mall, plus a smaller amount of affordable or social housing than was there before. The market for the new flats will mostly not be the Sierra Leonean community. The video does not acknowledge that the area's marvels of creativity and diversity grew up in the old structures now vilified and destroyed, but uses these qualities, like rustic huts in a landscape garden, to decorate appropriation. But less beautifully. It has no interest, needless to say, in voices alternative to the official narrative.

Theatre in Barking

Examples of what might be called theatre in the making of urban spaces – in the sense that they offer spaces for the imagination which their users can augment and reinterpret – can be found in the works of muf architecture/art, a practice led by the architect Liza Fior and the artist Katherine Clarke. 'The practice philosophy,' they say, 'is driven by an ambition to realize the potential pleasures that exist at the intersection between the lived and the built . . . Access is not a concession but the gorgeous norm; we create spaces that have an equivalence of experience for all who navigate them both physically and conceptually.'

Like *Elephant Creative Vision*, muf occupy the slivers of financial and physical space offered by regeneration projects to 'art', 'creativity' and 'the community', a realm in which it is all too easy for the tokenistic, the gestural, the palliative, the sop, the bribe and the downright deceptive to flourish. A large part of muf's work goes into the politics and diplomacy required to bypass these perils: on the occasions when they are hired to deliver placebo art or Potemkin participation, they fight to make something genuine. Their methods include the taking seriously of the rhetoric of regeneration: with deliberate naivety they act as if the people who write statements about inclusiveness and public art really mean it (which, sometimes, they do). They aim to establish 'constructive relationships' with all involved, treating developers, planners and community groups alike, as people whose agendas deserve both respect and challenge. Their methods include frankness. If something seems wrong to them, they will say so – their diplomacy is not of a conventional kind. Their approach requires a willingness to lose commissions when neces-sary and to earn very much less money than practices who make less significant contributions to the public spaces of London. Theirs is a difficult way to make a living.

With Barking town centre in east London, they 'worked very, very hard to create a square with a degree of mystery, with the pos-sibility for escape. It is meant as a place with many meanings and functions.' Barking has been battered and neglected and despite good transport links is considered remote, but has elements which if reassembled in a country town would make it desirable – its asso-ciations with William the Conqueror and St Erkenwald, its river, abbey ruins, theatre, market and park. The remaking of its town centre, completed in 2010, is part of a regeneration project where, as at Elephant and Castle, the local authority went into partnership with a property company, only more constructively so.

A block of flats, hotel and learning centre were built, by the architects Allford Hall Monaghan Morris, whose plan repaired the gaps, rough edges and poor connections in the existing fabric. It

Barking: ruin and arboretum

formed public spaces – a T-shape of two adjoining oblongs, in which the crossbar runs alongside the existing town hall and the upright is formed between two new blocks. A generous arcade runs down one side. As with many buildings of the early third millennium, AHMM exploit the ease with which the computerized production of cladding systems allows a range of colours to be chosen. On this project there are a lot of yellows, in somewhat clumsy reference to a lemonade factory that used to stand here.

muf worked with AHMM to shape and animate the public spaces. They ennobled the public realm by introducing some of the accoutrements of a stately home: a chequerboard floor and contemporary chandeliers made the arcade a little like a ballroom, and an arboretum was installed in the upright of the T. The crossbar became a town square, a simple open area of paving. It was made unusual with a 'folly' at one end, a faux ruin in the tradition of English landscape gardens, a wall of brick and salvaged sculptures, built by apprentices from the local bricklayers' college. muf say that the folly 'recreates a fragment of the imaginary lost past of Barking'. It also screens the ugly back of an Iceland supermarket.

Into these democratized aristocratic spaces they introduced other suggestive elements: fallen tree trunks, paved inlets in the arboretum and conventional park benches built at unusual length and curved round trees, which are simple ways both of elevating the ordinary and proposing sociability. At the junction of the bars of the T is an open stage. They encourage without prescribing ways to inhabit and reinterpret the space, to make it temporarily your own, which people do: karate on the stage, climbing the trees, reading books, having picnics, taking wedding photographs. The place is designed by muf and AHMM, but it is also made out of an unsnobbish welcoming of the accidents of its history and by the local people who (in the case of the apprentices) built it and who daily occupy it.

Some architecture in London

There are other ways to make space for the imagination and for atmosphere, and places that engage their users and inhabitants, for example:

Serpentine temporary pavilion, 2009. A thin plane of steel, with amoeba curves, propped on poles, that wrapped reflections of people and greenery into its mirrored underside. When it rained, it was enclosed by a curtain of water. Designed by the Japanese architects SANAA.

A House for Essex, 2015. You have to travel seventy miles east of London for this, to the estuary of the river Stour, as the capital had difficulty doing justice to some of the finest of its creative progeny, the architectural practice FAT. FAT disbanded in 2014, but not before they had collaborated with the artist Grayson Perry on designing a house for the Living Architecture programme, whereby people can rent for holidays or weekends exceptional works of architecture in beautiful places.

The house is decorated inside and out with imagery of the life of Julie, a fictional Essex everywoman invented by Perry. It has green-and-white glazed tiles outside, a gold roof, silver statues and big round-vaulted dormers. Inside, there are tapestries and ceramics, and thwarted axes and surprise openings in the manner of Lutyens and Soane. Its shape, ultra-symmetrical about one axis and with pitched-roof elements of ascending size, is reminiscent of a Russian stave church. It is singular and untypical in a place where singularity is common, and therefore after all typical.

It explores areas where many architects fear to go – sadness, longing, joy, perversity, ornament. You might call it kitsch, but its generosity and emotional openness make it the opposite.

Serpentine

House for Essex

Sugarhouse

Sugarhouse Studios, 2014. A temporary shared workspace built just off Stratford High Street for £80,000, created by the architecture collective Assemble. A barn/basilica shape whose timber frame was erected largely with unskilled labour. Inside, it is wooden, practical and sociable. Outside, a facade of hand-moulded concrete shingles in multiple colours. A building that wears its making on its sleeve.

Buildings can sometimes do well to offer a degree of muteness or suggestive reticence, a holding-back that allows space for other interpretations. By lowering the architectural decibels other properties can be heard and relationships made apparent. People like Georgian architecture for reasons such as this: the light on a plane tree in leaf could sometimes be more beautiful for the plainness of the buildings around it. A mist might be better sensed when measured by a fading rhythm of windows, a shadow when cast by a simple shape, or reflected light when captured by a white soffit. Plain buildings can manifest their own making – their lintels and arches, the parts that are structural or decorative – and subsequent weathering, repaintings and revisions. They become registers of time and of the continuous human actions that make a city. Too much reticence can get boring, but it's not a bad way to make much of a city's substance.

Makers of plain buildings include those for whom it is a considered intellectual or conceptual approach, sometimes called The Whisperers because of the low, earnest tones in which they like to speak. An early example is the Lisson Gallery of 1992 by Tony Fretton, in what was then a scruffy part of Paddington. It whispered in fact less than most, being white, plain and rectangular in a time when many architects were twiddling with references to the past. It stood out. But it works through relationships rather than rhetoric: a gallery space is set a few feet below pavement level, meaning that the wall

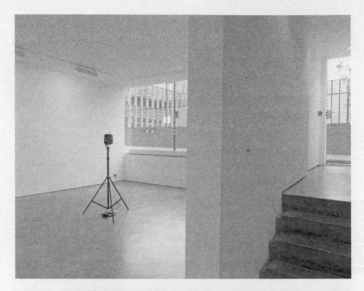

up to this point is solid, but from there to the ceiling it is all glass, which creates a connection between the street and the art that is direct but complex. From the street you get an unexpected revelation of a different world. In the gallery you feel that you are in a dug-out space, both vulnerable and protected: the outside world might then be viewed with an altered perception, having been raised by the change in level to the sort of height in relation to the eye at which one is used to viewing works of art. As is usual among Whisperers, there is an accepting attitude to the already-there, in this case the street and a school playground on its far side, with a chain-link fence. The glass plane extends over the first floor, above which is a band of solid wall, punctuated by a matter-of-fact square opening. Heavy is placed on light, solid on void, in a deadpan reversal of expectations.

There are also those for whom plain building is a pragmatic option, a sensible way of getting a construction up without upsetting too many people. There are shades in between. By the second decade of the new century Whispering – or at least a certain restraint – was being adopted not only for thoughtful galleries and private houses, but also for office blocks, towers and entire new residential areas in ex-industrial sites. Becoming mainstream, it interpreted the pioneers' intentions with varying degrees of faithfulness or flimsiness. Practitioners included the quietly but hugely successful Allies and Morrison, and Lifschutz Davidson Sandilands, with their good student housing near the architecturally less-good libeskindian hotel in City Road. Developers like Berkeley Homes picked it up, to make blocks of flats which, if lacking the resonances of the Lisson Gallery, at least make a background for the life of a city.

With commercial buildings the architect Eric Parry developed regularity as a way of combining his clients' desire for prestige with the civic role of urban architecture. With 5 Aldermanbury Square, an eighteen-storey office block in the City that was completed in 2007,

a right-angled order is created within which scales of scale, modulations of rhythm and surreptitious sensuality are allowed to happen. A curving entasis, like that of a classical column, becomes apparent towards the top. If the proportions are roughly classical the material – stainless steel – is post-industrial. The building fronts a simple square that is one of the more convincing 'public spaces' in Peter Rees's City of London, and a triple-height through-route, given nobility by the pillars bearing the mass above, runs under the bulk of the building. It is separated from an atrium of equal height by a glass wall, which allows both passers-by and visitors to the offices to share a space, within which are layers of different degrees of publicness. Materials run from the shine of the stainless steel, to a reflective soffit over the through-route, to running water, to board-marked concrete of a ruggedness that is both precise and fetishistic.

This is a building with little desire to challenge the status quo, but to make the most of it. Which, often, is a role architecture plays: it serves the power and money that created it and cannot without hypocrisy pretend otherwise, but can work on, negotiate and expand the interactions with the people who use and experience it. At times architecture's role is to be a fall-guy, to propose an official orderliness which can then be subverted and challenged through use. Parry's steel rectangles and muf's fallen tree trunks have this much in common – they share the understanding that buildings do not make cities by themselves, but are propositions and settings for lives that cannot be predicted and without which they are not complete.

In all this work, whether by Parry, Fretton, muf, SANAA or FAT, there is an essential quality, one with the power to liberate from the tyrannies of oversimplification, monomania, literalism. It gives room to those qualities and possibilities that exist between verbal or numerical descriptions. By its nature, however, it tends to recede from attention and so needs to be given special emphasis. It is called

NUA

NCE.

The substance of knowledge

Knowledge is a subtle substance, and a city can be read through the spaces in which information or learning is offered and withheld.

In the case of London one could start such a reading with Dippy the diplodocus, whose Jurassic-Gothic skeleton was placed at the centre of an eddy of stone striations and bony structures which, expanding into the iron-ribbed vault of a central hall and multiplying into subsidiary galleries, finally rectangularizes into the fossil-hard citadel, terracotta-clad to resist the filthy Victorian air, that is the Natural History Museum, set within a moat of living green nature on the north side of Cromwell Road, South Kensington.

The museum was created by a coalition of science and imperium not unlike that which made the zoo. Its architecture (1873–81, by Alfred Waterhouse) is associative: its style is a version of Romanesque, approximately French, for reasons that are not obvious but might include the thought that, relative to later Gothic and the Renaissance styles, it is dinosaurian – an illusory parallel of art history and natural history. It imparts a sense of unusual age. The exterior decoration is layered in a way which, to interpret too far, reminds of a passage in *The Voyage of the Beagle* where the author sees the geological strata of Chilean cliffs, heaved up out of the water, and reflects that the world cannot be as young as the Bible says it is. About the main entrance are patterned colonettes, pedantically variegated such that they resemble specimens of geology or biology. Or else there are different explanations for the above, such as sheer random taste: it is just that the architecture is so purposeful, in parallel with the equally directed science, that it's tempting to speculate about connections.

The entrance is flanked with cathedral-like towers, for the avoidance of doubt that this is an important place. At the same time you are welcomed in, across the moat and through the portal, and

invited to explore. There is stiff charm in the polychrome building. This is the Victorian way of enlightening the public: having established the great significance of wisdom, to permit a respectful approach.

The 1990s way, Lottery funded, was more about access at all costs, inclusivity, the elimination of barriers that might be felt elitist, the sugaring of learning with fun, or rather 'fun'. There was a word for it, edutainment. This attitude gave the Natural History Museum a premonition of the disastrous Millennium Dome, in which the former Geological Museum, an annexe considered fusty and boring, was renamed the 'Earth Galleries' and converted into a grinding, screeching theme-park experience. Here you enter past another dinosaur, a stegosaurus, somewhat randomly but never mind, as dinosaurs sell. A long escalator penetrates an abstracted metal sphere and gets you to an ADHD clatter of plasticized display panels, cramped and churning with Hi-Viz school parties, splattered with facts aimed at attention spans of five seco . . . It was thought amusing to recreate a convenience store hit by the 1995 Kobe earthquake, its seismic patterns reproduced, with the actual CCTV tape from an actual store showing. Perhaps this ride teaches something, but there is little pause to reflect on the 6,400 people who died in Kobe. If the catastrophe had been nearer home, in Manchester say, you feel there would have been more respect.

Pause for reflection on anything, indeed, is what the Earth Galleries annihilate. As in London Zoo's BUGS, wonder is suffocated. Space is flattened. Materials are numbed. You are taken on a prescribed route that gives little chance to wander and discover. So much of the display is of pasted-up and glued-together nondescript stuff, that when you see a real exhibit you're not sure that it is. The Earth Galleries use what were then new developments of digitized colour printing; now that the World Wide Web is so much better at providing layers of information, they look dated.

Things improve on a floor with magnificent specimens of rare stones – pyrargyrite, argentiferous galena, skutterudite, vanadinite, carrollite, chalcedony, riband jasper – where, although the display has notes of duty-free jewellers, the presentation is at least straightforward. The experience declines again on the other side of the Waterhouse building, where the museum suffered another dose of Lottery clap, the Darwin Centre, where the architects put into practice just what the great man didn't say. The building's form is a giant cocoon, which is then placed inside a glass box, resulting in bizarre profligacy of space and material and a tortuous circulation (down steps, up lift, across bridge, down ramps, across bridge, down lift . . .) around nugatory displays which, along with the ramps, are not helped by having to contend with the curved walls of the cocoon. There are views of real live scientists at work, which don't in fact reveal very much (they sometimes wear white coats, they use computers, some are men and some are women, most of them have hair). Darwin, of course, talked about the way natural organisms adapt to their environments. A cocoon has its uses as something light, strong, small, temporary and economic. This is why in nature you don't find cocoons several storeys high and made of reinforced concrete.

Neither the Earth Galleries nor the Darwin Centre is designed to achieve the most efficient use of space. Both have spare volumes, overhead, around their circulation systems or occupied by non-essential installations. Nor did Waterhouse have these concerns when he enclosed the ample air in which Dippy would later stand by the glazed vault of the church-like entrance hall. Both reflect the fact that the non-functional void is a feature taken for granted in public places. The roles that it plays, when the commercial values of square feet are both high and minutely measured, are a crucial part of the exchanges between citizens – which term should in London include both residents and visitors – and their city.

About fifteen minutes' walk from the Natural History Museum is Bousfield Primary School, completed in 1956 to the designs of Chamberlain Powell and Bon, the architects of the Golden Lane housing estate and the Barbican. It is in The Boltons, an area soaked in wealth the way tar sands are with oil. The school is nonchalant in its use of land area, a low building in ample grounds, not bothered that the real estate it occupies might have a notional value of tens or possibly hundreds of millions of pounds. Like the museum, it stands alone in a moat of green.

Unlike the museum, the approach is informal and the building light. It is a glass pavilion which, like Japanese architecture, looks less substantial than the nature, here large plane trees, around it. It is animated by panels in shades of blue and yellow, with some green, which the architects hoped would teach the principles of colour mixing. From the street to its inner courtyards it is experienced as a series of layers of building and garden; the boundary was dissolved into planters, a pond and pieces of wall, and the glass allowed transparencies through indoors and outdoors. Child-high opening windows create connections between classrooms and green space.

Its lightness is anchored to mass, like a balloon tied to a brick. In one corner of the site concrete terraces descend into the ground: this is an outdoor theatre formed out of a reservoir made in the hole left by a Second World War bomb. In a moment of light relief a high yellow lollipop stands in the playground, the 'watersphere' that once held the school's reserve of water. The layers are therefore vertical as well as lateral, from the bottom of the bomb-theatre to the top of the sphere. The school itself, placed in the middle of these x- and y-axes looks fragile. It lives on trust.

John Stamp, the school's site manager, likes best the hardwood shoe shelves and stair balustrades, and the hardwearing floor

surfaces, still doing their job as well as when first installed. He is less keen on the way in which the single-glazed walls, installed in more spartan times, fail to keep out the cold; as is common in these architects' works, there are also eccentricities of level changes and circulation. Stamp describes how changing attitudes to risk have affected the building: railings have been installed to stop passers-by, potentially well-lawyered, from falling into the pond; the theatre was closed when the steps of its terraces were thought too high and reopened when new philosophies recognized that it's good for children to grow up with some degree of danger, so they can learn what it is. The theatre, unfortunately, isn't used as such, as the surroundings generate too much noise and its rake is acoustically un-ideal.

The school's design, which shows learnings from Mies van der Rohe and the Bauhaus, is high-minded, based on the belief that places of education deserve seriousness, but it also unbends towards the scale and thoughts of children. It uses its generosities of space to create an enriching and enrichable domain, a place that can be explored, inhabited and reinterpreted through use, with 'lots of nature and places to go outside', as one child put it. They also permit it to be sheltering, intimate and open at once. The school extends far enough to be a special and distinct place, but because its boundaries are softened it feels part of its surroundings.

These qualities can be hard to find in the creations of the school-building boom that took place under Tony Blair's government, when the emphasis was on conditioning children for a life of office work, by putting them in places with quasi-corporate atria. Many of them were built under the Private Finance Initiative, which hands design and management to large contracting companies, who would have given short shrift to the niceties of Bousfield.

Nor do the Earth Galleries use volume in the Bousfield way, but as something emptily impressive up which the escalator pipes disengaged crowds; nor does the Darwin Centre, where it is occupied by architectural rhetoric, coercive patterns of circulation and sheer waste. In Waterhouse, spare space is part of the dignity of the institution and its contents, but it is made approachable through gradations of decoration and scale and by the ways in which you are invited to move through it. The stairs at the far end of the entrance hall, for example, grow out of the architecture in such a way that, if you put your foot on the bottom step and your hand on the balustrade, you feel like a part of it.

Other spaces of knowledge include:

British Library, 1996. Slow to build and attacked by an idiot critic who would never visit it as an 'academy for secret police'. Actually a gracious and uplifting interior by the architect Colin St John Wilson, contemplative where it needs to be, which breathes respect for knowledge while encouraging inhabitation by its users. Its finishes – a curved Purbeck marble counter in the cloakroom, brass handrails wrapped in leather, stone and good brick throughout – belong to a remote age of quality in public buildings.

Board Schools. One of the great public inventions, out of almost nothing, by which London has progressed; the response to the sudden need, created by the introduction of universal education in 1870, for hundreds of new schools. In the designs of E. R. Robson, chief architect to the School Board of London, and his colleagues, standardized details and elements – brick, lofty windows, gables, white paint and sometimes terracotta – can be adapted to different sites, sizes and needs. Diversity within repetition. Airy. Dignified but approachable. Beacons of quality and equality whatever the wealth or status of the areas in which they were built. In passing, a demonstration of the freedoms and uniformities of the London Building Acts.

British Library and Board school

Bexley and Saw Swee Hock

Bexley Business Academy, 2003. According to its architects, Foster and Partners, it 'applied the philosophy of the practice's office buildings, which pioneered the humanization of the workplace in the early 1970s, to the design of a business academy that would engender a sense of community and institutional pride'. According to 'Why Architects Need to Use Their Ears', a TED talk by the sound consultant Julian Treasure, 'designed like a corporate headquarters with a vast central atrium and classrooms leading off it with no back walls at all. The children couldn't hear their teachers. They had to go back in and spend £600,000 putting the walls in. Let's stop this madness of open plan classrooms right now please.'

Saw Swee Hock Student Centre, London School of Economics, 2013. Local and global. It translates the crooked streets occupied by a famous academic institution into a vertical sequence of social spaces within a crooked brick building. At the same time it gives an identity to the LSE's diffuse and anonymous presence, which helps in the global competition with the likes of Harvard for the best students. The architects O'Donnell + Tuomey have fun with different properties of brick: perforated, sharp-edged, massive, floating. Assisted by a donation from the alumnus after whom it is named.

Digital and physical

There is also virtual space. If you head west down Cromwell Road, past the Natural History Museum, on until the route becomes the Great West Road, then the M4 motorway and on past Heathrow airport you can eventually reach London's Kuiper belt, where you might find the scattered planetoids that house high-tech businesses and data centres. It would not, however, be a rewarding journey. They are mute objects, inaccessible as Beckton sewage works, landscaped to deflect interest, which tell you only that their contents are to be accessed virtually, and that there is little to be gained or learned from contemplating the machines inside the sheds. At most you might realize, if you hadn't already, that this way of holding knowledge is specialized and complex, expensive and protected. You don't gain access by addressing the buildings, but through the familiar costs and protocols required by phones, tablets and computers.

It is commonplace that knowledge, or communication, or entertainment, can be divorced from physical space. You can carry in your hand a library, a cinema, a department store, a party or a post office. The internet of things further dissolves the physical shells of human actions: Airbnb makes diffuse hotels which cannot be identified by individual buildings or signs; Uber makes a cloud of vehicles that materialize when called upon. These phenomena are not absolutely different from the bygone practices of phoning up minicabs, or looking up rooms in printed directories, but they are smoother to a degree that makes them into a different species. They tend to make the forms of the city into a carapace, whose inner structures have been liquefied. Pipeless currents of choices and connections flow through and around, ideally frictionless, all the while siphoning the tithes that make tech companies' business plans prosper.

The consequences for built space are inconsistent. On the one hand cinemas and museums are in theory threatened by their digital rivals and a certain negligence towards public places arises, if people can always live in the bubble of light around their succulent devices. London's phone boxes, rotting like dead trees, are evidence of the callousness of new technology to structures that can't keep up. On the other hand, the same devices can enrich the same spaces through their multiple connections with other planes, through the ways that they enable their users to be in several places at once.

They help people to navigate and explore the city. It is also a true truism that the digital creates a new appetite for the physical, for being there and not somewhere else: bands have to earn their living from concerts, not recordings, and art galleries, bars, spas, clubs and public events are valued for giving the experiences that screens can't. The digital has not killed the city – in some ways has intensified it – but it changes relationships. It makes the match of form and content, never perfect, looser: a concert hall or library can exist in a building designated as such, but also – with obvious changes to the nature of the experience – on a pavement or in a cafe. It tends to polarize the physical into those parts that become more degraded and those more special – sought out as relief from the empires of the bytes.

The digital world goes to extremes of transparency and opacity – even as everything is apparently available, the technology is incomprehensible to almost everyone, and the workings of the giant companies are as secret as can be. Google, Apple and Facebook want you to share everything, except their own patents and plans; wandering through the groves of the internet, you bang your nose against the undeclared and unstormable citadels of information and power. These extremes are translated into the physical environment in different ways. The Garden Bridge is a project of the digital age to the extent that its hyper-realistic computerized images seem to tell you everything you want to know about the project at the same time that they conceal significant aspects of its impact. You can also experience the contemporary city as an internet-like flow of accessible space interrupted by zones of security or exclusivity, the epitome being the glass door of a bank or the glass gates with which the 'public spaces' of new developments are made not-public. In this community of silicates – semi-conductors and glass – the ambiguous chemical element on which modern civilization depends allows your sight to pass through, but not your body.

The implication for architecture is that it might provide the qualities that digitalia don't; and to offer relationships and degrees of access that are not all-or-nothing. One such island of the there is ORTUS, in Camberwell, south London, which opened in 2013. It is a facility of the Maudsley Charity, which is the charitable arm of the South London and Maudsley NHS Foundation Trust (SLaM), who say they are 'proud to provide the widest range of mental health services in the UK'. It is also, in the ways in which it complements rather than mimics contemporary technology, a true building of the digital age.

Kumar Jacob, chair of the Maudsley Charity Committee and a driving force behind ORTUS, says that 'it is a place where everybody goes to learn', by which he means doctors, academics, patients, delegates, casual visitors, lunchers in its cafe, parents before and after the school run, all of whom occupy the building. The hope was that 'you learn from talking to other people', through informal meetings on its stairs and in-between spaces, 'not just in the classrooms'. Different types of professional, isolated in their silos, might engage with each other. Patients would 'love the fact that they are not treated differently from anyone else'.

ORTUS consists of a number of rooms for meetings and conferences, all well equipped with presentation technologies, which can be booked in different combinations for different purposes. Some of these events might be training courses or conferences relating to issues of mental health, some might be about something else altogether, such as film or music nights, mindfulness sessions, community events and corporate hires, where the objective is to earn money for the charity. The building is open to anyone, apart from reasonable restrictions on the meeting rooms.

Its spaces could have been anything. The soul of the flipchart might, as it often does, have seeped into the suspended ceilings and the carpet tiles, the venetian blinds and the extractor vents.

The lobby of a conference hotel might have been taken as a role model. Instead, ORTUS is a resonant work – whispering, but muscular with it – by the architects Duggan Morris. It allows itself to be liberated by the fact that, once the technical requirements have been dealt with, the brief is pure: it is to make places for people to speak to each other, as they might once have done in a garden outside Athens, or on a hill in Palestine. With due adjustment for logistics and climate, the task is to make simple rooms to serve these actions, and the stairs and spaces that connect them. The lightness of Wi-Fi, tablets and laptops aids the simplicity of the space, allowing as they do the ability to roam and access information anywhere. Here the digital and the physical are complicit with each other.

The building is an approximate cube that stands in the grounds of the Maudsley Hospital. It expresses its structure externally, a concrete frame with vertical, faintly Georgian proportions that have some relation to a terrace of houses across the street, with infill of brick or glass. Verticals and horizontals, and major and minor elements, are tuned. The rhythm is regular, except for a jigger in the elevation which reflects the internal arrangement, whereby the floors of the southern half of the building are set a half-level different from those of the northern. The cube is set on sloping ground, of which the jigger is an architectural echo.

The architecture does not advertise the fact that it is open to all. You have to find your way in, a pleasant walk up the slope and round a corner, past a sliver of meadow planted with yarrow, betony, vetch and other indigenous species. Inside, the role of the shifts in levels becomes clear: it encourages an upward flow, from half-level to half-level, and a relationship between different parts of the building which would be harder if they were separated by quanta of a storey at a time. At ground level the cafe area rises up in a series of theatrical terraces, running counter to the slope outside, to create

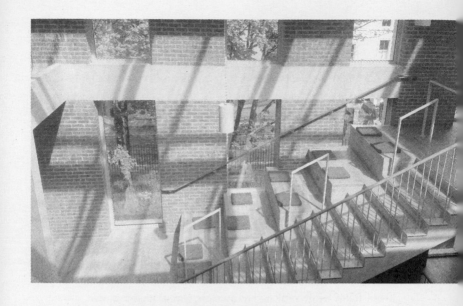

an open-ended space for events, meeting, or passing the time, an indoor agora. Above it rises the generous open stairwell, with further pauses for thinking and talking, that connects with all the other parts of the building. It ascends to a rooftop from where the global skyline of London can be surveyed.

The interior resembles the outside: more brick and concrete, but with added timber. This is something architects like, the feeling that a building is made of a unified substance throughout, inside and out, like a ruined temple, but here achieved with sleight of hand. The requirements of thermal insulation mean that the enclosure comprises separate inner and outer skins, joined to look like one, although if you are paying attention you will pick up the fact that the inner concrete is of a different type from the outer, being cast on site rather than off. The masonry also makes the interior feel like an outdoor urban space that happens to have a roof, an internalized street, and it forms a foil for the sunlight that rakes across it.

ORTUS is not quite perfect – it accommodates displays of patients' artwork in frigid glass cases, and the lifts for wheelchair users feel set apart from the joys of the split-level circulation – but it is a beautiful way to wield the physical in a digital time, and to share knowledge in ways that are neither technocratic nor excluding. It confounds some clichés of contemporary architecture: that flow has to be achieved by dynamic forms and transparency by expanses of glass. ORTUS is right-angled and often opaque and reveals itself by degrees, but its spaces are both fluid and permeable.

Dippy vs Wally

Having been comfortable with several degrees of bogusness in the Earth Galleries and the Darwin Centre, the Natural History Museum decided to come over strict and pedantic over Dippy's authenticity.

For he is not a diplodocus, nor a skeleton of one, nor a fossil of a skeleton of one, but a plaster cast of a fossil of a skeleton of a diplodocus, donated by the American Industrialist Andrew Carnegie in 1905. In this sense he is not 'real'. Which in 2015 was cited as a reason for his removal, to be replaced by the real skeleton of a real blue whale, to be hung from the ceiling. 'It's just a copy', said the museum's director, Michael Dixon, and

> what makes this museum special is that we have real objects from the natural world – over 80 million of them – and they enable our scientists and thousands like them from around the world to do real research . . . Going forward we want to tell more of these stories about the societally relevant research that we do.

It was speculated that an additional attraction of the change would be to free up floor space, of which Dippy occupied quite a lot, so that more money could be made by holding bigger corporate functions. Be that as it may, the announcement provoked a reaction. There was a #savedippy campaign. 'When I was little,' went a tweet that spoke for many, 'it was the dinosaurs at the Nat Hist Museum that got us heading to London on the train, not some sodding whale.'

Swirling round here are questions of fact and theatre. It is not a bad thing in itself to put up a whale – let's call him Wally – who in time might embed himself in the affections and memories of future generations, but the museum seems to be missing important points. If you want to imprint on young minds concepts such as extinction, evolution and the depth of biological time, not to mention sheer wonder that such creatures could have existed and then disappeared, there is no better way than with the skeleton of a large dinosaur. 'It's about asking real questions of contemporary relevance,' said Dixon, but what could be more important than these issues? They matter more than a 3-D mission statement about the museum's activities, important though they are, which is what he seems to want from the whale.

The skeleton is not 'just a copy'. Its molecular composition – that it is Edwardian plaster rather than an actual fossil – is secondary. In fact it adds something, in that it tells you something not only about dinosaurs but also about the modern fascination and investigations that they have inspired. The object is embedded, too, in the personal histories of the millions who have seen it, and there would be value in its staying put, such that children could find that their parents and grandparents had been as moved as they are moved by the diplodocus. It would be a way of situating yourself in time, which is part of the role of a museum.

Dippy is also situated in space, by virtue of the echoes between his bones and Waterhouse's structures. That these likenesses are coincidences, unintended by the architect, does not matter; they are happy ones. Exhibits and architecture resonate in a way that the escalator of the Earth Galleries and its enclosure do not; resonance means that the differences between things are not blunt dislocated contrasts, but exist in layers of connection, affinity and distinction, within which visitors might find their own places. The likenesses help create a situation made up of space and time that can be shared across generations and nationalities. Here the already-there, accidents included, enriches. It belongs to the great republic of visitors over time, who, if a piece of their shared memory is thoughtlessly replaced, are subtly disenfranchised.

The choice of bones in a museum entrance may not seem like the most important issue facing a city with large and obvious problems of (for example) housing. But decisions like this are emblematic and, cumulatively, they change the ways in which a city is inhabited. It is a question of ownership of its subtle substances. When its imaginative spaces are too much scripted, targeted, harvested and appropriated, its citizens become disengaged by degrees. Slivers of availability and openness are lost. The freedom for people to make up their own minds and find their own place in the city is diminished. If museums cannot protect such qualities at a time when they are assaulted in less privileged zones, the city is in trouble.

14. You Burned Your Own Town

A green rectangle in north London late in 2011, enclosed by functional stands, mostly built before the time that satellite television doused English football with wealth. The white shirts of Tottenham Hotspur are warming up, among them the hard-tackling Brazilian Sandro, number 30, known as The Beast. In blue are Chelsea, owned by the oligarch Roman Abramovich, the sporting embodiment of London's welcome to foreign money from whatever source. The two teams are multinational crews, assembled by the operations of the player transfer market, of a kind that has become standard: they come from the United States, France, Croatia, the Netherlands, Togo, Ivory Coast, Cameroon, the Czech Republic, Serbia, Portugal, Nigeria, Brazil, Wales and England.

From the away supporters surges a familiar drone, the notes, if they can be so called, of football's most adaptable chant. It could accompany 'Luis Suarez, your teeth are offside', or 'Ryan Giggs, he shags who he wants' or, with some fiddling with the metre, 'Manchester's a shit-hole, we want to go home.'

'You burned your own town, you burned your own town', it goes, 'you stupid bastards, you burned your own town.'

The home fans direct their responses at the England and Chelsea captain, charged the previous day by the Crown Prosecution Service with using racist language ('you fucking black cunt', it was alleged). 'John Terry, you know what you are,' they sing. And to a different tune: 'John Terry, your mum's a thief', a reference to his family's police cautions for shoplifting. The effect is to make him play well in what ends up as a 1–1 draw. It also fails to obscure the painful truth of the Chelsea fans' taunt.

In August that year about 200 people had gathered outside the police station in Tottenham High Road to protest about the fatal shooting of a twenty-nine-year-old local man called Mark Duggan. The crowd was peaceful until, at about 8.30 p.m., a sixteen-year-old girl threw – oddly enough – a champagne bottle, which provoked a police response thought excessive by some, which escalated into the throwing of missiles and then, within a few hours, to the burning of buildings, cars and businesses up and down the High Road, the looting of shops and attacks on the TV crews which arrived to film the riots. Aldi was ransacked, and Carpetright, the latter housed in an art deco landmark. The stone torch of its tower became an emblem of the riots; its charred steel frame, sagging like on old bed, of its aftermath.

Violence expanded in the early hours of the morning into the nearby Tottenham Hale retail park. Boots the Chemist, JD Sports, O_2, Currys, Argos, Orange, PC World and Comet were among the brands pillaged by the hordes. As if in a Black Friday painted by John Martin, a trolley dash through Gomorrah, looters carried TVs and sound systems, phones, trainers and food around the burning streets. 'The make-up of the rioters was racially mixed', said one report, 'but families and other local residents representative of the area – black, Asian and white, including some from Tottenham's Hasidic Jewish community – also gathered to watch and jeer at police.'

It was important to remember, as the local MP David Lammy later said, that 'while 600 people burned shops and homes and looted, 99 per cent of Tottenham's young people were terrified in their homes'. One was the teenager Zehra Harrison: 'I was home alone with my cousins,' she recalled in 2015, 'and suddenly there were waves and waves of sirens. There were helicopters. The phone networks shut down. It was really scary. And then waves and waves of people came down the road. Afterwards everywhere was a tip, smashed up.'

The troubles spread to nearby Wood Green and to other parts of London. Croydon, on the opposite side of the city, south to Tottenham's north, was one of the worst hit. Over the next few days they reached other English cities. Five people died across the country, several were injured; there were thousands of arrests and hundreds of millions of pounds' worth of damage.

As usual with such events, there were explanations and agonizing about the sort of country where such things could happen. On the one hand deprivation and police aggression were blamed, on the other the greed and viciousness of the rioters. The role of BlackBerry Messenger in spreading news and inspiring copycats was dissected. The consumerist aspect of the looting was noted, the riots being seen as a retail experience with menaces. For some this revealed a society where shopping had become the only form of enfranchisement, such that people who could not afford it took part by force.

A participant in one of the follow-up riots, in Hackney, saw it as an expression of rage against multiple corruptions, later saying:

> I heard the furious voices of kids on our burning streets: angry about the phone-hacking scandal; angry about the MPs' expenses scandal; angry about the bank bailouts; angry about police corruption and the abuse of stop-and-search powers. This was no party. And for most, it wasn't about consumerism either – I saw a girl steal a pint of milk for her mum because she said her family were too poor to buy food.

For the historian David Starkey,

> the whites have become black. A particular sort of destructive nihilistic gangster culture has become the fashion, and black and

white, boy and girl, operate in this language together. This language which is wholly false, which is a Jamaican patois that's been intruded in England and this is why so many of us have this sense of literally a foreign country.

It was a conclusion with a remarkable absence, for a historian, of historical evidence. Its implication that English whites were incapable of mass violence without black influence ignores (for example) football hooliganism in the 1980s, the Hyde Park riots of 1855 or the Gordon Riots of 1780.

There was particular anxiety because the following year London was due to host the Olympic Games, in a location not far from Tottenham. The bid had been won with the help of proud celebrations of London's diversity and of its successful inclusion of minorities. The riots were the Games' evil twin, a festival attracting the attention of the world's media, the Carpetright tower its unofficial Olympic flame, revealing a side of the city that the London 2012 boosters didn't want to talk about.

The consensus was that, while violence could not be condoned, the riots had revealed real problems in the social structures of British cities. As is also common after such events, it was decided that something must be done, especially in Tottenham, and the machinery of regeneration began to be assembled. The developer Stuart Lipton was put in charge of an independent panel of advisers, who produced a report. Council leaders made their obeisances to MIPIM, with some assistance from companies behind local developments. Pots of money were successfully applied for from London and national government. Aspirations were stated: that by 2025 'Tottenham will have more than 10,000 new high-quality homes and 5,000 new jobs, with almost a million square feet of employment and commercial space added'; that the area can be 'London's next contemporary suburb'; that it 'has the potential to be London's next big

The Carpetright phoenix: in 2011 and 2015

growth opportunity'. The scale of transformation would be 'equivalent to a new town'.

The issues to be addressed included what Claire Kober, the leader of the local council, called 'really ingrained structural problems' and 'structural economic decline since the 1970s'. Once a successful industrial area that made gas pipelines, pencils and large quantities of furniture, it had lost tens of thousands of jobs. Unemployment and deprivation were among the highest in London. There was overcrowded housing and gang warfare. The shops of Tottenham High Road had never recovered from the blow they received in the 1970s, when Wood Green Shopping City opened two miles to the west.

It is also a place with distinctive characteristics. It is diverse: 200 or 300 languages, depending on whom you ask, are spoken in Tottenham. It has a lively and well-attended range of religious offerings: International Ministries for the Living Word, the Calvary Church of God in Christ, the New Life Holy Ghost Ministries (London Miracle Centre), the Fresh Anointing Christian Centre, the Rainbow Church, the Global Light Revival Church. Despite its industrial decline, people still make things there – luxury shoes, self-cleaning coatings for glass, bread, pitta bread, the casings that allow tablet computers to be displayed in public places. It has history – the long straight High Road follows the line of Roman Ermine Street, which ran from London to York; there are a Tudor manor, handsome Georgian houses, Gothic and neo-Gothic churches and Victorian terraces. It has nature and open space, around the marshes and reservoirs on its eastern edge.

It has football, in the form of Tottenham Hotspur, the sixth richest and often, thanks to the sport's close link between resources and success, the fifth or sixth best club in the English Premier League. As this is the most watched national league on the world's televisions, and as Spurs had a knack of attracting both dazzling

individual players and newsworthy disasters and near-triumphs, the name of Tottenham has a global reach ever more loosely connected to the place it historically identified. From 2013 the sponsors of the club's shirts were AIA, the Hong Kong-based insurance company who don't do much business in Britain, but who benefit from their presence on Spurs players seen on screens in the Asia Pacific region.

By 2015 the achievements of the post-riot regeneration drive were mixed. Some lumpy blocks of flats had gone up, with the promise of more and better-designed homes in what Boris Johnson calls 'housing zones'. A nasty traffic gyratory system had been tamed and the open space of Tottenham Green, once the symbolic centre of the area, had been refurbished. The Carpetright Tower went up again. The football club had built a new supermarket and a university technical college and demolished chunks of the High Road, as preliminaries to a planned new stadium with 56,250 seats. There were plans for a zone branded as 'High Road West', where council housing and an industrial estate would be replaced by new, better, more numerous homes and by a 'world class public realm' which would connect the new stadium to the refurbished White Hart Lane railway station. There was 'pulling together' and 'cross-party consensus' between the different institutions.

The drawback was that there didn't seem to be enough respect in all this for the place that Tottenham already was. The developers, Grainger, were given permission to erase a block that contained a lively indoor market and a distinctive South American restaurant, the Pueblito Paisa cafe, and replace it with a development aimed, to judge by the computer visualizations, at attracting Pizza Express. The council say it will be a 'gateway' to a new kind of Tottenham. The council also stated their view that there were too many small shops on the High Road, even though each represents lives and livelihoods for someone.

The proposed Spurs stadium, silvery, scaly, bulbous and vast, looked like something from another galaxy (at least until the summer of 2015, when replaced by a still larger but slightly less extraterrestrial design). In the aftermath of the riots the football club stated that they would rather not pay the £16.4m agreed as their contribution to such improvements as upgrading local railway stations, but instead £500,000. The council, desperate for signs of progress, assented. The proposed 'world class public realm' was a zone of generic paving and street furniture that required the obliteration of existing shops. It looked like a device for getting high-paying Spurs customers to and from games with minimal contact with anything too much like Tottenham, that would suck their spending into the premium outlets lining the route rather than local businesses. It would be a perfect diagram of the gap between the global brand of the football club and the locality whose name it carries.

In all the regeneration talk, little love was expressed for the industries that were still an essential part of Tottenham's economy. The stadium required the relocation of seventy-two businesses and High Road West many more. The 'Physical Development Framework' produced by the planning and design consultants Arup doesn't talk about industry, and local politicians tend not to mention it. The usage of 'world class', ubiquitous in regeneration-speak, doesn't mean 'very good' so much as 'could be anywhere' and 'nothing much to do with Tottenham'. It describes types of space with which investors feel comfortable, because they've seen it before in the Gulf, in China or in North America. It excludes the genuinely global, such as the Pueblito Paisa cafe.

Mark Brearley and Jane Clossick of Cass Cities at the London Metropolitan University, who are studying Tottenham, say that 'this is an ideal place. It's fantastic. It's got massive problems, but the urban structure is organized in a really good way. If you're looking for the big urban idea for our century – here it is in Tottenham.' Too much of the proposed change, they say, is based on a 'misunderstanding' of what's there already.

What Brearley and Clossick like are the relationships of the front parts of buildings to their backs and of upper to lower floors, a 'depth of structure' in blocks facing the High Road that allows them to house in different parts shops, small offices and other businesses: 'painters, upholsterers, that sort of thing; community-serving uses such as churches, church halls, schools; billiard halls, local solicitors, studios, banqueting, libraries'. This is what Brearley calls a 'normal structure that makes sense and works well.' It encourages an 'entrepreneurial culture' where people can 'start trying things, start making things, start repairing things'. It allows interfaces between businesses and the public and between each other. It makes work visible: 'it's a good thing when people see a lot of aspects of the economy, when kids grow up seeing how things work'. But, he says, 'our society is still very hooked on disaggregation'. And the tendency is to strip out and erase the complexity of such places.

When the Chelsea fans sang of burning your own town, they could have been describing the whole of London. For, in the second decade of the twenty-first century, the city appeared to be consuming itself. This was a function of land values: when large profits are to be made from converting anything – factories, air space, the clay beneath existing terraces, school playgrounds, shops, pubs, office blocks, social housing, open space, places of worship, artists' studios, art schools, back gardens, the spaces of Peter Rees's erotic economy – into residential developments, then this is what will happen unless measures are taken to guide it otherwise. Since a city is more than a gigantic housing estate and needs things other than flats in order to prosper, it will suffer when it loses these places of work, knowledge and pleasure. Once gone, they will not come back.

A city needs places like A & C Continental Delicatessen, lodged in a railway arch in Atlantic Road, Brixton, and nearby shops selling fish and Afro-Caribbean hair products, all serving the multiple needs of the local communities and all threatened by the planned renovation of the arches and a likely hike in rents. The delicatessen sells outstanding produce, but it is not a shrine to delectable exorbitance like Leila's in Shoreditch. Jose Cardoso, of Portuguese descent, whose father took over the shop from a Greek family in 1990, says he serves everyone 'from the white middle class buying Parma ham and olives' to 'immigrants getting day-to-day stuff and green coffee'. Cardoso is almost in tears as he contemplates his possible new sources of livelihood. A taxi driver, perhaps, he thinks. But it is clear that nothing will replace the pleasure and society of the shop, for him or his neighbours. 'The fishmongers are in their third generation,' he says. 'Some of the businesses have been here for twenty, thirty or forty years.'

A city also needs places like Holborn Studios, a waterside community of workplaces described by Helmut Newton as 'the Abbey Road of photography'. Or the blocks of artists' studios provided by Space or ACAVA, who are agencies with impressive records of setting up and running such places. Or a pub like the Canterbury Arms in Brixton, described by one who knew it as 'a social hub for so many years', now 'flattened and turned into flats'. Or LGBTQ pubs closed or endangered. Or the makers of food and drink in Hackney Wick, just across a canalized branch of the River Lea from the Olympic Stadium, who are also faced with uprooting. Most of the time it is for the same reason, which is that there is money to be made from converting these locations into flats, while such resistance as the planning system offers was reduced by relaxations in policy by the Coalition government of 2010–15. Anna Harding of Space Studios says that there has long been pressure to turn the sort of industrial spaces that artists occupy into loft apartments, but 'now it is in hyperinflation mode. Owners can knock them down and put up forty-two-storey towers and make a fortune.'

For Harding, artists are part of 'the whole eco-system that makes the city functional'. Another provider of studios, Duncan Smith of ACAVA, points out that artists come with networks of associated skills –'web designers, advertising people, film-makers and all the rest'. Brearley speaks of the 'vast diversity of smaller businesses that are unstoppably, entrepreneurially driven', except that they may have nowhere left to go. 'The jobs that I provide,' says a Hackney Wick drinks maker, 'don't require a university education, but they are skilled and provide career progression. We are not call centres. They are jobs with futures. They establish long-term relationships with local communities. But you can't do that if you are always being pinged around the city, from one place to the next.'

In these circumstances new development will not necessarily be in the interests of the city as a whole, unless guided otherwise, or of business, or even of the property market. It will only reflect the immediate interests of individual landowners and their investors. Individual landowners might themselves benefit from external intervention: if they are made to work with their neighbours, for example to create a coherent and pleasant street between developments, they all might expect to sell their flats more easily. But they are unlikely to do such a thing on their own.

These issues were made more pressing by London's increasing population. If it were to become a city of ten million, an increase by 50 per cent on its mid-1980s size, while still being contained by its green belt, the consequence would be more and more pressure on the spaces within. Which, if undirected by any sort of planning intelligence, would crush the fragile but vital elements on which the city depends. At the same time the needs of housing would not be met in the best or smartest way.

VNEB

You can get a premonition of this future in the zone known as VNEB, which stands for Vauxhall Nine Elms Battersea. It is an area haunted by the memory of Vauxhall Pleasure Gardens, where for two centuries up to 1859 the subtle substances of diversion, society and desire were tended, but whose posterity is a series of large-scale interventions which, decade after decade, make the assassination of sensibility a primary aim – a railway viaduct, a traffic gyratory, a concrete cold-storage building, a spy headquarters, the block surmounted by the penthouse of the convicted perjurer Jeffrey Archer. Some shoots of creativity and pleasure survived these brutal structures. The Very Reverend Dr D. Wayne Love, of the band Alabama 3, in the book about the industrial band Test Dept titled *Test Dept, Total State Machine*, describes it thus:

> Vauxhall in South London has never been what you might call a 'desirable' neighbourhood, but back in 1982 it was positively seedy and totally compelling. Bonnington Square in Vauxhall was a few paces from the train station and two of the roughest gay bars in London. The square had been claimed by a vibrant crowd of writers, artists, musicians, and junkies, and every single one of them squatted the quaint old but thoroughly decrepit buildings in the square. It was awash with rodents, wet and dry rot, sinking roofs, treacherous floorboards, stinking smack dens and a bunch of the shadiest characters you're ever likely to meet outside of a William Burroughs novel; but that was also part of its addictive charm. There was a real community spirit about the place. Everyone fiddled with the electricity, burnt the rotting floorboards to keep the houses warm in winter, and the sprinkling of hippies that lived on the edges of the square even ran a community shop. One of the great things about Bonnington Square was the amount of raw talent that flourished

there. Like exotic mushrooms from a dungheap, the amount of artists that emerged from those few decaying squats is really quite astonishing ...

In the previous year Michael Heseltine, Secretary of State for the Environment in Margaret Thatcher's government, called the area 'as outstanding an opportunity as is offered anywhere in the Western world, straddling as it does a major approach to the capital'. He was talking in particular about a pair of riverside sites on either side of the approach to Vauxhall Bridge that had already defied two decades of proposals for development. The downstream site had been the location of the 'Green Giant', a proposed 500-foot tower of offices and flats whose ground floor was to house the Tate Gallery's collection of modern sculpture, a sort of proto-Tate Modern. But the tower had been called a 'monstrosity and a gross overdevelopment' and a public inquiry had found against it.

Because Thatcherism liked competition, Heseltine liked competitions, and one was held for the planning and design of the two sites. 'Shortlists were announced', to quote an insightful account written in 1992, 'public opinion canvassed and ignored and a winner chosen. The new owners said, "This is one scheme that will happen" – and went into receivership.' One of the entries, by Terry Farrell, proposed a series of structures that stepped down to the river to maximize views, and were arranged 'regularly like pearls on a necklace around a central public spine.' It was all about mixed use, homes, offices and shops together, access to the water and creating neighbourhoods around networks of streets that would help stitch together a fragmented area. (Networks don't stitch, but mixed metaphors, like cliches, come as standard when talking about regeneration.)

The developers Regalian then bought the Green Giant site, hired Farrell, decided to make it all offices, and did a deal with government to locate MI6 there, a sequence of events that erased all the architect's good intentions and left a stepping, pomo-deco ziggurat shape, like Arnold Schwarzenegger all pectorals and big shoulders, pin headed, flesh-coloured on a steel frame. It wasn't a mixed-use neighbourhood any more but an office monolith. It wasn't permeable, but windowless on its bottom floors and protected with dry and wet moats. Cut off from the other site, it didn't stitch. Its 'public spaces' became internal circulation systems for the intelligence community. But, hey, it kept its architectural form, which, as the wheel of fashion turns, will one day become a listed building.

MI6 was completed in 1994. In due course the developers St George, a subsidiary of the Berkeley Group, built St George Wharf, a series of residential blocks designed by Broadway Malyan, which approximately followed the pattern of Farrell's plan – repeating blocks, stepping up towards the back, enclosing courtyard gardens and through-routes. The plan was not all terrible, but unfortunately chose to grab an assortment of shapes apparently from a made-in-Shenzen toy box and then used an algorithm, it seemed, that stuck together random forms with those others that would clash the most. The bottom-heavy composition was topped with stubby wings, as if of a doomed flightless bird, before descending with a series of beak-shaped projections to a boot-like base. The concrete was the colour of dirty bandages and half-washed bloodstains, teamed with greenish glass. It was for such reasons that the *Architects' Journal*'s poll twice damned it.

In 2005 John Prescott approved the neighbouring St George Wharf Tower, by the same architects and developers; it was completed in 2014. Also in 2005 the attractiveness of the area was improved not at all by a gesticulating bus station in the middle of the gyratory. Bonnington Square meanwhile completed its journey from the hippy/junkie/squatter bedlam described by Dr Love to a charming housing cooperative, whose shared garden would be

MI6 and bus station

described by the travel section of the *Smithsonian* magazine as 'a ragtag oasis of trees, vines and flowering shrubs' that 'reflects its eccentric past, planted as it is with a tangle of mimosa, beech and mulberry trees as well as lavender, giant ferns, low-growing palms – and the appropriately vegan Bonnington Café'. Where developers and planners conspired in visual and spatial violence, the wild people of the square made harmony and peace.

Just under a mile upriver the vast carcass of Battersea Power Station, left roofless by an abortive attempt to make it into a theme park, went through owners: John Broome, the theme park man; the Hong Kong developer Victor Hwang; the Irish developers Treasury Holdings; the Irish government, who took on Treasury's overvalued assets following their country's financial apocalypse; a Malaysian consortium called the Battersea Power Station Development Company. Visions and architects came and went and the site became London's most intractable, until a plan was reached with massive apartment blocks and associated 'public realm', to be designed by Norman Foster, Frank Gehry and the megalomaniac and would-be sexy Danish-global practice BIG.

Between Vauxhall and Battersea is Nine Elms, an area where stood, owing to the protection of industrial uses in the past, a mail sorting office and the fruit, vegetable and flower market that was once in Covent Garden. It also has some isolated riverside apartment blocks from the 1980s. Taken together, Vauxhall, Nine Elms and Battersea were declared an 'opportunity area' by Ken Livingstone, 'with significant capacity for new housing, commercial and other development'. In 2008 it was announced that the United States embassy would move there from Grosvenor Square, Mayfair, attracted by the opportunities for enhanced security that came with building anew in the open spaces of Nine Elms. It was a momentous coup for the area. The Dutch later announced their intention to move their embassy there too. An extension to the

Northern Line was planned, to improve VNEB's poor transport links, and a possible new footbridge to the blessed lands on the north side of the river.

It could be a wonderful place: the location on the outside of a lazy bend in the Thames, the views of the Palace of Westminster, the benign influence of the embassies, the wealth to be unlocked through realizing land values, the range of architectural talent in both Britain and abroad, the heritage. Battersea Park, created through an Act of Parliament in 1846 and laid out by James Penne-thorne, is nearby. There are Portuguese cafes in the railway arches. There is the delightful example offered by Bonnington Square of ways to improve a place. But at the time of writing VNEB is one of the most miserable zones in London.

What makes it so now are the car-boot sale of obsolescent property around Vauxhall, the untamed traffic of Nine Elms Lane and the fragmentary nature of attempts at improvement: conflict-ing fashions in paving and light fittings going back to the 1980s, odd dollops of lawn or flowerbed, the failure of residential develop-ments to coordinate with each other or even themselves. Topiary is enlisted, spheres and slabs of green cut with special ferocity, as if the imposition of geometry on botany can make up for the calami-ties of town planning. *We may not be able to manage a city, but we can command a shrub.*

There is a bricky and pitched-roofed but nonetheless multi-storey block – a late flowering of the 'neo-vernacular' style of the late 1970s and early 80s – and a pitiful stab at postmodernism on the edges of the forty-two-acre power station site. The form of the St George Tower, according to a Wikipedia entry whose neutrality might be contested, 'has been designed to be elegant and un-gimmicky', but at its base it crumbles into a confusion of granite, water features and planting, of thwarted paths, service zones and radiating shapes that go nowhere, of mismatches of opacity and

. . . but we can command a shrub

STEAX promenade and cruise club exterior

transparency, of gates in conflicting styles (Weybridge-traditional metalwork; contemporary planar glass) that capture for private use what might have been public or at least publoid space.

The main activities on the riverside promenade are jogging-with-earphones, deal-making by phone and spilling out of the Steax bar and restaurant. Or rather, as the bold and light type of their sign wittily puts it, **STEAX**. All involve an attention not fully engaged with the immediate environment. All reduce the possibilities of lingering, or openness to what and who is around. In a tacit pact of mutual impoverishment between spaces and people, the environment gives little reason for either lingering or openness.

Vauxhall is achieving the atomization of sensuality and space. Wikipedia tells us that the St George Tower has 'the highest swimming pool in London'; the area has the gay sex clubs and the more heterosexual delights suggested by **STEAX**. It would be surprising if the attraction of the high-rise waterside apartments were not, for at least some of the buyers, their pulling power. But between these hidden depots of relief there is a radical absence of intermediate shades of pleasure which because less private can be shared. Vauxhall is an arid diagram of property speculation within which each must find or buy a personal oasis.

Part of the misery of VNEB in 2015 was the fact that much of it was still under construction or awaiting development, which gave hope that it might be better in the future. Around the power station, billboards displayed high-grade property PR babble:

INDUSTRIAL MAGIC
Battersea Power Station is London's quintessential industrial landmark. Its rawness and atmosphere are its authenticity and must drive aesthetic decisions

LIVEABLE AND LOVEABLE
Battersea Power Station will be a real place for real people.

To be considered 'home' we must make a neighbourhood where there are unparalleled opportunities for people

SYMBOLIC ACTION

The reputation of Battersea Power Station is based on the principle that actions speak louder than words. We must make actions that are generous, truthful and unmissable

SHOWSTOPPER

As a destination, Battersea Power Station must offer a guaranteed good time. People will come because there is a myriad of new, different and interesting experiences all year round

THE GOOD LIFE

At Battersea Power Station sustainability is a given. It must embrace all that is positive about low energy living

And, eeeuuuuw,

MASSIVE ICON, INTIMATE PLACE

Battersea Power Station must come across as both an icon and an intimate place. At one moment monumental and awe-inspiring, at the other browsable and fine grain.

You can take your massive icon round to my intimate place any time you like, dearie.

Whatever optimism these promises might inspire, however, had to be qualified by the just-finishing Riverlight. This was by the esteemed practice of Rogers Stirk Harbour and has similarities to their Neo Bankside project next to Tate Modern, but something had happened to the usual crispness of their detailing. It was as if a Rogers design had gone through Google Translate. Most of what

remained was the needless aggression of their 45-degree angles, the harsh slashes of the cross-bracing, a rigidity that makes impossible happy relationships with future neighbours. Rogers tics – Pompidou ventilators, glass lifts, felt-tip colours – appeared randomly, like items on a charm bracelet, but without the charm. Splats of landscaping failed to restore absent intimacy.

Optimism also had to be qualified by proposals for the future. At the Vauxhall end of VNEB there was to be a prick party of towers, as if a contextual nod to events in nearby railway arches. But joyless withal. If the Green Giant at 500 feet had been considered a gross overdevelopment and a public inquiry had found the 600 feet of the St George Tower unacceptable, both were now exceeded by the height and mass of planned new blocks. The proposed height of One Nine Elms, for the Chinese property developers Dalian Wanda, would after successive negotiations upwards with the planners reach 656 feet. Compared to many American and Asian cities these heights are modest, but in a location considered sensitive because of its nearness to the Palace of Westminster, they are not.

As important as the effect on historic monuments are the ways in which individual projects work together to make a new part of London, and the natures of places formed between them. Here height is a factor because it requires greater skill to shape the ground-level spaces around tall buildings than it does about lower structures – much as it is harder to moor an oil tanker than a dinghy – which skill often seems to be available in inverse proportion to the scale of the building. Vauxhall doesn't promise to buck the trend. Despite claims of 'significant improvements to the existing public realm and experience', most of the tower proposals offer skimpy sketches of the received opinion of what public space is. A bit of grass, a bit of paving, a gesture to art or play; the boundary between public and private made in glass, not because that is what makes a street into a better place, but because commercial cliché demands it.

There is no recognition of the fact that successful public places are made not only by the clearing of a space and the specification of its surfaces, but also by the exteriors of the buildings that surround it, the ways they combine, and by the gradations and layerings between outside and inside, front and back. Consider any street or square that you like and you are likely to see these qualities. Instead, the new towers of Vauxhall compete with each other to clash their forms – if one is an ellipse, another must be square, one sheer, another stepped – while maintaining the deeper monotony that comes from using similar industrialized cladding, which cladding reduces the interface of outside and in to a hard septum. They don't collaborate, but jostle for attention like middle managers at an office party.

The central area of VNEB, where a height limit of 70m applies, is more sober, with brownish blocky developments that conform to generic ideas of good urbanism. They frame greenish vegetated areas, also generic. They restrict their means of expression to re-arranging their grids of balconies, such that they gesticulate less than the towers, but they still exhibit a competitive agitation that precludes calm and cohesion. In the centre is the big cube of the American embassy, which aims to deal more charmingly with its security issues than MI6. The hope is to 'build an embassy that reflects the core values of democracy – transparency, openness and equality – and is welcoming, secure and highly sustainable'.

When completed it will be a castle keep protected by a moat, but promises to 'integrate aspects of British landscaping and site design, rather than high fences, to create security'. The 'pond' – moat – 'serves as a subtle security barrier' but 'also plays an integral role in the site's stormwater strategy'. Like the landscape, the building itself 'is designed to be visually engaging while imperceptibly integrating security measures'. An outer envelope of ethylene tetra-fluoroethylene, with a staggered 1960s styling reminiscent of the building that Eero Saarinen designed for the US Embassy in Grosvenor Square, would wrap the glass box of the building, modifying solar energy and downdraughts in an environmentally responsible way.

It is possibly an impossible job, to design an embassy for a superpower, with obvious security risks attached, in such a way that it is a welcoming and enriching contribution to its immediate neighbourhood. Kieran Timberlake, the building's Philadelphia-based architects, have maybe done as well as might be expected. But the spaces proposed around it are unconvincing, because of not only the controlled zones surrounding the keep, but also the lack of affinity between it and the brownish, aimlessly variegated buildings around it.

If Vauxhall will be a havoc of towers and Nine Elms blocks of bricks, the third component of VNEB, the site around Battersea Power Station, has been so richly fed on world-class architecture, on visions and square footage, that like a burdened bowel it must at last discharge into thick lumps of residential property. Like Brint Moltke in David Foster Wallace's story *The Suffering Channel*, who could sculpt Michelangelo's *Pietà* with his sphincter, the role of genius was to give intricate form to the raw material. Foster, Gehry and BIG, to adopt a more tasteful tone of architectural criticism, brought extravagant curving forms to the close-packed sixteen-storey blocks inherited from a masterplan by Rafael Viñoly. These managed a feat that might have been thought impossible, which was to make the power station look small; it appears unexpected at the end of canyon-like streets like, if one were to be generous, the Treasury at Petra. This is more fun than the blocks of Nine Elms and the Shenzen toys of Vauxhall. It has a certain oomph, a thumping drama, but it has to be asked why, in the presence of the majestic

US Embassy and Power Station development

power station, it was good to add such a surcharge of iconicity. The substance of the new buildings shows no particular respect for the old but rather love for their own signatures. The egos of each architect overwhelm the cohesion of the place; what could be a magnificent conversation becomes a shouting match.

In Nine Elms and Battersea, it should be said, the quality of much of the new building and open spaces promises to be higher than it would have been fifteen or thirty years before. There has been progress since St George Wharf. There was also an attempt to give shape to development and make it more than a real-estate spreadsheet made flesh. The Greater London Authority produced a 'planning framework', which proposed, for example, a 'linear park' running through the zone. Public transport, such as the planned extension to the Northern Line, was coordinated and a competition held for the new bridge over the Thames. There are hopes of civilizing the Vauxhall gyratory.

This is an advance on the post-Heseltine phases of Vauxhall and on much development across London, but it is sketchy. A prospective new town of 16,000 homes is shown as a set of diagrams, with no positive idea of what sort of a place it would be or for whom. The linear park is conceived as a ubiquitous piece of greenery: it is compared, predictably, to the High Line in New York, but the power of the latter was in its particular response to the specific situation of disused infrastructure. The VNEB park is to be developed in fragments by the developers of the sites through which it passes, which means that, even if there were the strong unifying vision that makes the New York example a success, it would be impossible to achieve. The 'High Line', it turns out, becomes a useful way of branding a strip of green, which otherwise might be derided for its narrowness, as something innovative and desirable. (And yet another 'High Line' – spare me – is promised on the roof of Foster's power station apartments.)

Attempts to define the public good proved flimsy. The framework set the height of the St George Tower as the limit for new development, but when Dalian Wanda asked for more they got it. The linear park grew skinnier as the plots around it enlarged. A competition was held for the promised bridge, which generated a predictable shortlist of rhetorical sticks and strings, but which turned out to be flawed by the fact that the City of Westminster, on whose territory the bridge was to land, announced that they did not and never had wanted it. One of the entrants, Reinier de Graaf of OMA, accurately stated that such competitions

> no longer serve their original purpose: a meticulous selection of the best possible building, but increasingly serve as promotional campaigns in the context of a political lobby. Competitions fill a void left by a public sector increasingly short of means, who, in an effort to save costs, defers an ever greater part of its responsibilities onto the private sector (in this case architecture and engineering firms).

Battersea Power Station was criticized for its modest provision of affordable housing, for which the defence was that the old building itself was so expensive to restore that there was insufficient profit left to pay for other social benefits. This was no sort of excuse: the site had been bought and sold and bought again in the knowledge that the power station had to stay, which therefore should have been factored into the price.

The Northern Line extension was also a money drain to which developers would have to contribute, thus generating a circular argument. Why does there have to be so much luxury development? To pay for the Underground line. Why do we need the Underground Line? To serve the luxury development. There might have been an alternative approach in which less intense, less expensive housing could have been served by cheaper transport such as buses and footpaths linking into existing infrastructure, but no one seems to have stood back and seriously considered such an option.

The result will be a mile-long tract in which things considered good appear as ciphers of themselves. The 'public realm' becomes a filler between chunks of real estate. A tree, a balcony or an artwork might appear in the computer visualizations, but without the qualities for which we like such things. The distribution of architectural energy is misdirected: it is applied not to the conception of the whole but to the massaging of the consequences of questionable decisions, to distracting for example from the lightlessness of the deep streets around the power station.

Where aspiration and creativity might have been applied to the shared spaces, there are instead marketing and spectacle that are strictly for the paying residents. One tower, the Aykon, was presented as London's first fashion-branded tower, 'a global symbol of opulence ... the ultimate in luxury, the ultimate in Versace', inspired 'by the Greek and Roman myths that are part of the Versace DNA'. Some media excitement was generated by the announcement, at Embassy Gardens, Nine Elms, of an all-glass rooftop swimming pool spanning the void between two ten-storey blocks, which it was promised would 'feel like floating through the air in central London'. Which perfectly summarizes the buzz of London's wealthfest: architectural daring goes into an exhibition of exclusivity, in which passers-by may only gawp at the privileged bodies above them.

Many of the thousands of 'homes' are also ciphers, in that they are aimed more at the international investment market in London residential property than at the needs of Londoners. It is important to be clear here: there is nothing wrong in itself with foreign investment, which has been sustaining London for centuries, but the official justification for developments such as this is that they are helping to meet the city's housing needs. When small flats are sold for a million pounds, often through property fairs in other countries before locals even get a chance to see them, they are not, in any meaningful sense, doing this.

A model to display to the world

Around Vauxhall there are suggestions of different ways of building cities. There is Bonnington Square, with its strengths of collaborative work, specificity to place and sheer joy in nature. There is a gallery designed by Caruso St John for Damien Hirst, leader of the art aristocracy that has been created over the last two decades by the astounding prices paid for their work. The gallery is free to enter and displays Hirst's personal collections of art other than his own, so gives something to the public. There is also the Social Justice Centre, a workspace for charities, social enterprises and voluntary and campaign groups, whose building is designed by Architecture 00.

Both gallery and workspace, as is common, augment formerly industrial buildings: theatre workshops in one case, a shoe-polish factory in the other. In both the new work is sympathetic to but enriching of the old, for example with some warmth in the brick-work or timber, or a glint in the aluminium. Both make something out of the unexpected properties of the existing. The factory had thick brick walls, to stop the potentially catastrophic interaction of combustible polish-making processes with large nearby gas holders, which walls become a strong presence in the atrium of the Social Justice Centre. The theatre workshops have idiosyncrasies of scale and proportion, to which Caruso St John add their own rhythms.

These two structures have characters and registers of scale that both grow out of the soil of the already-there, and are fertilized by the new lives of the buildings. Both have generosities in their internal circulation, with ample concrete spirals in the gallery and a hefty wooden stair in the atrium of the workplace. They set up

Newport Street Gallery and Social Justice Centre

relationships of actions and space. They consider light and materials. They have layers and depth. They have nuance. It is easier to achieve these qualities in bespoke, smaller projects than in large developments, but if more of the same intelligence had been applied to VNEB, together with some of the spirit of Bonnington Square, it would be a model to display to the world.

The subtleties of the gallery or the workspace might seem trivial compared with the pressure of numbers presented by the population statistics and the weight of investment, but the two are linked. A city needs both quantity and quality; the failure to respond adequately to the first can lead to the crushing of the second. If London's housing is seen purely as a problem of numbers, it will end up with the homes and places that it doesn't want and doesn't need.

And, if the city's leaders understand nothing else, its self-eating will in the end destroy the things that help it succeed. It is 'without question the most popular city for investors', as I was told in early 2015, in the Singapore office of the property agents Savills, by their then Head of International Property Sales, Gavin Sung. 'It has a strong government,' he said, explaining why people from his city-state want to buy in London, 'a great legal system, the currency is relatively safe. It has a really nice lifestyle, there is the West End, diversity of food, it's multicultural.' At least some of that diversity, lifestyle and multiculturalism will disappear if too much of the city ends up like VNEB.

15. Slow Burn City

Embodied energy is a basic concept of sustainability, but one which the modern industries and legislation of 'sustainable development' struggle to acknowledge. It describes the fact that any existing building embodies energy in its fabric: the smelting of its metals, the firing of its bricks, the melting of its glass, the polymerization of its plastics, the transport of its materials from quarry to processing works to building site, their lifting into place, the multiple journeys of workmen. When a building is destroyed this energy and the attendant costs in pollution and mineral extraction are thrown away, with those of demolition and the disposal of waste added. A new building incurs these costs again. In assessing whether a project is 'sustainable' it is meaningless to ignore them. It is like judging the cost of a car only by its petrol consumption.

Yet, while many developers and architects proclaim the wind turbines and ground-source heating of their works, their use of renewables, low-energy lighting, natural ventilation and other ways of limiting the consumption of energy in the running of a building, they tend to be quieter about their implications for embodied energy. This lacuna arises partly because, a lot of the time, it would make developers' and architects' lives more complicated to take embodied energy into account. It would often tell them to refurbish rather than rebuild. It would discourage them from building towers, whose structure and services require more energy than lower buildings.

The notion of embodied energy is important within the confines of sustainable design. Applied seriously to construction, it discourages redundant gestures and needless destruction, and encourages respect for the existing and for realities beyond an architect's personal style. It challenges mental habits and requires thought. It disrupts the standardized and generic. More than this, it is a valuable concept if applied more widely and loosely to the development of cities: if 'energy' is taken to mean the experience, memories, chances and usefulness inherent within a city's fabric, which are easily overlooked but should not lightly be destroyed, then it is also desirable that they too are given value in the development of London.

Cities change. They renew through consuming themselves. Districts are remade and repurposed, populations churn, buildings are adapted or demolished and rebuilt. A city's fabric is made out of the raw material supplied by the past and becomes the raw material for the future. This includes its cultural fabric – traditions of art, music or cuisine grow up which will be exploited and reinterpreted. Its places are formed, inhabited, acquire value, are appropriated, decline, are recreated. London has a particular ability to change in this way: areas that can move from one social group to another and between ethnicities, or from industrial to artistic. The common land of a heath might have agricultural purposes, be exploited for quarrying and housebuilding, be rescued for a wider populace, be inhabited by visionaries, radicals, kite flyers, clerks, cruisers, families.

In the first decade and a half of the twenty-first century London started consuming itself with accelerating voracity. Change tended in one direction, towards the conversion of all qualities into investment value, especially that of residential property. Such change tends towards sterilization and irreversibility, without a crash or an external catastrophe such as a war. It threatened qualities that might have been thought fundamental to the city: its availability, generosity, fluidity and social diversity. It looked as if London could consume itself at a rate that might liquefy into profit its vital organs of work and society. Most obviously its desirable areas, its quite nice areas and even those that were just about tolerable were being priced out of range of most of its citizens. More subtle were the ways in which its freedoms and pleasures, even as they grew in sophistication and abundance, were priced and scripted.

The ideal is that cities burn slowly. Their social ecologies and physical forms should renew through change, not be devastated by it. A community and a place cannot be bound together forever, but neither should city-dwellers be threatened with uprooting every few years. Being an ideal, such a city is something never perfectly attained – no one can regulate the temperature of a city as if it were a gas ring on a cooker. London, with its adaptability, its variegation and its areas of slackness and redundancy, has long been an outstanding example of a slow-burning city, but its phases of growth and crisis have also had their drastic aspect.

Put simply, the pattern has been one where private interests have been given freedom to create, to exploit and to grow up to and beyond the point of disaster – fire, disease, overcrowding, sprawl, pollution. There is then major public intervention, in its own way unprecedented, such as the London Building Acts, Bazalgette's sewerage, council housing, the green belt, the Clean Air Acts, the protection of heritage through conservation areas and listed buildings. These interventions are not only technical, but also political, social and cultural. To make the sewers, for example, required the invention of a new form of city government.

After thirty-five years in which private interests have again led the growth of the city, it is time for another adjustment. There is already something wrong with a place that expels its poor and puts decent homes beyond the reach of many of its citizens. Even if the problem is seen only in functional and not human terms, a city will struggle to succeed if it can no longer house the people who teach, clean, nurse, treat, make, repair, build, plan, design, create, cook, serve, police, drive and entertain. If the city is to grow to ten million, the current responses will be – as they already are – inadequate. In their failures, they are also causing damage to the physical environment of the city, wasting its opportunities and endangering its richness.

It might seem strange to speak of slowness when London is dynamic and its challenges urgent and when past forms of intervention – the sewers, council housing – have been dramatic. The actions needed now are not modest. But, paradoxically, large-scale intervention can be needed, as dykes and sea-walls might protect agriculture, to allow a city's human ecologies to flourish.

We might even hope that London could do better than Bazalgette, a century and a half on, and, while working at a scale equal to its largest-ever size, encourage growth through local and individual initiatives. Take, for example, self-build housing, a concept promoted by governments right-wing and left, but, despite the inspiring work of Walter Segal long ago, almost never achieved. This is because would-be self-builders can't compete with the land-buying powers of property companies. It would require public authorities to designate land on which individuals could build their own homes.

By, say, the time of the oil crisis that followed the Yom Kippur war of 1973, the Victorian projects of improving the city and their twentieth-century developments and reinterpretations, the consequences of struggles and campaigns, were in some senses complete.

Bazalgette's sewers were handling the unceasing evacuation of the city's bowels. Thanks to the preservation of commons and parks, the creation of new green spaces and the private gardens which London's scattered structure encouraged, it was known internationally as a verdant city. The Clean Air Acts had cleaned the air. Street lighting and supplies of electricity and potable water could be taken for granted. There were free schools and universities, free hospitals and surgeries, free libraries and great museums and art galleries that were free to enter. New centres of culture, such as on the South Bank, were being created. There were public swimming pools and sports centres. Historic buildings were being increasingly protected and restored. An extensive, intelligible and still good-looking public transport system covered the city. An elected government, now called the Greater London Council, ruled.

In keeping with Abercrombie's plan, the population was gently falling, allowing new open spaces to be created. A green belt was preventing the city from encroaching further into the countryside and, beyond that, a ring of new towns was developing roughly according to Howard's principles.

The precedent of the Boundary Estate had been followed, with hundreds of thousands of new council homes built. No longer were they restricted to the slightly better-off and more well-behaved workers, but in principle were available even to the poorest. It could be claimed that slums, in the Victorian sense, no longer existed. People on middle incomes had a wide choice of homes to buy, from suburbs at the outer reaches of the Underground lines, to flats, to whole houses in central terraces and squares, including in places like Camden Town and Notting Hill, close to great parks and the centre of the city. Social institutions such as pubs and markets continued to serve their original purposes. The city's freedoms – of access, protest, movement, privacy – were, apart from instances of police misbehaviour, strong.

There were signs that the reign of Roseberyan astyphobia was coming to an end. The influence of Jane Jacobs, in praise of traditional streets and urban life, was seeping through. Nascent conservation movements were fighting against clearances for road-building and comprehensive redevelopment. Covent Garden market was saved from demolition and converted into a retail destination. In 1974 Jonathan Raban wrote *Soft City*, based on his experiences of London, which talked of 'the continual creative play of urban living. The city as we imagine it, the soft city of illusion, myth, aspiration, nightmare . . . maybe more real than the hard city one can locate on maps, in statistics, in monographs on urban sociology and demography and architecture.' Cities were 'plastic by nature. We mould them in our images: they, in their turn, shape us by the resistance they offer when we try to impose our own personal form on them.'

Emptied out by depopulation and deindustrialization, London was rich with places to be taken over, squatted, done up, converted – such as the making of the Roundhouse into a performance venue in 1964, the 1970s rescue of Georgian Spitalfields from developers and dereliction, and the occupation of the floors of Wapping warehouses. There were wastelands on which people set up adventure playgrounds, ecological parks and city farms.

Had you proposed that this was some sort of golden age, people would have given you strange looks, accelerated their gait and crossed the street. There was a feeling of vanishing national greatness and with it the means to sustain the Victorian inheritance. Things seemed to be getting shabbier, dirtier and more prone to break down. Food was mostly terrible. There was a fear of rising urban crime, of the kind seen in the United States. There was racial hatred. Public authority was overreaching itself: the heirs in spirit and title to the Metropolitan Board of Works were still acting with nineteenth-century high-handedness, in driving motorways and viaducts through communities and making mass clearances for new housing, but finding the populace less willing to accept it.

Modernity was seen as sterilizing and destructive. It was creating a type of space – a subway, a walkway, a windswept plaza, a housing estate greensward, a tower-block lift lobby, a highway margin – that belonged to everyone and no one and so became neglected, litter strewn, graffiti'd and threatening. Architects, seen as accomplices of this degradation, were widely hated. In British Rail, the nationalized train company, whatever there might have been of the spirit of Pick was at best dilute. Instead, they wanted to destroy the great Victorian stations of Euston, where they succeeded, and St Pancras, where they were thwarted by public opposition.

In the 1980s, except for the building of the M25 motorway around London, faith in major public intervention disappeared. Construction of new council housing was stopped. At the same time house price inflation became the instrument of national economic policy that it has been ever since. 'Inner city' was a phrase that commonly prefixed words like 'decay', 'deprivation' and 'violence', but the games of spotting up and coming areas had started, of finding places where the attractive terraces and interesting ethnic cuisine were in just the right ratio to street crime and dirt. Restaurants started to get better. In the Thatcher period radical economics came dressed with traditionalist architecture, but in the 1990s the city began to pride itself on its contemporary design. Modernism returned in a different form, as a desirable lifestyle choice.

In the twenty-first century these tendencies intensified. The inner and not-so-inner city became more and more valued commodities. The ingenuity of chefs, designers and mixologists grew in parallel to that of inventors of financial instruments. Despite promises of beautiful new public spaces the quality of the streets struggled to keep up. It no longer became necessary for an area to be physically attractive before it was gentrified, or to improve much as a result. The consequence was a place like Redchurch Street in Shoreditch, the one where you can buy blankets and buckets at premium prices, whose interiors of tuned mellowness are reached across pavements as grotty as they have been since the early years of the London County Council.

Playpen and propaganda

Tech City, taken as a whole, offers an example of the London-wide phenomenon whereby creativity, ingenuity and delight are lavished on private initiatives, at the same time that shared spaces are degraded. South of Redchurch Street is Hanbury Street, where there is an exotic flowering of street art (a giant stork, shouting faces, a naked crouching angel) and a corrective text in plain white letters that quotes the late trades unionist Bob Crow: IF WE ALL SPIT TOGETHER WE CAN DROWN THE BASTARDS. There is also Second Home, one of the newest of London's spaces of knowledge, created with the help of a dynamic and eloquent former adviser to David Cameron, one described by the *Financial Times* as a 'networker extraordinaire', called Rohan Silva. It is a shared workspace where the 'creative nomads' of tech companies such as SurveyMonkey, TaskRabbit, Kovert Designs and Chineasy come together in a space where, in the style of Silicon Valley, business is conducted in the atmosphere of a sophisticated playpen. The rather good Spanish architects SelgasCano (who have caught the Google-friendly bug of omitting the space between their names) have installed in a former carpet factory an environment of curving transparent screens, stimulating colours, a diffused grove of 1,000 hydroponic pot plants, an eclectic tribe of classic modern chairs, a meeting table that rises to the ceiling when not in use. It is delightful, friendly, welcoming, social. The Jago restaurant projects back into the dirty old street, a long curved-sided, orange-decked, largely transparent object like a railway carriage from the future. The cuisine is 'Southern European, Middle Eastern and Ashkenazi' (chargrilled calcots & romesco; duck hearts, prunes, & fennel). The arguably tasteless name refers to *A Child of the Jago*, the horrifying 1896 novel about the nearby Old Nichol slum, the one that spoke of 'slinking forms, as of great rats, [that] followed one another quickly between the posts in the gut by the High Street'.

The contrast is great between the attention lavished on the small internal world of Second Home and the disorder of the Silicon Roundabout from which Tech City gets its alternative name, at the intersection of Old Street and City Road. This is made of several decades of mistakes: horrible traffic engineering, drain-like pedestrian underpasses, 1970s and 80s office blocks of special mediocrity, and the buttocks-shaped Bézier Apartments, Carbuncle Cup finalist in 2010, which places its balconies on its north face, away from the sun and towards the traffic. Its double-convex form was precisely what wasn't needed to repair the shattered unity of the space.

It has been noticed for a long time that the roundabout wasn't the nicest place. Some planting tries to ameliorate. In the early 1990s a four-sided advertising box was hoisted above it off white-painted parabolic steel, with, to the side, jiggery, calatravesque glass-and-steel canopies pretending to keep off the rain. The revenue from the advertising at least helped pay for improvements in surrounding streets, but the work was an early example of the fantasy that you can distract people from unresolved botch-ups with dynamic metalwork. In 2015 Google took over the advertising space with their 'be together not the same' campaign, assaulting the traffic with lowercase declarations of faux localism. Android-style cartoons were made of the area's folk, with cute-patronizing descriptions and the hashtag #oldstreetlocals:

tom, burgher buff
bringing killer disco & bacon jam
to the upcoming burgher bear

cain, software studio ceo
staging secret parties & bringing code to life
at red badger

thierry noir, street artist
painting radical murals, from berlin to old street

joseph, pie shop owner
serving pie, mash and local history at f. cooke

pauline, lollipop lady
helping kids cross bath street for thirty-three years

Somehow, these documents of the infantilizing propaganda of a conquistadorial corporation did not redeem the continued awfulness of the space. From 2000 onwards it was recognized under successive mayoralties that the Old Street roundabout needed help, yet despite substantial redevelopment around it as the area rose in value good intentions were not converted into reality. In 2012 David Cameron announced that £50m would be made available from the otherwise austerity-hit exchequer to build on the roundabout 'the largest civic space in Europe – a place for start-up companies and the local community to come together and become the next generation of entrepreneurs.' It was designed by Architecture 00, the people who would later do a nice job of the Social Justice Centre in Vauxhall, but attracted the suspicion that it would make official and monumental the spontaneity of the area: 'the idea of building a place where we put all the tech people', said the great thinker on urban vitality Richard Sennett, 'contravenes why that area grew up in the first place. The reason the area is a centre for innovation already is that most of the firms that are here weren't meant to be here. It was somewhere planners never expected them to go.' Three years later, an aeon in the hyperspeed of tech businesses, there was no sign of this new hub appearing.

Old Street does not in fact need the degree of preciousness found at Second Home, but it does need simple coherence and the possibility of basic enjoyment of its spaces. As at Vauxhall and Stratford High Street, there was a failure to define public space and the public interest with sufficient clarity and force, with the result that the hundreds of millions invested in development are not directed to the best interests of citizens or even businesses and investors. The physical lousiness of these places must, after all, be bad for property values and employee satisfaction. The political response is then an expensive and unhelpful gesture (the 'civic space', the Stratford Shoal, the Nine Elms phantom bridge – and, for London as a whole, the Garden Bridge). *We are sorry our pilotless plane killed your grandmother*, said the airline, *but here's Europe's biggest carnation to put on her grave.*

These diagrams of public squalor call to mind Rasmussen's statement, in his 1959 book *Experiencing Architecture*, that 'the Londoner calls his sidewalk the "pavement" and a more cultivated example of paving can hardly be found'. The accompanying photographs unfavourably compare a Danish example with one in Bloomsbury, the former a harsh combination of concrete, asphalt and granite, the latter a harmonious pattern of York stone, 'pleasing to the eye and comfortable under foot' and neatly punctuated by the cast-iron covers of coalholes and inspection chambers. Copenhagen has so long ago overtaken London in the field of civic design that it is outlandish to think that things might once have been the other way round. The modern London pavement is more likely to be a conflict zone of taking-up and putting-down, whether by utility companies, data providers or local authorities, of pink paviours garbled with grey, black gobs of asphalt, cracks, spots of gum and phlegm, mismatched bollards and sometimes the residue of hopeful art projects, where the void in the *res publica* was to be filled by a morsel of underfunded wit.

One response would be to call for the restoration of the prewar municipal virtues that made the pavements that Rasmussen admired. This would be a good start. If local officials and politicians could be persuaded of the benefits of doing things simply and well, that the exercise of a little intelligence early in the planning of a place can save expensive stupidity later on and that basic dignity should be the minimum for shared spaces, it would be a leap forward. It might seem quixotic to think of such a thing at a time when the attitude of national to local government is one of pummelling, binding and starving. But such things can change.

At the same time London needs more than a Scandinavian perception of its 1930s order, no matter how enlightened. It should be remembered that the municipal is not always virtuous and that at least some of the damage at Old Street roundabout was done in the name of planning. The arguments of Sennett and Raban in favour of spontaneity and against overdetermination by officials need to be heard. Here one is back to the swing between plan and non-plan, between Patrick Abercrombie and Cedric Price, that was the underlying pattern of post-war development. Both have proved emancipating and beneficial and both have been prone to abuse and appropriation by special interests. Plan kept at bay the kind of housing crisis that London now faces, built Churchill Gardens and Golden Lane, created open spaces and new towns, built roads which, however clumsy, serve a purpose, and enabled places of education with the qualities of a Bousfield. It also created the waste and rigidity against which Raban and others kicked. The spirit of non-plan is in both Bonnington Square and Canary Wharf, adventure playgrounds and the Thames skyline. At best it enables both bottom-up initiative and entrepreneurial wealth creation. At worst it allows the seizure of common assets for profit.

The truth is that London needs all of everything: plan and non-plan; popular action, public intervention and commercial investment. They have their own forms, their own benefits and disbenefits, their own extremes. The ideal for London is not the smoothing-over of these differences in the name of an overall homogeneous order, but their vigorous co-existence. Better the self-declaration of a Canary Wharf than the stealth-wealth of other parts, as long as the spaces for those outside the financial services industry also have their strength and dignity, and due attention is paid to the connections between such zones. Let there be Versace towers, if they rise out of public spaces of equal ambition and conceivably better design.

London is made of everything already. The transport system is a creation of both Yerkes's piracy and Pick's ordering. The high property values of Hampstead rest on the public protection of the Heath, the actions of private citizens' campaigns that brought it about, the sculpting of its land by Maryon-Wilson's and others' exploitations, its protection in Tudor times for the purposes of royal hunting rights. Canary Wharf owes its success not only to the entrepreneurship of its developers, but also to the 1799 Act of Parliament that created the West India Docks, to the tax and rent breaks of the London Dockland Development Corporation and to the construction with (mostly) public funding of the Jubilee Line extension.

Whatever is done in London has to take into account existing interests, with whom some sort of pact is usually required. The multiple exceptions made for the City of London, which was there before everything else, bear witness. Victorian philanthropy towards the poor was partly motivated by fear, preferred some of the working classes to others and was often more about getting slum-dwellers out of sight than about helping them. Change of policy requires struggle, as can be seen in the decades-long effort to preserve the commons, whose motivation was not wholly altruistic but included the desire of proto-nimbies to protect the spaces near their homes. Political structures have to be respected or at least understood, in particular the ways in which the thirty-two boroughs, plus the City of London, have more effect on the shaping of the capital than the mayor or anyone else.

But unprecedented change can happen if enough people, like those who demolished the Hyde Park railings, push for it. The present city owes its parks, its freedoms, its health, its efficiencies and its desirability to such change in the past.

A Manifesto

The ideal of London is that it is available and open. It gives opportunities and freedoms. Its common assets can be shared by all. It is competitive but generous. All identities are possible, but not mutually exclusive.

The city has two main needs:

- new and accessible homes
- enhancement of the qualities that make a city worth inhabiting.

MAKE HOMES

It is clear that, in the early twenty-first century, the most critical issues facing the city are to do with housing. It is a crisis of price and supply that:

- creates a class of people who can no longer afford to live in the city
- creates a class of people who continue to live in the city at the cost of accepting exceptionally poor living spaces
- generates favelas: beds-in-sheds, grossly overcrowded flats.

It has other damaging effects. It:

- distorts choices in personal lives, in relationships, in decisions whether and when to have children

- inhibits the free movement of people, and of labour
- exiles people vital to the functioning of the city.

It has been created by:

- national government policy that has encouraged house price inflation for a generation
- restricted supply and high demand
- the inability of the private sector, at any time since the 1930s, to meet need by itself.

It will only get worse as the population increases. Therefore:

- more space must be made available for new neighbourhoods
- government (national, London-wide, local) must build when the private sector won't; governments should own land and guide building on it in the public interest
- national government must stop pushing up the price of homes.

Ways to make more space include:

- making existing streets denser: two storeys can become three, four can become six
- intensification of outer suburbs, especially in their centres, without destroying their essential characters
- building on formerly industrial land, but not at the expense of vital businesses
- building the transport, schools and other essentials for making new neighbourhoods work
- towers, if they fulfil their promise of being well designed and in the right place
- building (with care) on the green belt.

The green belt, invented for the benefit of Londoners, is now causing the city to suffer. Building there could not only create more places to live, but also give more people access to nature. The traditions of making town houses with gardens, admired by Rasmussen, could be revived. A dull field, given to the city, can make a richer contribution to human life than when left alone.

These options do not exclude each other. All are needed. All require planning.

People who oppose building near their homes often have good reason to do so. They should therefore be able to share in the benefits that come from new development.

MAKE NEW PLACES. PROTECT THE EXISTING

Reverse the degradation and erosion of the city's shared spaces and encourage new ones to match its expansion. As the best parts of London are removed from the reach of most of its citizens, it is essential to make good new places to replace them.

Stop further devastation caused by tall buildings to the Thames and other parts of London, both long distance and close up. Enforce the principle that the more conspicuous a building is, the more care should be taken in its design.

Planning has to support the qualities that make shared spaces succeed, including the relationships of buildings to each other and the qualities of the surfaces.

A city is not a gigantic housing estate. Support the vital places that are not homes: for working, sociability, knowledge, health, imagination. These include high streets, gardens, factories, clubs, markets.

The city should include slack space – places where people can do their own thing, create urban gardens, allotments and playgrounds. Again, an acre of such space is worth more than an average acre of green belt.

Value the already-there when making the new.

PLAN

Simplify planning rules; reduce the roles of opinion and obscurity.

Employ more planners; value and pay them better. The amounts spent on guiding development well are tiny compared with the billions spent on construction. Investment in intelligence early on saves waste later.

Require that definitions of sustainability take embodied energy into account.

Conceive areas of new development as places not diagrams. Consider the spaces made in three dimensions. Recognize the qualities that make a place distinctive and successful. (Clue: it may not be topiary.)

End abuse of terms. Something described as 'public space' should be fully public. Ignore words of puff such as 'iconic' and 'world class'.

Planning is not just the mitigation of damaging proposals, but the active encouragement of areas and buildings that enhance the city.

DON'T PLAN

Planning does not mean that planners make all decisions themselves, but create conditions in which local and individual initiatives can flourish.

Let there be places for large and small enterprises. Let there be zones of hyperdensity, if the market wants it, and self-build housing, Canary Wharfs and Walters Ways. Make space for experiment and transience.

Give London the freedom to make the most of its resources and energies. Give its citizens the freedom to live well there and make the most of the city.

There is a view that London has never been more marvellous than now, in its energy and wealth, in its concentration of creativity and concentration, in its pleasures and freedoms. Suggestions that there might also be problems are met with accusations of party-pooping, and the assurance that the bounties of the market will benefit all. Towers and iceberg houses, goes the argument, should be celebrated as signs of success. And, indeed, the city is fascinating and exciting. An exceptionally active imagination might be able to see VNEB not as a work of inadequate planning but as the embryo of a fantastical, delirious district, where the Gehry architecture, the ruined power station, the jostling towers, the soft-coated fortress of the embassy and the Damien Hirst gallery, combine to form a new kind of urban phantasmagoria.

VNEB, in truth, is a long way from being such a place, but the bigger point is this: if London is so brilliant, why not apply that brilliance more widely, such that it can boast to the world of its public housing and city planning, the unrivalled intelligence and beauty with which its new towers are directed, its city-transforming ways of draining rainwater, its encouragement of thousands of projects to build homes, grow gardens and improve streets? Why not apply the ingenuity that currently goes into massaging the planning system, such that multi-level basements might be permitted beneath historic houses, to addressing the city's larger needs. Which would in the end benefit everyone, including those overseas investors that London's politicians have been so anxious to court. For whatever thrill might be had from a glass swimming pool would be more thrilling if part of a wider environment that was itself exceptional. London has an amazing ability to reinvent itself decade by decade: why not make its next invention be the rediscovery of its generosity?

There are reasons to think that London can direct itself better. The campaigns by Richard Rogers and others for better design and public realm have left the importance of such things written into policy, into the behaviour of property companies and into the job descriptions of public officials. There are good architects. There are developers who sincerely want to improve the city. There are planners who, despite the ways in which their jobs are made almost impossible, want to do the same. The *London Housing Design Guide* shows that public intervention can raise the standards of the city's living spaces. The Olympics showed that large-scale projects can be achieved; it remains to apply this ability to works of greater social benefit than a giant but short-lived sporting event.

The city has energy, pride and intelligence. There is a feeling, growing every day, that its inequalities and exclusions must be challenged. London has shown its ability to address problems in the past, including recently: it has responded to pressure on transport, if imperfectly, with a series of actions with buses, trains, cars and cycling.

Against these signs of hope are the growing imbalance between weakening local government and the power of investment, a flow of poor decisions that shows no sign of slowing, politicians who continue to prefer futile gestures to effective actions. The scale of the city's growth requires seriousness and ambition that its politicians have not shown for decades. Its complexities require a level of understanding that is also rare.

It might be asked: why worry? If London glitters and shines as never before, and if it continues to be a magnet for people and money, why not just seek more of the same? For the sake of those inside the city but nonetheless outside its velvet rope is one answer. Because it can always be better is another. As important as either are the effects on its citizens if London loses its openness and defines itself by its divisions. Even for the winners, would it be such a good place to live?

London is a point where the globalized and specific meet with special force. In this it is not alone – Mumbai, Delhi, New York and Shanghai could make the same claim – but the history and fabric of the city give special characteristics to the encounter. London, important in itself, represents qualities that are everywhere challenged. Abundant, dynamic and flawed, it has the genius to create examples that can change the world.

List of Illustrations

10 Snowdon Aviary, London Zoo, Lord Snowdon, Cedric Price and Frank Newby, 1965.

14 Giraffe House, London Zoo, Decimus Burton, 1830s; Mappin Terraces, London Zoo, Belcher and Joass, 1914.

17 Penguin Pool, London Zoo, Tecton, 1934.

19 St Mark's church, Primrose Hill, Thomas Little, 1852; Regent's Park Mosque, Frederick Gibberd, 1978.

32 View from Primrose Hill.

37 HSBC boardroom, Foster and Partners, 2002, and history wall, Thomas Heatherwick, 2002, Canary Wharf. (Top image © Nigel Young / Foster + Partners; bottom image © Andrew Pulter.)

41 Canary Wharf.

44 HSBC, Canary Wharf.

47 Non-Plan special issue of *New Society*, 1969.

50 *Aerial view of proposed Canary Wharf in the year 2025* by Carlos Diniz, 1988. (Image courtesy of Drawing Matter Collections, copyright the Famlly of Carlos Diniz.)

54 London Wall, 1962 and 2015. (Top image © John Maltby / RIBA Collections.)

56 HSBC, Canary Wharf, by Foster and Partners, 2002.

57 The Gherkin, by Foster and Partners, 2004.

60 Paternoster Square, William Whitfield and others, 2003.

62 Route from St James's Park to Regent's Park, as planned by John Nash. (From John Summerson, *Georgian London*, London, 1945.)

64 Nash, Park Crescent, 1822.

66 Regent's Park.

69 Bromley-by-Bow.

75 Heron Tower, KPF, 2011/Sushisamba. (Top and middle images: courtesy of SUSHISAMBA.)

78 Rick Owens party; Smiljan Radić Serpentine pavilion, 2014.

79 London Fields lido; Café Oto, Assemble, 2013. (Top image © WENN Ltd / Alamy Stock Photo.)

89 Chapel Market; Shakespeare's Head. (Top image © Frank Tewkesbury / Stringer / Getty Images.)

92 City Road: Canaletto, UNStudio, 2016; Texaco; Montcalm Hotel, Squire and Partners, 2015.

93 Mixed-use development, East Road, by Lifschutz Davidson Sandilands, 2011; Silicon Roundabout with Bezier building, TP Bennett, 2010.

95 Leila's.

96 Lounge Bohemia (courtesy Lounge Bohemia archive); Old Street at night.

104 Wanstead Park; River Roding at Barking.

109 Bazalgette's sewage system.

114 Albert Embankment; cross-section through Victoria Embankment. (© Science & Society Picture Library / Getty.)

119 Royal Festival Hall, London County Council, 1951; Hayward Gallery, Greater London Council, 1968; Queen Elizabeth Hall, GLC, 1967.

121 Tuning London, The Southbank Centre, Ron Herron and Diana Jowsey. (© 1972 Archigram Architects. Courtesy Archigram Archives 2016.)

123 Beckton Sewage Works (© Armitage Press Centre); Greenway; Abbey Mills pumping station, Joseph Bazalgette and others, 1868.

126 The Castle, Stoke Newington (William Chadwell Mylne and Robert William Billings, 1856); West Reservoir with Woodberry Down development; New River, Enfield.

128 William Hogarth. *Times of the Day: Evening*, 1738. (Image © Private Collection / Ken Welsh / Bridgeman Images.)

133 Percy Circus, Islington.

136 Bedford Square, Bloomsbury; Fournier Street, Spitalfields.

139 Bevin Court, Tecton, 1954.

142 Abram Games, *Your Britain, Fight for it Now*. (Image © Estate of Abram Games, 1942.)

146 Image of Hampstead Heath from Rasmussen, *London. The Unique City*.

147 Hampstead Heath.

155 Maryon Park, still from *Blow-Up*. (Image licensed by: Warner Bros. Entertainment Inc. All Rights Reserved.)

157 William Curtis ecological park, by Tower Bridge, 1976–85. (Image: David Hope / Greater London Council.)

171 Cross-section through the Metropolitan Railway at Baker Street. (Image © Mary Evans Picture Library / Alamy Stock Photo.)

175 London Underground train carriage interior and station platform, from Rasmussen, *London. The Unique City*.

180 Chiswick Park underground station, Charles Holden, 1932.

187 Lodging house in Field Lane, from Hector Gavin, *Sanitary Ramblings*, 1848.

189 Arnold Circus, Shoreditch, London County Council, 1900.

197 The Heygate Estate, Elephant and Castle, London Borough of Southwark, 1974.

209 Site of former Heygate Estate, with Strata SE1 tower, BLFS, 2010; posters promoting redevelopment of Heygate.

210 Base of Strata SE1 with promotional posters, Elephant and Castle.

221 Carpenters Estate, Stratford, occupied by Focus E15, 2014. (Image © Jess Hurd / reportdigital.co.uk.)

224 Lillington Gardens Estate, Darbourne and Darke, 1964–72.

226 Trellick Tower, Ernö Goldfinger, 1972.

227 Dawson's Heights, Kate Macintosh and London Borough of Southwark, 1972.

228 *and* 229 Central Hill, Rosemary Stjernstedt and London Borough of Lambeth, 1973.

230 Golden Lane Estate, Chamberlain Powell and Bon, 1957–62.

231 Spa Green Estate, Tecton, 1950.

232 Alton Estate, Roehampton, J. Leslie Martin and London County Council, 1959.

234 Alexandra and Ainsworth Estate, St John's Wood, Neave Brown
and London Borough of Camden, 1979.

235 Churchill Gardens, Pimlico, Powell and Moya, 1946–62.

240 Hampstead Garden Suburb; Northwood Hills.

244 Highfort Court, Kingsbury, Ernest George Trobridge, 1937; BAPS
Shri Swaminarayan Mandir, Neasden, 1995; Dollis Hill Synagogue,
Owen Williams, 1938.

248 Walters Way, Lewisham, Walter Segal, early 1980s; Barbican, City
of London, Chamberlain Powell and Bon, 1965–76; Peabody Estate,
Whitechapel, Henry Darbishire, 1881.

249 Albert Hall Mansions, Kensington. Norman Shaw, 1879–86;
Pulman Court, Streatham, Frederick Gibberd, 1935; Du Cane Court,
Balham, G. Kay Green, 1938.

252 Terrace housing in Newham, early twentieth century; Becontree
Estate, 1921–35; London County Council housing, near Lisson
Grove.

253 SPAN housing, Blackheath, Eric Lyons, 1965–67; converted
warehouses at Shad Thames; Setchell Road Estate, Bermondsey,
by Neylan and Ungless, 1972–78.

255 Housing near Abbey Mills; The Circle, Bermondsey, CZWG, 1989;
Scape East, Mile End Road, Jefferson Sheard Architects, 2012.

256 1–3 Willow Road, Ernö Goldfinger, 1939; Straw Bale House,
Islington, Sarah Wigglesworth and Jeremy Till, 2000; The Blue
House, FAT, Hackney, 2002.

259 Brick House, Paddington, Caruso St John, 2005; Hopkins House,
Hampstead, Michael and Patty Hopkins, 1976; Dirty House,
Shoreditch, David Adjaye, 2002.

260 Bonnington Square, Vauxhall; the Old Dispensary, Stratford;
Athletes' Village, Stratford.

263 Mint Street housing, Bethnal Green, Pitman Tozer, 2014; Pocket
Living, Marcon Place, Hackney, 2015; the Lawn, Harlow New Town,
Frederick Gibberd, 1951.

264 St Andrew's, Bromley-by-Bow, Allies and Morrison, 2010.

269 Cross-section through a typical 'iceberg house'.

274 Stills from promotional video for Redrow London, 2014.

277 Diagram of three-bedroom house with twenty-six residents, Newham, 2015.

281 Graph of London house-building numbers 1971–2014, courtesy Greater London Authority 2015.

299 Cannes during MIPIM and Palais Bulles, Antti Lovag. (Bottom image © aerialphotos.com / Alamy.)

303 Finsbury Avenue Square, Broadgate, City of London, Arup Associates, 1980s.

307 One New Change, City of London, Jean Nouvel, 2010.

308 Richard Rogers, *London as it could be*, 1986. (Image courtesy Rogers Stirk Harbour + Partners.)

313 Number One Poultry, City of London, Stirling Wilford, 1997.

315 Foster and Partners, London Millennium Tower, 1996. (Image © Foster + Partners.)

319 The Shard, London Bridge, Renzo Piano, opening laser show, 2012. (Image © Joseph Okpako / Getty.)

320 Foster and Partners, The Gherkin, City of London, 2004.

327 St George Wharf and St George Wharf Tower, 2014, Vauxhall, Broadway Malyan.

337 20 Fenchurch Street, or 'Walkie-Talkie', City of London, Rafael Vinoly, 2014; 'Sky Garden' at ditto. (Bottom image © Jim Dyson / Getty Images.)

343 Customers at the York Minster pub in Soho, London, October 1941; Granada Theatre, Tooting, London, October 1976. (Top image © Kurt Hutton / Stringer / Getty. Bottom image © Evening Standard / Stringer / Getty.)

345 Tate Modern, Bankside, Herzog and de Meuron, 2000, exterior and Turbine Hall.

349 Millennium Bridge, Foster and Partners, 2000; Neo Bankside, Rogers Stirk Harbour and Partners, 2012; Neo Bankside, Tate Modern and Blue Fin building, Allies and Morrison, 2007.

354 Camley Street Natural Park, King's Cross; Granary Square, King's Cross; One Pancras Square, King's Cross, David Chipperfield, 2013.

359 One Commercial Street, Aldgate; Whitechapel Art Gallery, Charles Harrison Townsend, 1899, with 'Tree of Life' artwork by Rachel

Whiteread, 2012; Altab Ali Park, Whitechapel, muf architecture + art, 2011.

362 Idea Store, Whitechapel, David Adjaye, 2004; Wickhams Department Store, Mile End Road, 1927; shops on Mile End Road.

364 St Mary and Holy Trinity, Bow, fourteenth and fifteenth centuries; Bow flyover.

366 Carpenters Estate, Stratford, with Olympic Stadium and Orbit, Anish Kapoor and others, 2012; Stratford High Street.

368 Westfield Stratford City 2011; The Shoal, Stratford, by Studio Egret West, 2012.

372 Aquatic Centre, Stratford, Zaha Hadid, 2011.

375 Queen Elizabeth Olympic Park.

377 Hanbury Street, Spitalfields.

383 Proposed Garden Bridge, Heatherwick Studio, 2013. Image courtesy Garden Bridge Trust.

391 National Theatre, South Bank, Denys Lasdun, 1976. (Top image © Lasdun Archive / RIBA Collections; bottom image © John Donat / RIBA Collections.)

394 Hackney Empire, Frank Matcham, 1901. (Image © Matt Humphrey.)

407 Barking Town Centre, muf architecture + art and AHMM, 2010.

410 Serpentine Gallery pavilion, Kensington Gardens, SANAA, 2009; a House for Essex, FAT and Grayson Perry, 2015; Yardhouse, Sugarhouse Studios, Assemble, 2014.

412 Lisson Gallery, near Lisson Grove, Tony Fretton, 1992. (Bottom image courtesy Lisson Gallery.)

414 Aldermanbury Square, City of London, Eric Parry, 2007.

419 Natural History Museum, South Kensington, Alfred Waterhouse, 1873–1881: interior with cast of diplodocus skeleton; detail of entrance.

421 Earth Galleries, Natural History Museum, 1996.

424 Bousfield School, Kensington, Chamberlain Powell and Bon, 1956.

427 British Library, St Pancras, Colin St John Wilson, 1996; Shaftesbury School, Newham, 1894 and 1904. (Top image © Nigel Bewley.)

428 Bexley Business Academy, Foster and Partners, 2003; Saw Swee

Hock student centre, London School of Economics, O'Donnell and Tuomey, 2014. (Top image © Nigel Young / Foster + Partners.)

434 ORTUS Learning and Events Centre, Camberwell, Duggan Morris, 2013.

443 Carpetright Tower, Tottenham: after the fire of the 2011 riots and in 2015, following restoration. (Top image © Peter Macdiarmid / Getty.)

445 Views of Tottenham High Road.

447 Seven Sisters Market, Wards Corner, Tottenham; Cox London factory; billboard promoting new stadium for Tottenham Hotspur, 2015. (Middle image © Philipp Ebeling.)

455 MI6 Building, Vauxhall, Terry Farrell, 2012; Bus station, Vauxhall, Arup Associates, 2005.

457 Embassy Gardens construction site, Nine Elms; Battersea Power Station.

459 Riverlight, Nine Elms, Rogers Stirk Harbour and Partners, 2015.

460 St George Wharf, Vauxhall, Broadway Malyan; the Hoist, Vauxhall.

463 Riverlight; proposed towers at Vauxhall. (Bottom image © Uniform.)

467 US Embassy by Kieran Timberlake, due for completion 2017; Electric Boulevard, Battersea Power Station, showing Foster and Partners' Battersea Roof Gardens (L) and Gehry Partners' Prospect Place (R). (Top image: Kieran Timberlake / Studio amd; bottom image copyright Battersea Power Station Development Company.)

472 Newport Street Gallery, Vauxhall, Caruso St John, 2015, interior; Social Justice Centre, Vauxhall, Architecture 00, 2014, interior. (Top image © Prudence Cumings Associates Ltd; bottom image © Rory Gardiner.)

481 Second Home, Spitalfields, SelgasCano, 2014; 'Silicon Roundabout', Old Street.

Bibliography and Sources

General

London: The Biography, Peter Ackroyd, Chatto and Windus, 2000

Lost London 1870–1945, Philip Davies, Transatlantic Press, 2009

http://michaeledwards.org.uk

A People's History of London, Lindsey German and John Rees, Verso, 2012

London: Bread and Circuses, Jonathan Glancey, Verso, 2002

Rebel Cities: From the Right to the City to the Urban Revolution, David Harvey, Verso, 2012

Space, Hope and Brutalism, Elain Harwood, Yale, 2015

The London Encyclopaedia, Christopher Hibbert, Ben Weinreb, John Keay, Julia Keay, Pan Macmillan, 3rd edition 2010

Guide To The Architecture Of London, Edward Jones and Christopher Woodward, Phoenix, 2013

This is London, Ben Judah, Picador, 2016

Critical Cities, Volumes 1–4, ed. Deep Naik and Trenton Oldfield, Myrdle Court Press, 2009–14

Nairn's London, Ian Nairn, Penguin, 1966

Pevsner Architectural Guides: Buildings of England, London, Volumes 1–5, Nikolaus Pevsner and others, Yale

London Orbital, Iain Sinclair, Granta, 2002

Hackney That Rose Red Empire, Iain Sinclair, Hamish Hamilton, 2009

A Guide to the New Ruins of Great Britain, Owen Hatherley, Verso, 2010

London: The Unique City, Steen Eiler Rasmussen, Macmillan, 1937

The Survey of London, multiple volumes, authors and dates, Yale,
    http://www.british-history.ac.uk/search/series/survey-london
Expulsions: Brutality and Complexity in the Global Economy, Saskia
    Sassen, Belknap Press, 2014
London in the Twentieth Century: A City and Its People, Jerry White,
    Random House, 2001
London in the Nineteenth Century: 'A Human Awful Wonder of God',
    Jerry White, Random House, 2008
Family and Kinship in East London, Michael Young and Peter Willmott,
    Penguin, 1957
The New East End: Kinship, Race and Conflict, Michael Young, Kate
    Gavron, Geoff Dench, Profile, 2006
Only writers of exceptional rigour and purity, and maybe not even
    them, can fail to benefit from Wikipedia, whose usefulness is
    hereby gratefully acknowledged.

1. City of the Present

London's Zoo, Gwynne Vevers (compiler), Bodley Head, 1976
The Buildings of London Zoo, Peter Guillery, Royal Commission on the
    Historic Monuments of England, 1993
Berthold Lubetkin: Architecture and the Tradition of Progress, John Allan,
    Merrell, 2002
Beastly London, Hanna Velten, Reaktion, 2013
London: the Unique City, Steen Eiler Rasmussen, Penguin, 1960
*A Different Nature; the Paradoxical World of Zoos and their Uncertain
    Future*, David Hancocks, University of California Press, 2001

2. The Disembodied Economy, Embodied

New Statesman lecture, Alex Salmond, 5 March 2014
Exploiting the Archive; Case Study: History Wall, http://www.
    managingbusinessarchives.co.uk
Gangster Bankers: Too Big to Jail, Matt Taibbi, *Rolling Stone*, 14 February
    2013
http://www.scribd.com/doc/235609643/1969-Nonplan-An-
    experiment-In-freedom-Banham-Barker-Hall-Price#scribd

The Smithsons on Housing, produced by B. S. Johnson, BBC, 1970

High Rise, J. G. Ballard, Jonathan Cape, 1975

'Canary Wharf epitomises enterprise culture', James Pickford, *Financial Times*, 13 May 2012

'Big money, fast spending, free fall', Scott Shane, *Baltimore Sun*, 4 July 1999

Hard Times: The Divisive Toll of the Economic Slump, Tom Clark and Anthony Heath, Yale, 2014

The Death and Life of Great American Cities, Jane Jacobs, Random House, New York, 1961

London: the Unique City, Steen Eiler Rasmussen, Penguin, 1960

Architecture in Britain 1530–1830, John Summerson, Penguin, 1963

'The myth that Canary Wharf did east London any good', Owen Hatherley, *Guardian*, 15 May 2012

Mapping Corporate Philanthropy and Community Engagement in East London, Johanna Wadsley and others, Queen Mary College, 2013

Interviews with Rushanara Ali and others

3. New Sybaris

The Super Rich and Us, Jacques Peretti, two-part BBC documentary, 2015

http://www.bbc.co.uk/programmes/b04xw4rw

Interviews with Peter Rees and others

http://www.theguardian.com/commentisfree/2014/dec/22/behind-the-restaurant-boom-urban-delusion

http://www.timeout.com/london/alternative-nightlife/killing-kittens-1

Albert Angelo, B. S. Johnson, Constable, 1964

http://www.thesun.co.uk/sol/homepage/news/79093/A-Kylie-unlikely-pub-trip.html

http://www.newstatesman.com/culture/2014/09/will-self-awful-cult-talentless-hipster-has-taken-over

http://www.bbc.co.uk/news/uk-england-london-34373485

The County Books: East London, Robert Sinclair, Robert Hale, 1950

4. Water

The Great Stink of London, Stephen Halliday, Sutton, 1999

The Ghost Map, Steven Johnson, Allen Lane, 2006

Tonic to the Nation: Festival of Britain, 1951, Mary Banham (Editor), Bevis Hillier (Editor), Thames and Hudson, 1976

http://archigram.westminster.ac.uk

London's New River, Robert Ward, Historical Publications, 2003

5. Fire, Air, Nature

A Cry from the Streets, dir. Lewis Gilbert, 1958

London: the Art of Georgian Building, Dan Cruickshank, Architectural Press, 1975

Survey of London, Volume 47, Northern Clerkenwell and Pentonville, Yale, 2008

Berthold Lubetkin: Architecture and the Tradition of Progress, John Allan, Merrell, 2002

A Complete Body of Architecture, Isaac Ware, 1756–57

http://archive.spectator.co.uk/article/4th-march-1916/8/henry-james

http://www.londongardenstrust.org/features/heath.htm

Commons, Forests and Footpaths, Lord Eversley, Cassell, 1910

London in the Nineteenth Century: 'A Human Awful Wonder of God', Jerry White, Random House, 2008

Blow-Up, dir. Michelangelo Antonioni, 1966

Conversations with Jo Gibbons, Mathew Frith, Peter Massini, David Goode

Nature in Towns and Cities, David Goode, Harper Collins, 2014

The Greening of the Cities, David Nicholson-Lord, Routledge & Kegan Paul, 1987

http://www.theguardian.com/lifeandstyle/gallery/2012/may/23/guerrilla-gardening-richard-reynolds

Characteristics of Men, Manners, Opinions, Times, Vol. 2, Anthony Ashley-Cooper, 3rd Earl of Shaftesbury, 1711

To-morrow: A Peaceful Path to Real Reform, Ebenezer Howard, London, 1898

Garden Cities of To-morrow, Ebenezer Howard, London, 1902

Greater London Plan, Patrick Abercrombie, London, 1944

London Fog: The Biography, Christine L. Corton, Belknap, 2015

6. Darkness

Robert Louis Stevenson, *Virginibus puerisque*, 1881

At Day's Close, Robert Ekirch, Norton, 2005

Urban Lighting, Light Pollution and Society, ed. Josiane Meier et al.,
     Routledge, 2014

Brilliant: the Evolution of Artificial Light, Jane Brox, Houghton Mifflin
     Harcourt. 2011

*Underground Writing: The London Tube from George Gissing to Virginia
     Woolf*, Dave Welsh, Liverpool University Press, 2010

'The Genii of the Lamps', John Hollingshead, *All the Year Round*, no. 129,
     1861

*The Subterranean Railway: How the London Underground Was Built and
     How it Changed the City Forever*, Christian Wolmar, Atlantic Books,
     2005

Charles Holden: Architect, Eitan Karol, Shaun Tyas, 2007

Rosebery: Statesman in Turmoil, Leo McKinstry, John Murray, 2005

Translations from Drawing to Building and Other Essays, Robin Evans,
     AA Documents, 1996

Sanitary Ramblings: Being Sketches and Illustrations of Bethnal Green,
     Hector Gavin, London, 1848

A Child of the Jago, Arthur Morrison, Methuen, 1896

Estates: an Intimate History, Lynsey Hanley, Granta, 2007

London in the Nineteenth Century: 'A Human Awful Wonder of God',
     Jerry White, Random House, 2008

Life and Labour of the People in London, Charles Booth, 2nd edition,
     Macmillan, 1892–97

Toward an Architecture, Le Corbusier, 1923, trans. John Goodman, Getty,
     2007

Subterranean Cities: the World Beneath Paris and London, 1800–1945,
     David L. Pike, Cornell, 2005

7. Exile

http://www.robertholden.org

http://heygatewashome.org

Interviews with Tim Tinker, Peter John, Fred Manson, Julie Greer, George Turner, Jerry Flynn, Adrian Glasspool and others

Heygate Heaven, produced by Chris Wood, 2012, http://www.wordthecat.com/heygate.html

'Hidden forest at the heart of London's Heygate estate regeneration', Matthew Wilson, *Financial Times*, 2 May 2014

'Secret twilight of the high-rise housing awaiting demolition', *Daily Mail*, 28 April 2013

http://www.lendlease.com/emea/united-kingdom/projects/elephant-and-castle-regeneration

'Look to the Heygate Estate for what's wrong with London's housing', Ian Steadman, *New Statesman*, 6 November 2013

The Report: Right to Buy, BBC Radio 4, 2014

https://mappinglondonshousingstruggles.wordpress.com

'Revealed: how developers exploit flawed planning system to minimise affordable housing', Oliver Wainwright, *Guardian*, 25 June 2015

'The families priced out of their London homes by benefit cap', Amelia Gentleman, *Guardian*, 5 March 2014

Private Island: Why Britain Now Belongs to Someone Else, James Meek, Verso, 2014

http://focuse15.org

'New Era Estate sold to affordable housing group', *BBC News*, 20 December 2014

8. At Home in London

https://municipaldreams.wordpress.com

Utopia London, dir. Tom Cordell, 2010

http://www.utopialondon.com

Nairn's London, Ian Nairn, Penguin, 1966

Pevsner Architectural Guides: Buildings of England, London, Volumes 1–5, Nikolaus Pevsner and others, Yale

Woodward and Jones, *Guide to the Architecture of London*

'Trellick Tower's Trendy Takeover', Katie Law, *Evening Standard*, 7
    October 2013

Interviews with Kate Macintosh, and residents of Central Hill and 369
    Leigham Court Road

One Below the Queen, several directors, 2010

London in the Twentieth Century: A City and Its People, Jerry White,
    Random House, 2001

Metro-land, written and narrated by John Betjeman, BBC, 1973

London Suburbs, Andrew Saint, Merrell Holberton, 1999

http://www.segalselfbuild.co.uk/home.html

Chamberlain Powell and Bon, Elain Harwood, RIBA publishing, 2011

A History of Du Cane Court: Land, Architecture, People and Politics,
    Gregory K. Vincent, Woodbine Press, 2008

Eric Lyons and Span, Barbara Simms, RIBA publishing 2012

London Housing Design Guide, Mayor of London, 2010

9. The Values of Value

*All That Is Solid: How the Great Housing Disaster Defines Our Times, and
    What We Can Do About It*, Danny Dorling, Allen Lane, 2014

From Russia With Cash, dir. Dan Reed, Channel 4, 2015

http://www.nortonrosefulbright.com/knowledge/publications/121493/
    residential-real-estate-in-the-uk

'London's Most Mysterious Mansion', Ed Caesar, *New Yorker*, 1 June 2015

'Billionaires' basements: the luxury bunkers making holes in London's
    streets', Oliver Wainwright, *Guardian*, 9 November 2012

http://www.telegraph.co.uk/news/newsvideo/
    weirdnewsvideo/11324969/Watch-Strange-advert-for-luxury-
    London-flats.html

http://strangeharvest.com/redrow-psycho

New Ideas for Housing London, Claire Bennie, NLA, 2015

Das englische Haus, Hermann Muthesius, E. Wasmuth, Berlin, 1904

10. Mipimism

Interviews with Ken Livingstone and others

Norman Foster: a Life in Architecture, Deyan Sudjic, Weidenfeld and
    Nicolson, 2010

A New London: Two Views, Richard Rogers and Mark Fisher, Penguin,
    1992

Cities for a Small Planet, Richard Rogers, Faber and Faber, 1997

Cities for a Small Country, Richard Rogers and Anne Power, Faber and
    Faber, 2000

Towards an Urban Renaissance, Members of the Urban Task Force,
    Spon, 1999

Our Towns and Cities: The Future: Delivering an Urban Renaissance,
    DETR and John Prescott, DETR, 2000

County of London Plan, J. H. Forshaw and Patrick Abercrombie,
    Macmillan, 1943

Greater London Plan, Patrick Abercrombie, HMSO, 1944

The London Plan, Mayor of London, with successive revisions, since
    2004

'Irvine Sellar: blue-sky thinker', Alastair Dawber, *Independent*, 6 July
    2012

www.palaisbulles.com

Super-Cannes, J. G. Ballard, Flamingo, 2000

11. Public and Publoid

https://libcom.org/library/1850-1994-battle-hyde-park-ruffians-
    radicals-ravers

London in the Nineteenth Century: 'A Human Awful Wonder of God',
    Jerry White, Random House, 2008

*Hippie Hippie Shake: The Dreams, The Trips, The Trials, The Love Ins, The
    Screw Ups , The Sixties*, Richard Neville, Bloomsbury, 1995

Ground Control, Anna Minton, Penguin, 2012

Building Tate Modern, Rowan Moore and Raymund Ryan, Tate, 2000

Shakespeare's Globe Rebuilt, J. Mulryne and Margaret Shewring,
    Cambridge, 1997

12. You've been Heatherwicked

Civilizing Caliban: Misuse of Art, 1875–1980, Frances Borzello, Camden
    Press, 1987

'The East End's Own Pompidou Centre', Rowan Moore, *Evening
    Standard*, 27 September 2005

Interview with Afham Ismail

'The empty cable car joins a string of Boris Johnson follies', Andrew
    Neather, *Evening Standard*, 18 July 2013

Will Hurst of the *Architects' Journal* has reported extensively on the
    Garden Bridge, for example, in 'Garden Bridge procurement was
    "neither open nor objective" ', 28 October 2015

http://www.phillywatersheds.org/what_were_doing/green_
    infrastructure

'Planned London super sewer branded waste of time and taxpayer
    money', Ian Griffiths, *Guardian*, 27 November 2014

Lina Bo Bardi, Zeuler Rocha Mello de Almeida Lima, Yale, 2013

Nicholas Hawksmoor: Rebuilding Ancient Wonders, Vaughan Hart, Yale,
    2002

Denys Lasdun: Architecture, City, Landscape, William J. R. Curtis,
    Phaidon, 1994

Frank Matcham: Theatre Architect, Brian Mercer Walker, Blackstaff, 1980

13. Subtle Substances

The Decay of Lying, Oscar Wilde, James R. Osgood McIlvaine, 1891

Elephant Creative Vision

http://www.muf.co.uk

The Voyage of the Beagle, Charles Darwin, 1839, 2nd ed. John Murray,
    1845

Interviews with John Stamp and some pupils of Bousfield School; and
    Kumar Jacob

A Vision of Britain, Prince Charles, Doubleday, 1989

https://www.ted.com/talks/julian_treasure_why_architects_need_to_
    use_their_ears

'Save Dippy: outcry over Natural History Museum plan to eject famous
    dinosaur', Anita Singh, *Daily Telegraph*, 29 January 2015

14. You Burned Your Own Town

http://londonist.com/2015/03/whats-happening-at-nine-elms.php

'Tottenham riots: a peaceful protest, then suddenly all hell broke loose', Paul Lewis, *Guardian*, 7 August 2011

'Historian Starkey in "racism" row over riot comments', David Barrett, *Daily Telegraph*, 14 August 2011

Interviews with Claire Kober, representatives of Tottenham Hotspur, David Lammy MP, Zehra Harrison and other Tottenham residents

https://wardscorner.wikispaces.com

Tottenham Physical Development Framework, Arup, 2014

The Physical Structure of the Economy of Tottenham High Road, Jane Clossick

Interviews with Jose Cardoso, Anna Harding, Duncan Smith, Mark Brearley and others

Test Dept – Total State Machine, PC Press, 2015

Vauxhall Gardens: a History, David Coke and Alan Borg, Yale, 2011

'George Smiley would have hated it', Rowan Moore, *Independent*, 15 September 1992

http://www.smithsonianmag.com/ist/?next=/travel/londons-secret-gardens

kierantimberlake.com/pages/view/88/embassy-of-the-united-states-of-america

Oblivion, David Foster Wallace, Abacus, 2004

https://www.batterseapowerstation.co.uk

'Definitely not a bridge', Reinier de Graaf, dezeen.com, 17 March 2015

Interview with Gavin Sung

15. Slow Burn City

The Death and Life of Great American Cities, Jane Jacobs, Random House, New York, 1961

Soft City, Jonathan Raban, The Harvill Press, 1974

Experiencing Architecture, Steen Eiler Rasmussen, Chapman and Hall, 1959

'Richard Sennett pours scorn on Tech City plans', Elizabeth Hopkirk,
    Building Design, 11 December 2012
Capital: the Eruption of Delhi, Rana Dasgupta, Canongate, 2014
Maximum City: Bombay Lost and Found, Suketu Mehta, Vintage, 2004

Acknowledgements

The following have given in different ways the time, help, knowledge, insights, guidance and/or support essential to writing this book:

Kris Doyle, Paul Baggaley, Wilf Dickie, Stuart Wilson, Nicholas Blake, Dusty Miller, Nuzha Nuseibeh and all at Picador. Jane Ferguson, Sarah Donaldson, Rob Yates, John Mulholland and all at the *Observer*. Architects for Social Housing. David Bass. Diane Berg. Bousfield School and John Stamp. Mark Brearley. The British Library. Greg Callus. Caruso St John. Clem Cecil and SAVE. Alessandra Cianchetta. Jane Clossick. Alan Colam. Albane Duvalier. Peter Eversden and London Forum. Angus Farquhar. Liza Fior. Jerry Flynn. Focus E15. Mathew Frith and the London Wildlife Trust. The Games family. Jo Gibbons. Adrian Glasspool. Julie Greer. Katy Harris. Niall Hobhouse. Nigel Hugill. Afham Ismail. Andrew Kidd. Susan Lasdun. Ian Lindsley. Amy Linford. Lucy Luck. Kate Macintosh. Fred Manson. My family, both close and extended. The Open Spaces Society. Ortus and Kumar Jacob. Peter Rees. Fred Scott. Rohan Silva. Andrew Smith. Jane Southern. Carolyn Steel. Edward Teeger. Thames Central Open Spaces. Tim Tinker. Robert Torday. Tony Travers. George Turner. Marc Vlessing. Barbara Weiss and Alan Leibovitz. Sarah Wigglesworth. Stephen Witherford. Ellis Woodman. Zoological Society of London.

In grateful memory of Peter Hall, Norman Moore, Janet Moore, Meriel Oliver, Dalibor Vesely and Jules Wright, all of them inspirations.

Index

A & C Continental Delicatessen 449–50
A House for Essex 409, **410**
Abbey Mills pumping station 108, **123**, 124–5
Abercrombie, Patrick 163, 310, 478, 486
Abramovich, Roman 439
Abramović, Marina 80
Abu Dhabi 217
ACAVA 450, 451
Acts of Parliament 31, 45, 63, 137, 165, 458, 487
Adelphi development 115
Adjaye, David 361
  Dirty House, Shoreditch 258, **259**
  Idea Store, Whitechapel **362**
  Moscow School of Management 361
  Museum of African American History 361
  Whitechapel Library 361
Adonis, Lord 214–15
advertising 176, 179
Aerial view of proposed Canary Wharf in the year 2025 (Carlos Diniz, 1988) **50–51**
AHMM *see* Allford Hall Monaghan Morris
AIA 446
AIDS 84
air pollution 164–6
Airbnb 430
al-Muhajiroun 363
al-Sabouni, Marwa xvi
Alban Gate 53
Albert Edward, Prince of Wales (later Edward VII) 108, 182
Albert Bridge 117
Albert Embankment 113, 115
Albert Hall Mansions, Kensington **249**, 250
5 Aldermanbury Square **414**, 413–15
Aldgate 376
Aldgate East Underground station 357
Aldi 440
Alexandra and Ainsworth Estate, St John's Wood 233–5, **234**
Alexandra Crescent 242

Ali, Rushanara 71
All London Green Grid 160
All Souls, Langham Place 65
Allan, John 140
Allen and Overy 52
Allford Hall Monaghan Morris (AHMM) 306, 406–8
Allies and Morrison 301, 350, 353, 413
  St Andrew's, Bromley-by-Bow **264**
Altab Ali Park **359**, 360
Alton Estate, Roehampton 232, **232**
Amersham 243
Ampomah, Angela 207
Amsterdam 85
Amwell 127
Amwell Society 296
Angel Association 296
animals, exotic 9–15, 20–3, 160
Antonioni, Michelangelo 154
ANZ 52
Apple 431
Apprentice, The (TV show) 72
Arad, Ron 42
ArcelorMittal Orbit 371–3
Archer, Jeffrey 452
Archigram 120
Architects Journal 317, 324, 454
Architecture 00 485
  Social Justice Centre 471, 485
Architecture of London, The (1983) 198–9
Architecture and Urbanism Unit 310
architettura povera 90
Argent 353
Arnold Circus 140, 188, **189**
arts-and-crafts 239, 241, 243, 286
Arup, Ove 16, 348
Arup Associates 302, 304, 448
  Battersea Power Station **457**
  Finsbury Avenue Square **303**
Assemble 80, 411
  Yardhouse, Sugarhouse Studios **410**

Athletes' Village, Stratford **260**, 371
Aykon 470
Aylesbury Estate 198–200, 205

B of the Bang sculpture, Manchester 396
Baker Street Underground Station 172, 243
Balham Society 296
Ballard, J. G.
 High Rise 46, 225
 Super-Cannes 328–9
Ballymore 97
Balmond, Cecil: ArcelorMittal Orbit 373
Baltic Exchange 311, 314, 316
Banham, Reyner 46
Bank of America 52
Bank of England 338
Bankside Power Station 348–52
 Turbine Hall 344, 346, 350
 see also Tate Modern
Banksy 378
BAPS Shri Swaminarayan Mandir **244**, 245
Barbican, City of London 231, 247, **248**, 423
Barcelona 310, 311
Barclays 52
Barfield, Julia: London Eye 305
Barker, Paul 46, 214
Barking 406–8
Barking Abbey 103
Barking Creek 103, 105, 110, 122–4
Barking Town Centre **407**
Barnet 215
Barnett, Henrietta 237–9, 242, 358
Barney, Matthew 77
Barratt 215
basements 268–70
Battersea 81, 316, 456, 468
Battersea Park 458
Battersea Power Station 456, **457**, 461–2, 466, **467**, 468, 469
Battersea Power Station Development Company 456
Battery Park City, Lower Manhattan 49
Bauhaus 55, 425
Bazalgette, Joseph 108, 110, 112–13, 115–17, 122, 125, 127, 129–30, 167, 192, 306, 356, 385, 387, 476, 477
 sewage system xx, 109
Bazalgette (sludge vessel) 105
Beaux-Arts planning 59
Beck, Harry 177
Beckton Alps 122
Beckton Sewage Treatment Works 103–5, 108, 110, 122, **123**, 430
Becontree 250–1, **252**

Bedford, Earl of 135
Bedford Estate 333–4
Bedford Square **136**
bedroom tax (under-occupancy charge) 216, 219
'Being a Dickhead's Cool' anthem 91
Beirut 53
Belcher and Joass 15, 20
 Mappin Terraces, London Zoo **14**
Belgravia 27, 61
benefit caps 215–16, 218–20
Bengali Language Movement 360
Bennett, Hubert
 Hayward Gallery 118, **119**
 Purcell Room 118, **119**
 Queen Elizabeth Hall 118
Benyon, Richard 222
Bepler, Jonathan 77
Berkeley Group 454
Berkeley Homes 413
Berkhamsted Common 152, 220
Berlage, H. P.: Holland House 322
Berlin 169, 311
Bermondsey 81, 254, 272
Bethnal Green, London Borough of 71, 138, 185, 219, 262
Betjeman, John 82, 176, 242–5
Bevin, Ernest 138
Bevin Court 138, **139**, 140, 141, 143, 165
Bexley 261
Bexley Business Academy 330, **428**
Bézier Apartments **93**, 482
BIG 456, 466
Big Ben 360
Binnie, Chris 385
biodiversity 160
Bishopsgate 316
Bishopsgate railway station 94, 97
Black Deep 105
Blackfriars 272
Blackfriars Bridge 348
Blackwall Tunnel 112
Blair, Tony 90, 98, 200–1, 301, 309–10
Blair years 27, 425
Blake, William 184
Blind Beggar pub 361
Bloomberg News 45
Blooms restaurant 358
Bloomsbury 61, 134, 242, 486
Blow-up (1966) 154
Blue Fin Building 348
Blue House, Hackney **256**, 257
Blumenfeld, R. D. 172
Bo Bardi, Lina 389
Board Schools 426

Boltons, The 423
Bonnington Square, Vauxhall 258–61, **260**, 452–6, 458, 471, 473, 487
Booth, Catherine 363
Booth, Charles 190
'Descriptive Map of London Poverty' 185
Booth, General William 363
Borzello, Frances 358
boulevards 342–4
Boundary Estate, Shoreditch 94, 140, 188–91, 195, 479
Bourne, Simon 384
Bousfield Primary School 423–5, **424**, 487
Bovis Lend Lease, The Athletes' Village 261
Bovril boats 105
Bow 71
Bow church 365
Boxpark 97
Branson, Richard 67
Brearley, Mark 448, 449, 451
Breslau 330
Brick House, Paddington 257, **259**
Brick Lane 80, 94
British Airways 378
British Empire 38–9
British Freehold Land Company 241
British imperialism 38–9
British Land 24, 26
British Library 426, **426**
British Museum 23
Great Court 305
British Rail 480
Brixton 199, 449–50
Broackes, Nigel 70
Broadgate 59, 302–4, 309, 321, 334, 352
Broadwater Farm Estate 199–200
Broadway Malyan 317, 454
St George Wharf 317, **320**, 324
Vauxhall Tower 324–5
Bromley 242
Bromley-by-Bow **69**
Brooks, Alison 306
Broome, John 456
Brown, Gordon 90
Brunel, Isambard Kingdom 116, 117
brutalism 118, 247
BT Tower 26
'bubble houses' 298
Bubley, Ernest 250
Bucharest 42
BUGS (Biodiversity Underpinning Global Survival), London Zoo 22, 420
Burgess Park, Southwark 148
Burton, Decimus: London Zoo 13–15, **14**, 18
Bus station, Vauxhall **457**

buses 178, 181
Butlers Wharf 254
Buy to Let 216–17, 219, 279
Bygraves, Max 132

CABE see Commission for Architecture and the Built Environment
Cable, Vince 34
Caesar, Julius 168
Café Oto **79**, 80
Caine, Michael 204
465 Caledonian Road 254
California 257
Camden, London Borough of 159, 233–5, 353, 355, 479
Alexandra and Ainsworth Estate, St John's Wood **234**
Cameron, David 217, 281, 482, 484–5
Camley Street xxv
Camley Street Natural Park 159, 353, **354**
Campaign (advertising publication) 38
Canada 49
One Canada Square 40–2, 55
Canaletto tower 91, **92**
Canary Wharf 25–7, 34–46, **41**, 48, 49–59, **50–51**, 67–73, 334–5, 352–3, 403, 487–8
Canary Wharf Group 45, 49, 52, 70, 218
Candy, Christian 65
Canterbury Arms, Brixton 450
Cantor Fitzgerald 52
carbon dioxide emissions, zero-carbon-growth developments 211
Carbuncle Cup 482
2010 211
Cardoso, Jose 450
Carmody Groarke 353
Carnaby Street 317
Carnegie, Andrew 436
Caro, Anthony 348
Carpenters Estate 220, **221**, 365, **366**
Carpetright 440, 442, **443**
Carroll, Lewis 144, 161, 172
Caruso St John 471
Brick House 251, **259**
Newport Street Gallery, Vauxhall **471**
Case Study Houses 258
Cass Cities 448
Casson, Hugh 22
Elephant House, London Zoo 18, 21
Castle, The, Stoke Newington **126**
Ceaușescu, Nicolae 42, 261
Central Hill **228**, 229, **229**
Central House of Artists 298
Cereal Killer, Brick Lane 94

cesspools 106
Chadwell Spring 127
Chadwick, Edwin 107
Chakrabortty, Aditya 86
Chalk, Warren 120
Chamberlain Powell and Bon
  Barbican 231, 247, **248**, 423
  Bousfield Primary School 423, **424**
  Golden Lane Estate 230–1, **230**, 423
Channel Tunnel 355
Channel Tunnel Rail Link 159
Chapel Market 87, 88, **89**, 90
Chaplin, Charlie 140
Charles, Prince 370
Charles II 331
Charlton sandpits 154
Cheesegrater (Leadenhall Building) 26, 58,
  316, 321, 336, 339
Chelsea Embankment 113, 125
Chelsea Football Club 439–40, 449
Chelsea Hospital 117, 363
Cherry, Bridget, *Buildings of England* (1983)
  199
Chicago 178
Child of the Jago, A (Arthur Morrison) 188,
  482
Chiltern Firehouse 276
China 38, 53
Chipperfield, David 306, 353
  Camley Street Natural Park **354**
  Granary Square **354**
  One Pancras Square **354**
Chiswick Park underground station **180**
cholera 30, 106–7, 108–12, 185
Chorley Wood 243
Chrysler Building 25
Churchill, Winston 141
Churchill Gardens, Pimlico, City of
  Westminster 235–6, **235**, 266, 487
CIL *see* Community Infrastructure Levy
Citi 52
Citi tower 43
'City, The' (The Square Mile) 34–5, 42, 58
City Corporation 154
City Hall 156, 200, 352
City of London 26, 34–5, 58–59, 70, 74, 81–2,
  200, 293, 302, 304–5, 338, 357, 488
  accommodation 230, 236, 247
  5 Aldermanbury Square 413–15
  Barbican 231, 247, 423
  Golden Lane Estate 230–1, 247, 423, 487
  Heron Tower 74–6, 81, 97, 125, 316, 318, 321,
    340
  IRA bombings 311
  lighting 167
  Number One Poultry 311–14

public spaces 335
  sewerage 107, 110, 112, 125, 129
  Underground stations 172
  versus Canary Wharf 49, 52
  Walkie-Talkie 340
City Road **92**, 272, 273, 413, 482
City of Westminster 293, 305, 469
  Churchill Gardens 235–6, 266, 487
  Lillington Gardens Estate 223–4, 266
Clarke, Katherine 403
Clean Air Acts 476, 478
  1956 166
Clerkenwell 190
Clifford Chance 52
Clifton Bridge, Bristol 117
Clinton, Bill 202
Clissold Park 127, 134
Clossick, Jane 448, 449
coalition government 2010–2015 215–16, 217,
  279, 450
Coca-Cola London Eye 378
Coe, Sebastian 374
commercial architects 304
One Commercial Street, Aldgate 273–5, **359**
commercial viability assessments 217–18, 326
Commission for Architecture and the Built
  Environment (CABE) 293–5, 300, 309–10,
  323–4, 338–9
commons, preservation of the 149–54,
  159–61, 181–2, 220, 488
Commons Preservation Society 149, 163
Community Infrastructure Levy (CIL) 295
Conrad, Joseph 36
Conran, Terence 379, 384
conservation areas 132, 271, 477
Conservative governments 278, 309
  1923 239
  2015 216, 220
Conservative Party 287, 311
Constable, John 145, 178
Cool Britannia 98
Copenhagen 486
Copley, Tom 217
Corbusian architecture 198, 232
Cornell, George 361
Corporation of London 151–2, 173
Coulthurst, Edmund 127
council housing 29–31, 68, 94, 138–40,
  188–91, 195–220, 223–37, 242, 245–6, 250–1,
  254, 276, 278, 280, 285, 446, 477, 479, 481
council tax 278
Covent Garden 456
  market 479
  Piazza 135, 342
Cranbrook Estate 219
Credit Suisse First Boston (CSFB) 48, 49

Crompton, Dennis 120
Cromwell Road 418, 429
Cross, Laura 204
Crossness 108, 110
Crossrail 295
Crossway United Reformed Church 207
Crow, Bob 481
Crown 151
Croydon 440
Cruickshank, Dan 132
Cry from the Streets, A (1958) 132
Crystal Palace, Great Exhibition 1851 (Paxton)
    122
Crystal Palace (re-erected), Sydenham Hill
    158
Crystal Palace area 228
CSFB *see* Credit Suisse First Boston
Cullen, Gordon 143
Curve, The 205
Cutler, Horace 46
cycling lanes 365–7
CZWG 254

Daily Express building 82
Daily Telegraph 334
Daiwa 55
Dalian Wanda 464, 469
Dalston 205–6
Dance, George 137
Darbishire, Henry: Peabody Estate,
    Whitechapel **248**
Darbishire Place, Whitechapel 262
Darbourne, John 223–4
Darbourne and Darke: Lillington Gardens
    Estate **224**
Darke, Geoffrey 224
Darwin Centre, Natural History Museum 422,
    426, 435
Dawson's Heights, East Dulwich 227, **227**
de Graaf, Reinier 469
de Rijke Marsh Morgan 306
de Rothschild, Hannah 182, 183
de Rothschild, Baron Mayer 182
'decent home', notion of 186
deer 151
Delancey 212
Delevingne, Cara 276
Department of Culture 309
Department of the Environment 156
Department of National Heritage 309
Derby (horse race) 181–3
Design Council 294
'design review' committees 323
Diana, Princess of Wales 84, 379

Dickens, Charles 127, 164, 168, 170, 246
digital world 430–2
Diniz, Carlos: proposed Canary Wharf **44–5**
Dirty House, Shoreditch 258, **259**
Disraeli, Benjamin 106, 107, 246
District Line 113, 177
Dixon, Michael 436
Docklands 46–55, 68–70, 73
    see also Canary Wharf
Dockland's Enterprise Zone 48
Docklands exuberant 254
Doha 27–8
Dollis Hill synagogue 82, **244**
Dolphin Square 236
Dolphin Square Charitable Foundation 222
Dome of Discovery 118
Doré, Gustave 169
Douglas, Lord Alfred 182
Downham Estate 242
'Downham Wall' 242
drains 108, 110
Draper House 272
Du Cane Court, Balham **249**, 250
Dubai 379
Dudok, Willem 179
Dufy, Raoul 297
Duggan, Mark 440
Duggan Morris: ORTUS 433, **434**

Eagle Black, City Road 273
Earl's Court 218
'Earth Galleries' 420–2, **421**, 425–6
    Natural History Museum 420–2, 425–6,
    435, 437
East End 70, 81, 153, 169–70, 358
East Enders 238
east London 72, 108–11, 199, 335, 406
East London Mosque 360
East London Water Company 110–11
East Village (Athletes' Village) 261
Eastbury Estate 173–4
École des Beaux-Arts 26
Economist (weekly newspaper) 111
Edison, Thomas 167, 169
education 30
Eiffel Tower 305, 321
'eighteenth-century picturesque' 18–20
Ekirch, Roger 168
electricity 169–70, 173, 178–9
Electricity Lighting Act 167
One The Elephant 211
Elephant and Castle 159, 195, 199, 201–2, 204,
    212–14, 323–4, 403–6
Elephant Creative Vision (video) 403–5

Elephant House, London Zoo 18, 21
Eliasson, Olafur 347
Eliot, T. S. 164
embankments 117, 122, 149, 167, 306, 344, 356,
    387, 390, 392
  Albert Embankment 113, 115
  Chelsea Embankment 113, 125
  Victoria Embankment 113–15, 125
Embassy Gardens, Nine Elms 470
embodied energy 382, 475–6, 491
Emirates Air Line 379
Empire Pool Wembley 82
Enfield 127, 219
English Heritage 20, 294, 295, 316, 338
English Palladianism 135
Epidaurus 392
Epping Forest 80, 151–2, 162
Epsom Downs 181–4
Erkenwald, St 406
Ermine Street 444
Estates Gazette (magazine) 202
ethnic minorities 245
  see also multiculturalism
Eton College 238
European Union (EU) 105
Euston station 233, 480
Euston Tower 26
Evans, Robin 185–8
  Rookeries and Model Dwellings (1978) 185
  Sanitary Ramblings 186
  'The Disease Mist' map (1847) 185–6
Evelyn, John 164
Evening Standard (newspaper) 199, 226,
    276–8
Everett, Kenny 84

Facebook 431
Fahd, King 360
Faraday, Michael 106
Farr, William 111–12
Farrell, Terry 453–4
  MI6 Building 455
FAT 257, 415
  Blue House, Hackney 256
  A House for Essex 409, 410
20 Fenchurch Street *see* Walkie-Talkie
Ferguson, Rachel 242
fertilizer 106
Festival of Britain 1951 118, 122, 235, 390
Financial Times (newspaper) 52, 267, 270, 279,
    482
Finch, George, Lambeth Towers 229
Findlay, Kathryn 373
Finsbury, London Borough of 138, 231

Finsbury Avenue Square 303
Finsbury Council, Public Health Committee
    141
Finsbury Health Centre 140, 143
Finsbury Plan 141
Finsterlin, Hermann 15
Fior, Liza 405
Fire Service 283–4
First World War 12, 178, 250
Fisher, Mark, *A New London* 309
Fitzrovia 61
Flamingo Court 212
Fleet River 125
Fleet Street 52, 82, 316
Fleming, Ian 257
Flynn, Jerry 206, 213
Focus E15 369, 370–1
fog 164–6, 396–7
Foggo, Peter 302, 304
Forestry Commission 205
Forster, Frank 107, 108
Forster, Pauline 288
Foster, Norman 22, 40, 58, 301–2, 304, 305,
    314, 317, 322, 456, 466
  Great Court of the British Museum 305
  HSBC tower 35–9, 43–5
  London Millennium Tower 315
  Millennium Bridge 305, 348
  power station apartments 468
  Project Orange 298
  Sackler Galleries 302
  Stansted Airport 302
  Tate Modern 350
Foster and Partners
  Bexley Business Academy 330, 428
  The Gherkin 57, 314–16, 320, 323
  HSBC boardroom 37, 44, 56
Foster employees 323–4
Fournier Street 136
Frankfurt 59
Fretton, Tony: Lisson Gallery 411, 412
Frith, Matthew 158, 160
Future Systems 42

Games, Abram 141–3
Gandhi, Mahatma 140
gangster culture 441–2
Garden Bridge 379–85, 383, 387–8, 395–6,
    402, 431, 485
'garden cities' 162–3, 174, 185, 232, 262, 282,
    286
Gardner, Nikola 219
Garratt, Lyndsey 222
gaslights 167, 168

'gated communities' 242
Gehry, Frank 15, 328, 456, 466, 492
  Battersea Power Station **467**
  Guggenheim 321
Geological Museum 420
George, Prince Regent (later George IV) 13,
  61–3, 73
George Tavern, Stepney 288
Georgian Society 296
Germanic expressionism 15
Germany 286
Gherkin (London Millennium Tower) 26, **57**,
  58, 74, 311, 314–16, 321–3, 324, 336, 340, 378
ghost streets 270–1, 275
Gibberd, Frederick
  Pulman Court **249**, 250
  Regent's Park Mosque 18, **19**
  St Mark's church, Primrose Hill 19
  The Lawn, Harlow **263**
Gibbons, Jo 161, 205
Giggs, Ryan 439
Ginsberg, Allen 332, 336
Giraffe House, London Zoo **14**, 15, 16, 18, 23
Gissing, George 170, 172, 173, 174, 179
Gladstone Park, Dollis Hill 82, 153, 243
Gladstone, William 113, 149
GLC see Greater London Council
Glencore 395
Globe Theatre replica 348, 350
Golden Lane Estate, City of London 230–1,
  230, 247, 423, 487
Golders Green 237
Goldfinger, Ernö 225
  1–3 Willow Road **256**, 257
  Trellick Tower **226**, 225–7
Golf magazine 152
Google 431, 484
  UK headquarters, King's Cross 353, 355
Gough, Piers 254, 348, 350, 365
Grainger 446
Granary Square, King's Cross **354**
grands projects 304
Great Arthur House 230–1
Great Exhibition 1851 122, 331, 333
Great Fire of London 1666 30, 137, 165
Great North Wood, Surrey 158, 229
Great Stink 105–8, 122, 402
Great West Road 429
Greater London 215–16, 267
Greater London Assembly 381
Greater London Authority 468
Greater London Council (GLC) 46, 118–20, 158,
  300, 301, 477
Greater London Plan 1944 163, 310
Green, G. Kay: Du Cane Court, Balham **249**

'green belt' xxi, 162–3, 267, 281, 284–5, 310,
  451, 477, 479, 490, 491
'Green Giant' 453, 464
'green girdle' 162
green infrastructure 385–7
green spaces 143–64, 238, 287, 382
  see also parks
Greenwich Peninsula 218
Griffiths, Sean, The Blue House 257
Grimsby 219
Gronow, Captain Rees 331–2
Grosvenor, Lord Robert 330
Grosvenor Square, Mayfair 456, 466
guano 106
Guantanamo 27
Guardian (newspaper) 68, 86, 218, 226
guerrilla gardening 159, 161, 381
Guggenheim, Bilbao 321
Gummer, John 316
Gunnersbury Triangle 158
Guryev, Andrey 268

Hackney 257, 441
Hackney Empire **394**
Hackney Wick 373, 450–1
Hadid, Zaha 301, 371
  Olympic Aquatic Centre 80, 371, **372**
Hagenbeck, Carl 15
'Hagenbeck Revolution' 15
Hainault Forest 151
Hakkasan restaurant 77
Hall, Peter 46
Halliday, Stephen, *The Great Stink of London*
  (1999) 105
Halo 365, 376
Hammersmith 125
Hammersmith Bridge 117
Hammerson 97
Hampstead 125, 150, 238, 257, 258, 355, 487
Hampstead Garden Suburb 162, 237–9, **240**,
  250–1, 286
Hampstead Heath 85, 145–9, **146**, **147**, 150–1,
  154, 162, 178, 318, 487
Hanbury Street **377**, 481
Handelsman, Harry 348, 351
Hanley, Lynsey: *Estates* 188–90
Harding, Anna 450–1
Harlow **263**
Harman, Mark 331–2
Harold, King 168
Harrison, Zehra 440–1
Hatherley, Owen 68, 239
Haussman, Baron 61, 115, 116
Hawksmoor, Nicholas 395

Haworth Tompkins 306
Hayward Gallery 118, **119**
Heatherwick, Thomas 36, 380–81, 384, 396–7
  B of the Bang sculpture 396
  History Wall, HSBC **37**, 38, 72, 403
Heatherwick Studio: Garden Bridge **383**
Help to Buy 279
Hemingway, Ernest 77
Hemmings, David, *Blow-Up* 20
Henley 105
Henry VIII 63, 331
Heron Tower 74–6, **75**, 81, 97, 125, 316, 318, 321, 340
Herron, Ron 120
Herzog and de Meuron: Tate Modern **345**, 346–50
Heseltine, Michael 46, 453
Heygate Estate 195–212, **197**, **209**, 214–15, 218, 247, 272, 285, 298, 403–4
High Line, New York 468
high-rises 271–6, 284, 295, 311–26, 336–40, 490–2
High Street 2012 357–60, 363
'high-tech' 301–2
Highfort Court, Kingsbury **244**
Highpoints 1 and 2 140, 284
Highways Department 196–8
Hilberseimer, Ludwig Karl 55
Hills, David 306
Hilversum 179
Hindus 245
Hirst, Damien xxi, 471, 492
Historic England 294
Hitler, Adolf 250
HMP Weare 365
Hodge, Margaret 385
Holborn Studios 450
Holborn Viaduct 167
Holden, Charles 177, 179, 239
Holden, Robert 195, 207
Holford House 137–8
Hollamby, Ted, Lambeth 228–9
Holland House 322
Holland Park 258
Höller, Carsten 347
home-ownership 241, 287–8
homelessness 190, 217, 381
homosexuality 81, 83–5, 98, 332
Hong Kong 35–6, 38
Hong Kong and Shanghai Banking
    Corporation (HSBC) 36–9, 42
  headquarters, Hong Kong 35–6, 43
  see also HSBC tower
Hopkins, Michael
  Hopkins House 258, **259**

Mound Stand, Lord's Cricket Ground 16, 258
Hopkins, Patty
  Hopkins House 258, **259**
  Mound Stand, Lord's Cricket Ground 16, 258
Hopkins Architects, Velodrome 371
Hopkins hats 22, 367
Hopkins House, Hampstead 258
horse racing 181–4
House for Essex, A 409
house-building 267, 280–1, 286, 489–90
houses for artists 258
Houses of Parliament 31, 112, 117
housing 132–43, 166, 186–92, 488–90
  absorption 280
  affordable 61, 208, 216–17, 222–4, 280, 295, 326, 353, 469
  bubble 35
  council 29–31, 68, 94, 138–40, 188–91, 195–220, 223–37, 242, 245–6, 250–1, 254, 276, 278, 280, 285, 446, 477, 479, 481
  crisis 68, 487
  Docklands exuberant 254
  early philanthropic 247
  East Village (Athletes' Village) 261
  ghost streets 270–1, 275
  high-rises 271–6
  home-ownership 241, 287–8
  iceberg houses 268–70, 271, 275, 492, 493
  lofts 251
  'lofts' 251
  low-budget 276–8
  mansion blocks 247–50
  modern one-offs 257–61
  new towns 262
  Peabody contemporary 262
  planning 280–5
  Pocket Living 262
  posh brutalism 247
  PTSD 254
  rural 261
  self-build 246–7
  semi-detached 239–41, 245
  shared ownership 208
  Span 251
  student 254
  suburban 237–46, 283, 479, 490
  terraced 132, 250
  two-storey terrace 250
  unaffordability 266–82, 287–90, 477–8, 481, 487, 489
  vernacular 251–4
'housing zones' 446
Howard, Ebenezer 162–3, 167, 174, 183–5, 190–2, 241, 262, 310, 479
Hoxton 344

HSBC *see* Hong Kong and Shanghai Banking
 Corporation
HSBC tower 35–9, 43–5, **44, 56**
 Boardroom 36, **37**
 History Wall 36–9, **37**, 72, 403
Huddart, Bella 227
Hugo, Victor 169
Hwang, Victor 456
Hyatt Hotel chain 58
Hyde Park 145, 148, 330–3
One Hyde Park 266
Hyde Park Railings Affair 1866 xx, 330–1, 488

iceberg houses 268–70, 271, 275, 492, 493
iconic architecture 58, 321–3, 396
Idea Store, Whitechapel **362**
Ilford 25–6
immigrants, illegal 276
immigration 80–1
Independent, The (newspaper) 204
Iraq 310
Irish Republican Army (IRA) 311
Ironmonger Row Turkish Baths 77
Islamist extremism 27
Isle of Dogs 49, 68, 72
Islington, London borough of 87–91, 127, 166,
 218, 219, 231, 257
Ismail, Afham 369–71
Ismail, Nazrah 370–1

Jack the Ripper sites 361
Jacob, Kumar 432
Jacob, Sam 275
Jacobescu, George 39
Jacobs, Jane 479
 Death and Life of American Cities (1961) 59
Jago restaurant 482
Jago-dwellers 188–90, 192
James, Henry 143–4, 182
James I 12, 129
Jefri Bolkiah, Prince of Brunei 65
Jespersen industrialized building system 196
Jewish community 245, 358, 440
Joass, John 15, 22
 Giraffe House 15
 Mappin Terraces 15
John, Peter 212, 298
Johnson, B. S. 46, 134, 166
 Albert Angelo 87–90, 131–2
Johnson, Boris 27, 160, 326–8, 373, 378–81,
 446
Johnston, Edward 176, 179
Jones, Brian 332

Jones, Inigo 135
journalism 52
Jubilee Line extension 488
Jubilee Line station (Stratford Regional
 Station) 367

Kapoor, Anish, ArcelorMittal Orbit 371–3
Karakusevic Carson 306
Katial, Dr Chuni Lal 140–1
Keats, John 145, 178
Kensington 225–7, 250, 266, 289, 418
Kensington Palace 331
Kenwood house and gardens 150
Kesteven, John, Heygate Estate 196
Khrushchev, Nikita 261
Kieran Timberlake 466
 US Embassy **467**
Killing Kittens club 86–7
King's Cross area 158–9, 170, 352–5
Kingsbury 243
Kingsley, Charles 190
Kingsway 342–4
Knight Dragon 218
Knightsbridge 270, 289
Kobe earthquake 420
Kober, Claire 444
KPF 321
 Heron Tower 316
Kray, Ronnie 361

Labour governments 167, 212, 278
Labour and Wait 94
Ladbroke Estate 174
Lambeth, London Borough of 228–9, 325
 Central Hill **228**, 229, **229**
Lambeth Towers 229
Lammy, David 440
Land Securities, Blue Fin Building 348
Lasdun, Denys 120–2
 National Theatre 120, 390, **391**, 392–5
Lawn, the, Harlow New Town **263**
Lawrence, Philip Henry 149, 150
Le Corbusier 191, 312, 328, 393
 Toward an Architecture 191
 Ville Radieuse 138–9, 141, 163, 165
Le Marché international des professionnels de
 l'immobilier (MIPIM) 297–300, 321, 323,
 442, 446
Lea River 450
Leadenhall Building (Cheesegrater) 26, 58,
 316, 321, 336, 339
Lear, Edward 144, 161
Lehman Brothers 35

Leicester Square 153
Leighton, Lord 258
Leila's grocery shop, Shoreditch 94, **95**, 450
Leith, Prue 376–8
Lend Lease 203, 206, 207–8, 212, 298
Lenin, Vladimir Ilyich 132, 138
Les Trois Garçons restaurant 94
Letchworth 162, 185
Lewis, Brandon 214–15
Lewisham, London Borough of 247
LGBTQ pubs 450
Liberal Democrats 212
Liberty Bell 360
Libeskind, Daniel 91
lido, London Fields 80
Lifschutz Davidson Sandilands 91, **93**, 413
lighting, artificial 167–70
Lillington Gardens Estate, Pimlico, City of
    Westminster 223–4, **224**, 266
Lincoln's Inn Fields 135, 145
Lion House, London Zoo 18
Lipton, Stuart 302–4, 309, 321, 442
Lisson Gallery 411–13, **412**
Lisson Grove **252**
listed buildings 9, 13, 20, 21, 22, 311–12, 314,
    454, 477
Living Architecture 409
Livingstone, Ken 158–60, 228, 300–1, 310, 318,
    325, 326–8, 378, 456
Lloyd George, David 250
Lloyds building 302
Lobster Kitchen 86
lofts 251
'lofts' 251
"lodging-house" from *Sanitary Ramblings*,
    1848 **181**
London As It Could Be 306
London Assembly 217
London Bridge 317
London Building Acts 261, 265, 426, 476
    'Black Act' 1774 137
London County Council 113, 118–20, 140, 152,
    154, 183, 188, 192, 198–9, 235–6, 481
    Alton Estate, Roehampton **232**
    Arnold Circus, Shoreditch 183
    Inter-war 251
London Daily News (newspaper) 226
London Docklands Development Corporation
    48, 70, 487–8
London Eye 304–5, 376, 378
London Fields lido **79**
London First 384
London Housing Design Guide 265, 493
London Metropolitan University 448
London Millennium Tower *see* Gherkin

London Passenger Transport Board xxii, 178,
    179, 181
London Plan 294, 310–11, 318
London School of Economics 34
London Stock Exchange 386
London Transport 30, 31
London Underground 52, 53, 148, 170–81, **175**,
    379
    advertising 176, 179
    maps 177
    suburban extensions 237–9
    writing 176, 179
London View Management Framework 31
London Wall 53–5, **54**
London Wildlife Trust 156
London Zoo 9–24, 27
    BUGS (Biodiversity Underpinning Global
        Survival) 22, 420
    Elephant House 18, 21
    Giraffe House **14**, 15, 16, 18, 23
    Lion House 18
    Mappin Terraces **14**, 15, 16, 18, 24, 25
    Millennium Conservation Centre 18
    Penguin Beach 16, 21, 23
    Penguin Pool 15–16, 20–1, 22–3, 138, 348
    Snowdon Aviary 9–11, **10**, 16–18, 23, 46
    tea-house 24, 26
    Zoo Lates 13
London-hate 191, 192
'Londonistan' 27
Lord's cricket ground, Mound Stand 22
Los Angeles 85
Lounge Bohemia 97
Louvre 305
Lovag, Antti, 'bubble houses' 298
Love, The Very Reverend Dr D. 452–3, 454–6
Lubetkin, Berthold 18, 22, 192
    Bevin Court 138, 143
    Highpoints 1 and 2 140
    Penguin Pool, London Zoo 15–16, 20–1,
        22–3, 138
Luftwaffe 124
Lumley, Joanna 379, 380–2, 388
Lutyens, Edwin 409
Luxembourg 386
Luzhkov, Yury 298
Lyons, Eric 251
    SPAN housing, Blackheath **253**

M1 motorway, phase one 82
M4 motorway 429
M25 motorway 480
McDonald's 91, 124
Mackintosh, Kate

269 Leigham Court Road 228
Dawson's Heights 227, **227**
McLaughlin, Niall: Darbishire Place 262
Magna Carta 111, 168
Maida Vale 261
Mailer, Norman 77
Maitland, Mr 152
Major, John 304, 311
Manifesto for London 488–92
mansion blocks 247–50
Manson, Fred 200–2, 206, 212–13, 218, 318, 380
manure 106
Mappin Terraces, London Zoo **14**, 15, 16, 18, 24, 25
Marks, David: London Eye 305
Martin, John 107, 108, 440
Martin, Leslie 198
    Alton Estate 232, **232**
Marx, Karl 330, 334
Marylebone 134, 242
Maryon Park 154, **155**
Maryon-Wilson, Thomas 149, 150, 487
Maryon-Wilson family 154
Matcham, Frank 77, 393
    Hackney Empire **394**
Mather, Rick, Heygate Estate 196
Maudsley Charity 432
Maudsley Charity Committee 432
Maudsley Hospital 433
Mayfair 82, 217
    Grosvenor Square 456, 466
Meek, James, *Private Island* 219
megastructures 113
mental health 432–3
Mercury, Freddie 84
Merrick, Joseph, 'the Elephant Man' 361
Mesopotamia 23
'Metro-Land' 82, 243–5, 266
Metropolis Local Management Amendment Act 106
Metropolitan Board of Works xxi, 107, 108, 112–13, 116, 117–18, 122, 150, 154, 164, 173, 188, 387, 402, 480
Metropolitan Court of Sewers 107
Metropolitan Green Belt 30, 284–5
Metropolitan Line 174, 242–3
Metropolitan Open Space 208
Metropolitan Police 107, 115, 204
Metropolitan Railway 170, 172
Metropolitan Underground 82
Metropolitan Water Board 129, 132
MI6 453–4, **455**, 465
miasma 107, 111, 164, 185
Middle Level Sewer 125

Middle Temple 384
middle classes 200–1, 213–14
Middleton, Kate, Duchess of Cambridge 86
Midland Railway Company 149
Mies van der Rohe, Ludwig 312, 314, 425
Mile End Park 365
Mile End Road 362
Mile End Waste 363
Mill, John Stuart 149, 151
millenarian architecture 304–5, 322
Millennium Bridge 200, 305, 348
Millennium Conservation Centre, London Zoo 18
Millennium Dome 310, 420
Milton Keynes 284
Ministry of Defence 115
Ministry of Health 141
Minogue, Kylie 91
minorities 81, 245
Mint Street, Bethnal Green 262, **263**
Minton, Anna, *Ground Control* (2009) 68, 333–4
MIPIM (Le Marché international des professionnels de l'immobilier) 297–300, 321, 323, 442, 446
Mitchell, Peter Chalmers 15
Mittal, Lakshmi 27, 373
Mitterrand, François 304
'model dwellings' 186
modernism 58, 59, 251–4, 301–2, 304, 390, 481
molly houses 84
Moltke, Brint 466
Montcalm Hotel **92**
Montevetro 316, 321
Moor Park 242, 243
Moorgate Street Underground Station 172
moral disease/contagion 185, 190–1
More London 333–4, 352
Morgan Stanley 49
Morris, William 179
Morrison, Herbert 178
Moscow School of Management 361
Mound Stand, Lord's Cricket Ground 258
Moya, Hidalgo
    Churchill Gardens **235**, 235–6
    Skylon 118, 235
muf architecture/art 405–8, 415
    Altab Ali Park, Whitechapel **359**
    Barking Town Centre **407**
multiculturalism 27, 473
    see also ethnic minorities
Mumbai 270, 494
Munby, Arthur 113, 173
Municipal Dreams (blog) 224, 236

Museum of African American History, Washington 361
Muslims 245
Muthesius, Hermann, *Das englische Haus* (*The English House*) 286
Myddelton, Hugh 127–30, 166
Mylne, Robert 134
Mylne, William Chadwell 134, 138
The Castle, Stoke Newington **126**

Nairn, Ian 232, 363, 369
Napoleon III 61, 115
Nash, John 61, 63–5, 135, 153
London Zoo 13
Park Crescent **64**
National Health Service (NHS) 140, 222, 360
National Lottery 304, 305, 310, 344, 352, 365, 420, 422
National Theatre 118, 120, 390–5, **391**
National Trust 257
'National Valhalla' 63
Natural History Museum **418**, 418–23, 429, 435–8
Darwin Centre 422, 426, 435
'Earth Galleries' 420–2, **421**, 425–6, 435, 437
Nature in London conference 1981 156
NatWest Tower 55
Nauman, Bruce 347
Neasden 245
Neave Brown and London Borough of Camden: Alexandra and Ainsworth Estate, St John's Wood **234**
Neo Bankside 348, 462
Neue Oder Zeitung 330
Neutra, Richard 328
Neville, Richard 332
One New Change **307**
New Era Estate, Hoxton 220–2
New Labour 90
New River, Enfield xxii, 125–30, **126**, 134, 163
New River Company 129, 132, 134, 165
New River Estate 137
New River Head 132, 190, 231
New Scotland Yard 115
New Society (magazine), 'Non-Plan: an Experiment in Freedom' 46, **47**, 48, 67, 214
new towns 162–3, 262, 282, 284, 479, 487
New York 49, 59, 301, 468, 494
New Yorker (magazine) 268
Newby, Frank: Snowdon Aviary 9, **10**
Newham 220, 278, 357, 370
Newport Street Gallery **471**, 471–3
newspapers 52
Newton, Helmut 450

Neylan and Ungless: Setchell Road Estate **253**, 254
NHS *see* National Health Service
Niemeyer, Oscar 76
Nightingale, Florence 106–7, 115
Nine Elms 456, 464, 466–8, 485
One Nine Elms 464
Nine Elms Lane 458
Noble, Tim 258
Nomura 55
'Non-Plan: an Experiment in Freedom' (*New Society* magazine) 46, 48, 67, 214
Norman Conquest 28
Northern High Level Sewer 125
Northern Line 237
extension 456–8, 468, 469–70
Northern Lower Level Sewer 125
Northern Outfall Sewer (Sewerbank/ Greenway) 124–5
Northumberland Avenue 112, 116
Northumberland House 116
Northwood Hills 241
Norton Rose Fulbright 268
Notting Hill 225, 289, 479
Nouvel, Jean: One New Change 305, **307**
Number One Poultry 311–14, **313**

O'Brien, Flann 28
Occupy movement 335
O'Donnell + Tuomey, Saw Swee Hock Student Centre, London School of Economics **428**, 429
Old Bailey, Central Criminal Court 305
Old Dispensary, Stratford **260**
Old Nichol slum, Bethnal Green 94, 185, 188, 482
Old Street 482, 484–5, 486
Old Street (Silicon) Roundabout 91, 482, 484–5, 486
Olympia and York 49
Olympic Aquatic Centre 80, 371, **372**
Olympic Games 46
Barcelona 1992 310, 311
London 2012 27, 220, 261, 311, 356–8, 367–9, 371, 373–4, 380, 442
Olympic Park 70, 367, 371, 373–4
Olympic Stadium 450
OMA 469
Rothschild Bank headquarters 305
One Below the Queen (2010) 233–5
One Canada Square 40–2, 55
One Commercial Street 273–5
One Hyde Park 266
One Nine Elms 464

One Pancras Square **354**
One The Elephant 211
One Tree Hill, Honor Oak 152–3
Open Spaces Society 151
Opium Wars 38–9
Orbit, The 27, 379
OROGOLD 77
Orton, Joe 84
ORTUS, Camberwell 432–5, **433**
Osborne, George 381
Osborne, John 242
Our Towns and Cities – the Future (White Paper) 309
Owens, Rick **78**, 80
Oxford Circus 63
Oz magazine 332

Paddington Basin 26
Paddington, London Borough of 125, 138, 257, 411
Palace of Westminster 31, 105, 115, 271–2, 295, 305, 458, 464
Palais des Festivals 297, 300
Palumbo, Peter 311–12
Paris 28, 61, 85, 115, 144, 257, 267, 301, 311
Paris Opera 403
Park Crescent **64**, 65
Parker Morris space standards 236
parks 143–9, 153–4, 161–2, 164, 330–3, 402–3
see also specific parks
Parliament 105–7, 151, 331
Parry, Eric 305
5 Aldermanbury Square 413–15, **414**
Parthenon 23
Paternoster Square 59, **60**, 335, 403
Pawson, John 90
Paxton, Joseph 116
Crystal Palace 122
Peabody, George 247, 262
Peabody contemporary 262
Peabody Estate, Whitechapel **248**
Peabody Trust 188, 262
Pearson, Charles 174
Suburban Residences for London Mechanics 174, 237
Pelli, César
Citi tower 43
One Canada Square 40–2
Penguin Beach, London Zoo 16, 21, 23
Penguin Pool, London Zoo 15–16, **17**, 20–1, 22–3, 138, 348
Pennethorne, James 458
Victoria Park 153
pensions 279

Percy family 116
Percy Circus 131–2, **133**, 138, 140, 165, 166, 174, 246
Perry, Grayson 409
A House for Essex **410**
Petherton Road 127
Petronius Arbiter 77
Pevsner, Nikolaus 232
Buildings of England (1983) 199
philanthropy 70–1, 186, 188, 247, 365, 488
phone boxes 430
Piano, Renzo: Shard 200, 317–22, **319**
Piccadilly Circus 63, 174–6
Piccadilly Line 177
Pick, Frank xxii, 179–81, 480, 487
Pimlico 235–6
Pinner 243
Pioneer Health Centre, Peckham 82
Pitman Tozer: Mint Street, Bethnal Green 262, **263**
Pizza Express 446
plain building 411–13
planning 293–6, 338, 490–1, 493
planning committees 293
planning gain 61, 217
pleasure, pursuit of 74–90, 98–9
Pocket Living, Hackney 262, **263**
Pole-Tylney-Long-Wellesley, William 103, 152
pollution 164–6
Pompidou Centre, Paris 55, 317, 464
population decline 162, 478
population growth 106, 110, 163, 241, 266–7, 310, 451, 489
Portland Place 65
poverty 185, 188, 190
Powell, Geoffry 230
Powell, Philip, Churchill Gardens **235**, 235–6
Prescott, John 310, 318, 321, 325, 454
Price, Cedric 46, 486
Snowdon Aviary 9–11, **10**, 16–18, 23, 46
Priestley, J. B. 241
Primrose Hill xx, 24–5, 31, **31–2**, 33, 35, 61, 156, 159, 289, 341
Primrose Hill Declaration 156
'Primrose Hill set' 24
Primrose Hill Village 24–5
Prince's Gate 266
prison ships 365
Pritzker Prize 58, 322, 323, 336, 350
Private Finance Initiative 360, 425
property business 27, 29
protest 330–6
Public Accounts Committee 385
public benefit 61, 63
public gardens 153

public land 283–4
public spaces 200, 309–10, 312, 314, 335–6, 338–56, 357, 360, 367, 387, 389, 403, 408, 431, 470, 481, 490–1, 492
Pueblito Paisa cafe 446, 448
Pulman Court, Streatham 249, 250
pumping stations 134
Purcell Room 118

Qatar 27, 261, 318, 381
Qatari Diar 218, 318–21
quantitative easing 279
Queen Elizabeth Hall 118
Queen Elizabeth Olympic Park 375
Queen Mary College, University of London 70
Queen Victoria Street 116
Queensberry, Marquess of 182
Quinn, Pat 219

Raban, Jonathan 191, 486
  Soft City 479
Radić, Smiljan 80
Raffles, Stamford 12
Rahman, Lutfur 360–1
railway arches 81, 83
Rainham Marshes 160
rainwater 385–6, 492
Rasmussen, Steen Eiler 61, 67, 132, 134–5, 144–8, 153, 161, 163–4, 178–9, 192, 238–9, 286–7, 333, 402, 490
  Experiencing Architecture 485–6
  London, the Unique City 28–30, 174–7
Ratrad 224
Redchurch Street, Shoreditch 481
Redpath, Ian 207
Redrow 273–5, 289–90, 357, 358, 376
Rees, Peter Wynne 58, 81, 85, 98, 273, 312, 338, 340, 415, 449
Regalian 453–4
Regent Street 63–5
Regent's Canal 9, 20
Regent's Park 12, 13, 18, 61, 65–7, 66, 161, 333, 402–3
Regent's Park Mosque 18, 19
Reichmann brothers 49
Reith lectures 1995 309
Revolt of the Ravers 1994 332
revolution 190–1
Revolutionary Communist Group 220
Reynolds, Richard 159
Rhubarb 339, 355
Richmond Park 158

Right to Buy 216, 219, 237, 278, 279
Rimbaud 164
riots 199–200, 440–2
Riverlight 459, 462–4
'Roastmaster' buses 397
Robson, E. R.: Board Schools 426
Roding River 103, 104, 125, 163
Roehampton 232
Rogers, Richard 53–5, 117, 301–2, 304, 305, 306–11, 317, 321, 351, 493
  A New London 309
  Cities for a Small Planet 309
  Leadenhall Building 316
  Lloyds building 302
  London As It Could Be 306, 308
  Montevetro 316
  Pompidou Centre 317, 464
  Tate Modern 350
Rogers Stirk Harbour and Partners
  Neo Bankside 348, 462
  Riverlight 459, 462–4, 463
Rolling Stones 332
Rome 61, 77, 85
Romford Road 261, 283
Ronan Point 199
Ronson, Gerald 97
rookeries 186
Rosebery, Lord (Archibald Primrose, fifth earl of Rosebery) 181, 182–5, 190, 191, 192
Rosebery Avenue 190
Rosenberg, Isaac 360
Rothschild Bank headquarters 305
Rotten Row 331
Roundhouse 480
Rousham 77
Routemaster buses 380, 397
Roux Brothers 48
Royal Academy 302, 306
Royal Festival Hall 118, 119, 120
Royal Fine Art Commission (RFAC) 294, 309
Royal Humane Society 129
Royal London Hospital 360–1
Royal Mail sorting office, Mount Pleasant 218
Royal Navy 158
Royal Parks Department 156
Royal Society for the Protection of Birds (RSPB) 382–3
Royal Vauxhall Tavern 84
Ruskin, John 179
Russell, Lord John 111

Saarinen, Eero 466
Sackler Galleries 302, 305
Sadler's Wells 125, 129, 190, 231

St Andrew's, Bromley-by-Bow **264**
St George (developers) 454
St George Wharf 317, 324, 454, **460**, 468
St George Wharf Tower (formerly Vauxhall
    Tower) 324–5, 454, 458–61, 464, 469
St James-the-Less 223
St James's Park 61, 266, 309
St James's Park Station 177
St John Wilson, Colin: British Library 426
St John's Wood 233–5
St Mark's, Primrose Hill 18, **19**, 25
30 St Mary Axe *see* Gherkin
St Mary and Holy Trinity, Bow **364**
St Pancras 149, 355, 480
St Paul's Cathedral 31, 55, 58, 271, 295, 316, 318,
    335, 344, 346, 355, 382, 392–3
St Thomas's Hospital 115
Salcedo, Doris 347
Salmond, Alex 34–5
Salvation Army 363
Salway, Catherine 226
Samuel, Herbert 16
San Francisco 85
SANAA 415
    Serpentine temporary pavilion 409, **410**
Sandro 439
Saunt, Deborah 306
SAVE Britain's Heritage 296
Savills 473
Savoy Hotel 115
Saw Swee Hock Student Centre, London
    School of Economics **428**, 429
Saxon customs 150, 182
Sayle, Emma 86
Scape East, Mile End Road 254, **255**
School Board of London 426
Scott, Giles Gilbert 344–6, 361
Scottish Independence 34–5
Scottish National Party 34
Second Home, Spitalfields 481–2, **484**, 485
Second World War 124, 141, 143, 191, 198–9,
    423
security issues 43–5
Segal Close xxiv, 247
Segal, Walter xxiv, 246–7, 477
    Walter's Way, Lewisham **248**
Seifert, Colonel Richard 304
Self, Will 91
Selfridges 80, 363
SelgasCano 482
    Second Home, Spitalfields **484**
Sellar, Irvine 317, 324
Sennett, Richard 485, 486
Serpentine Gallery 80, 376, **410**
Serpentine temporary pavilion 409

Setchell Estate 254
Seven Sisters Market **447**
sewerage 30, 103–10, 112–13, 115, 117, 122,
    124–5, 129–30, 163, 385, 387, 477, 478
sex clubs 83–7, 98
Shad Thames **253**
Shaftesbury, Earl of 161, 165
Shaftesbury School, Newham **426**
Shakespeare, William 164, 348
Shakespeare's Head pub, Islington 88–91
Shanghai 38, 494
Shangri-La hotel group 318
Shard, The 25–7, 200, 317–25, **319**, 336, 378,
    380
Shaw, Norman: Albert Hall Mansions,
    Kensington **249**
Shaw Lefevre, George (later Lord Eversley)
    149–53, 192, 238
    Commons, Forest and Footpaths 153
Shell Centre 218
Shell-Mex headquarters 115
Shepherd Market 82
shipping container constructions 97
Shoal, The, Stratford **368**, 369, 485
Shoreditch 74, 82, 91, 94–8, 258, 272, 344, 378,
    450, 481
    Boundary Estate 94, 140, 188–91, 195, 479
Shoreditch House 94
Shrimpy's 353
Sidcup Road 283
Sikhs 245
Silicon (Old Street) Roundabout 91, **93**, 482,
    484, 484–5, 486
Silva, Rohan 482
Sinaloa drugs cartel 39
Sinclair, Robert 94–6
Sinclair C5 332
Singapore 12, 285
Sixtus V, Pope 61
'Sky Garden' at the Walkie-Talkie **337**
Skylon 118, 235
slack space 491
SLaM *see* South London and Maudsley NHS
    Foundation Trust
SLR Ltd 202
slums 30, 94, 112, 162, 169, 185–90, 214, 241–2,
    247, 250, 479, 488–9
Smiljan Radic Serpentine pavilion **78**
Smith, Augustus 152
Smith, Duncan 451
Smith, W. H. 113, 149–50
Smithfield Agricultural Show 165
Smithson, Alison 46
Smithson, Peter 46, 118
Smithsonian magazine 456

smog 30, 164–5, 170
smoke 164–6
Snow, Dr John 106, 111
Snowdon, Lord: Snowdon Aviary 9–11
Snowdon Aviary, London Zoo 9–11, **10**, 16–18, 23, 46
social change 191–2
Social Justice Centre, Vauxhall **471**, 471–3, 485
Soho 82, 106
SOM 58
Somerset House 115, 391
South Bank 117–22, 306, 384, 478
South Bank Centre **121**, 344, 356, 478
South Kensington 418
South London and Maudsley NHS Foundation Trust (SLaM) 432
Southwark, London Borough of 195, 196, 198–215, 227, 228, 298, 317, 351, 403
Dawson's Heights **227**
Southwark council 201–3, 206, 212–14
Southwark council Strategic Committee 201
Southwark Street 116
Soviet Union 138
Spa Green Estate, Sadler's Wells 190, 231, **231**
Space Studios 450
SPAN housing, Blackheath **253**
Speaker's Corner, Hyde Park 331, 333
Spiegelhalters 363
Spitalfields 480
Square Mile 58
Stalin, Josef 361
Stamp, John 423–5
Stanley, Albert (later Lord Ashfield) 178, 179
Stansted Airport 127, 302
Starkey, David 441–2
steam engines 170–2
Steax bar and restaurant 461
Steiner, Rudolf 15
Stephenson, Robert 116
Stevenson, Robert Louis 167–8, 169, 177, 178, 238
Stirling, James 312–14
Stirling Wilford: Number One Poultry **313**
Stjernstedt, Rosemary: Central Hill **228**, 229, **229**
Stoke Newington Secondary School 156
Stour Estuary 409
Stowe 80
Strata SE1 **210**, 211, 272, 323–5
Stratford City 335, 365–76
Stratford High Street 283, 357, 365–7, **366**, 376, 411, 485
Stratford Regional Station 367
Straw Bale House, Islington **250**, 257

Suarez, Luis 439
suburban housing 237–46, 283, 479, 490
Subway club, Leicester Square 84
Sugarhouse Studios 411
Sunday Trading Bill 330, 333
Sung, Gavin 473
Survey of London 134
Sushisamba 76–7, 85, 97, 125
sustainability 475–6, 491
Swiss Re 314, 316
Sydenham Hill 158

Tan, Abigail 86
Tate Gallery 453
Tate Modern 200, 288, 305, 344, **345**, 346–50, 352, 462
see also Bankside Power Station
Tattenham Corner 181
Taut, Bruno 15
Taylor, Robert 137
Team Four 301
'tech cities' 30, 481–2
Tech City 481–2
Tecton 192
Bevin Court 138, **139**
Cranbrook Estate 219
Finsbury Health Centre 140
Penguin Pool, London Zoo **17**
Spa Green Estate 190, 231, **231**
TED 429
telephone boxes 31
terrorism 361–3, 370
Terry, John 439–40
Texaco 91, **92**
Thames 103, 105–8, 110, 112–13, 117–22, 149, 228, 235, 272, 324–6, 380, 384, 388, 390, 392, 458, 468, 487, 491
Thames cable car 379
Thames Tideway Tunnel xxiii–xxiv, 385–7
Thames Water 386–7
Thatcher, Margaret 46, 48, 55, 216, 236, 278, 279, 287, 300, 301, 453
Thatcherism 48, 453, 481
Third Way 310
Till, Jeremy: Straw Bale House **256**, 257
Time Out magazine 86
Times, The (newspaper) 107, 331, 333
Tinker, Tim: Heygate Estate 196, 198, 205, 207, 211
Toovey, John, Lion House 18
Tottenham 200, 440–9
Tottenham Green 446
Tottenham Hale retail park 440

Tottenham High Road   440, 444, **445**, 446,
   449
Tottenham Hotspur Football Club   439–40,
   444–8
   stadium   **447**, 448
   training ground   127
Tower 42   74, 340
Tower Bridge   112, 156, 254, 333–4
Tower Hamlets   70, 357, 360–1
Tower of London   11, 338
towers   26, 35–9, 43–5, 55, 58, 74–6, 81, 91, 97,
   125, 225–7, 229, 311–26, 336–40, 378, 454,
   458–61, 464, 469, 490–2
Townsend, Charles Harrison: Whitechapel Art
   Gallery   358, **359**
Townsend, Geoffrey   251
Trafalgar Square   306, 309, 376–8
transport   30, 40, 487, 493
Transport for London (TfL)   379, 381, 382, 384
   offices   318
Travelstead, G. Ware   48–9, 52, 53
Travers, Tony   34, 326
Treasure, Julian   429
Treasury Holdings   456
Trellick Tower, North Kensington   **226**, 225–7
Tretyakov Gallery   298
Treves, Frederick   361
trickle-down economics   68
Trinity Green   363
Trobridge, Ernest George   243
   Highfort Court, Kingsbury   **243**
Trotsky, Leon   82
tuberculosis   141, 164
Turner, George   218, 326
Twentieth Century Society   296

Uber   430
under-occupancy charge (bedroom tax)   216,
   219
UNESCO World Heritage Sites   338, 339
United Arab Emirates   379, 381
United Electric Railways Company of London
   178, 179
Universal Studios   160
University of the Arts   353
University of London   70
Unwin, Raymond   237–9
Urban Task Force, 'Towards an Urban
   Renaissance'   309
urbanism   59
urbanization   184
URBED   285
US Embassy   466, **467**

'vacant building credit'   217
Vauxhall   82, 83, 98, 218, 258–61, 272, 456–61,
   464–8, 471, 485
Vauxhall Bridge   453
Vauxhall gyratory   452, 454, 468
Vauxhall Nine Elms Battersea (VNEB)   xxvii,
   452–73, 492
   VNEB park   468
Vauxhall Pleasure Gardens   452
Vauxhall Tower see St George Wharf Tower
Velodrome   371
Velten, Hannah, Beastly London   11
vice   185
Victoria   331
Victoria Embankment   113–15, **114**, 125
Victoria Park   80, 153
Victorian Society   296
View Management Framework   294–5
Ville Radieuse   138–9, 141, 163, 165
Viñoly, Rafael   466
   Walkie-Talkie (20 Fenchurch Street)   **337**,
      336–40
Vogt, Gunther   348, 351
Volic, Ademir   270
Volume 3   268–70
von Clemm, Michael   48, 67
Voysey, C. F. A.   243

Waddington-Ball, Oliver   227
Wainwright, Oliver   218
Wales, Robin   220
Walkie-Talkie (20 Fenchurch Street)   26, 58,
   337, 336–40, 403
'Wall Street's Guantanamo'   27
Wallace, David Foster   466
Walter's Way, Lewisham   xxiv, 247, **248**
Wanamaker, Sam   348, 351
Wandsworth, London Borough of   232
Wanstead House   103, 135, 152
Wanstead Park   80, 103, **104**
Wapping   480
Wapping Project   288
Ward, Reg   48
Ware, Isaac   137
water pollution   106–12
Waterhouse, Alfred: Natural History Museum
   418, 418, 422, 426, 437
Waterloo   218, 272
Waterloo Bridge   392–3
Watford Observer (newspaper)   173–4
Watson, Kevin   204
Webster, Sue   258
Welfare State   140

Well Hall Estate 239
Welsh, David, *Underground Writing* 170–2
Welsh, Irvine 35
Welwyn 162, 185
Wentworth, Richard 355
Wesker, Arnold 358–60
West Ham United Football Club 374
West Hendon Estate 215
West India Docks 45, 487
West Reservoir, Enfield **126**
Westbourne Park 174
Westbrook Partners 222
Western Avenue 283
Westfield, Stratford City 335, **368**, 373
Westminster, City of 235–6
Westminster Abbey 135
Westway 225
Wharmby Kozdon 18
  Penguin Beach 16, 21
Whisperers, The 411, 413
White Chapel 360
White Hart Lane railway station 446
White, Jerry 242
  London in the Nineteenth Century 116, 154,
    190, 331
Whitechapel Art Gallery 29, 358–60, **359**
Whitechapel Library 358, 361
Whitechapel Road 357, 361
Whitehall Court 115
Whiteread, Rachel 358, **359**, 360
Wickhams department store **362**, 363
Wigglesworth, Sarah: Straw Bale House **256**,
  257
Wilde, Oscar 182, 401
'wilding' 156–61
Wilkinson Eyre, Jubilee Line station (Stratford
  Regional Station) 367

William I 28, 34, 103, 406
William IV 67, 376
William Curtis Ecological Park 156, **157**
Williams, Owen 82
  Dollis Hill Synagogue **244**
Williams, Stanton 305
Willingdale (tree-lopper) 152
1–3 Willow Road, Hampstead **256**, 257
Wilson, Colin St John: British Library **426**
Wilson, Fergus 279
Wilson, Gordon 34–5
Wilson, Judith 279
Wimbledon Common 149
Winfrey, Oprah 207
Witanhurst 268
Wood Green 441
Wood Green Shopping City 444
88 Wood Street 55
Wood Wharf 52
Woodberry Down 127
World Economic Forum, Davos 27
World Trade Center 49
Wren, Christopher 24, 363
  Chelsea Hospital 363

Yardhouse, Sugarhouse Studios **410**
Yates, Peter 138
Yerkes, Charles Tyson xxii, 178, 238, 487
Yom Kippur war 1973 477
Your Britain, Fight for it Now (Abram Games)
  142

zero-carbon-growth developments 211
Ziamani, Brusthom 361–3
Zone Z homes 276
Zoological Society of London 12–13, 15, 21, 24

picador.com

blog
videos
interviews
extracts